Nietzsche on Ethics and Politics

Nietzsche on Ethics and Politics

Maudemarie Clark

OXFORD
UNIVERSITY PRESS

Oxford University Press is a department of the University of Oxford.
It furthers the University's objective of excellence in research, scholarship,
and education by publishing worldwide.

Oxford   New York
Auckland   Cape Town   Dar es Salaam   Hong Kong   Karachi
Kuala Lumpur   Madrid   Melbourne   Mexico City   Nairobi
New Delhi   Shanghai   Taipei   Toronto

With offices in
Argentina   Austria   Brazil   Chile   Czech Republic   France   Greece
Guatemala   Hungary   Italy   Japan   Poland   Portugal   Singapore
South Korea   Switzerland   Thailand   Turkey   Ukraine   Vietnam

Oxford is a registered trade mark of Oxford University Press
in the UK and certain other countries.

Published in the United States of America by
Oxford University Press
198 Madison Avenue, New York, NY 10016

© Oxford University Press 2015

All rights reserved. No part of this publication may be reproduced,
stored in a retrieval system, or transmitted, in any form or by any means,
without the prior permission in writing of Oxford University Press,
or as expressly permitted by law, by license, or under terms agreed with the
appropriate reproduction rights organization. Inquiries concerning reproduction
outside the scope of the above should be sent to the Rights Department,
Oxford University Press, at the address above.

You must not circulate this work in any other form
and you must impose this same condition on any acquirer.

Library of Congress Cataloging-in-Publication Data
Clark, Maudemarie.
Nietzsche on ethics and politics / Maudemarie Clark.
p. cm.
Includes bibliographical references and index.
ISBN 978–0–19–937184–6 (hardcover : alk. paper)
1. Nietzsche, Friedrich Wilhelm, 1844–1900. 2. Ethics. 3. Political science—Philosophy.
4. Metaphysics. I. Title.
B3317.C56 2015
193—dc23
2014012113

1 3 5 7 9 8 6 4 2

Printed in the United States of America
on acid-free paper

To Connie
Again and Always

{ CONTENTS }

Abbreviations ix

Introduction 1

PART I **Ethics**

1. Nietzsche's Immoralism and the Concept of Morality 23
2. On the Rejection of Morality: Bernard Williams's Debt to Nietzsche 41
3. Nietzsche's Contribution to Ethics 62
4. Nietzsche on Free Will, Causality, and Responsibility 75
5. Nietzsche and Moral Objectivity: The Development of Nietzsche's Metaethics (co-authored with David Dudrick) 97

PART II **Politics**

6. Bloom and Nietzsche 133
7. Nietzsche's Misogyny 141
8. On Queering Nietzsche 151
9. Nietzsche's Antidemocratic Rhetoric 164
10. The Good of Community (co-authored with Monique Wonderly) 184

PART III **Metaphysics**

11. Deconstructing *The Birth of Tragedy* 203
12. On Knowledge, Truth, and Value: Nietzsche's Debt to Schopenhauer and the Development of his Empiricism 213
13. Nietzsche as Anti-metaphysician 250

14. **Nietzsche's Philosophical Psychology: Will to Power
    as Theory of the Soul (co-authored with David Dudrick)**   **260**

Sources and Acknowledgments   287
Bibliography   289
Index of Passages from Nietzsche's Works   297
Index of Names and Subjects   301

{ ABBREVIATIONS }

Nietzsche's works are cited using the following abbreviations. "P" is used for "Preface." Works are cited by section number except where noted. Translations used and consulted are indicated in some notes and listed in the Bibliography. Works not listed below are cited by author and date and are listed in the Bibliography. Other works cited by abbreviation are in a second list below.

A	*The Antichrist*
BGE	*Beyond Good and Evil*
BT	*The Birth of Tragedy*
D	*Daybreak: Thoughts on the Prejudices of Morality*
EH	*Ecce Homo*
GM	*On the Genealogy of Morality*
GS	*The Gay Science*
HA	*Human, All Too Human*
KSA	*Sämtliche Werke. Kritische Studienausgabe*
KSB	*Sämtliche Briefe. Kritische Studienausgabe*
OS	"On Schopenhauer"
TI	*Twilight of the Idols*
TL	"Truth and Lies in the Non-Moral Sense"
UM	*Untimely Meditations*
Z	*Thus Spoke Zarathustra*

Other Works cited by Abbreviation
CPR	Kant, *Critique of Pure Reason*
ELP	Bernard Williams, *Ethics and the Limits of Philosophy*
SN	Bernard Williams, *Shame and Necessity*
WWR	Schopenhauer, *The World as Will and Representation*

Introduction

This book brings together fourteen of my papers, three of which are published here for the first time. The previously published papers are left in their original form, except for minor changes to fix typos and make citations more consistent throughout. In these introductory comments, I offer an overview of how the papers fit together and, in a few cases, remarks on their continuing relevance.

Although my two books on Nietzsche (Clark 1990 and Clark and Dudrick 2012) focus on truth, knowledge, and metaphysical claims, my work on Nietzsche actually began with a PhD thesis on Nietzsche's critique of morality. Since then I have published a considerable amount on Nietzsche's ethics and his related views on political matters, probably more than even most Nietzsche scholars are aware. The papers included here do not add up to an overall view of Nietzsche on ethics or politics, and I do not intend them to be my last word on either. Yet, published together, they not only exhibit important developments in my views on these topics but also fit together in a way that expresses a distinctive voice in the moral-political area of Nietzsche studies. A final section adds four essays on metaphysics. These reflect the development of my views on the metaphysical and epistemological issues to which my two books are devoted and allow readers to see connections between those issues and the normative claims that are the focus of this volume.

As one anonymous reviewer put it, the papers on ethics and politics published here "articulate, overall, a rather surprising combination of two positions each surprising in itself." The papers on politics read Nietzsche as "much less 'conservative' regarding equality, feminism, homosexuality, and other such social issues than he's generally taken to be," whereas the papers on ethics read him as "less comprehensively critical of 'morality' than is usually supposed: he's not hostile to the ideals of justice, the common good, and responsibility, for example, but only to the historically current interpretations of these." So Nietzsche is not as socially or politically conservative as he seems, yet he does aim to *conserve* more of morality than it may seem. My "large-scale tendency" in these papers, according to the same referee, is the same as in my 1990 book *Nietzsche on Truth and Philosophy*, which is "to rescue Nietzsche from the radical and alarming positions he sometimes seems to express: from extreme skepticism, extreme immoralism, and extreme conservatism." I do not disagree with this characterization as long as the claim is not that my *aim* has been to "rescue" Nietzsche from anything. My aim has always been to make as much *sense* of his texts as possible. And, as will become clear when I discuss my papers on ethics, I actually started out attempting to attribute to Nietzsche as radical a position as I could concerning morality, namely, that he rejected morality itself. Although I still think that is an apt description of his position, as I tried to make sense of that position over the years, I came to realize that it could equally be described as a matter of rejecting the "historically current interpretation of morality." That is because the interpretation has become part of the thing itself.

Nietzsche suggests that this is actually the usual course with things (at least things with a history; cf. *GM* II:12) by saying that "*what things are called*" (i.e., how they are interpreted) "is unspeakably more important than what they are." He explains that the interpretation

> originally almost always mistaken and arbitrary, thrown over things like a dress, and quite foreign to their nature and even their skin—has, through the belief in it and its growth from generation to generation, gradually grown onto and into the thing and become its very body. What at first was appearance becomes in the end, almost invariably, the essence and is effective as such. (*GS* 58)

So while there is truth in the idea that Nietzsche is only rejecting a particular conception of morality, this is because how morality was thought of or interpreted has entered into the very phenomenon of morality. To overcome that interpretation of morality, therefore, would ultimately or eventually be to change not merely a certain understanding of morality, but morality itself.

Ethics

My work on Nietzsche's ethics began by attempting to understand the stance he takes in opposition to morality. Nietzsche repeatedly proclaims himself an immoralist (*D* P:4; *BGE* 32, 206; *HA* P 1; *GS* 381; *EH* IV:4, 6), indeed, the "first immoralist" (*EH* III, *UM*:2; *EH* IV:2). And he makes explicit that his philosophy involves a "campaign against morality" (*EH* III, D:1). His position is not the same as amoralism; immoralism claims not simply that morality has no right to our adherence, but that morality is of negative value, that it is something to be overcome. This is not an easy position to understand and take seriously. It makes sense only if morality is being judged from the viewpoint of some value standard. But if that standard is a nonmoral one, such as self-interest, it is unclear why morality should be expected to live up to it; and if the standard is a moral one, then Nietzsche's immoralism is not a challenge to morality itself, but can only be an attack on one morality from the viewpoint of another one. The latter position is the one interpreters tended to assume when I began writing a dissertation on Nietzsche and morality at the University of Wisconsin. For instance, both Walter Kaufmann and Robert Solomon thought that Nietzsche was rejecting only a particular morality (Christian morality) or a kind of morality (altruistic morality), but not morality itself. To me, their views did not capture the radical nature of the position Nietzsche appeared to be endorsing when he put himself forward as an immoralist. In my dissertation I therefore attempted to make sense of his position as an attack on morality itself. By the time I was ready to publish something on this topic (I had in the meantime written my 1990 book on Nietzsche on truth and epistemological issues), there were a number of interpreters who shared my view that Nietzsche rejects morality itself. But their way of making sense of this position differed from mine. I therefore devoted my first paper on the topic, "Nietzsche's Immoralism and the Concept of Morality"—paper 1 in the present book—to arguing for my own way of making sense of his rejection of morality in opposition to the ones being offered by these other interpreters: Alexander Nehamas, Frithjof Bergmann, and Philippa Foot.

My approach was to begin with Nietzsche's own analysis of the concept of morality. After all, to understand his "campaign against morality," we need to identify the object against which it is directed, the phenomenon against which he is campaigning. And his own analysis of the concept of morality, should he offer one, would tell us what he takes that object to be. The three interpreters discussed in paper 1 either fail to consider the possibility that Nietzsche offered such an analysis or deny that he did. They base their accounts of the object of Nietzsche's immoralism on their own understanding of morality. Foot interprets Nietzsche's immoralism as a rejection of a concern for justice and the common good because this is what she takes to be essential to morality. Nehamas takes the essential ingredient of morality to be universal values and therefore interprets Nietzsche's immoralism as a rejection of such values. Bergmann holds that Nietzsche's immoralism amounts to rejecting the assumption that human beings have free will because he takes that assumption to be the essential or defining feature of morality.

The approach shared by these interpreters is understandable and even necessary if Nietzsche does not supply his own analysis of the concept of morality. But I argue that he does. I argue that his *Genealogy of Morality* (*GM*) is not only a unified account of the origin and development of morality—the dominant view now but not one that was accepted or even articulated when I wrote this essay—but is at the same time an analysis of the concept of morality. The point of this analysis is to understand not the use of the word "morality," but the object picked out by the use of that word. According to *GM*'s account, both morality and the corresponding concept are products of a complicated history that has woven various elements together in a way that makes them very difficult to disentangle. *GM* aims to disentangle these elements so that we can see how they are synthesized in the phenomenon and concept of morality, which is why I called it an "analysis" of the latter.

The main point of paper 1, then, is to show that *GM* is plausibly and helpfully seen as an account not only of the history of morality, but also of what morality is. And when we pay attention to the latter account, it becomes plausible that Nietzsche's immoralism is not directed against a concern for justice and the common good or universal values or various other elements that we may associate with morality, but only against a particular historically conditioned understanding of these elements, one that is due to their mutual entanglement in what we now call "morality." In other words, "nonmoral" versions of justice, universal values, freedom, guilt, duty, and obligation, are possible, and a major point of Nietzsche's *GM* is to bring such possibilities to light. When I refer to a "nonmoral" version of justice, for instance, I am making use of Nietzsche's own distinction between a wider and a narrower sense of morality (*BGE* 30). It is only in the narrower sense of "moral" that Nietzsche's conception of justice can be considered "nonmoral," and only in this sense that Nietzsche seeks to overcome morality. And it is precisely the nature and development of morality in that narrower sense of which *GM* offers an account.

Paper 2, "On the Rejection of Morality: Bernard Williams's Debt to Nietzsche," develops the account of Nietzsche's immoralism offered in paper 1. It employs Williams's distinction between "ethics" and "morality" as a clearer and less confusing way of capturing Nietzsche's distinction between a wider and a narrower sense of morality. What Nietzsche and Williams reject as "morality," I argue, is indeed what we call "morality," and not merely one kind of morality. Yet morality is not the only possible form of ethical life. I think it is largely because they did not recognize this point that Foot and Nehamas were driven to suppose that Nietzsche rejects moral values in favor of aesthetic ones. I claim instead that Nietzsche rejects morality in favor of a different form (or forms) of ethical life, and indeed, does so at least in part because morality undermines other possibilities for such life. To put Nietzsche's claim about morality into Williams's terminology, morality is a particular form of ethical life that has managed to pass itself off as the only possible form. Nietzsche's *GM* offers an idealized history of how this form of ethical life came to be and to hide from view other possibilities for ethical life. It did so through a process whereby various components of ethical life, in particular, practices of judging virtue, on the one hand, and right and wrong, on the other, become linked together and synthesized by means of a certain interpretation of value. Nietzsche calls this interpretation the "ascetic ideal," whereas Williams calls it an "insistence on purity," but it amounts to the same thing. According to Nietzsche and Williams, then, morality is not simply a set of practices, but a set of practices informed by and developed by means of an ascetic interpretation of ethical life, according to which everything of true ("moral") value must be "pure," "separated out from the normal 'muck' of human life," as I put it in this essay. This is how we get, for instance, the idea that the virtuous must be altruistic and that the source of right and wrong must be something pure, like the categorical imperative or the voice of God, and why there can be no "moral luck."

But what is wrong with the ascetic demand for "purity"? What is Nietzsche's objection to the moralized version of ethical life informed by it? One point on which Nietzsche and Williams agree is that morality is bound up with a set of illusions, for instance, the idea of free will in what Nietzsche calls "the superlative metaphysical sense" (*BGE* 21) as well as a necessary lack of transparency. Yet Nietzsche claims that even if morality were based on an error (such as free will), it would not "touch the problem of its value" (*GS* 345). So we must look elsewhere for his ultimate objection to morality. In paper 2, I argue that we find it in Nietzsche's claim that morality brings about its own demise through the will to truth that it encourages. The naturalistic worldview that Nietzsche claims eventually emerges under morality's influence deprives of authority the one form of ethical life we recognize. And because this form of ethical life has been taken to be the only one, it also undermines possibilities for developing new forms. Accordingly, the suggestion offered in paper 2 is that Nietzsche's objection to morality is that it is "nihilistic": in the way just described, it threatens to undermine commitment to any form of ethical value.

Paper 3, "Nietzsche's Contribution to Ethics," is my most complete and succinct account of Nietzsche's naturalistic account of the origins and development of morality. It also adds importantly to the argument of paper 2, which may seem to suggest that Nietzsche's ultimate objection to morality is that it did not last long enough. But surely Nietzsche has a problem with morality such that it is a good thing that it did not last longer (ignoring here the question as to when it died)! Paper 2 therefore gives at best an incomplete account of Nietzsche's objection to morality, and paper 3 can be seen as supplementing it. It argues that his ultimate objection to morality is that it is not adequate medicine for the sickness it was meant to cure. The sickness at issue is the depression and lethargy that resulted when some group of our nomadic ancestors found themselves all of a sudden in a situation in which they were unable to act on the instincts, especially the aggressive ones, that had served them well in the wilderness. They needed a way to re-channel these impulses and the ascetic priest provided one. By reinterpreting ethical life in terms of the ascetic ideal, the priest provided a basis for redirecting aggressive impulses against the self in the form of guilt, various forms of self-torture, and attempts to purify the self of its natural impulses. Nietzsche believes that the redirection of aggressive impulses against the self led to many of the great achievements of human life. But his claim, as I present it in paper 3, is that morality (the ascetic interpretation of ethical life) is a hopeless project because it ultimately fails to provide a helpful or nondestructive way of dealing with aggressive impulses: every success at internalization produces more aggression, resulting in more need for internalization. Nietzsche appears to think that this burden can be borne only with the help of various externalizations of aggression, either the various crude forms we find (increasingly it would seem) in ordinary life or the more spiritualized versions that he claims to find among more spiritual types. The latter were able to externalize their aggression by creating religious and philosophical doctrines and sometimes works of art that devalued nature and existence itself (*GM* II:21). At one time, some of these creations also served less spiritual types, helping them to release their aggression against themselves in various forms of self-discipline (*GM* III:16–21). But at this point in the history of the internalization/externalization of aggression and cruelty, the creations of more spiritual types are increasingly directed against the very possibility of a higher type of human being, thereby undermining respect for higher culture and ultimately its very possibility. So the objection to morality, as discussed in paper 2 (that it ultimately undermines all forms of ethical life) is related to the objection discussed in paper 3 (that morality is not good medicine for the disease that prompts its use). The former problem is a sign and symptom of the latter.

Another noteworthy aspect of paper 3 is its brief discussion of Brian Leiter's 2002 *Nietzsche on Morality*. Leiter's account is complicated, and I do not pretend to do it justice here or in the paper, or to provide any argument against it. But I will say a few words about it because, starting from the same questions from which I had started, Leiter offers an influential alternative to the account of morality presented in the three papers I have been discussing, and this raises the question as to whether my approach is still relevant and worth considering. I want to sketch a few reasons for thinking that it most definitely is.

Leiter agrees with me that Nietzsche is not simply rejecting a particular kind of morality and that he sometimes uses the word "morality" for what he praises—for example, "higher" moralities that "ought to be possible" (*BGE* 202). What then is the "scope" of Nietzsche's rejection of morality? Leiter's answer, like my own, involves distinguishing two senses of "morality" and saying that Nietzsche rejects morality in only one of these senses. He dubs that sense "morality in the pejorative sense" or "MPS," an acronym that has proven very useful for referring to morality in the sense in which Nietzsche rejects it. Here is where Leiter's approach differs from my own: MPS is a heuristic category, as he makes clear, not an historical one. Leiter's approach, unlike mine, is not concerned with how Nietzsche understands the actual historical object that he calls "morality." MPS is a construct, one formed on the basis of Nietzsche's criticisms of various things that we associate with morality, for example, his "disparate critical remarks—about altruism, happiness, pity, equality, Kantian respect for persons, utilitarianism" (Leiter 2002: 129). To oversimplify a bit, an MPS is an ethical system that, in additional to certain metaphysical commitments (e.g., to free will), takes a pro-attitude toward happiness, altruism, and equality, and a con-attitude toward suffering, selfishness, and inequality. Leiter justifies taking MPS to be the "unified target" of Nietzsche's attack on morality (Leiter 2002: 77) on the grounds that the norms just mentioned (and a few others I am ignoring) have something in common, namely, that a culture in which they "prevail as morality" is "harmful to higher men" because "it eliminates the conditions for the realization of human excellence" (Leiter 2002: 126, 129). But even if all of this is correct, it leaves unclear how MPS is related to morality, that is, why *morality* should be blamed for undermining human excellence. Leiter's most plausible example of a cultural norm working this way is the pro-happiness norm. It does seem plausible that a culture holding out individual happiness as all-important will make it more difficult for higher or more creative types (evidently the only ones capable of excellence, according to Leiter's reading of Nietzsche) to even endure, much less welcome, the suffering necessary for the realization of the excellence of which they are capable. And contemporary western culture may well fit this description. But if our culture embraces the norm of individual happiness, this is surely not due to morality, but to the secularized and (one is tempted to say) "post-moral" character of our culture. Indeed a culture emphasizing individual happiness seems to be the antithesis of a moral culture, which would presumably promote duty and striving to be a good person, not striving for one's own happiness.

So a disadvantage of Leiter's nonhistorical account of MPS is that it does not explain why Nietzsche takes the features of contemporary western culture that he finds objectionable to be due to morality, to the actual historical phenomenon he analyzes in *GM*. One advantage of my approach, which focuses on Nietzsche's own account of what morality is, is that it does suggest an explanation. In paper 3, I argue that it is the demise of the ascetic ideal—so the breakdown of morality in the narrow sense—that leads to the culture of herd happiness and the "last man," which Nietzsche finds objectionable to the point of near despair. And morality is to blame for its own demise (as I argue in paper 2) because, in obedience to the ascetic ideal, it both set itself up as the only possible form of ethical life and then led to the undermining of its own authority. If this is correct, focusing on Nietzsche's own account of what morality is also has the advantage of allowing us to recognize the resources he thinks we have—the pre-moralized resources—for developing a new form (or forms) of ethical life. And, finally, I consider it another advantage of my account (though Leiter obviously would not) that Nietzsche's objection to morality is not simply that it is not good for higher types, but that it is ultimately not good for anyone.

Paper 4, "Nietzsche on 'Free Will,' Causality, and Responsibility," published here for the first time, provides an example of what I have in mind regarding resources for new forms of ethical life that Nietzsche attempts to bring into view. I argue against the now common view that Nietzsche is an incompatibilist concerning ethical responsibility (that he denies that responsibility in this sense is compatible with determinism or, as Leiter would have it, fatalism).

He certainly rejects the claim that we are responsible in what he calls the "metaphysical superlative sense" (*BGE* 21), which I argue is precisely the libertarian-incompatibilist sense. But in *GM* II he sketches the early development of something that seems very close to the compatibilist idea of responsibility defended by Peter Strawson in "Freedom and Resentment." The loss of the incompatibilist idea of responsibility therefore does not leave us bereft of any justifiable concept of responsibility. *GM* II provides an account of an idea of responsibility that precedes its moralization, that most of us still share, and that is not undermined by the factors that many, including Williams and Nietzsche, see as undermining responsibility in the metaphysical sense of concern to incompatibilists. It is due to the ascetic ideal that this older notion of responsibility has receded from view and that only its moralized, purified form, the incompatibilist notion, seems to remain. So one aim of Nietzsche's immoralism, understood as his rejection of the ascetic interpretation of ethical life, is to allow a compatibilist notion of responsibility to emerge as a resource for a "post-moral" ethics.

According to my interpretation, then, Nietzsche's immoralism involves not only the rejection of a moralized or ascetic interpretation of ethics, but is also an attempt to lay the groundwork for a "post-moral" form of ethics. And, presumably, the evaluative viewpoint from which he rejects morality already belongs to that post-moral ethics. But does Nietzsche believe that his own values, the values of such a "post-moral" ethics, are objective, or at least more objective than the moral values he rejects? This is a question I take up in paper 5, "Nietzsche and Moral Objectivity," coauthored with David Dudrick. We argue against Brian Leiter's claim that Nietzsche does not believe in the objectivity of any values, and that he therefore does not consider his own values any more objective than the moral values against which he campaigns.

Leiter treats the questions concerning the objectivity of Nietzsche's values as "broadly speaking, metaethical in nature," as questions concerning the metaphysical or epistemological status of those values (Leiter 2002: 136–7). We argue against his answers to these questions by offering an account of the development of Nietzsche's metaethics from *Human, All-Too-Human* through his later works. Nietzsche is often taken to be an error theorist about morality, holding that in making moral claims, we are making false claims that certain properties exist in the world (e.g., rightness, goodness). We argue that this is plausible in the case of *HA*. In fact, because in *HA* Nietzsche was not yet distinguishing between morality in the wide and narrow sense, between ethics and morality, his position was really an error theory with regard to ethics in general and not just morality. Ethical properties do not exist in the world according to the naturalist understanding of the world that Nietzsche begins developing in *HA*. But to derive an error theory of morality from this, Nietzsche would also have to hold a cognitivist account of moral discourse, interpreting claims such as "murder is wrong" as assertions about such properties. Leiter notes that Nietzsche offers no semantics of moral discourse and denies that we have good enough evidence as to the semantics he would have embraced if faced with the options available today. And this may very well be correct. And, yet, surely Nietzsche had to have a view as to how ethics (including morality, of course) fits into nature. If there are no normative facts or properties in the world for people to talk about or respond to, what is going on when people engage in ethical practices, including ethical discourse?

It seems plausible that when he wrote *HA*, Nietzsche considered involvement in ethical practices, including proneness to ethical attitudes and to making ethical judgments, to be guided by false beliefs, beliefs in entities that do not exist. He makes very explicit in *HA* 34 that the person who had overcome all false beliefs would live without such involvement. So, whether or not he had any semantics of moral discourse, it seems hard to deny that he held something close to an error-theoretic view of ethics and morality. Yet, by the time he wrote *The Gay Science*, his position had clearly changed. In understanding how ethics fits into nature, his emphasis is no longer on false beliefs about nonexistent entities, but on the interests and affects that color the world for us, making it into a value-laden world. Dudrick and I argue for interpreting Nietzsche, from *GS* on, as a metaethical non-cognitivist. But our concern is not with the semantics for ethical discourse to which Nietzsche may be committed, but rather with how his view had changed concerning how ethics fits into the natural world, a world that does not contain any ethical facts or properties. Our answer is in terms of the role he now sees ethics as playing in the expression of affective states, above all, of commitments. Of course, Nietzsche still thinks that some ethical practices are deeply involved in error and lack of transparency, as paper 2 argues he thinks is true of morality in the narrow sense. And the exposure of the errors and of what is actually going on in morality is likely to undermine it precisely by weakening the affective basis for morality's particular commitments. But, if my interpretation is correct, Nietzsche does not think that this would undermine all ethical commitment. Or, if it would, it is only because the ascetic ideal's demand for purity has led us to feel that values cannot be "objective" unless they reflect something like a god's eye point of view. Dudrick and I argue against this assumption. We take Nietzsche to have recognized that the error theory in *HA* was itself a product of the ascetic ideal, and we interpret his perspectivism as a way of understanding how he can take his values to be more objective than those he criticizes while also recognizing that when viewed from a naturalistic perspective, both are simply expressions of affect.

Politics

His rejection of morality notwithstanding, Nietzsche's normative perspective is often taken to be highly conservative, based on such evidence as his negative comments about democracy, equality, feminism, modernity, and liberalism, especially in *BGE*, arguably the most important statement of his mature philosophy. Admittedly *Human-All-Too-Human* seems to lean more to the left, to be inspired above all by the Enlightenment. Dedicated to the memory of Voltaire on the occasion of his 100th anniversary, it clearly stands behind much of what Voltaire and the Enlightenment stood for, in particular, the importance of science and democracy. Yet Nietzsche later came to reject much of this book, and this seems to include his political views—which apparently moved quite rightward thereafter. Nothing I have said in discussing the papers in the previous section gives reason to deny this. In fact, it may seem that I add to the reasons that support it. After all, if Nietzsche wants to reform ethical life by exploiting pre-moral resources, it makes sense that he would want to go back to a more traditional organization of society. The papers in this section, written over a period of twenty-five years, examine different aspects of the assumption concerning Nietzsche's rightward trend and constitute different aspects of the case that Nietzsche's later political views lean further left, being more in tune with the Enlightenment, than it appears.[1]

If Nietzsche is often taken to be politically conservative, he is also often used as a whipping boy by conservatives, who defend their own values by pointing to Nietzsche as an example of the danger of diverging from conservative political views. Nietzsche played both of these roles in a prominent neoconservative book of 1987, Allan Bloom's *The Closing of the American Mind*, the subject of paper 6, "Bloom and Nietzsche." Bloom was a follower of Leo Strauss and his esotericism, the view that philosophers do, and should, write in such a way that they will be understood differently by the people and by the philosophically minded.[2] Although I do not mention Strauss in this essay, I do in effect interpret Bloom's treatment of Nietzsche as exhibiting his influence. At first Nietzsche's role seems to be simply that of the villain of the piece, the major intellectual voice behind the 1960s rebellion against traditional culture in the United States and therefore the one ultimately responsible for the degradation of culture that Bloom thinks resulted. One upshot of this process, according to Bloom, was the movement toward liberalization of the college curriculum by the inclusion of minority voices and a greater openness to cultures other than that of the United States. This movement is what Bloom's book was particularly concerned to combat, which it does, at least in part, by associating the movement

---

[1] See Abbey for an analysis of Nietzsche's middle-period works, according to which these are "rich and fruitful works, deserving of close attention" (xii). Indeed, Abbey claims that these works, which constitute the "genealogist's apprenticeship" (xvii), present us with a more attractive Nietzsche than do the later works with which we associate Nietzsche because they show him as more willing to engage with the western philosophical tradition and appreciative of liberal institutions. If my account of Nietzsche's political views is correct, then Nietzsche's later thought continues to embody these characteristics that Abbey finds attractive, but they are more hidden from view.

[2] Strauss's followers are perhaps best known these days for their apparent role in leading the United States into the war in Iraq in the wake of 9/11.

with Nietzsche. To oversimplify: Nietzsche attacked reason, leaving no source for values, and relativism therefore ensued, as exhibited by the "anything goes" attitude of the 1960s as well as the attacks on the traditional curriculum. College students and their teachers sympathized with attacks on cultural imperialism because relativism had destroyed their faith in their own culture's values.

But Nietzsche as archrival of conservatism (or the "neo" version thereof) is only half of Bloom's story. The other side, I argue, is that Bloom sees in Nietzsche someone who actually agrees with his views: the "nihilistic" views of which he accuses Nietzsche are actually his own. The "esoteric" message of Bloom's book is that Nietzsche made the mistake of imparting to the people the content of the philosopher's point of view (when he should have kept it to himself), unlike Strauss's neoconservative followers, who think that the future of thought depends on lying to the people about what philosophers really think. It is because Nietzsche was so honest about, for instance, the nonexistence of God and the inability of reason to provide a basis for values that he can be held responsible for the breakdown of traditional culture in the United States (maybe not single-handedly, but with the help of other all-too-honest European intellectuals).

Although I think Nietzsche would have sympathized with Bloom's worries about what has and will become of intellectual culture (see papers 3, 6, and 9 for what I have to say about Nietzsche's diagnosis of the problem), I was clearly offended by his book and argue strongly against his neoconservative view of Nietzsche in this short paper. It is not Bloom's commitment to writing esoterically that offended me. Indeed, as later papers in Part II and my 2012 book show, I interpret Nietzsche himself as an esoteric writer (Clark and Dudrick 2012). What offended me was Bloom's elitism and disdain for ordinary human life. Some may think that Nietzsche shares these attitudes with Bloom. I do not.[3] I argue that the philosophical life, as Bloom describes it, has no positive content, no content beyond a negation of what he takes ordinary humans to believe, that there are gods that provide cosmic support for what humans care about. Given this structure, I interpreted Bloom's position as just another reflection of the ascetic ideal.[4] The same can be said about his claim that Nietzsche (and other honest intellectuals) drove culture to nihilism and relativism by convincing people that reason cannot provide support for values. It is the ascetic ideal, I claim, that leads one to think that only reason is "pure" enough to provide support for values, that desire and affect cannot provide such a foundation

---

[3] Here it is important to be clear that there are, of course, some ways of understanding "elitist" such that Nietzsche would count as one. Paper 9 suggests one sense in which he is, even though I do not use the word there.

[4] In retrospect, it seems too self-indulgent to be simply an expression of the ascetic ideal and is certainly not the expression of the ascetic ideal for which Nietzsche has the greatest respect (*GM* III:24–5). But, in fact, until that ultimate expression of the ascetic ideal that Nietzsche finds in the will to truth is reached, all versions of the ascetic ideal mix asceticism and self-indulgence.

(contrary to the Nietzschean position set out in paper 5). And, finally, much of what Bloom accuses Nietzsche of being too honest about is not what Nietzsche actually believes. This includes his immoralism, as Bloom understands it, which he in effect interprets as a denial of all ethical constraints, all obligations or duties. As my papers in the previous part should make clear, Nietzsche's rejection of morality is not aimed at liberation from all bonds of obligation and duty; it is rather a protest against the degradation of human life and culture (the nihilism) that "had to grow out of" morality, understood as the ascetic interpretation of ethical life (*GM* II:24). Like responsibility (see paper 4), duty and obligation are notions that have roots much older than the ascetic interpretation of them, and Nietzsche aims to strengthen these, not to undermine them. But this is not going to happen by having philosophers spout the same old doctrines while keeping quiet about they really believe.

In "Nietzsche's Misogyny" (paper 7), I argue against an interpretation of Nietzsche that is not only dear to conservatives but is accepted by most on the Left as well, that Nietzsche is against the liberation of women. Progressives tend to regard Nietzsche's thoughts on women as sexist, anti-feminist, and even misogynistic. Conservatives do not disagree with them about the content of his views, but often deny that they show Nietzsche to have prejudiced views of women, much less to be a misogynist. He does not hate women, I have heard some say (these were political scientists, not philosophers), he "loves women," but just does not want them to embarrass or devalue themselves by trying to act like men, trying to be the equals of men. In this paper, I look at Nietzsche's most extended piece of writing on woman or women, the second half of Part Seven of *BGE* (*BGE* VII). I argue that if we read it carefully, we can see that Nietzsche is not making the claims he seems to be making about women. This starts to become clear if we distinguish what he says about women (*die Frauen*) from what he says about woman (*das Weib*). Unfortunately, translations do not always make the distinction clear. It is even more obvious that we should distinguish what he says about women from what he says about "woman as such," or, perhaps more accurately, "the female in itself" (*das Weib an sich*). Given the similarity to the "thing in itself" (*das Ding an sich*), which Nietzsche dismisses in *BGE* 16 as a contradiction in terms, I argue that his talk of *das Weib an sich* refers to the social construction of the female or feminine (which the "sage" of *GS* 73 claims is the work of men) and is not about individual women who may or may not exemplify it. Indeed, a major point of these sections may be to point to the contradictions in our idea of the feminine—which, Nietzsche shows us here, includes being both more natural hence more animal-like and more spiritual than the male—which makes it impossible for any individual woman to exemplify it (Clark 2002).

I do not deny that there is evidence of misogyny or at least of resentment of women in *BGE* VII. But I claim that it is on the level of feeling or affect, and that Nietzsche uses his expression of it to show us how such feelings can be overcome without the kind of moralizing he rejects. From the viewpoint of my 2012 book with David Dudrick, it seems clear that I already viewed Nietzsche as writing esoterically when I wrote this paper, and the upshot of my esoteric reading of *BGE* VII is that Nietzsche is much more sympathetic than it seems to feminism and the liberation of women.

That this paper remains quite relevant today can be seen by considering the article "Nietzsche and Women" in the very recent *Oxford Handbook on Nietzsche*, which aims to give us the state of the art view on each of its topics. Julian Young begins this piece with Nietzsche's 1874 vote in favor of admitting women to the University, while acting as Dean of Humanities at the University of Basel. Nietzsche voted to admit women (and lost 6–4), Young notes, even though one of his heroes, Jacob Burckhardt, voted on the other side (Young 2013: 46). Adding to this event Nietzsche's friendship with several feminists and an analysis of his writings and letters, Young concludes that "up until 1882 . . . Nietzsche can reasonably be described—certainly by nineteenth century standards—as not only an admirer of feminists but as himself an at least cautious feminist" (Young 2013: 48). But things changed radically after that, he claims: "by 1883 and even more strongly by 1886, Nietzsche has moved from a position of general support for emancipationist demands to violent, total, and *abusive* hostility" (Young 2013: 49). His evidence for this accusation comes, first of all, from the remarks of Nietzsche's characters in *Thus Spoke Zarathustra*, most notoriously the suggestion from an "old woman" that one going to woman should not forget "the whip." If we ignore these—and I think we should because it is more than a little tricky to decide what an author believes on the basis of what he has fictional characters say, especially without an analysis of the work as a piece of fiction—Young's textual evidence comes down almost exclusively to the section of *Beyond Good and* Evil analyzed in my paper. What is Young's response to my analysis? Well, strangely, he does not say[5]—although he does pay attention to what I stress as the contextualizing passage for Nietzsche's remarks about women (which no one else not influenced by my paper has done), and provides an alternative to my reading of it, which he would clearly classify as a "creative misreading" (Young 2013: 58).

I begin with Young's explanation for Nietzsche's "turn" away from women and feminism. It is precisely the one I say in my paper I had always assumed for

---

[5] This is strange because he sent me an email in 2008 (when working on his biography) asking for a copy of the paper and I sent him one (though not electronically, so I cannot be sure that it arrived). Further, much that he says suggests that he did read it. It is also strange that a male positioning himself as the defender of women and feminism against Nietzsche's "pathology" would find, as far as I can tell, no contemporary women worth citing for this article or for his 2010 biography of Nietzsche. Among works not cited are Carol Diethe's *Nietzsche's Women: Beyond the Whip* (1996) and, in the case of the biography, Clark (1990), despite the fact that Young's own claims regarding truth and the will to power seem variations on its influential accounts of the same.

Nietzsche's apparent misogyny (until I worked through his remarks in *BGE* VII): his resentment toward Lou Salomé. Young certainly provides evidence from Nietzsche's correspondence of the nasty and resentful things he said about Salomé after she dumped him to run off with his best friend, Paul Ree. But is it likely that Nietzsche, of all people—the same Nietzsche whom Freud credited with a greater self-knowledge than any man who had ever lived or was likely to live—would allow himself to turn his resentment into not only hatred of women but also a view of women that was quite at odds with his view only a few years earlier? In the midst of the rancor and self-pity that beset him after his relationship with Salomé collapsed, he wrote: "If I don't turn this muck into gold, I am lost." He did turn it into "gold," it seems to me, specifically into *GM*'s analysis of *ressentiment*, including its emphasis on the way in which this affect "falsifies the image" of its object (*GM* I:10). Could he really not have known that this is what he was doing in the case of women?

Actually, even Young does not think so. After asserting, on the basis of no evidence whatsoever, that "one of Nietzsche's weaknesses as a philosopher was his occasional inability to distinguish between the philosophical and the pathological,"[6] he suggests that he nevertheless had, in the case of *BGE*'s remarks on women, "a shrewd suspicion that a personal pathology had invaded his philosophy." Citing *BGE* 231—the passage that I analyze as contextualizing Nietzsche's remarks about women as "only [his] truths" and an expression of the "great stupidity" he is, and therefore as "steps to self-knowledge" (*BGE* 231) rather than as informative about women—Young offers an interpretation that comes close to mine: "Because this most self-aware of men knows that he has not recovered from the Salomé affair, he warns readers that his view on women may well be infected by pathology and prejudice" (Young 2013: 56). This leaves Young with two questions: why didn't Nietzsche "excise" the suspect remarks from his work, and given that he did not, why did he leave in the warning of *BGE* 231? To the first, Young answers that Nietzsche wrote his books "not for a timeless audience located somewhere in outer space but for 'the very few,' five or six contemporaries, five or six actual or potential 'friends' (*GS* 381) he hopes to attract to his cause of cultural regeneration." And since these "friends," after all, "may literally have to live with him in a monastery for free spirits . . . it is important that they should know who he is, warts and all." To the second, Young explains that by the time he wrote *BGE*, most of Nietzsche's good friends were women, and indeed feminists. So because he realized that he had given them a problem of consistency, "of explaining how a Nietzschean feminist could be anything other than a self-contradiction" (a strange echo of the first paragraph of my paper), he invited them to "scrutinize his views on women

---

[6] Note that this seems to contradict the final line of Young's biography regarding Nietzsche's philosophy: that "there is nothing 'pathological' about it—apart from the views on women" (Young 2010: 562).

with an eye to separating the philosophical from the pathological" (Young 2013: 56–7).

Young's answer to the first question seems sheer speculation and based on a false dichotomy. Of course, he was not writing for those in "outer space," but there is little reason to think that the "friends" referred to in *GS* 381 are confined to, or even include, contemporaries, as opposed to future readers, and good reason to think that Nietzsche did not expect *BGE* to find understanding readers for over a hundred years.[7] That the poem at the end of *BGE* makes use of a poem he originally sent to Heinrich von Stein, perhaps in the hopes of getting him to "join him in the high mountains of Sils Marie," provides no evidence that *BGE* "is written for, above all, Heinrich von Stein" (Young 2013: 56). Given the kind of careful reading that *BGE* requires and repays (Clark and Dudrick 2012), it is hardly surprising that Nietzsche thought that it might take a long time before it could be understood. Further, contrary to what Young clearly assumes, the fact that Nietzsche told his feminist friends that he meant the sexist and misogynistic things he said does not give much support to Young's reading. Yes, he meant them. The question is what they mean. And if, as Clark and Dudrick (2012) argue, he wrote *BGE* to teach "to read well . . . to read slowly, deeply, looking cautiously before and aft, with reservations, with doors left open, with delicate eyes and fingers" (*D* P:5), and to reward with insights those who learned what he was trying to teach, there is no reason to think he would have thought he was doing his feminist friends a favor by offering them a shortcut.

Even more implausible is Young's answer to his second question. It seems completely implausible that Nietzsche had enough self-knowledge to strategize in the way Young claims about revealing his warts and helping his feminist friends to see through his misogynistic remarks if he had not seen through them himself. It surely would have been reasonable for Young to raise a third question, which is whether there is a way of reading what Nietzsche actually says in *BGE* VII such that it reflects the fact that Nietzsche actually did see through his *ressentiment*. This is the question to which my paper responds. And given Young's evidence that Nietzsche was very close to being a feminist before the fiasco with Salomé, his agreement with me that Nietzsche invites us to figure out the perspective from which his comments about women are coming, and his recognition of Nietzsche's superior self-knowledge, it is difficult to understand why Young did not even bother to try to follow out Nietzsche's own thinking in *BGE* VII. Perhaps he was having too much fun organizing Nietzsche's comments in a way that most fully brings out their apparent sexism and misogyny (Young 2013: 49). In any case, it is difficult for me to consider my careful

---

[7] See Nietzsche's letter to Malwida von Meysenbug, 24 September 1886, which suggests (in jest, presumably) that reading BGE not be allowed until the year 2000.

esoteric reading of Nietzsche's text less plausible than what appears to me to be Young's tortured psychological explanation.

In addition to being more sympathetic to feminism than he appears, Nietzsche is also more sympathetic to gay liberation than is assumed by conservatives. This is my claim in "On Queering Nietzsche" (paper 11), an unpublished paper I wrote for a meeting of the Society for Gay and Lesbian Philosophy in 1997. It is a response to two other papers given at that meeting, and therefore would not work well as a self-standing journal article. But it seemed to me to make sense to publish it as part of this collection because what I have to say here about Nietzsche and sex combines well with the previous paper on Nietzsche's attitudes toward women and it contributes to the case made in this part that Nietzsche leans much more left in his social and political sympathies than appearances and the secondary literature often suggest.

One of the papers to which I am responding is by Kevin Hill, who argues that Nietzsche was a closeted gay, hidden even from himself, and that his closeted status led him to many of his philosophical doctrines that can seem problematic. I look at Nietzsche's views concerning sex and homosexuality, arguing that his writings reveal him to be much more sympathetic to homosexuality than we would except from someone who was hiding his own tendencies from himself. Further, although being in the closet is a plausible explanation for some of the views that Hill attributes to him, the problem is that, on my reading, Nietzsche did not hold such views. These are mainly views concerning the impossibility of communication and the uncleanliness or "filth" of common culture. To my mind, Nietzsche's writings indicate that he attaches great import to culture and to a common culture. In particular, I claim that the basic practices concerning right and wrong must emerge from a common culture. If the philosopher is to "create values," it is not *ex nihilo*, but only by transforming existing practices through *interpretation* (see my discussion of *GS* 58 above).

In "Nietzsche's Antidemocratic Rhetoric" (paper 9), I piece together the evidence for the widely shared view that Nietzsche supports an antidemocratic, in fact aristocratic, political system. I argue that, as in the case of the previous two papers, careful reading of what Nietzsche actually says shows that he is not committed to the position attributed to him. I argue that his philosophical concerns are compatible with the existence and/or endorsement of a democratic political system. They would not be compatible if Nietzsche were opposed to political equality. I argue that he is not. When he complains about the modern "doctrine of equality," he is referring to the doctrine that all human beings are of equal worth, not to the claim that they have or deserve equal political rights and representation. At the end of this paper, I offer an account of his objection to egalitarianism, understood as the doctrine that human beings are of equal worth.

More important about paper 9 is that it fills in the story as to how Nietzsche thinks the denigration of culture that Bloom (paper 6) was attempting to diagnose follows from the collapse of the ascetic interpretation of ethical life. The moral doctrine of the equality of persons—originally established out of *ressentiment* against those who hold themselves up as superior human beings and translated into the idea that we are all equally children of God—was, after all, coupled with the idea that there are higher states of soul and that only some of us, the best among us, can really achieve them.

"The Good of Community" (paper 10), coauthored with Monique Wonderly, makes two contributions to the argument of the papers on politics in this collection. First, it argues against a new and perhaps more benign way of classifying Nietzsche as a political conservative. Second, it adds to the argument of the previous paper that even though I interpret Nietzsche as more leftist than he appears, he is not an egalitarian. It does so by making an extended and detailed case against Julian Young's claim (which he defends at length in two recent books, Young 2006 and 2010) that the flourishing of the community is Nietzsche's highest value. According to the more traditional view, which we defend here, Nietzsche values the exceptional individual above all. Young attributes to Nietzsche the more politically conservative view that exceptional individuals have value only insofar as they contribute to the flourishing of the community. I take this to be politically conservative because it holds that the interest of the community takes precedence over that of individuals, even that of the exceptional individual. The argument of paper 10 in opposition is that Nietzsche regards communities as valuable *most obviously* because of the goods they make available, and that the greatest of these, for Nietzsche, is individuality and, above all, exceptional individuality. The community is thus instrumentally valuable, whereas the individual is intrinsically valuable. In the final section, however, we suggest that Nietzsche holds that the community, as well as the individual, is intrinsically valuable, and not merely valuable *as a means* to the flourishing of the other. This emphasis on the value of the *exceptional* individual complements the conclusion of paper 9, in addition to making clear that I am not attributing to Nietzsche a liberal position, according to which individual personhood is itself (i.e., apart from the excellence it achieves) the source of value.

Metaphysical Background

A final part adds four essays on metaphysics. The point of including them is to suggest connections between the metaphysical issues with which I deal, especially in my two books, and the normative claims I have been discussing here. In paper 11, "Deconstructing *The Birth of Tragedy*," the earliest paper of those in this collection, my aim was to put my finger on the problem with Nietzsche's first book, the problem that led him to call it an "impossible book" by the time he wrote the new preface to it fifteen years later (*BT* P). I claim that this problem was a contradiction in his understanding and evaluation of the Dionysian. Simply put, in *BT* Dionysus functions as the god of both truth and the affirmation of life. Given Nietzsche's understanding of truth in *BT*, however, life is not really affirmable: appreciation of truth cannot coexist with the affirmation of life; we need illusion in order to affirm life. I still think the detailed analysis offered in paper 11 for this point about the contradiction in *BT*'s position is basically right. Further, my 2012 book with Dudrick provides resources for understanding Nietzsche's ultimate interpretation of how he got himself into this contradiction, a much deeper understanding than the paper itself was able to provide. This recent book allows us to recognize that the contradiction in Nietzsche's early idea of the Dionysian expresses a tension between the will to truth, on the one hand, and the will to value (the will to understand the world in a way that gives support to one's values), on the other—a tension that becomes a contradiction when value is understood from the perspective of the ascetic ideal. In Clark and Dudrick (2012), we argue that Nietzsche understood his middle period work as expressive of this contradiction. Republishing this early paper should help to make clear that this analysis can be extended to Nietzsche's early work.

One aspect of paper 11 that I now reject is its claim that when he was writing *BT* Nietzsche still accepted Schopenhauer's metaphysical claim that the thing in itself is will. Paper 12 rectifies that error, arguing that at this early point in his career, Nietzsche had already rejected the possibility of gaining knowledge of the thing in itself in favor of a more Kantian position. I argue that as Nietzsche overcame the influence of Schopenhauer's metaphysics, he became a Humean empiricist and non-cognitivist on moral issues. Paper 12 is thus a forerunner to paper 5, on Nietzsche's metaethics. It is also an extensive exploration of one side of what *BGE* calls the "magnificent tension of the spirit," which Nietzsche hopes will give rise to the "philosophy of the future" of the book's subtitle. According to Clark and Dudrick (2012), that tension is between the will to truth, the will to represent reality in terms of what is actually there, and the will to value, the will to represent reality in a way that supports one's values (other than truth). And the will to truth side of the tension, we argue, leads to an empiricist-naturalistic picture of reality. That is what Nietzsche developed in his middle-period works (*HA*, *D*, and *GS*) as he broke away from Schopenhauer, and it is the development of that picture that I explore in paper 12.

But it turned out that I only had half of the story when I wrote paper 12. I was not yet clued into Nietzsche's claim in *BGE*, to which Clark and Dudrick (2012) is devoted, that the will to truth and the will to value have existed in tension in his philosophy (and in all of the important philosophy with which he is concerned). Whereas paper 12 denies that Nietzsche has a metaphysics once he abandons the thing in itself, paper 13 indicates that a metaphysics, or at least something analogous to one, emerges in Nietzsche's thought once he takes the will to value into account and finds a way to satisfy it. This is a metaphysics from a first (and second) person point of view and one based on normative premises. Finally, paper 14, coauthored with David Dudrick, lays out the philosophical psychology that Clark and Dudrick (2012) claim emerges from this normative point of view and defends attributing it to Nietzsche against an alternative interpretation of Nietzsche's psychology offered by Paul Katsafanas.

{ PART I }

Ethics

{ 1 }

Nietzsche's Immoralism and the Concept of Morality

Although Nietzsche quite explicitly claims to be an immoralist (e.g., *EH* IV: 2–4; *BT* P:5),[1] many serious and sympathetic interpreters have denied that he is. This is understandable because immoralism is a difficult position to take seriously. An immoralist does not simply ignore morality, or deny its right to our compliance, but claims that morality is a bad thing that should be rejected. Immoralism therefore seems to be defensible only from the viewpoint of a morality, which makes it appear to be as self-refuting as another notorious Nietzschean claim, that truths are illusions. I have argued elsewhere that Nietzsche actually overcame this paradoxical claim about truth in his later works, starting with his *Genealogy of Morals* (Clark 1990). But this approach will not work for his immoralism, which is clearly expressed in the *Genealogy* and in later works, and in fact is more clearly expressed in later works than in earlier ones. Nietzsche moved toward, not away from, immoralism over the course of his work. Sympathetic interpreters have therefore usually tried another tact, suggesting that Nietzsche is an immoralist only in a very qualified sense: namely, that he rejects a particular kind of morality (say, Christian morality) or a particular theory or conception of morality, but not morality itself.[2]

There is now evidence of a change of direction on this issue within Anglo-American Nietzsche scholarship. At least three important Nietzsche scholars, Philippa Foot, Alexander Nehamas, and Frithjof Bergmann, have argued that the qualified interpretation trivializes Nietzsche's position on morality.

---

[1] Nietzsche's books are cited by the initials of their standard English translations, followed by the section number, which is the same in all editions. I have followed Kaufmann's translation of the *Genealogy*, but have made minor changes based on volume 5 of the *Studienausgabe*, ed. G. Colli and M. Montinari (Berlin: Walter de Gruyter, 1980).

[2] I would include among those who accept such a qualified interpretation of Nietzsche's immoralism Walter Kaufmann, Arthur Danto, Robert Solomon, John Wilcox, Richard Schacht, and Frederick Olafson.

Consider, for instance, his prediction in the preface to the *Genealogy* that one who begins as he did by raising questions about the morality of compassion, but also stays with the issue and learns to ask questions, will experience what he experienced: "A tremendous new prospect opens up . . . belief in morality, in all morality, falters—finally a new demand becomes audible . . . we need a *critique of moral values, the value of these values must itself for once be called into question*" (*GM* P:6). Nietzsche here makes clear that he distinguishes "all morality" from specific moralities—in this case from one he had earlier, under Schopenhauer's influence, identified with morality itself.[3]

The qualified interpretation of his immoralism therefore seems to trivialize what Nietzsche himself wants to say. Those who interpret him instead as a full-fledged immoralist agree that his position is perplexing and confusing. But they also suspect that there is a major issue here that will never get confronted unless we try to understand why Nietzsche thought that morality itself, rather than a specific morality, was the object of his attack. Although Foot certainly does not expect to agree with Nietzsche, she emphasizes that we are bound to receive some enlightenment about morality if we try to confront such a brilliant critic's rejection of it (Foot 1991: 18–21). To do this, we need to try to understand how Nietzsche could find it plausible that he rejected all morality.

That is what I shall begin doing in this essay. I will be concerned not with Nietzsche's arguments against morality but only with his perplexing claim to be against morality itself. I want to make clear, however, that I do not take this as a claim to reject all morality (or morality itself) given every possible understanding of "morality." If, for instance, one counts any set of rules or prohibitions as a "morality," Nietzsche is certainly not claiming to reject all morality. Nor does he do so if one counts as "a morality" any system for evaluating the goodness of persons. Nietzsche himself sometimes uses the word "morality" in such a way that he is not rejecting all morality and thus cannot count himself as an immoralist, for instance, when he praises "noble morality" or insists that "higher moralities" should be possible.

When Nietzsche calls himself an "immoralist," on the other hand, he uses the word in such a way that he does reject all morality. Given this use of the word, I shall argue later, he counts the noble mode of valuation as a nonmoral mode of evaluating persons rather than as a morality. This latter usage—the usage in accord with which he is an immoralist or rejects all morality—is, by far, his most common, especially in the works he published. This is to be explained, I suggest, by Nietzsche's belief that this sense of morality (the sense

---

[3] In *Human, All Too Human,* Nietzsche follows Schopenhauer in identifying acting morally with acting unegoistically (of which acting from compassion is taken as a primary example), but had clearly broken from Schopenhauer's narrow construal of morality by the time he wrote the *Genealogy*. I argued for both of these points in my unpublished dissertation, "Nietzsche's Attack on Morality" (University of Wisconsin, 1976).

given which he counts himself an "immoralist") corresponds pretty much to how we primarily use the term "morality" (or, if you prefer, what it would introduce the greatest amount of clarity in what we do say for us to consistently call "morality").[4]

My explanation is supported by *BGE* 32, in which Nietzsche includes himself among "immoralists" after distinguishing premoral, moral, and extramoral periods of human history. He refers to the second of these as a period that may be called "moral" in the narrower or strict (*engeren*) sense, then asks if we don't stand on the threshold of the third period, "of a period that should be designated negatively, to begin with, as extramoral (*aussermoralische*)." When he then refers to the "overcoming of morality," this clearly means the overcoming of morality in the narrower sense. But why does he call himself an immoralist (at least "to begin with"—that characterization of himself clearly stands or falls with the characterization of the period he wants to inaugurate as "extramoral") if he is only rejecting morality in this narrower sense? Because, as he makes clear in this passage, precisely this is morality in the traditional sense, or, more literally, in the sense "morality" has had until now ("*Moral, im bisherigen Sinne*").

So when Nietzsche occasionally writes of "higher moralities," I take him, in accord with *BGE* 32, to be using "morality" in a nontraditional and wider sense, which makes it equivalent to "codes for evaluating human beings and their conduct." I take the fact that he uses the term in this wider sense relatively infrequently to reflect his understanding of his immoralism as a rejection of precisely what we have traditionally embraced under the term "morality." My question is how Nietzsche made it comprehensible and plausible to himself that he was rejecting precisely what we have embraced as "morality."

To have a chance of finding a reasonable answer, we must begin by assuming that for Nietzsche what we call "morality" does not exhaust the realm of value. If moral values are to be called into question and found wanting, it must be from the viewpoint of some other species of value. To understand how Nietzsche could have considered himself an immoralist, we then need to know at least what he thinks moral values are, and why he did not take his own values to be moral values. I believe this approach is already implicit in the work of the three philosophers I have mentioned who interpret Nietzsche as an immoralist. However, I do not believe they have given adequate accounts of how Nietzsche

---

[4] *BGE* 202 supports this explanation. I take Nietzsche to claim in *BGE* 202 that we Europeans use the word "morality" so that codes of conduct and valuations he considers "higher" cannot count as moralities. He also proposes a revision in our linguistic practice, so that his higher codes can count as moralities. Why would he propose this? Because he thinks our current use of the word "morality" hides from us our prejudices concerning values and that if we got over these (or perhaps even got them out on the table), there would no longer be any point in restricting the term in the way we do now. But since we do now restrict the term that way, the least misleading thing for Nietzsche to say is that he rejects morality itself, that he is an immoralist.

understands moral values, or why he does not regard his values as moral values. I will therefore begin with a quick sketch of their views and of the factors that supply *prima facie* reasons to look for an alternative account within the general framework on which they agree.

Foot begins the serious attempt to treat Nietzsche as an immoralist by insisting that valuing a kind of person (or certain traits of character) does not commit one to specifically moral values.[5] Yes, Nietzsche praised and valued strong, independent, courageous people, but Foot thinks his values may be more aesthetic or quasi-aesthetic than moral. For she claims that morality is necessarily connected to the mores or rules of behavior of a society, and that Nietzsche denies that there are any social norms that should be taught to all. True, she says, Nietzsche refuses to praise anyone who is not strong and courageous. However, she thinks that what Nietzsche praises would give rise to an injunction no more specific than "seek your own health," which does nothing to reestablish social norms, and which in any case he would only preach to the exceptional ones truly capable of strength and health.

Foot argues that taking Nietzsche to be an immoralist rather than a special kind of moralist is further supported by the fact that "he was prepared to throw out rules of justice in the interests of producing a stronger and more splendid type of man," whereas morality is "necessarily connected to such things as justice and the common good, and it is a conceptual matter that this is so" (Foot 1978: 92). But she provides no evidence for this claim, and Nietzsche reserves his highest words of praise in the *Genealogy* for justice and the just person (*GM* II:11). We therefore have good reason to look for an alternative to at least part of Foot's account.

Nehamas does not mention the justice issue, but seems to accept and be working out the implications of the rest of Foot's account of why Nietzsche is an immoralist. Nietzsche's problem with morality, according to Nehamas, is that it is universalistic or unconditional—that it consists of "codes that are imposed not only on those for whom they are suited but on everyone else as well" (Nehamas 1985: 224). It would seem to follow that an immoralist need not reject all codes of conduct, but only all universal codes. There is, however, a problem with understanding morality in these terms. After all, a moralist need not think (and perhaps few have) that everyone has the same obligations or duties. Plato surely thought that the duties of the philosopher-king differed from those of the common person, yet Nietzsche seems right in regarding Plato as a moralist. Therefore, recommending different codes of conduct to persons

---

[5] Philippa Foot, "Nietzsche: The Revaluation of Values," in *Virtues and Vices* (Berkeley, Los Angeles, London: University of California Press, 1978), pp. 81–95. This paper was originally published in *Nietzsche: A Collection of Critical Essays*, ed. Robert Solomon (New York: Doubleday, 1973), and Foot has made its arguments accessible to a wider audience in her "Nietzsche's Immoralism."

in different positions or situations would not be sufficient to save Nietzsche from counting as a moralist. Recommending different codes to persons in the same position and situation would be sufficient, but would also render Nietzsche's position unworthy of serious consideration.

Nehamas avoids the resulting problem by insisting that Nietzsche does not teach a code of conduct to anyone. His assumption seems to be that Nietzsche could not recommend a code of conduct without imposing his values on others, thus being a moralist. This, I believe, is why Nehamas is attracted to the view that Nietzsche's books present us with a literary character, the character "Nietzsche," created by the writer Nietzsche. His writings can then function to *show* (some of) us that this character is praiseworthy without *asserting* that he is. Nietzsche can thus have his value stance without being a moralist—that is, without imposing his values on others. One problem with Nehamas's account is lack of evidence that Nietzsche was so worried about imposing his values on others. Further, how could this be so important to him, unless he accepted the moral premise that thou shalt not impose thy values on others? I therefore suspect that Nietzsche's rejection of morality on the grounds Nehamas suggests would be deeply incoherent.

Bergmann (1988), however, denies what Foot and Nehamas take for granted: that a code of conduct that is supposed to apply to all members of a society must be a moral code or morality. People usually see no hope for Nietzsche's immoralism, according to Bergmann, because they think we need morality to restrain the powerful, and establish justice and control. But perhaps it is a mistake, he suggests, to suppose that all other cultures have a morality. For the Balinese, according to Bergmann, even the most appalling and serious transgression provokes a reaction and judgment that is radically different in quality from what we are accustomed to. Even outrageous violations are interpreted as what we might call "stupidities." The point is not that the judgment made of these violations is milder than moral judgment, but that the underlying conceptions presupposed by these judgments are quite different. Whereas moral judgments presuppose the idea of freedom and a correlative notion of responsibility, according to Bergmann, these are not presupposed by the judgment of a violation as a stupidity. Whereas morality presupposes the idea of a self that is independent and marked off against nature, the other cultures he has in mind take human beings to be integral parts of nature through whom the flow of causally linked events runs.

Now if a code of conduct does not count as a morality unless it presupposes freedom in the radical sense Bergmann has in mind, we can understand why Nietzsche claimed to reject morality, for he clearly rejects the idea that human beings are free in a sense that sets us over against nature. The problem is that Bergmann offers us no reason to think morality *does* presuppose freedom in this sense. Further, there clearly were important philosophers of whom Nietzsche was aware—Hobbes and Hume, for instance—who claim to accept morality but reject radical freedom. So while I am in sympathy with much of Bergmann's account, I do not think he succeeds in explaining how Nietzsche could have convinced himself that he was an immoralist.

The new approach I want to propose for making Nietzsche's claim comprehensible is to look at his own analysis of the concept of morality. Although this may seem fairly obvious, it has actually not been tried by other interpreters. The three I have discussed rely on their own understanding of the concept of morality to make sense of Nietzsche's immoralism. Foot thinks that justice is essential to morality, so she assumes with very little help from Nietzsche's books that he claims to be an immoralist because he rejects justice. Nehamas and Bergmann do the same thing for universalizing one's values and freedom.

This procedure is perfectly understandable, and even necessary, if Nietzsche does not supply his own analysis of the concept of morality. But I believe that he does. This is not obvious to be sure, but I will argue that his *Genealogy of Morals* (or more literally, *Genealogy of Morality*) supplies a very original analysis of the concept of morality as an essential part of a theory of the origin of morality. It may turn out, of course, that this analysis is quite wrongheaded, and that given an adequate understanding of morality, we should count Nietzsche as a moralist. But I do not see how we can seriously confront his thinking about morality unless we try first to understand his immoralism in terms of what he himself has to say about the concept of morality.

My interpretation of the *Genealogy* as a unified theory will seem rather idiosyncratic these days. After all, the book consists of three separate essays, each one evidently devoted to a different moral phenomenon. Kaufmann summarizes the three essays as follows: "The first essay, which contrasts 'Good and Evil' with 'Good and Bad,' juxtaposes master and slave morality; the second essay considers 'guilt,' 'bad conscience,' and related matters; and the third, ascetic ideals" (Kaufmann 1968: 446). The problem for my interpretation is that Nietzsche makes no explicit attempt to connect up these different essays. Within each essay, the situation is similar: each turns out to consist of several different stories or pieces of stories, and Nietzsche does not seem concerned to patch them together into a unified account.

This has helped encourage the now common view (expressed, for instance, in Alasdair MacIntyre's recent book (MacIntyre 1990)) that genealogy is a new kind of moral inquiry, an exercise in perspectivism, one that is supposed to let in all sorts of different views without privileging one over others. We are supposed to learn from the *Genealogy* that there are only different stories, some better than others for certain purposes, to be sure, but none containing more truth than others. In an atmosphere pervaded by such ideas, viewing the *Genealogy* as a unified account of the origin of morality will seem bad enough. That I also see it as an extended analysis of the concept of morality will make me seem blind to what Nietzsche is up to, and perhaps deserving of Arthur Danto's barb that "to treat the *Genealogy* as though it were precocious analytical philosophy is to have swallowed the bait without having yet felt the hook" (Danto 1988: 19). I will nevertheless try to convince you that my approach to the *Genealogy* has some merit. I shall begin by discussing the view of conceptual analysis Nietzsche articulates at the very center of the book (in the middle section of the middle essay) in connection with an analysis of the concept of punishment. He begins his analysis of punishment by distinguishing between

> on the one hand, that in it which is relatively *enduring*, the custom, the act, the "drama," a strict sequence of procedures; on the other, that in it which is *fluid*, the meaning, the purpose, the expectation associated with the performance of such procedures. (*GM* II:13).

Nietzsche adds that "the procedure itself will be something older, earlier than its employment in punishment, that the latter is *projected* and interpreted *into* the procedure (which has long existed but been employed in a different sense)." This is an application of the major point of historical method he has been developing in the essay: namely, that "the cause of the origin of a thing and its eventual utility, its actual employment and place in a system of purposes, lie worlds apart" (*GM* II:12).

I suggest that what Nietzsche calls the "stable element" in punishment is the act of inflicting a harm or loss on a person based on a judgment that the person deserves this loss owing to something he or she has done.[6] Nietzsche's analysis of the debtor–creditor relation earlier in this essay makes apparent his belief that people inflicted harm based on judgments of desert before such judgments became part of punishing. He suggests, in effect, that the stable element in punishment originated in the agreement made by debtors that if unable to pay off debts, they would provide a substitute repayment in the form of some harm or physical suffering the creditor would be allowed to inflict on them (*GM* II:5).

It seems right to deny that such infliction of suffering (e.g., the taking of a pound of flesh from the person who cannot repay a debt) constitutes a case of punishment, even though it occurs as a result of a judgment that the debtor owes this suffering (or the opportunity to inflict it) to the creditor. The purpose of inflicting suffering in this case seems to be not to punish the debtor but

---

[6] It might seem more reasonable to construe the stable element in punishment as the actual procedure for inflicting suffering. Nietzsche discusses such procedures earlier in the same essay (*GM* II:3), and he would then be making the obviously true claim that techniques for inflicting suffering existed prior to their employment in punishment. However, it is difficult to see why Nietzsche would equate such techniques of violence with "a strict sequence of procedures," or why he would consider the procedure the "stable element" and the purpose the "fluid" aspect of punishment when there are at least as many different procedures for inflicting suffering as there are purposes for punishing. I therefore suggest that the enduring element, "the custom, the act, the 'drama,' a strict sequence of procedures," he refers to is the sequence of accusing someone of a wrong or violation, judging that the violation has taken place, determining the penalty that is appropriate or deserved, and inflicting that penalty. This amounts to inflicting a penalty as a result of a judgment that the person deserves it owing to something he or she has done.

rather to extract a substitute repayment. The distinction made in civil cases between compensatory and punitive damages also suggests that judgments of desert are not sufficient to make inflicting a loss a case of punishment.

But then what is sufficient? What distinguishes the punitive from the nonpunitive infliction of such harm? Nietzsche answers as follows:

> As for the other element in punishment, the fluid element, its "meaning," in a very late condition of culture (for instance, modern Europe) the concept "punishment" possesses in fact not *one* meaning but a whole synthesis of "meanings": the previous history of punishment in general, the history of its employment for the most diverse purposes, finally crystallizes into a kind of unity that is hard to disentangle, hard to analyze, and, as must be emphasized especially, totally indefinable. (Today it is impossible to say for certain *why* people are really punished: all concepts in which an entire process is semiotically concentrated elude definition; only that which has no history is definable.) At an earlier stage, on the contrary, this synthesis of "meanings" can still be disentangled, as well as changed; one can perceive how in each case the elements of the synthesis undergo a shift in value and rearrange themselves accordingly, so that now this, now that element comes to the fore and dominates at the expense of others; and under certain circumstances one element (the purpose of deterrence perhaps) appears to overcome all the remaining elements. (*GM* II:13)

In thus denying that "punishment" can be defined, Nietzsche denies that there is an essence of punishing, in the sense of a set of necessary and sufficient conditions that distinguishes the punitive from the nonpunitive infliction of harm. We can say that such harm must be inflicted for a punitive purpose to count as punishment; but Nietzsche's point is that there is no single purpose that constitutes the purpose of punishing—that our idea of punishing is an unstable synthesis of various purposes that have been served by inflicting harm based on judgments of desert. A Nietzschean history of punishment would try to show how different purposes came to be associated with inflicting such harm, and how these purposes replaced or combined with each other to explain the meaning or justification of doing so.

Analyzing the concept of punishment, however, would involve disentangling various of these purposes and exposing how they have been run together or conflated. Nietzsche suggests that concepts influenced by history are like ropes held together by the intertwining of strands, rather than by a single strand running through the whole thing. To analyze such concepts is not to find necessary and sufficient conditions for their use but to disentangle the various strands that may have become so tightly woven together by the process of historical development that they seem inseparable. Such analysis would take place most effectively in conjunction with historical theorizing, because it is the historical synthesis of strands that hides their separability from view, and it is thus by going back and forth between historical and conceptual considerations that one can hope to make progress in either the history or the conceptual analysis. Historical theorizing and conceptual analysis would thus be two sides of a complex theory as to the origin and development of punishment.

Now Nietzsche must believe that this connection between history and concepts also exists in the case of morality. After all, he articulates it in the very middle of a book titled literally *On the Genealogy of Morality*. Kaufmann's translation of the singular "*Moral*" as "morals," while not wrong, has tended to encourage those who deny that the book offers any kind of unified theory. But given the discussion of concepts at the physical center of the book, we should expect Nietzsche's view to be that a unified theory of the origins of morality would uncover the origin and trace the development of different and originally independent strands of morality that history has woven together. This, I believe, is exactly what the *Genealogy* attempts. I suggest that the sometimes disjointed or fragmentary character of the *Genealogy* has nothing to do with telling different stories or allowing in various perspectives, but is due instead to a self-conscious attempt to analyze a concept with a complex history—to disentangle originally independent elements that we can no longer see as such.

Genealogy is nothing mysterious or newfangled. Nietzsche's history of morality is a genealogy because it is the history of couplings. Something that already exists combines with something else that has its own history to give birth to a third thing, which then combines with something else that is also the product of such couplings. Genealogy is simply a natural history. If there is something new in Nietzsche's use of genealogy, it is the suggestion that concepts are formed in the same way as other living things—and, in particular, that this is true of the concept of morality. I will now try to indicate something of the implication of this view for an analysis of the concept of morality.

Consider the First Essay, titled "'Good and Evil,' 'Good and Bad.'" Following Kaufmann, this essay is usually assumed to be a comparison of master and slave morality, an attempt to distinguish "moralities that originated in the ruling class from moralities that originated among the oppressed" (Kaufmann 1968: 440). I consider this misleading for two reasons. First, even in the case of good and evil, Nietzsche is not looking at a whole morality in this essay. Standards of right and wrong, for instance, receive no attention. The essay compares not two moralities, but two different ways of determining who is good and who isn't. Further, as I shall argue, Nietzsche's "good/bad" is not a moral distinction.

Nietzsche begins by arguing on philological grounds that "good" originally meant the same as "noble," or "of the ruling class," whereas "bad" meant "common" (*GM* I:4). But then how could "good" express a value judgment? Nietzsche answers that the nobles' self-affirmation showed through in the words they used to refer to themselves. Happy with their own existence (after all, they had power, wealth, and so forth), they naturally experienced their own lives as preferable or superior to the lives of those they ruled. Nietzsche explains the origin of regarding particular characteristics as "good"—the origin of judgments of virtue—along the same lines, claiming that the nobles called "good" the characteristics they perceived as belonging to themselves and distinguishing them from the commoners. Their self-affirmation or happiness was such that they took any characteristic they saw as peculiar to themselves to be part of their goodness, that is, an aspect of their superiority to the common human being.

At first, they perceived the distinction in crude physical terms, like wealth and power. As time went on, their view of the distinction between themselves and commoners came to center more on traits of soul or character, such as loyalty, truthfulness, and courage. They began to designate themselves as "the truthful," as "distinct from the *lying* common man" (*GM* I:5). In this process, Nietzsche claims, "good" finally lost all connection to political class and became identical with superiority of soul. However, it is unclear whether this is supposed to have happened sometime in the past, or is being held out as a possible future development of the good/bad distinction.

In either case, it seems to me that good/bad here is not a moral distinction. Although he does not draw this conclusion, Danto provides the basis for it when he writes:

> From the masters' perspective, those unlike themselves are merely bad humans; that is to say, humans that do not come up to the mark. This is similar to the way bad eggs are low in the scale of egghood. There is nothing *morally* bad in being a bad egg, or, in this usage, a bad human. It is just the way one is. Too bad, then, for the bad. They hardly can be blamed for being what they are; but they are bad. (Danto 1965: 159)

In other words, calling commoners "bad" is certainly making a value judgment about them, but it is not judging them to be "morally bad" or "immoral." But then it should follow that the nobles are not proclaiming their own moral virtue when they call themselves "good," and that good/bad does not express a distinction of moral value, a distinction made from the viewpoint of morality. This is most obvious in the earliest stage of the noble mode of valuation. When noble birth, power, and wealth are the criteria for being "good," it is easy to see that goodness is not equivalent to moral virtue. In whatever way the moral point of view is characterized, it is not the viewpoint from which the nobles declare power and wealth to be marks of the good human being.

It may seem less obvious that moral distinctions are not involved when traits such as truthfulness become marks of "the good," and especially when goodness is constituted solely by traits of soul unrelated to political or social position. According to Nietzsche's story, however, there is no change in the point of view from which goodness is judged when it expands to include character traits. It is still merely the natural viewpoint of a group of individuals well pleased with themselves when comparing themselves to a group they would not be happy to be part of. Goodness is still constituted by what members of the self-affirming group perceive as marking themselves off from those they would not want to be.

Further, Nietzsche claims that the German equivalent of the word "bad" had no inculpatory connotations until the time of the Thirty Years' War (*GM* I:4). We should therefore take him to be using "bad" in such a way that being bad is not something one is to be blamed for, whether it is a matter of being poor and politically weak, or of lying and cowardice. From within the good/bad mode of valuation, the attitude toward the liar is not one of moral disapproval. Instead, Nietzsche claims that the noble feels "contempt for the cowardly, the anxious, the petty, those intent on narrow utility," and "above all, the liars: it is part of the faith of all aristocrats that the common people lie. 'We truthful ones'—thus the nobility of ancient Greece referred to itself" (*BGE* 260).

Schopenhauer had already distinguished this attitude toward liars from moral disapproval. "According to the principle of knightly honor, the reproach of being a liar is regarded as extremely grave," Schopenhauer wrote, "not because the lie is *wrong*," but because it is taken as evidence of fear and lack of strength (Schopenhauer 1965: 162). Nietzsche's noble and Schopenhauer's knight "look down on" or feel superior to the liar because lying demonstrates lack of power, and thus the absence of something the nobility spontaneously affirms in its own life. Since this explains why liars are considered "bad" without recourse to moral concepts, we can deny that the distinction Nietzsche calls "good/bad" constitutes a moral distinction, even when made within the realm of character.

Good versus evil, however, is clearly supposed to be a moral distinction. Like good versus bad, it distinguishes superior from inferior people. Unlike bad, evil is equivalent to immoral or morally bad. The main difference seems to be that the evil are blamed or thought deserving of punishment for being the kind of people they are, whereas the bad are not blamed for being bad, any more than the nobles consider themselves deserving of reward for being good. Only when contrasted with "evil" does goodness become something for which it makes sense to think one deserves a reward. By that point, goodness has become equivalent to moral goodness.

According to Nietzsche's theory, this way of judging goodness originated in resentment directed against the nobles and their easy sense of superiority. The resentful call the nobles "evil" and themselves "good." Rather than reflecting the goods' natural sense of their own superiority, these judgments constitute an act of "imaginary revenge" against the nobles (*GM* I:10). I think this means they involve a sublimated or spiritualized equivalent of burning someone in effigy. As burning in effigy acts out or plays at depriving someone of his life, and in so doing helps satisfy pent-up resentment, calling someone "evil" can satisfy the same kind of feelings by playing at depriving others of their self-proclaimed goodness or superiority.

Calling another "bad" or "contemptible" can sometimes function in the same way, but would not have been very effective against the nobles who in Nietzsche's story possess precisely what the resentful want.[7] This would make very difficult any wide-scale pretense to regard them as inferior. But things change once the idea of blame or culpability is used to transform "bad" into "evil." If they can be *blamed* for what they are, they can be thought deserving of punishment on that basis. And especially since it will then seem natural to regard the good as deserving of reward for being good, it will be much easier for the good to convince themselves that they really are superior and do not want to be like the nobles at all.

If this reading is correct, the First Essay of the *Genealogy* does not compare two different moralities. Instead, it attempts to isolate from the historically conditioned synthesis we call "morality" a particular strand—the idea of moral worth or goodness—and to show how it developed from something that existed prior to morality. The revolt against the noble mode of valuation lies, according to Nietzsche's story, at the beginning of the specifically moral evaluation of persons. The *Genealogy's* First Essay is an account of how a nonmoral mode of evaluating persons was transformed into a specifically moral mode, of how pagan virtue became moral virtue.

But it would also be misleading to say that this account is supposed to explain the origin of morality. Morality is a very complex affair on Nietzsche's account; and the moralization of virtue could not have taken place without earlier developments that also contribute central strands to our concept of morality—strands left completely out of account in the *Genealogy's* First Essay. This point can be appreciated by considering the incompleteness of its account of the revolt against the noble mode of valuation. I have so far suggested that it is the idea of blaming people for what they are that transforms the noble mode of valuation into a moral mode. But the practice of blaming people for what they are did not arise out of thin air. Blaming too must have a history and must already be present in some form to be used to transform "bad" into "evil." One obvious suggestion is that blaming people for what they are probably developed as a transformation of the practice of blaming people for what they do. But blaming people for their actions only makes sense if there are standards for acceptable behavior. Yet Nietzsche's First Essay tells us nothing about such practices and standards, much less where they come from. The rest

---

[7] What this is depends on the person in question. Whereas the people probably envied most the nobles' power and wealth, the priests may well have envied most of all their unquestioning sense of their own worth.

of the *Genealogy* does suggest answers on both counts—but we must be willing to piece them together for ourselves.

Its Second Essay suggests that the oldest strand woven into the concept of morality is rules or codes of conduct that set out standards of right, of socially permitted and forbidden behavior. For it traces the phenomena with which it deals, "guilt, bad conscience, and the like," to what Nietzsche had earlier called "the morality of mores"—the system of laws and customary practices found in ancient communities (*GM* II:2).

When he introduced this term in *Daybreak* (*D* 9), he believed that the mores functioned within such communities as the naturalistic equivalent of moral rules or categorical imperatives that were obeyed not from prudential motives, but from a kind of reverence based on superstition.[8] Nietzsche rejects this theory in the *Genealogy*, claiming that the task of what he had called the "morality of mores" was to create a memory and that this was done with the use of severe punishments. Through the experience and threat of punishment, Nietzsche claims, "one finally remembers five or six 'I will not's' in regard to which one had given one's promise so as to participate in the advantages of society" (*GM* II:3). The rules are "I will not's" rather than "ought not's," I presume, because they are kept in place as rules demanding obedience largely by the threat of punishment, and therefore function as hypothetical—rather than as categorical or moral—imperatives. A major (if unspoken) issue of the *Genealogy's* Second Essay is how rules originally regarded as hypothetical imperatives came to be regarded as moral imperatives.

The big story of the Second Essay is the development of bad conscience, initially characterized as "the consciousness of guilt" (*GM* II:4). This suggests that on Nietzsche's view the mores become moral rules when they are connected with guilt—when people come to believe that those who violate the rules incur guilt. But where did this idea come from? Nietzsche claims that "the feeling of guilt, of personal obligation" had its origin in the debtor-creditor relation (*GM* II:8). That is, being guilty originally was nothing more than owing a debt, as is suggested already by the fact that the same German word (*Schuld*) is used to translate both "debt" and "guilt."[9] Originating in the sphere of trade, the idea of having a debt or owing something then transferred itself to the first forms of social organization. The community is viewed as "standing to its members in the same vital relation of creditor to its debtors" (*GM* II:9). The members enjoy the advantages of community (advantages Nietzsche says we sometimes underrate today), "dwelling protected, cared for, in peace and

---

[8] I have argued for this interpretation in chapter 1 of "Nietzsche's Attack On Morality."

[9] It should be kept in mind that this makes the translation of *Schuld* in the essay difficult, for it is ambiguous between the moral and material concepts Nietzsche distinguishes in *GM* II:4. Kaufmann sometimes resorts to "guilty indebtedness" in an attempt to capture the ambiguity of "*Schuldgefühl*."

trustfulness, without fear of certain injuries and hostile acts . . . since [they have] bound and pledged [themselves] to the community precisely with a view to injuries and hostile acts" (*GM* II:9).

What happens, Nietzsche asks, if this pledge is broken? "The community, the disappointed creditor will get what repayment it can, one may depend on that." In the beginning, the criminal is thrown out of the community, back to the savage and outlaw state against which he has been protected, and every kind of hostility may be vented upon him.

> The direct harm caused by the culprit is here a minor matter . . . the lawbreaker is above all a "breaker," a breaker of his contract and his word *with the whole* in respect to all the benefits and comforts of communal life in which he has hitherto had a share. The lawbreaker is a debtor who has not merely failed to make good the advantages and advance payment bestowed on him but has actually attacked his creditor: therefore he is not only deprived henceforth of all these advantages and benefits, as is fair, he is also reminded *what these benefits are really worth*. (*GM* II:9)

As the society grows stronger, it takes offenses less seriously because they are less dangerous to it. Rather than casting out the criminal and allowing anger to be vented unrestrainedly upon him, the community sets up a system of punishments. Many purposes are served by this, but above all, according to Nietzsche, "the increasingly definite will to treat each crime as dischargeable, and thus at least to a certain extent to isolate the criminal and his deed from each other" (*GM* II:10). In other words, the person did something that breaks his pledge to the community and therefore to some extent threatens its stability, angering its members. In the old days, they would have cast him out and treated him as no longer due community protection. But since the community is now stronger, its members no longer feel sufficiently threatened, or angry enough (though the persons directly affected by the crime well may), to need to throw the criminal out. So they set up a system of punishments that allows the criminal to pay off his debt and remain within the community. This is what Nietzsche thinks guilt is in its origins: a debt or substitute payment owed to society for failure to obey the community's rules.

Despite the contempt with which Nietzsche sometimes treats ideas of a social contract, he is clearly working with such an idea here. He rejects the idea that the state begins with an actual contract, an explicit promise that the members make to obey community laws (*GM* II:17). But he believes that from fairly early times, the relation between individual members and community was viewed on the model of such a contract: If you accept the advantages of the community life, you are in effect making a bargain with the community, agreeing to go along with the rules that make community life possible. You now have an obligation to the community to obey the rules, and if you renege on it, you deserve punishment, that is, "owe" it as a matter of fairness or justice (*GM* II:9).

It is difficult to find in Nietzsche's discussion here any suggestion that he objects to such judgments of fairness, or any basis he could think he has for doing so. He seems to present judgments of fairness as completely natural to human beings and in no way based on mistakes or errors. Nor does anything he says suggest that he thinks, or could reasonably think, that human beings will or should eventually outgrow a concern for fairness.[10] But then how can Nietzsche consider himself an immoralist? The only plausible answer I can find for him is that he denies that regarding obedience to the rules as a matter of fairness is equivalent to granting them the status of moral rules.

On textual grounds, I believe that this is in fact Nietzsche's position. As I discuss below, he claims that debt is moralized into guilt, and duty into moral duty, through the development of the bad conscience and of the idea of having a debt to God (*GM* II:21). But neither of these notions plays any part in or is presupposed by his account of judgments of fairness. Nietzsche evidently believes, therefore, that we can regard obedience to the rules necessary for communal existence as a matter of fairness *without* the help of ideas of moral duty or guilt, and therefore without regarding them as moral rules.

This may seem implausible. It may be thought that a system of rules involving an idea of fairness must have room for acting from conscience and that conscience necessarily brings with it ideas of guilt. Nietzsche admits the role of conscience, but explicitly distinguishes conscience from "*bad* conscience," the consciousness of guilt (*GM* II:3-4). Nietzsche's person of conscience obeys the rules that make community existence possible—but not out of fear of punishment. Rather, they are obeyed from an identification with the aims of the community and from pride in being a person who can be relied on to keep promises—which Nietzsche calls "the proud awareness of the extraordinary privilege of *responsibility*" (*GM* II:2).[11]

Within the system against the background of which conscience appears, breaking one's promise to obey the rules of society amounts to a failure to pay one's debt to society. Punishment, as a means of substitute repayment, is now the debt one owes to society. But Nietzsche's analysis suggests that this is only what he calls the "very material" concept of debt, which he distinguishes from

---

[10] In *GM* II:10, he does write of the overcoming of justice by mercy. This constitutes an overcoming not of a sense of fairness, however, but only of the need to punish. This is in line with Nietzsche's thought that the stronger the community is, the less threatened it will be by violations of the community norms, and therefore the less in need of causing pain to violators. But the possibility Nietzsche thus entertains of going beyond a concern for justice in this (retributive) sense in no way implies that we can or should overcome the idea that people owe obedience to the rules as a matter of fairness. It only suggests the possibility of giving up holding violators to a particular kind of substitute repayment.

[11] Nietzsche does not himself make explicit that identification with community aims is one of the pieces of motivation here. I bring it in because I believe that the motive Nietzsche does make explicit, the pride the conscientious take in the extraordinary privilege of responsibility, makes psychological sense only given their identification with the community and its aims.

the moral concept of guilt (*GM* II:4). One sign of the difference is that a material debt is completely dischargeable. Once you have paid it off, no debt or guilt remains. In the case of moral guilt, however, it seems that we remain guilty of whatever wrongs we have done, even if we have suffered an appropriate punishment. A related point is that material indebtedness, unlike guilt, does not automatically lower one's worth as a person. People of conscience may consider you bad and look down on you because you don't have what it takes to keep your word; but your indebtedness is not itself a matter of your worth, as it clearly is in the case of moral guilt. Indebtedness and worth may be interconnected, but are two separable issues; whereas, this is not the case once debt becomes guilt.[12]

If this is correct, the Second Essay of the *Genealogy* tries to show us the possibility—indeed the historical reality—of a nonmoral version of a social contract, involving what we can recognize to be nonmoral ideas of fairness, justice, obligation, indebtedness, and conscience. This suggests that Nietzsche's objection is not to justice or the common good (contrary to Foot), nor to social norms that apply to all (contrary to Nehamas), but rather to the *moralization* of these ideas and norms.[13] I turn now, all too briefly, to his account of how that moralization took place.

There are two evidently independent parts of the story Nietzsche tells about the moralization of debt into guilt. First, he gives an account of the origin of the bad conscience that is very similar to Freud's later one. Nietzsche claims that the bad conscience develops when restrictions on the external expression of hostile impulses become so severe that they can be satisfied only through internalization (*GM* II:17–18). Debt is moralized into guilt, Nietzsche claims, when it is pushed back into the bad conscience (*GM* II:21).[14] I take this to mean that the moralization of debt into guilt occurs through the taking over of the idea of debt by the bad conscience, the project of internalizing aggression. Debt becomes guilt insofar as people start using the idea of being indebted to

---

[12] I want to make it clear that I am not here attempting to determine the essence of guilt, or giving necessary and sufficient conditions for debt being a matter of guilt. I assume Nietzsche thinks this cannot be done. I am suggesting only that we can come up with clear cases of the material concept of debt, on the one hand, and the moral concept of guilt, on the other, and can specify differences between them. The burden of Nietzsche's historical analysis is to specify the processes that led from the obvious case of pure debt to the equally obvious cases of moral guilt. However, I assume that these obvious cases are the extremes, and that there are many cases in between, and that Nietzsche would deny that there is some exact point at which debt turns into guilt.

[13] In the context of Nietzsche's *Genealogy*, "moralization" refers to the process whereby something becomes part of the synthesis we call "morality." There is, of course, no common essence of the process of moralization because different elements become part of the synthesis we call "morality" through different processes.

[14] Actually he says pushed back into conscience. But it is clear from what he goes on to say that he means the bad conscience.

inflict suffering on themselves. But how did they do this? And how does using the idea of debt for self-punishment turn it into guilt?

Nietzsche evidently expects us to find our answers in the second part of his story, which concerns the idea of owing a debt to God (*GM* II:21). The relation to ancestors, he claims, was interpreted along the lines of the debtor–creditor relation (*GM* II:19). The conviction reigns that the tribe exists only through the sacrifices and accomplishments of ancestors. The tribe therefore owes them a debt that constantly grows greater, since these forebears never cease (in their continued existence as powerful spirits) to accord the tribe new advantages. Eventually the ancestor grows into a god, and finally into God, the God before whom all human beings are guilty (*GM* II:20).

But why isn't the debt we owe to God just a debt? What makes it a matter of guilt? In Nietzsche's initial telling of this story, the debt owed to God appears to be just a debt, for he suggests that with the dawning of atheism, human beings would get over their sense of guilt and acquire a second innocence (*GM* II:20). But he then tells us in effect that he has been pulling our leg, writing as if the moralization of the idea had not taken place—whereas the reality is to "a fearful degree otherwise" (*GM* II:21). If the moralization of the concept *had not* taken place, atheism *would* rid us of guilt, because guilt would just be a debt supposedly owed to God, and given no God, there would be no guilt. Given that moralization, guilt can remain without someone to whom it is owed. We need to understand more about what Nietzsche thinks is involved in this moralization if we are to understand how the bad conscience transformed debt into guilt.

Nietzsche claims explicitly that the moralization of the concepts of debt and duty occurred through the involvement of the bad conscience with the idea of God (*GM* II:21). I take this to mean that the project of the bad conscience—of internalizing aggression—determined the form the idea of God would take. God was to be understood as pure spirit, the opposite of human beings who are sunk in nature, afflicted by desires, senses, animality. Nietzsche claims, in effect, that one of the major factors behind the transformation of pagan gods who are merely human beings writ large and more powerful into a purely spiritual God was the need for a weapon against the self—a standard of good we could never live up to, and in relation to which we could enjoy judging, condemning, and chastising ourselves and others. The debt we owe to this nonnatural God is one that can never be paid off and one that is definitely tied to our worth as persons. We owe God a debt not just for what we do, but for what we are.

Nietzsche thus denies that owing a debt to a divine being is enough to make this debt a matter of moral guilt. The material concept of debt was transformed into the fully moral concept of guilt when the divine being to whom the debt was owed was conceived nonnaturalistically or ascetically, as a repudiation of the value of natural human existence. What transforms debt into guilt—makes it unpayable and a matter of our worth as persons—is the ascetic ideal and its attendant ascetic conception of virtue, which Nietzsche discusses at length in the Third Essay of the *Genealogy*. I do not have time to go into that here, but I hope I have said enough to indicate why he would consider his essay on the ascetic ideal a central part of his account of morality itself. This is because he thinks that through the historical processes he discusses in the *Genealogy* the ascetic ideal became tied to and intertwined with the very concept of morality. Briefly put, rules became moral rules when their violation was thought to incur guilt, and the idea of guilt is a transformation of the idea of debt by means of the ascetic ideal. Further, the noble nonmoral conception of virtue or goodness becomes moral virtue precisely insofar as people are blamed for what they are—that is, are considered guilty.

Despite the incompleteness of my account of the *Genealogy*, I believe that the approach to it suggested here provides the basis for a better explanation than has been given previously as to why Nietzsche believed he was rejecting morality itself. Specifically, I have tried to show that he thinks the ascetic ideal is tightly intertwined with our idea of morality, and I have argued elsewhere that he rejects the ascetic ideal (Clark 1990: 159–203). More generally, I have tried to show that much of Nietzsche's work on morality involves prying apart central components of our concept of morality and showing how these strands came together in the course of human history. This work gives him a basis for insisting that what we call "morality" is not something that has always been with human beings but is instead an extremely complex affair that developed in the course of human history through the multiple couplings of originally separate strands that we can no longer see as independent.

By separating them, I think Nietzsche tries to show us the possibility of tying these strands together differently, and thus the possibility of gaining much of what morality gives us, indeed what we cannot do without, in alternative ways, and specifically without the tie to the ascetic ideal. As an immoralist, he claims that some such alternative is superior to the present synthesis that we call "morality." Explaining this alternative and Nietzsche's arguments for its superiority are complicated matters that I will be working on in the future. Here I have tried only to show that examining his own analysis of the concept of morality helps to make comprehensible why he believed he was rejecting morality itself.[15]

---

[15] Earlier versions of this paper were read at Colgate University and the University of Pennsylvania. This version has benefited from helpful comments and discussions on both occasions, and from Brian Leiter's written comments on it.

{ 2 }

On the Rejection of Morality
Bernard Williams's Debt to Nietzsche

That there is some connection between Bernard Williams's views on morality and Nietzsche's has long seemed clear. The most obvious point of comparison is that both thinkers are opponents of morality. Nietzsche presents himself as an "immoralist"—a term he claims for himself as a "symbol and badge of honor," one that "distinguishes [him] from the whole of humanity" (*EH* IV:6). Although Williams makes no comparable claim for himself, his abolitionist stance toward morality is suggested by the title of the final chapter of his 1985 *Ethics and the Limits of Philosophy*—"Morality, the Peculiar Institution"— which applies to morality the epithet given to slavery in the antebellum South.[1] What has not been so clear is whether Williams's reasons for advocating the abolition of morality are indebted to Nietzsche's, or even very similar to them. The debt and similarity may seem minimal at best. After all, Williams's tone and vocabulary for talking about morality and his focus on moral obligation place him squarely in the tradition of English moral philosophy, which seems far removed from Nietzsche's concerns. And the most obvious debt of his critique of morality is to Elizabeth Anscombe.[2] This suggests that, far from drawing his objections to morality from Nietzschean sources, Williams may not even be using "morality" to refer to the same thing that Nietzsche's immoralism rejects.

Yet, despite the continuing and obvious differences in philosophical style, Williams's more recent work makes Nietzsche's influence evident. This is especially true of his 1993 *Shame and Necessity*—not only in its relatively frequent references to Nietzsche, but also in its content. In this book, Williams's understanding of the ancient Greeks and his account of shame and guilt seem so much in Nietzsche's spirit that readers might suspect that Williams had been

---

[1] As Stephen Darwall points out in "Abolishing Morality," *Synthese* 72 (1987): 73.
[2] That is, to "Modern Moral Philosophy." See G. E. M. Anscombe, *Collected Philosophical Papers* (Minneapolis: University of Minnesota Press, 1981), vol. 3, pp. 26–42.

working under Nietzsche's influence all along, and that much of his earlier work in ethics was (among other things, of course) an attempt to figure out what Nietzsche was on to in his critique of morality.[3] My aim in this essay is to support this suspicion by showing that the understanding and critique of morality found in the final chapter of *Ethics and the Limits of Philosophy* (henceforth *ELP*) is deeply Nietzschean. I will also argue that it is not quite Nietzschean enough, that Williams moves closer to Nietzsche's account of morality in *Shame and Necessity* (henceforth *SN*), and that doing so helps to answer important objections to the critique of morality found in the earlier book.

Morality and Ethics

A distinction between morality and ethics is a crucial aspect of Williams's opposition to morality. Although he is an abolitionist regarding morality, he does not think we should or can abolish ethics, which he treats as the wider category into which morality falls. What counts as "ethical" is "any scheme for regulating the relations between people that works through informal sanctions and internalized dispositions."[4] Morality, on the other hand, is a particular ethical orientation—or better, a "range of ethical outlooks." "Morality is so much with us," Williams writes, "that moral philosophy spends much of its time discussing the differences between these outlooks, rather than the difference between all of them and everything else" (*ELP*, p. 174). Yet, all of these different moral outlooks are variations on a particular kind of ethical orientation that he thinks we would be "better off without."

Williams's distinction parallels one that is crucial for understanding Nietzsche's immoralism—the distinction between a narrower and a wider sense of "morality." When he calls himself an "immoralist," and, in fact, "the first immoralist," he seems to mean that he is the first philosopher to consider morality something bad, something we would be better off without. Yet he sometimes uses "morality" for what he seems to favor—for instance, "noble morality"

---

[3] When I suggested this to Williams, he said that my suspicion might be right, that he had actually been under contract to write a book on Nietzsche (during the 1970s, I believe), and that he had arranged time away from teaching to do so. He did not write it, however, because he was unable to solve "the problem of Nietzsche's style." He added that he now believes that Alexander Nehamas's account of Nietzsche's use of hyperbole in *Nietzsche: Life as Literature* (Cambridge, Mass.: Harvard University Press, 1985) would have helped him solve the problem. This suggests that Williams was very sympathetic from early on to what he took to be the content of Nietzsche's thought, but not to what he perceived as its rhetorical excesses. It also explains why we do not find frequent references to Nietzsche in Williams's earlier work even if, as I believe, he was a major influence on it.

[4] This is Williams's formulation in "Moral Luck: A Postscript," in *Making Sense of Humanity* (Cambridge: Cambridge University Press, 1995), p. 241; and I believe this is also what he means by the "ethical" in *ELP*.

(*GM* I) and "higher moralities," which he insists ought to be possible (*BGE* 202). This has led to significant disagreement among interpreters as to whether Nietzsche is really claiming to reject all morality. To be most faithful to his own usage and clear about his position, I believe we should say that he is.[5] Use of "morality" for what he favors is relatively rare in his writings, whereas an expression of skepticism toward morality is quite common, as is the demand for a liberation from all moral values, from all that has been honored under the name "morality." His occasional use of "morality" for what he himself embraces or promotes can be explained if we recognize that he uses the word in two different senses. *BGE* 32 explicitly connects immoralism with a demand for the overcoming of morality in what he calls "the narrower sense," which he also identifies as the sense morality has had until now ("*das Moral, im bisherigen Sinne*").

This implies, of course, that we could use "morality" in a new and wider sense—one that is equivalent, I believe, to what Williams calls "ethics." If so (and this whole essay should be seen as an argument that it is), Nietzsche's immoralism is a rejection of what Williams calls "morality" (and of what Nietzsche thinks his readers largely understand as "morality") but not of ethical life or of morality construed more broadly. It is only in the broader sense that an ethical orientation Nietzsche embraces or urges us toward counts as an instance of "morality."

The same can be said of the pre-moral form of ethical life he calls "noble morality." The historical version of it that he describes in the first treatise of *On the Genealogy of Morality* is certainly a form of ethical life. The ancient nobles who shared it had ideas of goodness or virtue and of behavior that is prohibited and deserving of blame. They also recognized obligations, experienced a version of guilt, and had a form of conscience. They thereby participated in what Williams characterizes as the "ethical" (a "scheme for regulating the relations between people that works through informal sanctions and internalized dispositions"), but not in what Nietzsche normally counts as "morality"—that is, "morality in the narrower sense." That he believes this seems clear, in any case, from the fact that he attacks morality in the narrower sense but not noble morality, and that he explicitly portrays the former as the "unconscious aftereffect" of the rule of the latter (*BGE* 32).

We thus have an easy way of dissolving the apparent inconsistency in Nietzsche's claims about morality.[6] When he attacks it, he uses "morality" in the narrower sense, which is equivalent to what Williams means by "morality";

---

[5] I argue for this claim and discuss some other interpretations in Clark 1994a, paper 1 in this volume. For a more extended treatment of other interpretations and an important view that differs from the one I defend, see Brian Leiter, "Morality in the Pejorative Sense: On the Logic of Nietzsche's Critique of Morality," *British Journal for the History of Philosophy* 3 (1995): 113–45.

[6] For an alternative and much more complex way of dissolving the apparent inconsistency, see the paper by B. Leiter cited in the previous note.

when he embraces or promotes it, he uses "morality" in the wider sense, which makes it equivalent to what Williams calls the "ethical." But we do not yet have an explanation of the point of making this distinction. To most people a scheme embodying or employing the concepts I have attributed to the noble form of ethical life—virtue, obligation, blame, guilt, conscience—is clearly an instance of "morality." What is the point of insisting that it is an instance of the "ethical" but not the "moral"? And what exactly does the latter amount to?

As to the point of making the distinction, something can be said in advance. Consider Nietzsche's claim that current European morality is

> merely one type of human morality beside which, before which, and after which many other types, above all *higher* moralities are, or ought to be, possible. But this morality resists such a "possibility," such an "ought" with all its power: it says stubbornly and inexorably, "I am morality itself, and nothing besides is morality." (BGE 202)

The point here is not that the term "morality" has come to name one particular form of ethical life so that other forms have to be called something else. It is rather that the term "morality" has been monopolized for a particular form of ethical life in such a way that we fail to recognize the possibility of other forms.[7] Or, as the passage I have already quoted from Williams suggests, morality in the narrow sense is "so much with us" that we have no sense of morality in the wider sense, which means that we take morality in the narrow sense to be the only possible ethical orientation. The point of distinguishing two senses of "morality," or "ethics" from "morality"—distinctions that do not conform exactly to existing linguistic practice—is precisely to help us to recognize possibilities for ethical life that are hidden from view by current linguistic practice. In fact, linguistic practice has changed among Anglo-American philosophers, who are now much more likely to recognize a distinction between the "ethical" and the "moral," or between a broad and a narrow construal of morality, than they were prior to the influence of Williams's work. When I began trying to understand Nietzsche's immoralism in the 1970s, no such distinction even seemed to be on the horizon: Morality was morality, and "ethics" was used as an equivalent term. The only opponent of morality most philosophers could conceive of was one who refused to accept it unless it could be given an egoistic justification. Although this demand for an egoistic foundation for morality was usually dismissed as misguided, at least philosophers could make sense of amoralism. Immoralism was a different story, for it does not merely reject the authority of morality but opposes it as something bad, which makes sense only if it presupposes an alternative set of values. But philosophers had difficulty seeing how it could make sense, for morality either monopolized their understanding of value

---

[7] For a more detailed account, see my comments on *BGE* 202 in "Nietzsche's Immoralism and the Concept of Morality," p. 32, n. 6 (paper 1 in this volume, p. 25, n. 4).

or was assumed to be by definition supreme (moral values being the set of values that override all others). Nietzsche's immoralism was therefore usually interpreted by sympathetic commentators as a rejection of a particular kind of morality, for instance, Christian or Kantian morality.

Philippa Foot's well-known paper on the topic made a significant contribution by showing that Nietzsche's immoralism could be interpreted both as a rejection of all morality and as a coherent position.[8] The way she found to do this, however, was to construe Nietzsche's criticism of morality as coming from an aesthetic or quasi-aesthetic perspective. She was able to interpret Nietzsche as an immoralist rather than a "special kind of moralist" by taking him to be rejecting something that she believed was conceptually tied to morality—namely, a concern for justice and the common good—for the sake of something that is not the concern of morality: namely, producing splendid human beings.[9] Therefore, she did not seem to fully appreciate the possibility that his opposition to morality was coming from the viewpoint of an alternative ethical orientation—one that had room for an alternative vision of justice, for instance. Although she expanded the normative realm that moral philosophers needed to take into account (at least for understanding Nietzsche), she still basically equated "ethics" and "morality."

Things have now changed, at least as far as terminology goes. A distinction between ethics and morality, and even between "morality" in a broad and narrower sense, is now widely accepted among philosophers. However, even though Williams's influence is largely responsible for this change, the way in which the distinction is drawn does not seem to yet be fully in line with Williams's way of drawing it. Consider the entry "Ethics and Morality" in the 1998 *Routledge Encyclopedia of Philosophy*. Its author, John Skorupski, takes ethics to be "the whole domain" of "normative thinking about action and feeling," whereas morality is a "distinct sphere within [that] domain."[10] How should we characterize the moral sphere?

Skorupski rejects two of the most influential suggestions for doing so: to characterize moral norms in terms of their function or content, or in terms of their supremacy or ability to override other kinds of norms. He accepts instead a third suggestion, derived from Hume and Mill and recently developed with great sophistication by Allan Gibbard: that the moral should be characterized

---

[8] I refer to her "Nietzsche: The Revaluation of Values," in *Nietzsche: A Collection of Critical Essays*, ed. Robert Solomon (Garden City, N.Y.: Anchor Books, 1973). The paper entitled "Nietzsche's Immoralism," which is reprinted in *Nietzsche, Genealogy, Morality,* is much later (it was originally published in 1991) and adds little to the earlier paper.

[9] Foot claims, for instance, that Nietzsche was willing "to throw out justice in the interests of producing a stronger and more splendid type of man" ("The Revaluation of Values," p. 166).

[10] For a more detailed account, see John Skorupski, "The Definition of Morality," in *Ethics*, Royal Institute of Philosophy Supplement 35, ed. A. Philip Griffiths (Cambridge: Cambridge University Press, 1993).

in terms of the appropriateness of certain sentiments—namely, those involved in blame, including self-blame or guilt. The morally wrong is essentially the blameworthy. If norms of permitted and prohibited behavior are *moral* norms—norms of moral right and wrong—it would be appropriate for violators to feel guilt for violating them, and for others to feel blame toward those who violate them.[11] Likewise, a moral obligation is one it would be appropriate or justified to blame a person for not fulfilling. Moral reasons are reasons it would be blameworthy not to have or act on; and moral virtues are ones it would be blameworthy not to have.

Skorupski explicitly recognizes that critics of morality, of which Nietzsche and Williams are his two examples, must level their critique "from a conception of ethical value, and assume that there is an [ethical] alternative to morality." This shows, I believe, that Williams's influence has brought moral philosophers much closer to the possibility of understanding Nietzsche's immoralism than they were when Foot first made her attempt. That they still have some distance to go is shown by Skorupski's further comment that if critics of morality do not accept the completely unrealistic "possibility of a communal life unmediated by any disciplinary forces at all," their assumption "must be that there could be a discipline that was better, ethically speaking, than the discipline of guilt and blame." Skorupski suggests that a nonmoral version of ethical life would need to employ shame or disdain in the place of guilt and blame, failing to see that (as I shall argue later in this essay) Nietzsche and Williams believe that there can be nonmoral versions of the latter, and thus that a nonmoral version of ethical life need not have to do without blame and guilt.

This misunderstanding reflects an important way in which Skorupski's distinction between morality and ethics differs from the distinction as it is drawn by Williams and Nietzsche. He thinks of morality as a particular part of the domain of the ethical (or normative), and so naturally thinks of nonmoral versions of ethical life as lacking certain concepts or emotions that belong to morality. But this is not how Nietzsche and Williams see the situation. Williams clearly presents morality as an *instance* rather than a part of the ethical, and therefore need not think that it lacks any of the components of morality. Using Nietzsche to understand Williams, I shall argue, can help us to see morality as a particular interpretation of ethical life, and to see how there could be a nonmoral version of ethical life that involves all the central components and concepts of morality but relates them to each other differently than does morality.

---

[11] According to Gibbard's analysis, we should add here something to the effect of "in the absence of extenuating circumstances." Otherwise we have no room to say that someone did something wrong, even though we do not think we would be justified in blaming them for this because of any of a number of special circumstances. See Allan Gibbard, *Wise Choices and Apt Feelings* (Cambridge, Mass.: Harvard University Press, 1990), esp. pp. 43–5.

Blame and the "Deep" Notion of the Voluntary

Although Williams cites blame as the "characteristic reaction of the morality system" (*ELP*, p. 177), this does not mean that he takes blame to be an essentially moral notion, one that has a place only within the "morality system." As I understand Williams, what places blame within the morality system—the system or interrelation of concepts that constitutes morality—is that it can only be directed toward what is voluntary and what in fact fits a particular idea of the voluntary. He writes, "there is pressure within [morality] to require a voluntariness that will be total and will cut through psychological or social determination, and allocate blame and responsibility on the ultimately fair basis of the agent's own contribution, no more and no less." So the specifically moral idea of responsibility is the idea of a responsibility that goes "all the way down." If I am morally culpable for some action, it must be the case not only that I could have acted otherwise if I had chosen to, but also that I could have chosen to—and thus that I could, if I had chosen, have had the kind of character or been the kind of person who would have chosen differently than I did. Blame belongs to the morality system by being coupled with this notion of the voluntary—that is, when there is pressure to consider it justified only in relation to what satisfies this "deep" notion of the voluntary.

One of Williams's objections to morality is that it is illusory to think that there is any responsibility of the type it requires. "This fact," he says, "is known to almost everyone, and it is hard to see a long future for a system committed to denying it" (*ELP*, p. 194):

> To the extent that the institution of blame works coherently, it does so because it attempts less than morality would like it to do. When we ask whether someone acted voluntarily, we are asking roughly, whether he really acted, whether he knew what he was doing, and whether he intended this or that aspect of what happened. The practice takes the agent together with his character, and does not raise the question about his freedom to have chosen some other character.

Within the morality system, on the other hand, blaming does raise this question. So moral blame—blame as it exists within the morality system—depends upon a defunct notion of the voluntary. This is the aspect of Williams's critique of morality that is *most obviously* like Nietzsche's. The first treatise of GM tells the story of the genesis of a specifically *moral* notion of goodness or virtue through the transformation of a previously existing aristocratic notion. The latter "good" is a nonmoral notion, for its contrasting term is "bad" (the equivalent of "common") and not "evil" (the equivalent of "immoral"). The big difference between "bad" and "evil," as Nietzsche uses these terms, is that "bad" has no accusatory or blaming connotation. The bad are bad, which is to say inferior, but they are not blamed or held responsible for being so.

Nietzsche's suggestion is thus that the moralization of goodness took place through the acceptance of the "deep" notion of the voluntary—one that "goes all the way down" to a "being behind doing," to a character-less self who, according to one of Nietzsche's infamous passages, freely chooses to be a bird of prey or a lamb (*GM* I:13). Nietzsche's reaction to the demand of morality for this kind of freedom is the same as Williams's: that almost everyone knows there is no such thing—and not because determinism is the case, but because such freedom would require an act of self-creation, creation ex nihilo, which Nietzsche calls "the best self-contradiction that has been conceived so far . . . a sort of rape and perversion of logic" (*BGE* 21). If the morality system does require the voluntary to go all the way down to such a free will, it is difficult not to agree with Williams (and Nietzsche) that there is not much future for it.

But why should we think that morality itself requires that our actions be voluntary in a way that requires an old-fashioned free will? Let's grant that morality has been bound up with such a notion in some major part of its history. But why tie morality itself to such a notion? Why not say simply that Nietzsche attacks an illusion about freedom and responsibility that Hume and many others had already attacked, and that morality gets on quite well without it—indeed, as Hume argued, much better without it? The dominant tradition within Anglo-American moral philosophy since Hume is certainly to deny that freedom and moral responsibility require anything very much like self-creation ex nihilo. Williams is forced to count Utilitarianism as a marginal member of the morality system because of its commitment to allocating credit and blame without relying on the "deep" notion of responsibility. But then why isn't the existence of Utilitarianism evidence precisely of the ability of morality to outlive the notion of responsibility that Nietzsche and Williams both reject? Perhaps they are simply quibbling about names: about whether to use the name "morality" for a system that gives up the deep notion of the voluntary. I do not think so, but I need to examine the rest of Williams's account of morality to explain why.

Moral Obligation

The main focus of Williams's account and critique of morality is his analysis of moral obligation. The morality system is distinguished from other ethical outlooks, Williams claims, by "the special notion of obligation it uses," the notion of a specifically *moral* obligation. He argues that this special notion involves the transformation of a more ordinary (and, in effect, nonmoral) notion of obligation, which is only one ethical consideration among others, into the central ethical notion. On the surface, this may appear to have little connection to Nietzsche's concerns. If so, appearances are deceiving in this case. I will argue that Williams's analysis of moral obligation is importantly connected to Nietzsche's account of morality, and that elucidating this connection helps answer some important objections to Williams's critique.

Williams's account of the transformation of the ordinary idea of obligation into moral obligation (about which more later) seems very similar to what Nietzsche attempts in the second treatise of *GM*. According to Nietzsche's account, the idea of specifically *moral* obligation develops from the realm of legal rights and obligations (*GM* II:6). If we concentrate on GM's account of how legal obligations were enforced through sometimes gruesome punishments, it may not seem concerned with ethical obligations. Yes, punishment certainly instills a disposition to give certain considerations high deliberative priority, but this is not the kind of "internalized disposition" that Williams sees as central to ethical life. But Nietzsche agrees that the recognition of ethical obligations requires more than a disposition to avoid punishment. He contrasts the person who obeys rules simply out of fear of punishment with the person of conscience: a person who keeps his word—and who, more generally, can be relied on to do what his obligations require of him—not out of fear of punishment, but because his identity as a person of responsibility (a person who is permitted to make promises) requires this of him (*GM* II:2). And this identity can only be understood in relation to an ethical community with whose aims he identifies.

Nietzsche thus makes room for an ethical realm that grows from, but also can grow beyond, the legal. His person of conscience recognizes obligations in an ethical sense even though obligation has not yet undergone the process of moralization he describes later in GM II (a process I discuss in the next section of this essay). For both Williams and Nietzsche the special notion of moral obligation results from the moralization of the ordinary and quite unmysterious notion of obligation, which is already an ethical notion. The upshot of this moralization for both is that different components of ethical life are woven together in such a way that they become almost impossible to sort out, so that we have great difficulty gaining clarity about ethical life, and in getting a handle on the factors operating on us through it. To show us this is one of the main aims of Nietzsche's genealogical treatment of the concept of morality. It also is one of the main lessons we should learn from Williams's account of the construction of moral obligation.

This connection between the two accounts is not obvious, however, because Williams's is presented as, and seems to be, an old-fashioned logical analysis. His strategy is to isolate a core or essence that distinguishes specifically moral obligation from ordinary obligations—obligation is moral obligation if it is the central ethical notion, so that an obligation can be overridden only by another obligation—and then to argue that the other features we attribute to the "moral" can be derived logically from this core. Nietzsche, however, denies that concepts that need analysis have a core or essence in terms of which they can be defined or analyzed. They need analysis precisely because they are products of complicated histories that have synthesized originally quite disparate elements into a unity that is difficult to untangle. Instead of isolating a core from which other characteristics can be derived, a Nietzschean analysis of a concept offers a genealogy of the concept's construction, the point of which is to sort out its different strands so that we can see what is actually involved in the concept and operating on us through it.[12] But I believe that Williams's analysis of moral obligation can be recast in genealogical terms, and that this would be to its advantage.

Williams's ordinary notion of obligation is that of a consideration given deliberative priority in order to secure reliability, that is, so that people can reasonably expect others to behave in certain ways (*ELP*, p. 187). The most familiar type of obligation is based on a promise, and here the connection between obligation and reliability is readily apparent. Although what I have promised to do may have little importance in itself, I am expected to give it a high deliberative importance—that is, I am obliged to do it—because the point of my promise is to give others reason to rely on my doing it. Because a similar connection between obligation and reliability is present in other cases, Williams thinks we also have ethical obligations that we have not taken on voluntarily. To lead a recognizably human life, we might say, people have to have reason to expect certain treatment by others: for instance, "not being killed or used as a resource."

One way people are given reason to count on such treatment is through the establishment of ethical life, which (among other things) instills a disposition to give the relevant considerations a high deliberative priority, and sometimes even a "virtually absolute priority, so that certain courses of action must come first, while others are ruled out from the beginning" (*ELP*, p. 185). A community thus instills in its members a disposition to recognize certain obligations. But, according to Williams, there need be no implication that one simply *must* do whatever one is obliged to do, or that only another more important obligation gives one a reason for not doing so. However brutal the means for getting individuals to remember their obligations—and Nietzsche details some of these at the beginning of the second treatise of *GM*—being obligated or bound to do something is a matter simply of what others have reason to expect of me and to count on me for, not of what I *must* do.

According to Williams, the morality system takes over this ordinary ethical notion of obligation and blows it up both in extent and importance, to the point that obligation becomes all-pervasive and inescapable. If I am *morally* obliged to do something, then I must do it. If I do not, I am subject to moral blame. The only excuse for not keeping a promise I have made is that I have another more stringent obligation, in which case I am not *morally* obliged to do as I promised. But since we can imagine all sorts of situations in which ethical concerns would justify breaking a promise, Williams thinks morality is under

---

[12] For a more detailed account, see paper 1 in this volume.

pressure to turn all such concerns into obligations. Because only an obligation can override an obligation, morality is forced to the idea of very general obligations, and thus to the idea that particular obligations are always instances of general obligations that apply to everyone. But these general obligations will now be "willing to provide work for idle hands, and the thought can gain a footing . . . that I could be better employed than in doing something I am under no obligation to do." In other words, the moralization of obligation, its transformation into the central ethical notion, leads to the idea that "I am under an obligation not to waste time doing things I am under no obligation to do." Obligation thus becomes an "intimidating structure" that threatens to "dominate life altogether" (*ELP*, p. 182).

It is widely assumed that Williams's major objection to morality is that it is overly demanding. As Darwall puts it, "Williams believes that the moralist is "committed to holding there to be almost no cases where general obligations do not plausibly apply," so that we are "always bound by morality." The moral life is thus a life of bondage (Darwall, pp. 75–7).[13] Darwall responds by arguing that while some moralists may have had such a picture of morality, there is "nothing in the notion of moral obligation to require, or even encourage" it. Moral common sense, he claims, rejects Williams's principle that an obligation can be overridden only by another obligation, for "it is widely assumed that one is not obliged to do many things one would otherwise be morally obliged to do, if doing them would require personal sacrifice, or even sacrifice to loved ones, beyond a certain threshold, even though it would not be *wrong* to do what would otherwise be obligatory and incur the sacrifice" (ibid., p. 78). Further, an ordinary or prima facie obligation can be overridden by something nonobligatory that is of more moral importance than the obligation, as when one is not obliged to keep a promise if one chooses to undertake a nonobligatory but morally more important action that makes keeping the promise impossible.[14] So it seems "that it can frequently happen that a moral obligation to do something can be canceled by further features of the situation other than an overriding obligation to act otherwise" (ibid., p. 79).

Darwall grants that nothing overrides what one is morally obliged to do, if that means what one *should* do (what it would be wrong not to do) all things considered. But, as we have already seen (from the considerations of personal

---

[13] Numbers in this paragraph and the next all refer to Darwall's "Abolishing Morality" (see note 1 above).

[14] Darwall cites Frances Kamm's example of a clear case where something of more moral importance overrides an obligation. Suppose I am morally obliged to do something because of a promise I have made, but en route to keeping my promise I am confronted with a situation in which I could save a stranger's life by doing something no one could reasonably think I was obligated to do: for example, giving up one of my kidneys. Moralists surely need not say that it is morally permissible to give up my kidney only if I am obligated to do so, because I am otherwise morally obliged to keep my promise.

sacrifice, for instance), morality can permit us to do what we are not obliged to do in this sense (what it would not be *wrong* not to do), and it allows obligations in the ordinary sense to be canceled by features of the situation other than obligation in the ordinary or the all-things-considered sense. Darwall suggests that Williams is confusing the two senses of "obligation" he himself distinguishes, taking the fact that obligation in the sense of an all-things-considered conclusion (our *actual* moral obligation) cannot be overridden as evidence that ordinary or prima facie obligations cannot be overridden by anything that is not conceived of as obligatory. Otherwise he cannot see how Williams could have found it plausible that only an obligation can override an obligation, and therefore that morality pushes us toward an overly demanding life of ubiquitous obligation (ibid., p. 81).

I believe that Williams's best chance of answering these criticisms is to give up his emphasis on the *logic* of moral obligation—and with it the principle that only an obligation can override an obligation—and go over to Nietzsche's more genealogical and psychological account of the concept. But wouldn't this undermine his criticism that morality is overly demanding by depriving him of any basis for claiming that morality must give rise to a series of general obligations and that it thus threatens to "dominate life altogether"? (*ELP*, p. 182). Perhaps, but I do not consider that a loss. Although Williams certainly stresses the demanding character of morality, this is not his objection to it. He formulates his objection to morality in very different terms: namely, that "many philosophical mistakes are woven into it" (*ELP*, p. 196). The first mistake, he says, is the misunderstanding of obligation, which is not recognized as "just one type of ethical consideration."

It is hardly surprising that the discussion of Williams's opposition to morality has not focused on this claim, for it is difficult to make sense of. As I understand Williams, the "morality system" is constituted by a specific interrelation of the ethical concepts found within it. Obligation becomes part of the morality system precisely when it is *no longer* just one type of ethical consideration but has become the central one (and when other concepts figure in this system by existing in certain logical relations to the supremacy of obligation—such as following from it). That is presumably how it can come to "dominate life altogether." I can understand why this would be a bad thing. But why is it a "philosophical mistake"? I began to make sense of this only when I remembered Nietzsche's line: "Morality is merely an interpretation of certain phenomena, more precisely, a misinterpretation" (*TI* VI:1).[15] Williams's objection to morality, I began to see, is that it involves a misinterpretation of ethical life.

---

[15] I must admit that, as Brian Leiter has pointed out to me, I have taken this sentence out of context. In context the sentence seems to mean that morality is a misinterpretation not of ethical life, as I go on to suggest, but of certain natural phenomena, such as of causality. However, the sentence worked on me with a suggestiveness that transcended its meaning in context, and

Williams in effect offers a genealogical account of moral obligation, arguing that the special notion of *moral* obligation was constructed by taking the ordinary idea of obligation and re-interpreting it as the central ethical consideration, thereby arriving at the all-things-considered judgment of morality. Obligations in the ordinary sense are still in play, but now we also apparently have *obligation in a new sense:* the all-things-considered judgment of what one morally ought to do. And we have conferred on this all-things-considered judgment all of the characteristics and expectations that belong to obligations in the ordinary sense—especially the blame, reproach, or guilt that attaches to nonfulfillment of the latter. The problem is to understand why Williams thinks this involves a philosophical mistake. What "mistake" is involved in modeling the all-things-considered judgment of morality after obligations in the ordinary sense?

I suggest that Williams believes it involves a conflation that keeps us from seeing the truth about ethical life. The conflation is between obligation in the ordinary sense and conclusions of practical necessity, judgments about what one categorically must do. Williams agrees with moralists that there are for human beings matters of unconditioned practical necessity, categorical imperatives in Kant's terms, but he denies that any imperatives are independent of desire. He thinks, in opposition to Kant, that an imperative can be unconditioned without being independent of desire, *if* the desire it depends on is essential to the agent and must be satisfied (*ELP*, p. 189).

Which desires are essential is presumably determined by the individual's identity. Christine Korsgaard has recently argued that obligations spring from what one's identity forbids.[16] Williams's point, in contrast, is that one's obligations spring from what other people have reason to expect of you, to rely on you for. What binds me, even in the case of a promise, is something outside of me, what another person has reason to expect from me. What my identity determines is what I categorically must do (as well as what it would be good or nice for me to do).[17] Obligation comes from without; practical necessity comes from within. Williams's claim, as I am now understanding it under Nietzsche's influence, is that morality runs these two together, thereby giving rise to the illusion of a moral law above or outside of the agent. The illusion involved here is a misperception of the voice of practical necessity as coming from without, when it actually comes from within. This is the first philosophical mistake that Williams finds woven into the moral interpretation of ethical life.

---

it allowed me to recognize something in *GM* for which there is plenty of evidence, but which I might otherwise not have been brought to see in it: that Nietzsche is there analyzing morality as an interpretation, specifically an ascetic interpretation, of ethical life.

[16] Christine Korsgaard, *The Sources of Normativity* (Cambridge: Cambridge University Press, 1996), esp. pp. 100–103.

[17] Williams pointed out the addition in parentheses to me in conversation after hearing an earlier version of this paper.

The second mistake is the misunderstanding of practical necessity, which is taken to be "peculiar to the ethical." In this case, Williams's claim is more obviously that morality is a misinterpretation of the ethical—a mistaken interpretation of the practical necessity found in ethical life as peculiar to the ethical sphere. That this is a mistake follows once we recognize the differing sources of obligation and conclusions of unconditioned practical necessity, of what one categorically must do. To the extent that my identity includes involvement in an ethical community, some conclusions of practical necessity will undoubtedly concern my obligations to others. There will be some obligations I simply must fulfill to be able to live with myself, that is, to be the person I take myself to be. Other conclusions of practical necessity will be ethical in character without being obligations: These concern what my identity requires of me in relation to others, even though others do not have a right to expect it from me.

However, a person's identity—the description under which she considers her life worth living[18]—can also be tied up with concerns that do not, or at least need not, count as ethical: for example, art or philosophy or sports. Once we accept that conclusions of practical necessity follow from one's identity, it becomes obvious that they cannot be confined to ethical conclusions. It is then difficult to uphold the thesis that ethical concerns are overriding, for nothing seems to prevent the possibility of what I must do, all things considered, being in conflict with my obligations and ethical commitments. That is precisely the case of Gauguin as presented in Williams's essay "Moral Luck."

If my Nietzschean-inspired interpretation is correct, Williams's case against morality does not rest (contrary to Darwall) on a conflation of the two types of obligation he himself distinguishes. It depends instead on being able to make it plausible that the moral interpretation of ethical experience (and in particular the idea of moral obligation as an all-things-considered conclusion) conflates and hides from view a distinction we ought to accept: between obligations, on the one hand, and conclusions of practical necessity, on the other. What is principally hidden from view by the idea of moral obligation is the fact that obligations are rooted outside of us, in other people's expectations and the conditions of ethical life, whereas conclusions of unconditional practical necessity are rooted in one's own identity. Williams needs to make it plausible that these two distinct notions are run together to produce the notion of specifically moral obligation, and that this results in a loss of clarity about the factors operating on us by means of our ethical consciousness. The importance of our own identity eludes us; we take our own voice as a command that comes from outside or "on high."

Serious problems still stand in Williams's way. For it seems likely that morality can survive the demystification that comes from realizing that the commanding voice of practical reason comes, as Williams puts it, from "deep within." Why can't moral commands be understood as ethical demands made

---

[18] This is borrowed from Korsgaard's *The Sources of Normativity*, p. 101.

by our identity—or our essential desires—against desires that we would merely like to act on? The existence of internal conflict would explain both the command aspect and the fact that the command seems to come from above.

Nor is it clear that morality must cover over the role played by ordinary obligations in ethical life. As Darwall puts this point:

> Williams himself believes we should recognize obligations (he refuses to call them "moral") and correlative rights that one "cannot ignore without blame." Like almost any moralist, he says that obligation "is grounded in the basic issue of what people should be able to rely on." And he includes under this rubric the traditional negative obligations and obligations to aid when the need is "immediate." How does this differ in substance from the status that moral obligations are ordinarily thought to have . . . ? The differences one might have expected are simply not there.[19]

Thus, as in the case of his critique of the deep notion of the voluntary, it is not clear that the points used here to support Williams's claim about the first mistake woven into morality—the conflation of obligation and conclusions of practical necessity—say anything of substance about ethical life with which those committed to morality must disagree.

The same problem emerges in relation to the second philosophical mistake that Williams finds in morality: the misinterpretation of practical necessity as peculiar to the ethical, which yields the conclusion that morality is overriding. Although many moral theorists defend the overridingness of moral concerns, others now seem willing to dispense with such privilege. For instance, Scheffler argues in *Human Morality* that the loss of overridingness is a problem for moralists only if they assume that morality must have a special source in order to have authority. He then argues that morality has sufficient authority in our lives even if it does not have a special source that makes it superior to all else.

This follows in large part from the widely accepted view that moral beliefs and concerns are woven throughout the fabric of human life, that they are "implicated in a wide range of human emotions and attitudes"—guilt, remorse, indignation, resentment, conscientiousness, and a sense of indebtedness, for instance—and that "a liability to experience these emotions and attitudes is in turn a prerequisite for participation in important human relations of various kinds."[20] Even if we cannot deny that it is ever rational to act against moral concerns—for Gauguin to leave his family and take off for Tahiti—morality plays a large enough part in our lives that moral concerns often enough attain what Scheffler calls "authoritative status," the status of Williams's categorical "must." Scheffler thinks the Freudian theory of the superego is a good example of a theory that finds enough motivational authority for conscience in the

---

[19] Darwall, p. 82.
[20] Scheffler, *Human Morality*, p. 69.

natural world that we do not need Kantian metaphysics or any other special source for moral obligation.

Williams, who writes as if some fairly deep changes are needed if we are to move beyond the illusions of morality, clearly cannot accept Scheffler's answer to his criticisms, for it implies that we need at most to make some fairly small changes in how we think about morality—in particular, changes that make it more forgiving and less demanding than it is when interpreted by (for instance) the more extreme Utilitarians. However, it is difficult to see what basis he has for substantive disagreement with Scheffler. Williams clearly thinks ethical concerns are woven into the fabric of human life, that they are essential to human emotions and relations, and that they have authority (if not overridingness) in human life. He does not want to call these ethical concerns "moral." But since he seems to say about the ethical everything Scheffler says about the moral, it looks as if, as in the case of Williams's claims about the connection between moral blame and the deep notion of the voluntary, what is at stake is merely a verbal matter—a dispute about how to use the word "moral."

Guilt and Shame

I suggest that this objection can be answered by a more Nietzschean interpretation of Williams's critique of morality than I have so far offered. My thought is that Williams is moving toward this account in *ELP*, but fully reaches it only in *SN*.

Nietzsche's account of the moralization of obligation is found in *GM*'s story of the origins of guilt, which begins with the "morality of custom" *(die Sittlichkeit der Sitte)*. The customs that belonged to the ancient morality (in the broad sense) that Nietzsche has in mind here become primitive versions of moral rules insofar as punishment is attached to violations. They function as societal standards of forbidden and acceptable behavior but lack certain features we associate with morality—for instance, a connection to guilt. These rules do not constitute standards of specifically *moral* right and wrong, we might say, because violators were not blamed or considered guilty—at least not in the moral sense.

According to Nietzsche's account, the most primitive version of guilt is debt. The relationship between the community and its members was thought of on the model of the creditor/debtor relationship, so that obedience to the rules was conceived of as something one *owes* the community, an obligation or debt one incurs in exchange for the advantages of community life. The community naturally reacts to the violation of its rules with anger, as "a deceived creditor [who will] exact payment as best it can":

> Here it is least of all a matter of the direct injury inflicted by the injuring party; quite apart from this, the criminal is above all a "breaker," one who

breaks his contract *with the whole*, in relation to all the goods and conveniences of communal life in which he has until this point had his share. The criminal is a debtor who not only fails to pay back his creditor, but also even lays a hand on his creditor; he therefore not only forfeits all of these goods and advantages from now on, as is fair,—he is now also reminded *how much there is to these goods.* The anger of the injured creditor, of the community, gives him back again to the wild and outlawed condition from which he was previously protected: it expels him from itself, and now every kind of hostility may vent itself on him. At this level of civilization "punishment" is simply the copy, the *mimus* of normal behavior towards the hated, disarmed, defeated enemy, who has forfeited not only every right and protection, but also every mercy; in other words, the law of war and the victory celebration of *vae victis!* [woe to the vanquished!] in all their ruthlessness and cruelty. (GM II:9)

When the community grows stronger and more secure, violations of its rules are no longer as dangerous to the "continued existence of the whole as they once were." The creditor now becomes "more humane" and finds a way to allow the debtor to pay off his debt and remain within the community, namely, through his own suffering. "Punishment" is no longer a mere venting of hostility on a defenseless "enemy of the people," but is a way in which one works off one's guilt, pays one's debt to society.[21]

Nietzsche clearly denies that the obligations or debts so far involved in his story have yet been moralized. Obligation is *moral* obligation only if the debt one owes for failure is *moral* guilt. The debt one pays off through punishment is only a primitive version of guilt, which is here a "material" concept rather than a moral one. But how exactly does moral guilt differ from primitive guilt—that is, from mere debt? Nietzsche's answer is complicated, but he makes clear that moralization of guilt and duty is a process of "their being pushed back into conscience, more precisely the entanglement of bad conscience with the concept of God" (GM II:21).

Nietzsche analyzes bad conscience, the sense of oneself as guilty, as the internalization of aggression. When community rules and the attached punishments prevented individuals from expressing aggressive and hostile impulses externally, they turned these same impulses back against themselves. I do not think this should be taken to mean that all internalization of hostile or aggressive impulses involves a sense of guilt. It is only when one internalizes the hostile attitude of one who thinks you *owe* him—in particular, that you deserve to suffer for what you have done—that it seems to be guilt.

---

[21] In paper number 4 in this volume I argue that Nietzsche takes this to be the beginning of punishment as retribution. I leave to the side here the issue of what Nietzsche thinks it shows about human psychology that suffering constitutes a typical way in which criminals are expected to pay off their debts to society.

What does the concept of God have to do with this? I think the point is that the moralization of debt into guilt takes place when the concept God becomes an instrument for the turning back of hostility against the self. The concept of God or the divine is a concept of value. The Greek gods, on the one hand, according to Nietzsche, were reflections of what the Greeks valued in themselves (combined with a lot more power than they themselves had). The Judeo-Christian God, on the other hand, is the projection of a value human beings can never come close to attaining, a being who is the opposite of their "ineluctable animal nature." This God is a product of the involvement of the concept of God with the bad conscience, the use of the concept of the divine as an instrument of self-torture. The debt humans are thought to owe this God is also an instrument of self-torture. What makes the debt one owes this God moral rather than material, I believe, is that it is taken to reflect one's worth as a person.

This is not true in the case of primitive guilt. There I owe a debt, I pay it off. People may be angry at me for violating the rules, they may enjoy inflicting punishment to collect the debt I owe, and maybe they even think less of me for one reason or another because I owe this debt; or maybe they do not. *The point is: My guilt is merely a debt I owe; it is not itself a matter of my worth as a person.* I may deserve to be punished—that is the debt I owe society—but the judgment that I deserve punishment need not carry with it a judgment of my worth as a person. In the moral case, however, guilt does carry with it a judgment of the person. I may be guilty because of something I did to you, but my guilt is a condition of my soul—a black mark upon it, as it were, something that should affect my sense of my own worth.

This fits with one of the central claims of Nietzsche's *Genealogy*, that standards of right or wrong and standards of personal worth (goodness in the sense of virtue) have quite different sources, and hence constitute distinct strands in the concept of morality. Moral guilt, as I have tried to understand it, is the site of the intertwining of the right and the good within what Williams calls the "morality system." And, as I will try to show, the intertwining that gives rise to specifically *moral* guilt, according to Nietzsche, hides the structure of ethical life from view in a way that is structurally similar to what Williams thinks goes on in the genealogy of specifically *moral* obligation.

In Nietzsche's account of moral guilt, there are two different relations: the relation of the individual to someone she has injured or failed in some way, and then the self's relation to the standards she accepts for a good person. Realizing— under the influence of Williams's *SN*—that moral guilt makes it easy to conflate these two relations finally allowed me to understand one of the sayings of Nietzsche's fictional character and alter-ego Zarathustra: "And if a friend does you evil, then say: 'I forgive you what you did to me; but that you have done that to yourself—how could I forgive that?' Thus speaks all great love: it overcomes even forgiveness and compassion" (*Z* II:3).

This had always struck me as arrogant. After all, who asked Zarathustra to forgive what his friend did to himself? I now realize Zarathustra's point to his friend is: I can forgive you your debt to me (let you off the hook, no longer hold it against you), but that is no solution to the problem moral guilt gives you with yourself. If what you did to me shows you are less than you thought you were, my forgiveness will not help with that, although seeking it may help to distract you from the issue. The moral interpretation of guilt makes it easy to distract oneself from one's problem with oneself by concentrating on one's anxiety or need for forgiveness in relation to another. But it can work the other way too: We are distracted from what we did to another person—and also from what we can do to help that person deal with what we did—because we are too involved in feeling bad about our own unworthiness; and what we really want from the one we have injured is a canceling of that unworthiness. The moralized version of guilt makes it very difficult to sort out these relations.

Nietzsche's account suggests that if they are sorted out, then if I regret what I did to another, it will be natural for me to consider myself in some version of indebtedness to that person—to want to make amends, for instance. But I will see the issue of what my action means about me and my worth to be a separate matter. And if it means that I have not lived up to what I expect of myself, then I will feel some version of disappointment or shame rather than guilt.[22]

I believe that Williams had a grip on this Nietzschean point all along, but he makes it explicit only in *SN*. Here he considers cases in which a person feels guilt when there is no question of wrong to others or reparation: "Robbed of these implications, guilt narrows down suspectly to a desire for punishment. It might then be helpfully replaced by what it should have been in the first place, shame" (*SN*, p. 93). Williams thus suggests that if we were not confused by the moral interpretation of ethical life, this is what we would have when we regret having caused harm to another person: some attempt at reparation in relation to the other, and a quite separate coming to terms with what that means about oneself. If it means that one has not lived up to what one expects of oneself, he thinks some version of shame is called for, not guilt.

In *ELP*, Williams located morality's conflation between relations to others and one's relation to one's own standards of goodness or worth in the conflation between obligations to others and the all-things-considered judgment of

---

[22] However, this does not mean that the ideal situation for Nietzsche is that we simply feel shame rather than guilt. In fact, it is clear that Nietzsche's ideal involves the overcoming of shame. Consider the ending lines of part three of *The Gay Science:* "Whom do you call bad? Those who always want to put to shame." "*What do you consider most humane?* To spare someone shame." "*What is the seal of liberation?* No longer being ashamed in front of oneself" (*GS* 273–5). Nietzsche's problem with the moralized version of guilt is that shame is hidden in it, and it must be exposed to be overcome. See John Kekes, "Shame and Moral Progress," *Midwest Studies in Philosophy* 13 (1988): 282–96, for an argument to the effect that "whatever value there is in shame can be achieved in less self-destructive ways."

practical necessity that he finds in the idea of specifically moral obligation. I have suggested that to answer the criticism that his critique of morality comes down to a merely verbal matter, he needs to give plausibility to the idea that the naturalistic accounts of morality offered by, for instance, Scheffler and Korsgaard still cover over something about ethical life. I have tried to show that he is able to do this with the help of the more Nietzschean analysis of this conflation in terms of guilt that he offers in *SN*. The latter's Nietzschean analysis of moral guilt completes the analysis of morality given in *ELP* in a way that supports that claim that the moral interpretation covers over something about ethical life. Williams can argue that Scheffler, for instance, continues this cover-up when he takes for granted that the natural response to violating one's own internalized standards is guilt, not shame.

Morality's Purity and the Ascetic Ideal

In this concluding section I turn, very briefly, to what I consider the most deeply Nietzschean element in Williams's critique of morality, and one that is fully present in *ELP*. Neither Williams nor Nietzsche believes that the mistakes or illusions of morality—its commitment to the deep notion of the voluntary and lack of clarity it induces concerning ethical life—constitute its ultimate problem. Although Williams spends most of his analysis on these philosophical mistakes, his ultimate charge against morality is that these mistakes are the most abstract expression of a nihilistic ideal. That is not Williams's own formulation, but my Nietzschean rendition of it. Williams actually says that the philosophical mistakes in question reflect a "deeply rooted and still powerful misconception of life," but it is clear that the vision of life he has in mind is the expression of an ideal or value. He explains that morality

> emphasizes a series of contrasts, between force and reason, persuasion and rational conviction, shame and guilt, dislike and disapproval, mere rejection and blame. The attitude that leads it to emphasize all these contrasts can be labeled its *purity*, [which is] its insistence on abstracting the moral consciousness from other kinds of emotional reaction or social influence. (*ELP*, p. 195)

What does morality's insistence on purity amount to? Williams says that the purity of morality expresses an ideal, the ideal that human existence can be ultimately just: "The ideal of morality is a value, moral value, that transcends luck." Insofar as it is to transcend luck, moral value must be pure in the sense that it must, as Williams puts it, "lie beyond any empirical determination." To hold purity as one's ideal, I take it, is to think that true value attaches only to what is separated out from the normal "muck" of human life. Moral (truly valuable) versions of worth, motivation, and emotions must therefore be separated from the non-moral as much as possible by virtue of the former's pure or non-empirical source.

The upshot is what Nietzsche calls "nihilism," because in this way, according to Williams, morality "makes people think that without its very special obligation, there is only inclination; without its utter voluntariness, there is only force; without its ultimately pure justice, there is no justice" (*ELP*, p. 196). In other words, the moral interpretation of ethical existence has been rooted in illusions, such as the deep notion of the voluntary, that are more and more exposed as illusions. It cannot therefore continue to serve our ethical needs. But as long as it remains in its remnant form, it serves to devalue any other alternative. It's ideal of purity has deprived the resources such an alternative could use of all value.

This is Nietzsche's ultimate problem with morality. Nietzsche calls the ideal he finds behind morality the ascetic ideal, and he considers this a nihilistic ideal because it devalues everything that is merely natural (as opposed to supernatural). But it also leads, through its encouragement to the will to truth, to the realization that there is nothing but the natural, that all belief in the supernatural or the nonempirical is a lie, on the same order as the lie involved in belief in God. The upshot is that the illusions on which morality is based are exposed by its own ideal. Although many people hold on to the illusions, there is a great weakening of confidence in morality. On Nietzsche's account, morality is dead in the same sense and to about the same extent that God is dead. The deed has already been done, and its effects will become more and more apparent as time goes on.

But why did Nietzsche devote so much of his life to fighting what was already dead anyway? I believe it was an attempt to show us where morality and its nihilistic ideal are still strong: in preventing the development of new ideals. The nihilism of the moral tradition leads to the death of morality, but also to the view that nothing else is good enough to replace it. And this part of Nietzsche's thought is what I believe Williams is on to in his critique of morality's purity.

{ 3 }

Nietzsche's Contribution to Ethics

This chapter will focus on two interconnected elements of Nietzsche's philosophy that are the most important for understanding his place in the history of ethics and his relevance to contemporary theorizing about morality: his critique of morality and his naturalistic account of the origins and development of morality.

Nietzsche's most striking contribution to ethics is his self-proclaimed "denial of morality." Claiming to be an "immoralist," indeed the "first immoralist," he not only denies that morality has a right to our adherence but also insists that morality is something bad that ought to be overcome. He thus denies both the authority and the value of morality. It is his articulation and defense of this immoralist stance that establishes Nietzsche's distinctive place in the history of ethics and will therefore be the focus here. His account of the origins and development of morality will be the other main topic of discussion because questions about both the scope and the substance of his critique of morality are best answered by considering this account, which is also of independent importance as a sophisticated example of what it is to naturalize morality that stands in some contrast to other attempts to show that we can understand morality's existence without supernatural or metaphysical assumptions.

The Scope Problem

The first thing we need to know about Nietzsche's anti-morality stance concerns its *object or scope*. Is it really morality itself that he rejects, or is it only a particular morality or type of morality, say, Christian morality? Some have chosen the latter option, wondering how one could coherently question the *value* of morality. If moral values are defined as those that are overriding, as some have claimed, then they cannot be coherently questioned or rejected. But in most relevant passages, Nietzsche seems to be rejecting morality itself, and he makes explicit in at least one passage that the object of his suspicion is "all moralities" (*GM* P). Philippa Foot was one of the first of recent interpreters to take Nietzsche at his word here. But because he insists that morality is bad, and not just that it lacks authority (that we have no reason to abide by it), Foot concluded that he himself must be arguing against morality from the viewpoint of some other species of value. She found a basis for taking Nietzsche at his word that he was an immoralist rather than a "special kind of moralist" by seeing him as willing "to throw out justice in the interests of producing a stronger and more splendid type of man" (Foot 1978: 166); for she saw justice, but not the production of splendid humans, as conceptually tied to morality. She took Nietzsche's admiration for such splendid beings as analogous to aesthetic evaluation and its judgments of beauty or sublimity. But Foot overlooked Nietzsche's claim that "higher moralities" are, or ought to be, possible (*BGE* 202), with its suggestion that Nietzsche rejects the value of morality from the viewpoint of such a "higher morality." We can still make sense of his claim to reject "all moralities" if he is using "morality" in two different senses, and this is exactly what he implies in *BGE* 32, where he makes explicit that it is only morality "in the narrower sense" that he seeks to overcome.

Bernard Williams's distinction between ethics and morality gives us a helpful way of formulating Nietzsche's implicit distinction between the wide and narrow sense of "morality." Some use "morality" to mark off a part of the larger domain of the ethical, namely, the part having to do with duty and obligation, and believe that they are following Williams in doing so. But Williams treats morality as an instance rather than as a part of the ethical. What counts as an *ethics* for Williams is "any scheme for regulating the relations between people that works through informal sanctions and internalized dispositions" (Williams 1995: 241), dispositions to accept the *legitimacy* of demands made upon one by the system. Morality, on the other hand, is a particular ethical orientation, or a "range" of such outlooks, which is "so much with us," according to Williams, "that moral philosophy spends much of its time discussing the differences between these outlooks, rather than the difference between all of them and everything else" (Williams 1985: 174). Yet, all of these different moral outlooks are variations on a particular kind of ethical orientation that Williams thinks we would be "better off without."

This is precisely Nietzsche's position. He thinks that what we call "morality" (or at least did call "morality" when he was writing) is "so much with us" because it presents itself as the only possible form of ethical life. He is an immoralist, only if one is using "morality" in the narrower sense; he does not reject all regulatory systems that rely on "informal sanctions and internalized dispositions." Yet he does reject both the authority and the value of the form of ethical life that now goes by the name "morality" and which he thinks claims to be the only form of ethical life. What Foot missed about Nietzsche's position when she tried to ground it in the priority of aesthetic values was the possibility that his rejection of morality was part of a defense of an alternative ethical orientation. At the very least, she shows no signs of appreciating that Nietzsche took morality to be only one of the possibilities for ethical life, perhaps because she herself took it to be the only one.

Defining Morality

What we need next is a definition or specification of morality, the form of ethical life that Nietzsche seeks to overcome. Unfortunately, this is not easy to provide, and Nietzsche tells us why, namely, that it is impossible to define anything that has a complicated history. One might try to sidestep this problem, as Brian Leiter influentially attempts to do, by going directly to Nietzsche's critique of morality, constructing the object of Nietzsche's critique from his objections to it. Leiter calls this object "morality in the pejorative sense" (MPS), which he offers as a heuristic category rather than a historical one. Leiter constructs the norms that belong to MPS from Nietzsche's "disparate critical remarks—about altruism, happiness, pity, equality, Kantian respect for persons, utilitarianism, etc." (Leiter 2002: 129). An MPS is thus an ethical system that has a pro-attitude toward, among other things, happiness, altruism, and equality. Although this approach has some appeal—after all, what we want to know is what Nietzsche is against—it also has a downside. For we also want to know if it is really morality that Nietzsche is attacking, and Leiter's account leaves it unclear whether Nietzsche's alleged objections to MPS are actually objections to morality. Leiter takes Nietzsche's objection to MPS to be that "a culture in which such norms prevail as morality will be a culture which eliminates the conditions for the realization of human excellence—the latter requiring, on Nietzsche's view, concern for self, suffering, a certain stoic indifference, a sense of hierarchy and difference, and the like." Leiter's most plausible example of how this can work concerns happiness. A culture permeated with a pro-attitude toward happiness and a con-attitude toward suffering will make it more difficult for creative human beings, great artists and thinkers—Nietzsche's higher human types, according to Leiter—to fulfill their potential: to endure and even welcome the suffering necessary for the realization of that potential, instead of squandering themselves in the pursuit of happiness. But does morality actually embrace happiness as a norm or create a culture that does? Although contemporary secular culture embraces happiness as a norm, it seems to be the antithesis of a moral culture, which would seem to promote the fulfillment of duty and the striving to be a good person, not the striving for one's own happiness. So granting that one of Nietzsche's major criticisms of morality is that it produces the contemptible "last man" who cares only about happiness, it is difficult to gather from Leiter's account how *morality* is supposed to be responsible for this. It is also difficult to understand why Nietzsche is so horrified by morality. Even if it does work against the existence of higher types, that doesn't seem enough to account for the sense one gets from Nietzsche that morality is "against life" and has turned humanity itself into a diseased and botched species.

Nietzsche's *Genealogy of Morality*

For an understanding of these matters, the best approach is to consult Nietzsche's *On the Genealogy of Morality* (*GM*), which offers a genealogy of the form of ethical life that he seeks to overcome. It does so, in part, because Nietzsche thinks genealogy is the only way to clarify the concept of morality, to get clear on what that particular form of ethical life is. In a late stage of development, he claims, the concept of any practice that has a history will involve "an entire synthesis of 'meanings'" that have "finally crystallize[d] into a kind of unity which is difficult to dissolve, difficult to analyze, and—one must emphasize—is completely and utterly undefinable" (*GM* II:13). But if we are thus unable to "define" morality, establishing necessary and sufficient conditions for a set of practices to count as an instance of this concept, Nietzsche proceeds to point out an alternative way of analyzing it: to look back to earlier stages of its development, where "that synthesis of meanings still appears more soluble, also more capable of shifts," and one can "still perceive" how the elements of the synthesis change their valence and rearrange themselves accordingly. The concept is thus like a rope, held together by the intertwining of its strands, so that analyzing it is not a matter of isolating a core or essence, but of disentangling its various strands so that one can see what is actually involved in it. This is what Nietzsche aims to do in *GM*. By going back to an "earlier stage," he attempts to sort out various strands that are synthesized into our concept of morality and to explain how they came to be synthesized in this way.

GM contains three treatises, each of which traces a particular strand of the concept of morality back to an earlier form. In a postcard to his friend Overbeck (4 January 1888; see Risse 2001: 55), Nietzsche explains that in *GM*, "it was necessary, for the sake of clarity, to isolate artificially the different roots of the complex structure that is called morality." Nietzsche thus indicates that the object for which he is attempting to provide a genealogy is a "complex structure," a synthesis of several distinct elements, and that *GM* deals with these elements in abstraction from their actual involvement with each other in the development of morality. The remainder of the postcard makes clear that Nietzsche is well aware that *GM* leaves out several elements that are involved in the synthesis that is morality, in particular, the "herd instinct," which he calls "the most essential one," and that it does not put them together to provide "a final account of morality." This has important implications for how we should understand *GM*.

The Slave Revolt in Morality

The first treatise (*GM* I) is infamous for its claim that our morality is the product of a "slave revolt" fueled by *ressentiment* directed against the nobles of the ancient world. The French *"ressentiment"* is close to the English "resentment," which is a human reaction to feeling slighted. According to Nietzsche's analysis, resentment becomes grudge-laden and poisonous among those who are powerless and therefore unable simply to shake off the (occasional) slight or to discharge the resulting resentment either by standing up to the offender and demanding proper treatment or by lashing out at him. The slave revolt he posits took place over a long period of time, and was originally led not by slaves, but by religious leaders who considered themselves good, and who felt envious of and slighted by the nobles who ruled them with all too much self-confidence in their own superiority. Unable to assert themselves directly against the nobles, they lashed out at them in the only way they could, by devaluing them. The ultimate upshot is a revaluation—a reversal—of the noble values. The poor, meek, and humble are declared "the good," and the nobles are claimed to be "'the evil, the cruel, the lustful, the insatiable, the godless, [who] will eternally be the wretched, accursed, and damned.'" Nietzsche claims that the slave revolt began with the Jews, but eventually led to the proclamation of the Christian beatitudes. Qualities that slaves needed to develop, such as meekness and humility, came to be seen as virtues (leading eventually to the view that altruism is the essence of virtue), whereas pride, the ultimate noble virtue (even in Aristotle), came to be seen as evil and the essence of sin—not because anyone admired the slavish virtues or wanted to exemplify them, but out of hatred toward and a need for revenge against the nobles, a need to "bring them down," if only in imagination.

However, it is important to recognize that it is not our entire morality—e.g., our notion of right and wrong—that Nietzsche takes to be a product of a slave revolt, but only our idea of goodness or virtue. *GM* I:2 argues on etymological grounds that "good" was originally equivalent to "noble" in a purely political sense. It was used by ancient ruling groups to designate themselves as members of the politically superior class, in opposition to commoners and slaves. At this point, it is not an ethical term, much less a specifically moral one. It becomes an ethical term when it evolves into an idea of nobility (i.e., superiority) of soul, so that its contrasting term is equivalent to "bad" in our sense, and not merely "common." This happens because of the nobles' self-affirmation, which shows through in the words they use to describe themselves. Happy with their own existence, they naturally experienced their own lives as superior to the lives of those they ruled. Accordingly, "good" begins to express their sense of their own superiority, as do the other terms they use to distinguish themselves from commoners. For instance, they are not only "the good" but also "the rich" and "the powerful." The nobles' conception of what distinguishes them from commoners is fairly crude at first, but later begins to center on traits of soul or character, such as loyalty, truthfulness, and courage. They are "the truthful," for instance, as "distinct from the *lying* common man" (*GM* I:5). In this process, Nietzsche claims, "good" eventually loses all connection to political class and becomes a purely ethical notion, equivalent to "virtuous" or "superior of soul." It is unclear, however, whether this is supposed to have actually happened already, or is being held out as a possible future development of the good/bad distinction. What is clear is that good/bad is not intended by Nietzsche as a moral distinction in the narrow sense. To call someone "bad" is certainly to call him a bad or inferior person, and not simply a commoner, and is therefore an ethical judgment. But it is not to call him "morally bad" or "evil."

The brilliance of Nietzsche's psychological analysis and the fact that his story has the leaders of the slave revolt exhibiting some of the same characteristics they themselves condemn make it tempting to locate his criticism of morality in his claim about its origins in resentment. But this would be an instance of the genetic fallacy, which he repudiates (*GS* 345). That humility was first put forward as a virtue by priests who were far from humble or that love was praised out of hatred does not show that humility and love are not virtues. And Nietzsche's whole approach makes clear that Christian virtues might be valued today for very different reasons than they were in the beginning.

The slave revolt plays such a central role in Nietzsche's account of the development of morality because it creates a *moralized* conception of a good person and a corresponding idea of an *"evil one"* (*GM* I:10), of a person who is not merely bad, but evil. To judge someone to be "bad," as Nietzsche is using that term, is to judge them to be inferior, but it does not imply that they are responsible for being inferior, much less that they deserve punishment for it. The appropriate response is pity or contempt, not condemnation. When "bad" is moralized into "evil," on the other hand, the person is held responsible for being the kind of person he is and condemned for it. This is how virtue and its opposite become connected to reward and punishment, which makes sense only on the assumption that we actually choose to be the kind of person we are, hence that we have free will in what Nietzsche calls "the metaphysical superlative sense," in which one is *"causa sui,"* cause of oneself (*BGE* 21). This is the aspect of the slave revolt that Nietzsche most clearly criticizes. When he demands that the philosopher "take his stand beyond good and evil and leave the illusion of moral judgment beneath himself" (*TI* VII:1), he is referring to the judgment of persons in the moralized terms of good and evil. And his most obvious reason for taking such judgments to involve "illusion" is that they presuppose free will in a sense that he considers absurd, namely, that we are *causa sui* (*BGE* 21). But even if this is true—and many philosophers deny that morality requires free will in that sense—it does not explain why Nietzsche denies the *value* of morality, for he insists that "even if a morality has grown out of an error, the realization of this fact would not as much as touch the problem of its value" (*GS* 345). Explaining that the value of a "thou shalt" is independent of "opinions about its origin, religious sanction, the superstition of free will, and things of that sort," he concludes that "nobody up to now examined the value of that most famous of all medicines which is called morality: and the first step would be—for once to *question* it. Well then, precisely this is our task."

Cruelty and Bad Conscience

We must dig deeper into the matter, therefore, if we are to understand Nietzsche's critique of morality. We need especially to understand why he calls morality a "medicine." The best text for this purpose is the second treatise of *GM*, which does for moral right and wrong what *GM* I does for good and evil, tracing it back to a pre-moral version. Nietzsche calls this version the "morality of custom" (*Sittlichkeit der Sitte*), which is a system of mores and laws that regulated behavior in ancient communities. It was not an ethical system, much less an instance of morality, because it does not work through what Williams calls "informal sanctions and internalized dispositions," but only through punishment and the fear of it. Nietzsche assumes that the disposition to obey the rules has an older source than fear of punishment, namely, the herd instinct, the disposition to conform one's behavior to what those around one do, which he calls the "most essential" aspect of morality in the postcard quoted previously. Customary practices thus constituted a kind of norm even before the institution of formal punishments. The disposition to conform one's behavior to customary practices would not count as an "internalized disposition," however, because it is purely a matter of instinct and does not yet carry with it ideas of authority or legitimacy. Rules obeyed only out of fear or instinct are not yet perceived as moral rules by those who are disposed to obey them. The main question Nietzsche pursues in *GM* II concerns how such non-moral rules, laws, and customs were transformed into moral ones.

His basic answer is that this happened through the development of guilt. Rules and practices have the status of moral rules for those who take those who violate them to be guilty. But what is guilt? Nietzsche's complicated answer has two sides, one conceptual, the other explanatory or causal. First, he argues, partly on etymological grounds, that "the central moral concept 'guilt'" originates in "the very material concept 'debt'" (*GM* II:4)—indeed, in German, the same word (*Schuld*) is used for both; second, he traces a process that transformed debt into guilt. His account begins on the conceptual side. The relationship between the community and its members was taken to be analogous to a creditor/debtor relationship. Obedience to the rules necessary for community life was conceived of as something one *owes* the community, a debt one incurs in exchange for the advantages of community life. This is the original idea of *obligation*. It is a primitive ethical idea because it is connected to ideas of legitimacy and fairness, as Nietzsche brings out by claiming that one who disobeys the rules is conceived of as "a debtor who not only fails to pay back his creditor, but also even lays a hand on his creditor; he therefore not only forfeits all of these goods and advantages from now on, as is fair,—he is now also reminded *how much there is to these goods.*"

> The anger of the injured creditor, of the community, gives him back again to the wild and outlawed condition from which he was previously protected: it expels him from itself, and now every kind of hostility may vent itself on him. At this level of civilization "punishment" is simply the copy, the *mimus* of normal behavior towards the hated, disarmed, defeated enemy, who has forfeited not only every right and protection, but also every mercy. (*GM* II:21)

So this "punishment" (the harm inflicted on the offender beyond banishment) is not yet thought of as something the offender deserves. It is simply what one is permitted to do to those who are not part of the community. This does not yet give us the thought that one who fails to live by the rules of the community is guilty, that he deserves blame and punishment.

That idea begins to come into view only when the community grows stronger, so that violations of its rules are no longer as dangerous to the "continued existence of the whole." Becoming "more humane," the creditor finds a way to separate the criminal from his deed, allowing him to remain in the community by offering him a substitute way of paying off his debt. Just as Shylock is permitted by law to take a pound of flesh as a substitute for the debt he is owed in *The Merchant of Venice*, the community extracts from those who have violated their agreement to abide by the rules a substitute payment in the form of the offender's suffering. Punishment is now no longer a mere venting of hostility on a defenseless "enemy of the people," but is a way in which one pays off one's debt to society. We have here the beginning of the idea that the offender *deserves* his punishment, which is also an *ethical* idea because of its connection to ideas of fairness and legitimacy. The offender did the deed, thereby breaking the rules and reneging on his promise; therefore it is fair that he be punished. But if we can therefore say that he is judged to be *guilty*, this is primitive guilt, still just a debt that can be paid off, and not the moralized idea of guilt that Nietzsche is after. To see how he thinks debt or guilt becomes moralized, it is necessary to consider the other side of his story.

Note first that Nietzsche's account of punishment as a way to pay off one's debt assumes that human beings find satisfaction in the suffering of others. It would otherwise make no sense that they accept someone's suffering as a substitute payment for obeying the community rules. This aspect of his theory is often connected to his idea of the will to power, but it is controversial how large a role this idea actually plays in his philosophy (Clark 1990; Reginster 2006) and there is no need to bring it in to understand the point at issue here. It is difficult to deny that violence and cruelty have played a huge part in human history, and Nietzsche's theory attempts to explain why. The key point here is that a stable society is impossible without restrictions on the expression of aggressive impulses. Such impulses, a product of natural selection because of the advantages they confer in the wild for hunting and dealing with predators, cannot be directed toward other members of the community, at least not in their original form. Nietzsche thinks societies discourage such behavior both by punishments and by providing alternative outlets for aggressive impulses. Among these outlets are various hierarchical arrangements, including military organizations, athletics and other contests, and the spectator sports of ancient Rome, in which the tendency of human beings toward cruelty is particularly apparent. This tendency toward cruelty is what allows the idea of paying one's debt to society through one's own suffering to make sense. But Nietzsche need not say that human beings are cruel by nature, nor deny that they have altruistic impulses by way of natural selection. His point is that cruel impulses develop under the influence of living in society because of the various things that happen to aggressive impulses, which human beings also have by means of natural selection, under the pressure of the need to suppress them and the further stimulation these impulses receive through the development of alternative means for satisfying them. These are ideas that were developed further by Freud.

Nietzsche is particularly interested in aggressive and cruel impulses because the redirection of these impulses back against the self is the other side of his story concerning the development of guilt. He presents bad conscience, the "consciousness of guilt" (*GM* II:4), as having its origin in the sudden imposition of the constraints of peaceful society on a previously nomadic population (*GM* II:16). Because it happened so suddenly, there was no time to develop new instincts through natural selection or new means of satisfying the old instincts through culture. There was only one way of satisfying such instincts, which was to internalize them, to turn them back against the self. Not all internalization of hostile or aggressive impulses involves a sense of guilt. The animal "that beats itself raw on the bars of his cage" (*GM* II:16) may be internalizing aggressive impulses, but is not feeling guilty or exhibiting a bad conscience. It is only when one internalizes (i.e., adopts against oneself) the hostile attitude of one who thinks you owe him something, and, more specifically, that you deserve to suffer for what you owe him, that it starts to be recognizable as guilt. The process that turns debt into moral guilt is one in which human beings learn to use the idea of having reneged on a debt or obligation, and therefore being deserving of punishment, to take a stand against themselves, to criticize themselves, hence to cause themselves "pain after the *more natural* outlet for this *desire to cause pain* was blocked" (*GM* II:22). When this process is completed, one has an internalized disposition to obey the rules. One has installed in oneself a critical faculty (like Freud's superego) that is on guard against violations of the rules, and that judges one to be guilty (at least blameworthy and often deserving of punishment) if one violates them anyway. The rules have the status of categorical or moral imperatives for those who have developed this critical faculty. They are motivated to obey the rules not out of mere instinct or fear of punishment, but because of the values they themselves hold.

What, then, is Nietzsche's objection to morality? Recall that his "task" is to evaluate morality as a "medicine," and that his immoralism implies that he does not consider it very effective medicine. We can understand this in the following terms: The "sickness" for which morality is a medicine is the bad conscience, the need to internalize aggression and cruelty, the "will to self-maltreatment" (*GM* II:18). Such internalization doesn't happen automatically; some kind of reason or basis for it is necessary. Indeed, Nietzsche portrays those who are prevented from expressing aggressive impulses externally but who lack a basis for internalization as suffering from "physiological depression" and "listlessness" (*GM* III:17–20). In the case at issue, if I am going to criticize and hold myself accountable for my behavior, there has to be some standard for correct behavior, and this is what morality supplies. But what, then, is the problem? Why isn't the moralization of guilt a perfect way of providing a safe channel for the expression of aggressive and even cruel impulses while at the same time giving a much-needed incentive for obedience to community standards?

If a "safe channel" is one that does not do damage to human beings and their potential, and morality provided such a channel for the expression of aggressive impulses, Nietzsche would have no objection. Contrary to the impression he makes on some readers, he does not wish to return us to the level of acting on brute instinct. He says that bad conscience is a sickness, "but a sickness as pregnancy is a sickness" (*GM* II:19), which means that he looks forward to the new birth to which it can lead, not backwards to a previous stage. But he believes that the moralization of guilt produced by the will to self-maltreatment leads to the infliction of gratuitous suffering, on self and others, in fact, that it promotes an endless cycle of aggression against self and others, which undermines vitality and creativity, and prevents human beings from realizing their highest potential. To get some idea of why he thinks this, we will consider all too briefly the role of the ascetic ideal in his account of morality.

The Ascetic Ideal

The ascetic ideal puts forward the life of self-denial as the ideal life. By devoting *GM* III to this ideal, Nietzsche indicates (as we can infer from the postcard quoted earlier) that he considers it one of the main strands of morality. We can make sense of this in light of his claim that the moralization of guilt occurred through the "entanglement of the bad conscience with the concept of god" (*GM* II:21), i.e., through the use of the concept of god for turning aggression back against the self, if we recognize that the concept of god in question is an ascetic one. Whereas the Greek gods were reflections of what the Greeks valued in themselves, according to Nietzsche, the Judeo-Christian God is the projection of a value human beings can never come close to attaining, a being who is the opposite of our own "inescapable animal instincts." This conception of the divine reflects the ascetic ideal and functions to internalize cruelty.

Nietzsche's idea is that contemplative types, originally priests, are the experts in internalizing aggressive impulses because their own nature disinclines them toward externalizing them. They therefore developed practices of self-denial and cruelty to self, which helps them to avoid the depression and listlessness that Nietzsche thinks would otherwise have affected them. But they needed a conscious reason to adopt the practices and found it in the ascetic ideal, which promotes the life of self-denial on the grounds that our life as animals, as part of "nature," has no value in itself, that it receives value only if "it were to turn against itself, *to negate itself*" (*GM* III:11), thus becoming a mere means to another mode of existence that is its opposite (e.g., nirvana, heaven). The ascetic life has no intrinsic appeal to most people. Nietzsche's suggestion is that ascetic priests taught non-reflective types, who were prevented from externalizing aggressive and cruel impulses almost exclusively by fear of punishment, how to use the idea of debt to internalize these impulses. They took over from non-ascetic or pagan priests the teaching that we owe a debt to some divine being and must pay it off with sacrifices or risk terrible consequences. The sacrifices demanded are material, e.g., the best cuts of meat (of which the priests make good use), although things can get much more serious, as when Agamemnon must sacrifice his own daughter to ensure the success of his fleet. The ascetic ideal is not at work here; there is no implication that the sacrifice is demanded because nature is of no value or that sensuality is to be overcome. But that is the implication when ascetic priests insist that we must sacrifice our nature as animal and therefore desiring beings. Ascetic priests use this framework to explain to the people the source of their suffering (which actually comes from having no way to organize and discharge instinctual drives): God is punishing them for disobeying him, indeed for rebelling against him. Their rebellion is a matter of affirming their "inescapable animal instincts," for God, as pure spirit, is the opposite of such instincts. In affirming them, as our nature inclines us to do, we are in effect saying that we do not need God, that "this life" is enough, which is pride, the essence of sin. We therefore deserve punishment. But the debt we therefore owe cannot be paid off, even in principle, because it is rooted in our very nature and is therefore connected to our worth as persons. This is what makes it *moral* guilt as opposed to primitive guilt or mere debt. And the debt that cannot be discharged gives rise to the idea of eternal punishment, in which Nietzsche sees "a kind of madness of the will in psychic cruelty that has absolutely no equal: the *will* of man to find himself guilty and reprehensible to the point that it cannot be atoned for . . . his *will* to erect an ideal—that of the 'holy God'—in order, in the face of the same, to be tangibly certain of his own unworthiness." Adding "Oh, this insane sad beast man," Nietzsche suggests that our ideas became "bestial" because we were prevented from acting like beasts (*GM* II:22).

Granting that the "self-crucifixion" at issue here is sad and insane, we may still wonder if this is really a problem for morality, for even if the ascetic ideal functioned to moralize guilt, secularized contemporary morality seems to get on quite well without it. Isn't Nietzsche's objection only to a particular and old-fashioned conception of morality, one that demands sacrifice of our natural instincts? He would deny this. The ascetic ideal seems absent from secularized morality due to the absence of factors that belong only to the exterior or appearance of the ideal—e.g., belief in God and an explicit demand for the denial of sensuality. But Nietzsche insists that the ascetic ideal itself is responsible for this situation and that its work is far from over once these factors are gone. It was an ever-deepening cruelty to self and demand for self-denial, imposed by the ascetic ideal on higher or more spiritual types in the form of a "will to truth" (*GM* II:23–8), Nietzsche claims, that led to the "sacrifice [of] everything comforting, holy, healing" in the ascetic ideal, "all hope, all faith in a concealed harmony, in a future bliss and justice" (*BGE* 55), thus everything that appeals to less spiritual people. Now all that remains for higher culture to do is to devote itself to destroying more and more of its own basis, which, according to Nietzsche, is the desire for higher states of soul, which in fact cannot be possessed by everyone. Using the conception of virtue derived from the slave revolt in morality as a basis for further internalization of cruelty, it turns against the desire for and belief in distinction, thereby depriving higher culture of much capacity to inspire, and depriving less spiritual types of any belief in the possibility of a higher type of human than they themselves are. Lower culture becomes unleashed from the ascetic ideal, becoming cruder and more oriented toward material things. Morality is now reduced to "herd animal morality," based largely on prudence and conformity. The reign of the "last man" threatens because we now lack any ideal that could inspire us to care about much beyond our own happiness.

Does Nietzsche have an alternative in mind? No doubt. His critique of morality, the attempt to show how morality and its "medicine" have gotten us into this depressing situation, is only part of his project, the no-saying part. There is also the yes-saying part, which is the attempt to show us glimpses of a new life-affirming ideal that could play the same kind of role in a new form of ethical life that the ascetic ideal played in bringing about the moralized form. Such an ideal cannot be adopted at will, however, but can only emerge in the new ways of seeing and feeling that come from thinking through the old ideal and its role in making us who we are now. Nor would a new ideal have to create a new form of ethical life from scratch. Nietzsche's genealogy of morality shows us that there are important ethical resources on which it can rely, e.g., pre-moral notions of virtue, obligation, and guilt. Synthesizing these notions in a new way would be an important part of its task (perhaps along the lines suggested in 2002a, paper 2 in this volume) as would pointing us toward new sublimated ways of dealing with the instinctual impulses that the ascetic ideal has directed back against the self. This is a major function of Nietzsche's books and goes a long way toward explaining why he writes the way he does.

{ 4 }

Nietzsche on Free Will, Causality, and Responsibility

It is now widely accepted that Nietzsche denies that human beings possess freedom or free will. Brian Leiter's arguments to this effect have been particularly influential (Leiter 2002). Some recent commentators depart from Leiter's view, taking Nietzsche to posit freedom as a normative ideal, one that is compatible with determinism, equivalent to autonomy, and attainable by some but probably not by all (e.g., Gemes 2009, Janaway 2009, Rutherford 2011). I endorse such attempts, but do not think that they go far enough in rejecting the standard view. For these commentators still agree that Nietzsche rejects free will in the sense required for moral responsibility. In this paper, I argue that he does not, at least not in his later and greater works.

Of course, whether Nietzsche rejects free will in the sense required for moral responsibility depends on what one means by "moral responsibility." Yet those who claim that Nietzsche rejects moral responsibility have not provided a careful specification of exactly what they take him to be rejecting. Nietzsche certainly rejects the idea of moral responsibility that attaches to the morality he seeks to overcome, which he calls "morality in the traditional sense" or "the narrower sense" and the "morality of intentions" (*BGE* 32). The idea of responsibility that he rejects is the one that is bound up with the idea of freedom in what *BGE* 21 calls the "metaphysical superlative sense." The question is whether Nietzsche thinks that a recognizable idea of moral responsibility is left standing once one rejects that idea of freedom. Brian Leiter assumes that he does not. I argue that, in his later works, he does.

I begin by looking briefly at an early passage, HA 39, in which Nietzsche does reject free will in the sense he then took to be required for responsibility. The incompatibilist position Nietzsche endorses in this passage is the one that Leiter believes he accepts in his later works as well. I begin my argument against Leiter's view by considering BGE 21, a later passage that plays a major role in his argument for interpreting Nietzsche as a forerunner of the "new wave of non-libertarian incompatibilism defended by philosophers like Derk Pereboom

(2001) and Galen Strawson (1994)" (Leiter 2007: 1). I argue to the contrary that *BGE* 21 is best interpreted as descending from Hume's compatibilism. I then turn to *On the Genealogy of Morality*, arguing that its account of the origins of judgments of responsibility makes Nietzsche a forerunner of Peter Strawson and his compatibilist account of holding responsible.

Context

I begin by providing some context for the present paper in two senses. First, I explain its relation to my earlier work on truth because this will be important for understanding my dispute with Leiter. Second, I say something about Nietzsche's early views on moral responsibility, which provide the context for his later views on this topic.

In *Nietzsche on Truth and Philosophy* (1990), I defended a developmental thesis regarding Nietzsche's views on truth. I took his early works to propound the Falsification Thesis (FT) according to which "truths are illusions," which I took to mean that all of our purported truths are false. I argued that Nietzsche's basis for FT was an understanding of truth as requiring correspondence to things as they are in themselves, combined with a denial that any of our truths achieve such correspondence. I argued further that problems concerning how we could *know* that our truths failed to achieve such correspondence eventually led Nietzsche to abandon FT, and that this is why his later works (from *GM* on) no longer call all purported truths "illusions" or "false." I concluded that the later Nietzsche rejects only a certain conception or theory of truth, namely, the metaphysical correspondence theory he began by assuming.

In this paper, I argue that Nietzsche's work shows a similar development in the case of free will in the sense required for moral responsibility. He begins by rejecting free will and responsibility completely, adopting the stance of the anti-libertarian incompatibilist. He ends by rejecting only a particular conception of free will, namely, the incompatibilist conception he began by assuming, as well as the idea of responsibility it supports.

Particularly clear evidence of Nietzsche's early incompatibilism is found in *HA* 39 ("*The fable of intelligible freedom*"), which aims to provide the history of the feelings "by virtue of which we consider a person responsible, the so-called moral feelings." Most noteworthy about this passage are the assumptions it leaves unexamined and the questions it fails to raise. In contrast to *GM*, for instance, it provides no account of the *origin* of the idea of responsibility, nor any account of how that idea became connected to the idea of goodness. Nietzsche simply *assumes* that judgments of responsibility are a necessary part of judging actions to be good or evil. He claims that human beings originally judged actions in terms of their consequences, but then forgot the origin of these judgments and took the qualities of good and evil to be "inherent in the actions themselves." (Nietzsche strongly criticizes the move he makes here in *GM* I:2 but attributes it to the "English psychologists."). Then we went further, assigning "goodness or evil to the motives" and taking the actions themselves to be "morally ambiguous [*zweideutig*]," that is, as good or evil depending on the motive. The next stage was to "go even further and cease to give to the particular motive the predicate good or evil, but give it rather to the whole nature of a man; the motive grows out of him as a plant grows out of the earth." Nietzsche assumes that in this history of our judgments regarding good and evil, "we make man responsible in turn for the effects of his actions, then for his actions, then for his motives and finally for his nature." It appears that the idea of responsibility at issue here is equivalent to full causal responsibility, and that the movement from one stage to the other in our judgments of good and evil and in the corresponding idea of responsibility is driven by the search for what ultimately causes human actions.

It therefore makes sense that Nietzsche thinks that the belief in responsibility is undone by an insight concerning causality.

> Now one finally discovers that this nature cannot be responsible either, in that it is altogether a necessary consequence, an outgrowth of the elements and influences of past and present things; that is, man cannot be made responsible for anything, neither for his nature, nor his motives, nor his actions, nor the effects of his actions. And thus we come to understand that the history of moral feelings is the history of an error, an error called "responsibility," which in turn rests on an error called "freedom of the will."

Nietzsche concludes from this argument that "no one is responsible for his deeds, no one for his nature; to judge is to be unjust. This is also true when the individual judges himself. The tenet is as bright as sunlight, and yet everyone prefers to walk back into the shadow and untruth—for fear of the consequences" (*HA* 39). Here Nietzsche seems to assume both determinism and incompatibilism. That is, he assumes that human behavior is causally determined by factors outside of the agent's control, and that freedom and responsibility are incompatible with one's actions being determined by such factors. Most of the work in the passage is being done by these assumptions. It certainly makes sense for Nietzsche to assume incompatibilism if, as it appears, he equates holding someone morally responsible for an action with holding them to have full causal responsibility for it.

I will argue that later Nietzsche moves away from the anti-libertarian incompatibilism of *HA* 39 and arrives at a much more subtle and interesting account of the origins of holding responsible in *GM*. This will require me to argue against part of my own earlier view. In my 1990 book, I made two quite different points about the next passage I will be analyzing here, *BGE* 21: first, that it offers a basically Humean analysis of causation, and second, that it insists that causality "falsifies" reality. I took the latter claim to be an indication that Nietzsche had not yet overcome the Falsification Thesis when he was writing *BGE*, and that this was because he was still in the grip of a naturalized neo-Kantian phenomenalism that he abandoned shortly thereafter. According to this phenomenalism, which Nietzsche took over largely from Schopenhauer and Friedrich Lange (but also from Afrikan Spir, as I came to realize),[1] the mind constructs the objects that we perceive by imposing on the data of sensation the components of knowledge that Kant considered a priori, most importantly, the categories of substance and causality. Because the data in question is the only part of experience that we do not construct or "make up," the construction of the normal objects of perception by the imposition of a priori categories on this data can be said to falsify reality, stabilizing the flow of sensation into things that persist and dividing it up into cause and effect (*GS* 112). I thought that this was why Nietzsche's middle-period works, *HA* through the first edition of *GS*, treat substance and causality as "fictions" or "falsifications." When I wrote my 1990 book, I believed that in *BGE* Nietzsche still continued to affirm FT and I treated *BGE* 21 as a major piece of evidence for this claim.

In the present paper, I reject my 1990 claim that *BGE* 21 is committed to a neo-Kantian phenomenalism and therefore to FT. I believe that I might have recognized the problem with my neo-Kantian reading of the passage sooner if I had done a more detailed reading of its Humean elements. And that is what I aim to do here, in part, because my reading of the passage has been used to support an incompatibilist interpretation of *BGE* 21. Leiter adopts my neo-Kantian reading of *BGE* 21 to interpret it as committed to the same non-libertarian incompatibilism that we find in Nietzsche's early work. By arguing against my earlier reading of *BGE* 21, I aim to establish that we have stronger reason to interpret the passage as endorsing a compatibilist position on the free will required to underwrite judgments of responsibility.

BGE 21

BGE 21 begins with an argument against what Nietzsche calls "freedom of the will" in the "metaphysical superlative sense":

> The causa sui [cause of itself] is the best self-contradiction that has been conceived so far, it is a sort of rape and perversion of logic; but the extravagant pride of man has managed to entangle itself profoundly and frightfully with just this nonsense. The desire for "freedom of the will" in the metaphysical superlative sense, which still holds sway, unfortunately,

---

[1] See Schopenhauer [1847] 1974: 76–84 for a vivid presentation of this theory. See Clark and Dudrick (2012: esp. 106–11, 124–9) for discussion of Lange's and Spir's influence on Nietzsche's thought.

in the minds of the half-educated; the desire to bear the entire and ultimate responsibility for one's actions oneself, and to absolve God, the world, ancestors, chance, and society involves nothing less than to be precisely this causa sui and, with more than Munchhausen's audacity, to pull oneself up into existence by the hair, out of the swamps of nothingness. (*BGE* 21)

The position against which Nietzsche is arguing here is clearly libertarianism, the claim that human beings possess "free will" in a sense that is incompatible with their actions being causally determined. Those who desire that kind of freedom need to absolve "God, the world, ancestors, chance, and society" of any responsibility for their actions because they want to make sure that their behavior is in no way determined by factors outside of their control. Nietzsche's argument against this position consists of two claims: (1) that free will in the "metaphysical superlative sense" at issue here requires that one be *causa sui*, and (2) that "the *causa sui* is the best self-contradiction hitherto imagined" (*BGE* 21). Nietzsche thus argues that the very idea of being *causa sui* is a contradiction in terms, hence that no one can be *causa sui*, that libertarianism takes us to be free in a sense that would make us *causa sui*, and therefore that libertarianism is false. He thereby rejects libertarianism without affirming determinism. The problem with libertarianism is that it requires one to be cause of oneself, and this is something one cannot be whether or not everything is determined.

In putting forward this argument, Nietzsche is indeed a forerunner of Galen Strawson, who cites Nietzsche's passage and uses his *causa sui* terminology in formulating his own position. Strawson begins from the premise that "when one acts, one acts in the way one does because of the way one is." But then, "to be truly morally responsible for one's actions, one would have to be truly responsible for the way one is: one would have to be causa sui . . . at least in certain crucial mental respects. But nothing can be causa sui—nothing can be the ultimate cause of itself in any respect. So nothing can be truly morally responsible" (Strawson 2005: 289). Strawson then quotes *BGE* 21 at some length. This is the half-truth in taking Nietzsche to be a forerunner of contemporary non-libertarian incompatibilists, namely, that they affirm his argument against libertarianism.

But rejecting libertarianism does not, of course, commit us to denying the existence of free will in a sense sufficient for responsibility. To get to that conclusion, we must also reject compatibilism, and *BGE* 21 says nothing that can plausibly be interpreted as such a rejection. Leiter seems to agree, for, commenting on that passage, he assures us that Nietzsche "simply takes [incompatibilism] for granted," and that "arguably, it is only certain philosophers who think the need to be a self-caused agent is superfluous" for moral responsibility (Leiter 2007: 7). But why shouldn't we take Nietzsche to be one of those philosophers? Leiter finds it so overwhelmingly obvious from passages such as *HA* 39 that Nietzsche is a non-libertarian incompatibilist that he thinks we can safely assume that this is also his position in *BGE* 21. Given the developmental thesis I am arguing, however, Leiter cannot make this assumption without begging the question against me. Nor can I take the mere fact that *BGE* 21 contains nothing obviously incompatibilist as a basis for rejecting Leiter's position without begging the question against him. To avoid begging the question either way, the issue between us must be how plausible it is to read the logic of the crucial argument of *BGE* 21 in compatibilist or incompatibilist terms. This "crucial argument" is introduced in the following portion of the passage:

> Suppose someone were thus to see through the boorish simplicity of this celebrated concept of "free will" and put it out of his head altogether, I beg of him to carry his "enlightenment" a step further, and so put out of his head the contrary of this monstrous conception of "free will": I mean "unfree will," which amounts to a misuse of cause and effect. (*BGE* 21)

Nietzsche thus claims that his denial of free will in the libertarian sense does not entail that the will is unfree. But then the obvious reading of his position would seem to be a compatibilist one: that *BGE* 21's denial of free will leaves open some sense in which the will is free. Indeed, this is already suggested by the fact that Nietzsche makes explicit that he rejects free will only in a *specific* sense, the "metaphysical superlative sense."

But this is not how Leiter reads the argument of the passage. Instead, he takes Nietzsche's denial of "unfree will" to be a denial that the will is causally determined. He uses my earlier neo-Kantian interpretation as a basis for taking Nietzsche's argument against "unfree will" to be that since nothing is causally determined, neither (of course) is the will (Leiter 2007: 6; 2002: 22–3).[2]

Now admittedly, the belief in "unfree will" that Nietzsche wants us "to put out of our head" would include a belief that the will's choices are causally determined, or, at least, that their ultimate sources lie outside of the agent's control. But that is only half of the picture. It must also involve the belief that determinism makes one unfree, that freedom is incompatible with having the ultimate sources of one's actions outside of one's control. In that case, the

---

[2] David Owens and Aaron Ridley (2003) have argued against Leiter's interpretation of *BGE* 21 that its rejection of "unfree will" provides evidence that he leaves room for a kind of freedom that he thinks is possible for human beings. The problem is that instead of taking the denial of "unfree will" to be Humean, as I will do, they agree with Leiter's interpretation of it as a rejection of determinism. If, as they claim, in denying "unfree will," Nietzsche denies that the will is determined and his denial is designed to leave open a kind of freedom that human beings can have, that freedom must be of the incompatibilist libertarian variety. But, as I will argue, it is simply not plausible that Nietzsche is affirming freedom in a libertarian or incompatibilist sense. The only way to defend the Owens-Ridley claim that Nietzsche's denial of unfree will leaves open the possibility of a kind of freedom and responsibility that we do or can have is to insist that it is not a denial that the will is causally determined. This is what I will argue.

position Nietzsche asks his more enlightened readers to put out of their heads is the *conjunction* of (A) determinism and (B) incompatibilism. But what is Nietzsche rejecting in the conjunction of A and B? Obviously, there are three choices: he could be rejecting either A or B or both A and B. According to Leiter, he rejects (A) determinism, but not (B) incompatibilism. My view is the reverse, that Nietzsche rejects incompatibilism but not determinism. Unlike Leiter, however, I can accommodate the other side, if a successful argument that Nietzsche rejects determinism is forthcoming, by granting that he rejects both A and B. In contrast, Leiter interprets Nietzsche as rejecting determinism precisely because that is the only possibility, given that he wants to interpret Nietzsche as an incompatibilist. I will argue that interpreting *BGE* 21 as rejecting determinism doesn't make good sense of either (1) the importance Nietzsche gives to rejecting "unfree will" or (2) his argument for rejecting it.

As to (1), consider that the rejection of "unfree will" seems to be the more important part of the passage; for one thing, it takes up over half of it (we will consider the yet unquoted portion of it below). More importantly, Nietzsche associates the kind of "free will" he is combating with the "half-educated." He assumes that more "enlightened" readers will have already seen through its "boorish simplicity." It seems reasonable to assume that the more important point of the passage is not to argue against an idea that only the half-educated accept, but to help Nietzsche's more enlightened readers to overcome something that they still accept, namely, that rejecting "free will" in the metaphysical superlative sense requires one to accept that the will is unfree. It is difficult to understand why overcoming this latter point would be so important if it is simply a denial that the will is determined. Why is that important if it does not imply that humans are therefore free or responsible in some sense? But now suppose Nietzsche's point is the Humean one, that to rid oneself of a metaphysically loaded notion of "free will" is compatible with accepting oneself to be free, at least in the sense necessary for responsibility. Then we can see why Nietzsche's argument for rejecting "unfree will" would be the most important part of the passage. Leiter has responded to this point as it appeared in a previous version of this paper by asking "where in the passage does Nietzsche invite us to conclude that we can be free in a sense sufficient for responsibility?" I grant that Nietzsche does not make his suggestion to this effect explicit. But neither does he explicitly deny that the will is determined in the passage. Leiter and I are both *interpreting* Nietzsche's denial that the will is unfree—and have no choice but to do so—on the basis of what makes sense of the *logic* of *BGE* 21's argument. And, as we will see, there is much in the argument that concerns responsibility.

So let's consider Nietzsche's specific argument against "unfree will," which is that it involves "a misuse of cause and effect." He goes on to explain this "misuse" as follows: "One should not wrongly reify 'cause' and 'effect,' as the natural scientists do (and whoever, like them, now 'naturalizes' in his thinking), according to the prevailing mechanistic doltishness that has the cause press and push until it 'effects' something" (*BGE* 21). Although this is far from self-explanatory, it does make clear that we should take what Nietzsche means by the "wrongful reification" and "misuse" of cause and effect as something that it is plausible to think of as a case of "naturaliz[ing] in [one's] thinking." Accordingly, I suggest that "reifying" is a matter of taking a causal connection between two events (as opposed to a mere correlation or constant conjunction between similar types of events) to be some naturalistic property of, or perceptible fact regarding, the things involved in the events. Thus, in the example of reification Nietzsche provides, the causal connection between events is supposed to be established by a thing involved in the first event "press[ing] and push[ing] until it 'effects' something."

Why does Nietzsche reject this account of causation? The obvious answer is that he is following Hume, which is what I claimed in 1990 (Clark 1990: 216). According to Hume, when we take a relation between two events to be causal, we take there to be a necessary connection between them. But we never actually perceive such a connection. What we find in the world itself are only regular patterns of succession, constant conjunctions of similar events. We may, however, think that we find more than that, *the connecting fact*, as Simon Blackburn puts it, "a fact making it so that when the first happens, the second must happen" (Blackburn 1993: 97–8). It seems plausible that this "connecting fact" is precisely what the "press-push" model of causation that Nietzsche rejects seeks to provide. According to Hume, thinking that one has found such a fact involves a projective error. We get our idea of necessary connection not from the perception of a pressing or pushing or any other fact "out there" in the world, but from something "in here," an impression in one's own mind, its determination, once it has been repeatedly exposed to the conjunction of two types of events, to infer or expect an event of one type from the appearance or memory of an event of the other type. As Don Garrett (2005) writes: "This impression [of the mind's own determination] is often then projectively mislocated in or between the cause and effect themselves, in much the same way that non-spatial tastes, smells and sounds are erroneously located in bodies with which they are associated." I propose that this is the kind of error Nietzsche calls "wrongly reify[ing] 'cause' and 'effect.'" If this is correct, Nietzsche's objection is not to making causal claims or to taking such claims to be true, but only to interpreting causal claims in a way that involves "wrongful reification" or projective mislocation.

In his statement of opposition to such reification, Nietzsche claims that "one should help oneself to 'cause' and 'effect' only as pure concepts, that is to say as conventional fictions for the purpose of designation and mutual understanding—*not* of explanation. In the 'in-itself,' there is nothing of 'causal connections,' of 'necessity,' of psychological non-freedom" (*BGE* 21). Once again, the point is hardly self-explanatory. Leiter takes it to be an expression of Nietzsche's "neo-Kantian skepticism about causation," an indication that Nietzsche is still "in the grip of the neo-Kantian view (acquired from his reading of Friedrich Lange) that 'cause and effect' are merely features of the phenomenal world, not of 'things in themselves'" (Leiter 2007: 6–7). This is what allows him to interpret Nietzsche's rejection of "unfree will" as a denial that the will is causally determined and as based *"entirely* on his neo-Kantianism skepticism" as to whether anything at all is causally determined (2007: 6). And because he believes that Nietzsche rightly came to reject this skepticism soon after he wrote *BGE* (in fact, the very next year, as I claimed in 1990), it also leaves him free to proclaim that we may disregard the whole second half of the passage if we are trying to understand Nietzsche's mature view (2007: 7), a part of the passage that strongly supports compatibilism, as I shall argue.

Leiter's key assumption here is that "in itself" is simply an abbreviated way of referring to the Kantian "thing in itself"—which is precisely what I assumed in 1990. But I now think I was wrong to do so.[3] In a nearby passage, *BGE* 16, Nietzsche has just claimed that the whole idea of the "thing in itself" is a contradiction in terms. He is therefore committed to denying that there is *anything at all* in the "in itself," if that is equivalent to the "thing in itself." It is therefore unclear how Nietzsche's alleged neo-Kantian position could possibly provide grounds for skepticism about causality in particular. Leiter agrees, calling Nietzsche's argument against causality here a "bad argument," which he fortunately soon got over. But to reject causality on the grounds that it does not exist in the thing in itself, when one has just denied that there is a thing in itself, would be such a bad argument that it is surely not one we should attribute to Nietzsche (or any other philosopher) without looking for an alternative.

Further and more importantly, it is difficult to see how the neo-Kantian interpretation can account for the argument Nietzsche makes against "unfree will," which is that it "amounts to an abuse of cause and effect" because it "wrongly reifies cause and effect." There are two problems here. First, assume with Leiter that Nietzsche's objection is to the belief that cause and effect belong to the thing in itself (perhaps are things in themselves). How does this belief "reify" cause and effect, making them more thing-like than they would be if they belonged only to the phenomenal realm? But even if Leiter can answer this,[4] there is a more difficult problem: how exactly does taking the will to be

---

[3] Clark and Dudrick (2004) gives reason to reject this claim.

[4] Leiter answers (in an unpublished response to an earlier version of this paper): "Clark claims puzzlement about how this constitutes reification, but it seems to me clear: we reify some entity when we give it an objective existence and standing independent of us that it does not really have, and surely thinking causality a feature of the noumenal world is, from a NeoKantian point of view, an outrageous reification!" But if we accept this response, it merely brings up another problem for Leiter's account, which is that it seems implausible that Nietzsche thinks "natural scientists" and "whoever, like them, now 'naturalizes' in his thinking" take causality to be a feature of the noumenal world, the existence of which they presumably deny. Further, Nietzsche makes explicit what he objects to in these naturalists, namely, "the prevailing mechanical doltishness which makes the cause press and push until it 'effects' something" [*bis sie "wirkt"*] (*BGE* 21). This certainly makes it sound as if they take causality to be a purely empirical matter that has nothing to do with the noumenal world.

unfree (equivalent to "determined" on Leiter's reading) involve a *particular* abuse of cause and effect? Nietzsche's argument that "unfree will" involves an abuse of cause and effect implies that there are legitimate or non-abusive uses of these concepts, ones that don't "reify" them (and we will soon see stronger evidence from the passage that this is the case). Therefore, the claim of *BGE* 21 is not that all belief in causal connection involves an "abuse" and "reification" of cause and effect, but only that the belief in "unfree will" does so. Nietzsche expresses and/or supports his opposition to such reification when he claims that "one should help oneself to 'cause' and 'effect' only as pure concepts, that is to say as conventional fictions for the purpose of designation and mutual understanding—*not* of explanation. In the 'in-itself,' there is nothing of 'causal connections,' of 'necessity,' of psychological unfreedom" (*BGE* 21). So I do not see that Leiter has a plausible explanation of Nietzsche's argument against unfree will. He takes it to be a mere application of Nietzsche's general point that there is no causal determinism (because the causes we pick out are not things in themselves). But not only is Nietzsche denying the very conceivability of a thing in itself, he is also clearly saying that there is a *particular* abuse involved in taking the will to be unfree (or in doing so because it does not have freedom in the libertarian sense) that is not involved in every claim that something is causally determined.

Therefore, because, as we've seen, we can give a plausible interpretation of Nietzsche's point about reification in Humean terms, we should consider whether the same terms might provide an account of the apparently neo-Kantian aspect of the passage. It seems that they do. Consider what Nietzsche might mean by the "in itself" if it is not the "thing in itself." A reasonable alternative is that he means the natural or empirical world, the world as it appears from the viewpoint of the natural sciences, which is simply the "thing in itself" in the empirical sense. Even Kant occasionally uses the phrase in this sense (CPR A45/B63). Whereas Nietzsche would contrast the thing in itself in Kant's more usual (transcendental) sense with the empirical world, in the empirical sense, he contrasts the thing in itself with the world as it appears from the viewpoint of our passions, emotions, and values. The latter world is what he calls "the eternally growing world of valuations, colors, accents, perspectives, scales, affirmations, negations" and "the world that concerns human beings" (*GS* 301; cf. *BGE* 226). If this is the world with which Nietzsche contrasts the "in itself," then he is using that term in the empirical sense and his claim about the "in itself" simply gives alternative expression to his claim that one "wrongly reif[ies] cause and effect" if one claims to find the necessary connection between them in some naturalistic fact or property "out there." This is once again the Humean point that the empirical world—the "in itself"—contains no such connecting facts, but only regular patterns of events.

Other aspects of the passage may seem less amenable to a Humean interpretation, for instance, the claim that "one should help oneself to 'cause' and 'effect' only as pure concepts," which suggests that Nietzsche agrees with Kant that "cause" is an a priori concept, rejecting the Humean view that it is derived from experience. In fact, various sections of *BGE*—including *BGE* 20, which ends by referring to Locke's "superficiality with regard to the origin of ideas"— suggest that Nietzsche rejects Hume's claim that all ideas or concepts are derived from experience. But this is not really a problem for the interpretation I am defending here; it simply allows me to say that Nietzsche actually rejects the least plausible element of Hume's account, the assumption that some internal impression must be the source of our idea of causation, given the absence of an external impression. My Humean interpretation of what Nietzsche means by "wrongly reify[ing] 'cause' and 'effect'" does not require him to accept that assumption, but only the more general point that *such reification involves making a projective error*, locating in the natural world (as a property of things in it) something that belongs to the subject. I will return to what that "something" is.

Consider now Nietzsche's gloss on his claim that we should understand cause and effect as "pure concepts": "that is to say, as conventional fictions for the purpose of designation, of mutual understanding—*not* of explanation." This sentence was my main basis in 1990 for taking *BGE* to claim that the use of causal notions involves falsification. But does that sentence support my 1990 claim? And does it therefore support Leiter's claim that the *BGE* 21 expresses a neo-Kantian skepticism about causation? I offer negative answers to both questions. First, recall that Leiter takes Nietzsche's alleged skepticism about causation to be based on the claim that it belongs only to the phenomenal world and not to the thing in itself. Yet, Nietzsche gives "cause" and "effect" the status of "fictions" not because they belong only to the phenomenal world, but because they are not derived from our experience of anything that is actually in that world—that is why he calls these concepts "pure." Second, calling them "fictions" can plausibly be interpreted as expressing skepticism not about causation, but only about a certain understanding of causation. The point is not that we are saying something false when we claim that the impact of one billiard ball caused another to move. The falsification occurs only when we hold a mistaken view as to the function of such causal claims, when we take it to be explanation rather than "mutual understanding."

In defense of this second point, it seems plausible to interpret Nietzsche as claiming that we are led to "wrongly *reify* 'cause' and 'effect'" precisely insofar as we take the function of causal talk to be explanation. But surely causality has something to do with explanation! Nietzsche can agree. But he can say, following Hume, that what does the explaining is the subsumption of the event in question under a general pattern or regularity, not the necessary connection between cause and effect. The function of talking about such necessary connections, he can add, as I suggest he does with his reference to "mutual understanding," is to be able to express and come to an understanding concerning something about *us*, about each other. Now what could this be? I do not think the neo-Kantian interpretation that I once defended has a plausible account to give at this point. My Humean interpretation is in better shape, although the position I am attributing to Nietzsche is actually more Kantian than I have so far suggested. This position is that the function of talking in causal terms is "mutual understanding" in the sense of expressing or making known to others our commitments, in particular, the inferences and counterfactuals we are committed to drawing and accepting. Nietzsche's denial that casual connections *explain* is thus perfectly compatible with saying that to indicate that there is a causal connection between two events (that they are not *merely* constantly conjoined) is to express one's commitment to accepting *that there is an explanation of the second event* (namely, that it is an instance of general pattern that supports counterfactuals). If I deny a causal connection between two events, even if I grant that the relation between the two events is an instance of some general pattern, I indicate that I am not committed to taking the general pattern to explain anything, i.e., to support the relevant counterfactual. If the sounding of the bell at noon is always followed by the rushing of people out of the factory, and yet, I deny that the former causes the latter, I indicate that I do not accept the following counterfactual: if the bell had not sounded, the people would not have poured out of the factory. If I say there is a causal connection, I express my commitment to that counterfactual.[5]

I take Nietzsche to be claiming that when we speak of "cause" and "effect," we are "objectifying" such commitments. That is, we express these commitments by talking about things "out there" in the world. In characterizing these things (or events) as "conventional fictions," Nietzsche need not deny the existence of causality (contrary to my 1990 account, and to Leiter's interpretation). The point is that our convention for expressing the commitments that constitute belief in causality is to talk about causes and their effects. Talking about these things "out there" is just a convenient way of talking about something that is not out there in the world. In this sense they are "conventional fictions." But this is not a problem (i.e., does not commit us to making false claims) as long as we do not begin to believe that we have experienced or located the "connecting fact"—the pressing or pushing that "effects" something, in Nietzsche's example—in some event or fact out there in the world. If we do begin to believe this, as the passage goes on to suggest, we are then likely to confuse causality with constraint, leading us to affirm "unfree will." All of this accords well both with Nietzsche's argument in *BGE* 21 and with the Humean

---

[5] This account owes a great deal to Simon Blackburn's account of causality in Blackburn 2003: 52–74 and 94–110. I could not have seen it in *BGE* 21 without the help of Blackburn's essays. It may seem implausible that Nietzsche could have come up with this account on his own (for I have found nothing like it in his sources) and so long ago. I can only say that it makes better sense of the details of the passage than any other account I can think of, and that it coheres very nicely with the other material in the first part of *BGE* (see Clark and Dudrick 2012).

account of causation.[6] Nietzsche does not make any of this *explicit* in *BGE* 21, but my interpretation of his remarks makes good sense of what he does say, much of which Leiter ignores—and does so without committing him to the implausibly "bad argument" that Leiter finds in the passage.

The Humean reading of *BGE* 21 also makes good sense of a striking feature of the passage that Leiter urges us to dismiss as just another reflection of Nietzsche's neo-Kantian skepticism about causation, his claim that the "'unfree will' is mythology; in real life it is only a matter of *strong* and *weak* wills." Leiter writes as if Nietzsche is using "mythology" loosely here, as synonymous with "false." But that seems unlikely. Nietzsche chooses his words very carefully throughout the first part of *BGE* and reflection on why he uses the word that he does usually pays off in a deeper reading of a passage. In the case of "mythology," Nietzsche has already indicated that when we accept the "press-push" view of causality, "we behave once more as we have always behaved, namely *mythologically*." This is easily explicable in terms of the Humean interpretation. Just as mythology is a kind of objectification of human powers and commitments, a projection of them onto non-human beings, so too is the press-push view of causality, according to the Humean account. It projects our expectations and commitments onto the world itself, with the result that we seem to perceive constraining facts "out there." That "unfree will" is mythology should be interpreted in the same way. In this, again, Nietzsche follows Hume, who was at pains to show that the notion that "the causing" is "in the world" contributes to the sense that *if* our actions are caused, *then* we are not free (Hume [1740] 1975a: Book II, Part III, sections 1–2). Consider Hume's first point concerning why people embrace "a fantastical system of liberty" (i.e., libertarianism) despite its "absurdity" or "unintelligibility." Note first that Nietzsche's analysis of libertarianism as implying that we are *causa sui* fits well with Hume's claim as to its "absurdity." Second, Hume's explanation as to why we are tempted to embrace it despite its absurdity is that we find it difficult to believe that our actions are "governed by necessity," and that therefore we could not have "acted otherwise," because necessity seems "to imply something of force, and violence, and constraint, of which we are not sensible" in regard to our own actions (ibid., section 2). Hume takes his account of causality to show that precisely such "force, violence, and constraint" is *not* involved in the idea of causation. He thinks it should therefore help us to recognize that the fact that our actions are caused does not mean that they are forced, nor therefore that they render us unfree in a sense that absolves us from responsibility. All there is to the causal relation is constant conjunction and the mind's tendency to infer one event from the other, both of which we (largely) agree are found in the case of human behavior. When we insist that the causal determinism

---

[6] In retaining a role for commitments, rather than simply expectations, my Humean interpretation is also Kantian. This aspect, however, in no way supports the naturalized neo-Kantian reading of the passage that is found in Clark (1990).

of behavior rules out responsibility, Hume takes it that we are in the grip of the wrong picture of causality. For Hume, then, libertarianism and what Nietzsche calls "unfree will" (incompatibilism plus determinism, as I have argued) are two sides of the same coin, that is, the two options for those trapped by such a picture of causal determinism as involving force or constraint.

Evidence that Nietzsche holds exactly this Humean view can be found in the following portion of *BGE* 21:

> It is almost always a symptom of what is lacking in himself when a thinker senses in every 'causal connection' and 'psychological necessity' something of compulsion, exigency, constraint, pressure, unfreedom: such feelings are traitors, the person who feels them gives himself away. And, if I have observed correctly, "unfreedom of the will" is in general conceived as a problem from two completely antithetical standpoints but always in a profoundly *personal* manner: one will at no price give up his 'responsibility,' his belief in *himself*, the personal right to *his* deserts (the vain races belong here—), the other, on the contrary, will not be responsible for anything, to blame for anything, and out of an inner self-contempt wants to be able to *shift off* his responsibility for himself somewhere else. (*BGE* 21)

This supports the Humean interpretation of the passage against Leiter's interpretation of it in several ways. First, it provides evidence that Nietzsche is not skeptical of causality itself, indeed that he takes for granted the existence of what we call "causal connection" and "psychological necessity," and therefore assumes that at least *some* human actions are causally determined. That he uses quote marks around the key terms here does not affect my point. Presumably the reason for doing so is to indicate that whatever it is that we call "causal connection" and "psychological necessity" are taken by some to involve force or compulsion, when in fact they do not. Second, and most clearly, it shows that Nietzsche's point in denying "unfree will" is the same as Hume's, namely, to call into question the association of causal determination with "compulsion" and "constraint," for the purpose of showing that causal determinism does not make us "unfree" in the sense of absolving us from responsibility. Third, it shows that Nietzsche recognizes "two completely antithetical standpoints" that are concerned with the "unfreedom of the will," one denying it, the other affirming it, and claims that both of these standpoints mistakenly take causal connection and psychological necessity to absolve agents of responsibility. These standpoints correspond to the varieties of incompatibilism: the one who refuses to give up "his belief in *himself*" is the libertarian. He conceives "unfreedom of the will" as a "problem" out of vanity, not wanting to give up any of the credit for his merits. Although Nietzsche clearly rejects this vain person's view, he shows perhaps even less sympathy with the other version of incompatibilism, for the one who "will not be responsible for anything, to blame for anything," who wants to "*shift off* his responsibility for himself somewhere else." This is clearly supposed to be the non-libertarian incompatibilist. When one takes together all of the striking connections between *BGE* 21 and the Humean position on causality and freedom, it seems clear that Nietzsche is *not* in sympathy with those who deny that we are ever justified in holding human beings responsible for their behavior.

To summarize this part of the paper, I have argued that it is not because Nietzsche denies determinism on implausible neo-Kantian grounds that he rejects "unfree will" in *BGE* 21. In fact it is not because he denies determinism at all in this passage. Like Hume, he denies what is sometimes and probably confusingly called "hard determinism," which is the conjunction of determinism and incompatibilism. And he does so, like Hume, because he denies that the truth of determinism would entail that human behavior is constrained or forced.

Nietzsche's *On the Genealogy of Morality*

I turn now to Nietzsche's discussion of responsibility in *On the Genealogy of Morality*, for two reasons. First, *GM* may seem to undermine my interpretation because it seems designed to undermine the concept of guilt. How can one be morally responsible without liability to guilt? Second, contemporary incompatibilists will find the Humean position I have attributed to Nietzsche weak. Their basic objection would be that if determinism is true, no one could ever have done otherwise than they did. Why, then, does it matter concerning whether one is morally responsible that determinism does not make one's behavior forced or "constrained," as Hume and Nietzsche argue, when it does make it the case that one could not have done otherwise?

This is where Peter Strawson's work comes in, because he recognized long ago (1962) that there is an answer to this question if we move from a theoretical viewpoint on responsibility to a practical one. That is, we can answer the objection of incompatibilists if we recognize claims as to a person's moral responsibility not as judgments made from a theoretical point of view—as, for instance, claims about causal responsibility would be—but as expressions of a practical attitude. The attitude in question is a demand for a certain kind of treatment from others, which is backed by the reactive attitudes, and in particular, by resentment. Holding people responsible is a matter of holding them to the basic demand and holding the expression of reactive attitudes towards them justified should they fail to satisfy that demand. There are complicated matters here, as Gary Watson (2004) in particular has shown, but the basic response to the incompatibilist's question is that if we understand claims of responsibility in Strawsonian terms, we can explain why force and constraint absolve one of responsibility—because they excuse violations of, or exempt one from, the "basic demand" for reasonable regard—in a way that determinism does not. I am going to use my last few pages here to suggest that Nietzsche's account of the origins of responsibility in *GM* fits nicely into a Strawsonian framework, that it gives an account of the origins of both the compatibilist notion of responsibility that Strawson is analyzing and of our incompatibilist intuitions. The latter are not "natural," contrary to what Galen Strawson claims, but are the result of a complicated cultural development at which I will barely be able to gesture here.

I rely for my account of moral responsibility on incompatibilist Derk Pereboom, who characterizes the sense of "moral responsibility" at issue in the traditional philosophical debate about free will and determinism as follows: for an agent to be morally responsible for an action is for the action to belong to her in such a way that she would deserve blame if she knew that it was morally wrong and credit (and perhaps praise) if she understood that it was morally exemplary. He calls the kind of desert at issue here "basic" in the sense "that the agent, to be morally responsible, would deserve blame or credit just because she performed the action (given that she understands its moral status) and not by virtue of any consequentialist considerations" (2007: 86). In what follows, I am going to ignore the positive or credit/praise side of this notion of responsibility and consider only the negative or blame side of it.

So what does Nietzsche say in *GM* that is relevant to the negative side of moral responsibility in Pereboom's sense? In raising the question as to how the consciousness of guilt came into the world, Nietzsche chastises previous genealogists of morality for failing to recognize "that punishment as *retribution* developed completely apart from any presupposition concerning freedom or unfreedom of the will," indeed, "to such a degree," he says, "that in fact a high degree of humanization is always necessary before the animal 'man' can begin to make those much more primitive distinctions 'intentional,' 'negligent,' 'accidental,' 'accountable,' and their opposites, and to take them into account when measuring out punishment" (*GM* II:4). The main alternative to a retributive theory of punishment being a consequentialist theory, we can take Nietzsche to be claiming that the idea that offenders deserve punishment for what they did, simply because the action was wrong or forbidden and not for any consequentialist reason, developed "quite apart from any presupposition concerning freedom or unfreedom of the will." And that presupposition, it becomes clear as Nietzsche continues, concerns whether the agent could have done otherwise:

> The thought, now so cheap and apparently so natural, so unavoidable, a thought that has even had to serve as an explanation of how the feeling of justice came into being at all on earth—"the criminal has earned his punishment [i.e., deserves it] because he could have acted otherwise"—is in fact a very late and sophisticated form of human judging and inferring;

whoever shifts it to the beginnings lays a hand on the psychology of older humanity in a particularly crude manner. (*GM* II:4)

So although it now seems "natural" and "unavoidable" that an offender *deserves* punishment only if he could have acted otherwise, Nietzsche claims, this was not always the case and is actually a quite late development. I take Nietzsche to be assuming here that one could not have done otherwise if one's behavior was causally determined. His claim, then, is that it is only very late—and certainly well after human beings began taking into account the distinctions between "intentional," "negligent," "accidental," "accountable," and their opposites—that the idea of deserving punishment became bound up with freedom of the will in the incompatibilist sense (the one he links to the desire to be *causa sui* in *BGE* 21). But this suggests that there was an idea of responsibility—and one that fits Pereboom's analysis—that developed without the presupposition of an incompatibilist free will. It is true that Pereboom talks of deserving blame whereas Nietzsche is concerned with deserving punishment, but it seems that the latter notion already involves the former. If you are thought to deserve punishment in the retributive sense for your action, it seems at the very least that you are being blamed for it and thought to deserve blame. Another apparent difference is that Pereboom makes understanding the moral status of the action a necessary condition of deserving blame in the "basic sense," whereas Nietzsche implies that there was originally no such condition for deserving punishment. But understanding the status of the action becomes a condition for deserving punishment once the set of distinctions between "intentional," "accidental," "negligent," "accountable," and their opposites, is brought into play, and Nietzsche claims this is well before there was any presupposition of free will. Therefore, Nietzsche can be seen as attempting to specify the origins of a compatibilist notion of responsibility in this passage.

His next sentence may seem problematic for this suggestion, however. Here is the sentence:

> Throughout the greatest part of human history punishment was definitely not imposed because one held the evil-doer responsible for his deed, that is, not under the presupposition that only the guilty one should be punished:—rather, as parents even today punish their children, from anger over an injury suffered, which is vented on the agent of the injury—anger held within bounds, however, and modified through the idea that every injury has its equivalent in something and can really be paid off, even if only through the pain of the culprit. (*GM* II:4)

Because Nietzsche explicitly denies that evil-doers were punished because one held them responsible for their deed, his point might seem to be that they were not held responsible in any sense until such time as human beings finally arrived at the idea that they could have acted otherwise. The truth in this suggestion is that Nietzsche does think that there is an incompatibilist idea of responsibility and guilt (liability to blame) that human beings did not arrive at until they came to believe that we have free will in the incompatibilist sense. These are the ideas of responsibility and guilt that Nietzsche denies were attached to the original retributive practice of punishing in the passage I have been quoting, and they are also ideas he is out to undermine, along with the idea of morality to which they are tied. But in *GM* he is principally concerned to uncover the genealogy of these ideas, and he is claiming that we cannot get clear on what is involved in them except by seeing them as transformations of already existing practices and ideas.

So here is my thesis: for Nietzsche, our basic or core idea of responsibility is a compatibilist notion. Although it involves no presupposition that one could have done otherwise, this core notion has been transformed in the course of human history into an incompatibilist notion that does involve this presupposition. I do not take this to be an admission that our current idea of responsibility is an incompatibilist notion. Nietzsche is claiming that the transformation of responsibility into an incompatibilist notion was accomplished by means of religious ideas that are quite dispensable and no longer defensible. So he does not deny that incompatibilist intuitions are alive and well and influential among us; but he does reject Galen Strawson's view that compatibilism "entirely fails to satisfy our natural convictions about the nature of moral responsibility." The convictions in question are not "natural," on Nietzsche's view, but result from the influence of religious views that many of us no longer accept. If we could remove the influence of these views, we would not be left with no notion of moral responsibility, but with the core compatibilist notion. Nietzsche is not claiming that this is an easy thing to do, or that we can get rid of incompatibilist intuitions simply by abandoning religious beliefs (*GM* II:21–2), but this does not affect my claim that if we could get rid of the influence of these beliefs, we would still have a core compatibilist idea of responsibility and one that corresponds fairly well to Pereboom's analysis.[7] And I think that many of us are operating with something like that core idea minus the incompatibilist overlay that we have rejected.

It is this core notion of responsibility that I think we can understand in terms of Peter Strawson's expressivist framework. As evidence, consider a few of the details of Nietzsche's account of the origins of punishment as retribution. His claim is that the foundation of this practice is the debtor/creditor relationship. The community is thought to stand "to its members in that

---

[7] So the position I am attributing to Nietzsche might sound like the revisionist position Manuel Vargas (2007) has recently defended: our notion of responsibility is incompatibilist, but we should revise it so that it is. However, I think Nietzsche's position does differ from that because he is claiming that if we could get rid of our incompatibilist intuitions, we would still be left with a notion of, and set of distinctions concerning, responsibility that are compatibilist.

important basic relationship, that of the creditor to its debtor." The idea is that the members are taken to have "pledged and obligated themselves to the community" in exchange for the advantages and protections that the community provides. So what happens if the pledge is broken?

> The community, the deceived creditor, will exact payment as best it can, one can count on that. Here it is least of all a matter of the direct injury inflicted by the injuring party; quite apart from that, the criminal is a "breaker," one who breaks his contract and word *with the whole*, in relation to all the goods and conveniences of communal life in which he has until this point had a share. The criminal is a debtor who not only fails to pay back the advantages and advances rendered him, but also even lays a hand on his creditor; he therefore not only forfeits all of these goods and advantages from now on, as is fair,—he is also now reminded *how much there is to these goods*. The anger of the injured creditor, of the community, gives him back again to the wild and outlawed condition from which he was previously protected: it expels him from itself,—and now every kind of hostility may vent itself upon him. At this level of civilization "punishment" is simply the copy, the *mimus* of normal behavior towards the hated, disarmed, defeated enemy, who has forfeited not only every right and protection, but also every mercy. (*GM* II:9)

Now I admit that this doesn't sound very much like Strawson, who defends the expression of the reactive attitudes in blaming and related matters as, in Watson's terms, forms of "moral address." But my claim is not that the passage just quoted describes a case of moral address, but that it sketches the origins of what becomes a primitive form of moral address at the next stage, which is the stage at which we find punishment as retribution. When punishment is exile, we don't yet have the idea that Nietzsche associates with retribution: "that every injury has its equivalent in something and can really be paid off, even if only through the pain of the culprit." Punishment is merely the withdrawal of community protection for one who has broken his agreement to abide by the rules necessary for the community's existence. The withdrawal of protection is considered fair, and I suppose it expresses and perhaps delivers a message, which is that the community is offended, if not outraged, by the lack of respect and appreciation the offender has shown for all that it has given him. But this doesn't seem quite enough for even the beginnings of moral address because it leaves no room for a response, no possibility of criminals repairing their relationship with the community. Any violence or further pain inflicted on the criminal is understood not as recompense or payment for the wrong that has been committed, but merely as what members of the community get to do to those who are not under community protection.

Of course, the explicit mixture of violence and the desire to inflict pain also keeps this from sounding much like a "moral" practice (as opposed to a merely natural one). It is of interest in this regard that in his sympathetic account of Strawson's theory, Gary Watson ends by suggesting that "our ordinary practices are not as unproblematic as Strawson supposes" (2004: 253), precisely because of the tendency towards animosity or violence that seems intertwined with them. In view of this tendency and Strawson's defense of proneness to the reactive attitudes as necessary if one is to treat others as moral agents, as opposed to viewing them from a detached or theoretical perspective, Watson asks: "Must we chose between [the] isolation [of the detached perspective] and animosity?" He thinks that some of Strawson's remarks suggest that we must. For Strawson thinks that the reactive attitudes such as indignation, disapprobation, and resentment "tend to promote at least partial and temporary withdrawal of good will," which includes "preparedness to acquiesce in that infliction of suffering on the offender which is an essential part of punishment," and that this is "the consequence of *continuing* to view [the offender] as a member of the moral community: only as one who has offended against it demands" (Strawson 2003: 90; Watson 2004: 256–7). Watson considers this troubling because it implies that an important ideal of love that such people as Gandhi and King have tried to live up to is not compatible with holding others responsible or making moral demands, which does not seem correct. His solution is to suggest that we not confuse

> Strawson's claims about the interpenetration of responsibility and the retributive sentiments . . . with the expressive theory itself. As [the] lives [of Gandhi and King] suggest, the retributive sentiments can in principle be stripped away from holding responsible and the demands and appeals in which this consists. What is left are various forms of reaction and appeal to others as moral agents. The boundaries of moral responsibility are the boundaries of intelligible moral address. (Watson 2004: 258)

I agree with Watson's conclusion and think that Nietzsche agrees with it. But there is an interesting difference: Nietzsche apparently has a somewhat more positive attitude towards the "retributive sentiments" than does Watson because he does not see them as the source of violence or the withdrawal of good will, but as a way of restraining and modifying the reactive attitudes that are the sources of that violence and withdrawal.

Here is the relevant passage:

> As its power grows, a community no longer takes the transgressions of the individual so seriously because they can no longer count as dangerous and subversive for the continued existence of the whole to the same extent as formerly: the evildoer is no longer "made an outlaw" and cast out; the general anger is no longer allowed to vent itself in the same unbridled manner as formerly—rather from now on, the evildoer is defended against this anger, particularly that of the ones directly injured, and taken under

the protection of the whole. Compromise with the anger of the one immediately affected by the misdeed; a striving to localize the case and prevent a further or indeed general participation and unrest; attempts to find equivalents and to settle the entire affair . . . above all the increasingly more resolute will to understand every offense as in some sense capable of being paid off, hence, at least to a certain extent, to *isolate* the criminal and his deed from each other—these are the traits that are imprinted with increasing clarity onto the further developments of penal law. (*GM* II:10)

This is Nietzsche's account of the beginnings of punishment *as retribution* and therefore, according to my account, of holding responsible, of taking the offender to *deserve* punishment for what he has done. Previously the withdrawal of community protection was thought to be deserved or fair, but any pain or suffering inflicted was simply the expression of a natural and hostile attitude towards outsiders. Now the pain and suffering inflicted is a means for keeping offenders within the community by giving them a way to "pay" for their offense. This can, but need not be, a monetary payment because, Nietzsche claims, pain and suffering is conceived of as a substitute payment to the community for the original debt that the offender has reneged on. With the belief that the infliction of pain and suffering is justified, that the offender owes or deserves it, it seems that we have a primitive case of holding responsible or accountable and of blaming behavior, and one that involves no incompatibilist assumptions.

It seems that we also have here the beginnings of a kind of moral address. The community repudiates the deed, but not the person, to whom it offers a way of restoring his relationship with it. Retributive ideas originally work to isolate the criminal from his deed, so only the deed must be repudiated. This is in line with Strawson's claim that the retributive sentiments are a consequence of continuing to take the person to be a member of the moral community. But Nietzsche also supports Watson's claim that our ordinary practices are not as unproblematic as Strawson suggests, because Nietzsche does not take the reactive attitudes themselves to be so unproblematic. In themselves, he thinks, the reactive attitudes reflect only the perspective of the aggrieved or injured one, "allowing only it to count," as he says specifically of revenge (*GM* II:11). He sees the retributive idea of pay-back or equivalence—an "eye for an eye"—as an attempt to rein in the excesses of the reactive attitudes, to impose an objective measure on them. For their strength does not reflect an objective assessment of the wrong committed, but a sense of the victim's own powerlessness.[8]

As the individual or community grow in power and self-confidence, Nietzsche thinks they become "more humane."

---

[8] Compare *GM* I:10: "For the *ressentiment* of the noble human being, when it appears in him, runs its course and does not poison—on the other hand it does not appear at all in countless cases where it is unavoidable in all the weak and powerless."

It would not be impossible to imagine a consciousness of power in society such that society might allow itself the noblest luxury there is for it—to leave the one who injures it go unpunished. "What concern are my parasites to me," it might then say. "Let them live and prosper; I am strong enough for that." ... The justice that begins with "everything can be paid off, everything must be paid off" ends by looking the other way and letting the one unable to pay go free; it ends like every good thing on earth, by cancelling itself (*sich selbst aufhebend*). (*GM* II:10)

Nietzsche's ideal of nobility thus involves the overcoming of retributive ideas by overcoming the reactive attitudes that make them necessary. But the idea is to "let the one unable to pay go free," which he proceeds to identify with mercy, not to overcome the whole idea of "payment." No society or individual could exist without making demands on others and having some idea of recompense, of what is required, in addition to repudiation of the offense, to restore relations with the community and individuals. That is what I take it would be left of holding responsible and blaming in a Nietzschean world and it would involve no incompatibilist assumptions. Of course, we don't live in a Nietzschean world, in part because incompatibilist assumptions have reversed the direction that retributive ideas began, that of separating the person from his crime, thereby appearing to justify directing reactive attitudes towards the person in a way that has no natural limit. But how Nietzsche thinks this happened with the help of religious ideas is another story, which will have to wait for another day.[9]

---

[9] Many thanks to Brian Leiter and Lanier Anderson for their presented comments on the version of this paper that was given as the first Bernd Magnus lecture at the University of California, Riverside. I received many helpful comments from the audience and am particularly grateful for those of Bernd Magnus, and for the written comments of John Perry and the late Paul Hoffman.

{ 5 }

Nietzsche and Moral Objectivity
The Development of Nietzsche's Metaethics
(co-authored with David Dudrick)

This essay begins from the uncontroversial assumption that Nietzsche holds certain ethical or moral values and expresses them in his work. Its question is whether his philosophy allows him to claim objectivity for these values. Many have thought that his metaethical position prohibits him from doing so, that it entails, in Brian Leiter's words, a denial that "there is any objective vindication for his [or any other] evaluative position." As Leiter notes, this is "the most familiar reading *outside* the secondary literature on Nietzsche," shared by such thinkers as Max Weber and Alasdair MacIntyre (Leiter 2002: 146). We will reconstruct the development of Nietzsche's metaethical position in order to show that this widely shared view is mistaken. The upshot is that Nietzsche does and can consistently claim that his evaluative position is objective and that this is a central component of his understanding of himself as a philosopher. We agree with Leiter that the secondary literature has not provided an adequate defense of this interpretation of Nietzsche. But since Leiter himself has made the most recent and compelling case against the position we want to argue for here, we will take him as our main interlocutor in this essay and organize it as an argument against his interpretation.

The essay has five sections. It begins from Leiter's interpretation. Leiter claims (*a*) that Nietzsche's naturalism entails a rejection of realism about moral values and assumes (*b*) that such anti-realism entails or is equivalent to a denial of moral objectivity. Section 1 argues that Leiter is right about (*a*), at least in the middle-period work, *Human, All Too Human* (1878). In this work, Nietzsche's naturalism leads him to anti-realism with regard to moral properties, a denial that such properties have what we call *ontological objectivity*. In section 2, we argue that in the same work Nietzsche also denies that moral claims have *normative objectivity*, that they deserve acceptance by others. However, this does not confirm (*b*), for the denial does not follow directly from his anti-realism, but from the "error theory" of moral discourse at work in *HA*. As it is at work in *HA*, this theory implies not just that moral claims refer to a realm that is cognitively superfluous, but that all evaluations are "partial" and so "unjust." Section 3 then argues that by the time he wrote the first edition of *The Gay Science* (1882), Nietzsche had overcome the error theory of *HA* by abandoning the cognitivism presupposed by it. Section 4 adds that *GS*'s non-cognitivism is a more complicated position than the one attributed to Nietzsche in section 3. This section offers an interpretation of Nietzsche's claim that values are created, and argues that he actually understands *value* claims (attributions of normative properties) as claims about *reasons*. To show that value claims are objective, therefore, Nietzsche needs to show not that there are ontologically objective facts that correspond to value claims, but that claims about what one has reason to do can be objective. In section 5, we argue that in *On the Genealogy of Morality* (1887) Nietzsche offers a conception of objectivity according to which such claims can be objective, and that Nietzsche's new conception of objectivity is connected to a new understanding of the nature of philosophy, and therefore of his own task.

1. Nietzsche's Value Anti-Realism

Leiter takes Nietzsche to object to a version of morality he labels "MPS" ("morality in the pejorative sense") on the grounds that MPS "is not conducive to the flourishing of human excellence" (Leiter 2002: 136). The question that motivates Leiter's discussion of Nietzsche's value anti-realism is what Nietzsche does or should say about the *value* of this flourishing: why it is more important than the values defended by MPS. Leiter explains that this question is a "metaethical" one concerning the metaphysical or epistemological status of the values Nietzsche uses to undertake his revaluation of moral values: whether they are "veridical" or "justified" in "some sense" in which the moral values he finds wanting are not. What "animates" these questions, Leiter claims, is "a worry about Nietzsche's critical project that might be summed up simply as follows: in offering a revaluation of morality is Nietzsche doing anything more than giving his idiosyncratic opinion from his idiosyncratic evaluative perspective? Is there, in short, anything about Nietzsche's evaluation of morality that ought to command *our* attention and assent?" (Leiter 2002: 137).

This is a question concerning the normative status of Nietzsche's position: is his critique of morality *worthy* of our attention and assent? Leiter suggests that the answer one can legitimately give to this normative question is dependent on one's metaethical position, in particular, on whether one is a realist or an anti-realist about moral values.[1] More specifically, Leiter holds that if Nietzsche

---

[1] Although, as we have noted, Leiter claims that the question of objectivity concerns the metaphysical and epistemological status of Nietzsche's values, he does not introduce independent considerations concerning the epistemological status of these values, thereby writing as if the objectivity of these values follows directly from their metaphysical status, from their lack of what he calls "naturalistic objectivity" in the material quoted below.

were a realist about moral values, he could claim that his evaluative position deserves the attention and assent of others. Because he is an anti-realist, however, he must admit that he speaks merely from his own "idiosyncratic evaluative perspective."

To evaluate Leiter's contention, we need an account of what is it to be a realist about value. According to Leiter, it is to hold "that there are *objective* facts about value" (Leiter 2002: 137). The "intuitive idea" behind this idea of objectivity, Leiter tells us, "is simple enough": "facts are objective just in case their character and existence is *independent* of the states of mind of persons in some appropriate sense. *Epistemic* independence is most often what is at issue: a fact is objective if its character and existence does not depend on what people believe or would have reason to believe about it."

Leiter takes Nietzsche to be a realist about prudential value: the facts concerning what is good *for* an individual are objective; they do not depend on "what people believe or would have reason to believe about" them. However, he takes Nietzsche to be an anti-realist about moral or ethical values—we use "value anti-realism" to designate this position concerning moral value throughout the essay.

What Leiter here calls "*epistemic* independence" is perhaps better termed *ontological* independence. The independence in question is certainly independence *from* epistemic considerations ("what people believe or would have reason to believe"), but it is a fact's "character and existence" that possesses this independence. What makes a fact "objective" is that its ontological status does not depend on what anyone believes or has reason to believe about it. That the objectivity Leiter has in mind is of the ontological variety is confirmed by his discussion of what he takes to be "Nietzsche's central argument for anti-realism about value." This argument, he says, "is *explanatory*: moral facts don't figure in the 'best explanation' of experience, and so are not real constituents of the objective world. Moral values, in short, can be 'explained away.' Such a conclusion follows from Nietzsche's naturalism" (Leiter 2002: 148). Nietzsche's naturalism, according to Leiter, is of the methodological variety; it holds that philosophy should cohere with the results and follow the methods of the sciences. Leiter assumes above that following such methods will show that moral facts can be "explained away" (need not be referred to in explanations of experience, including moral experience). That moral facts therefore do not belong to "the real constituents of the objective world" (the world that exists independently of what we believe or have reason to believe about it) is precisely the value anti-realism Leiter attributes to Nietzsche. It is the reasoning that establishes it that he calls "Nietzsche's central argument for anti-realism about value."

Before considering Leiter's claim that Nietzsche's anti-realism implies a denial of moral objectivity, we need a better picture of this anti-realism. Although Leiter cites a few specific passages as evidence for attributing value anti-realism to Nietzsche, his main evidence is a general feature of Nietzsche's work, his explanation of value judgments in terms of naturalistic factors. How else, Leiter asks, can we explain Nietzsche's "relentless pursuit of the psycho-physiological roots of our value judgments" if it is not an attempt to show that so-called moral facts—the goodness or badness of acts and characteristics judged to be good and bad—can be "explained away" and are therefore not part of the objective world? This rhetorical question may not be convincing if we are thinking of Nietzsche's major works (e.g., *GM* and *Beyond Good and Evil* (henceforth *BGE*)). There is little reason to think that the account of the origin of moral value judgments—the genealogy of morality—in these works is designed to show that moral properties aren't part of the objective world. However, that may be because Nietzsche takes that point for granted after *HA*. In the remainder of this section, we will therefore explain how *HA* exhibits anti-realism about moral value.

HA is widely acknowledged as marking a turning point in Nietzsche's career, the point at which he turns his back on the metaphysical or quasi-metaphysical commitments of his early works and embraces science as that which provides access to the "disclosed" or "real nature of the world" (*HA* 10; *HA* 29).[2] Nietzsche explicitly acknowledges that this has consequences for philosophy, specifically that the "historical philosophy" he takes himself to be practicing in *HA* is "no longer to be separated from natural science" (*HA* 1). *HA* thus shows that Nietzsche embraces the doctrine Leiter terms "methodological naturalism," that philosophy should cohere with the results of and follow the methods of the sciences, and that he embraces it precisely because he takes science to be, in Leiter's words, our guide to the "real constituents of the objective world."

Nietzsche does not merely "embrace" this doctrine in *Human, All Too Human*, he argues for it. The book's main project is to undermine metaphysics, which Nietzsche takes to involve commitment to the existence of a second world, a metaphysical or "true" world, in comparison with which the empirical world disclosed by science counts as "mere appearance." These two worlds are distinguished in terms of the methods that give access to them. The empirical world is precisely the world to which the empirical methods of the sciences give access, whereas the metaphysical world is one that can be accessed only through non-empirical or a priori methods. Nietzsche argues that the postulation of this latter world is cognitively superfluous. Taking for granted the adequacy of empirical methods to explain what goes on in the nonhuman world (presumably, on the basis of the success of science), *HA* focuses its attack on the assumption that the postulation of a metaphysical world—Plato's Forms, Kant's thing-in-itself—is necessary to explain certain value-related aspects of the human world. Nietzsche employs two main strategies against this assumption.

---

[2] We take responsibility for all translations and list the various published translations we have consulted in the References.

In some cases he argues that the belief that has led thinkers to posit a non-empirical world is an error; the object of the belief does not exist. For instance, the beliefs in free will and in unchanging entities (which becomes the basis for belief in an immortal soul)—both of which he implausibly claims were originally shared with "everything organic"—are mistakes which arose "in the course of the overall evolution of organic being" because they contributed to our ancestors' survival and reproduction, and we therefore now inherit them as part of our cognitive equipment (*HA* 18). Nietzsche assumes that it is already clear to his readers that the objects of these beliefs do not exist, that the beliefs in these objects are contradicted by the "real nature of the world," the world as disclosed to us by modern science (*HA* 29; *HA* 10). His contribution is to remove any remaining tendency to think there must be some truth in them—for how else can one explain why they are so commonly believed?—by showing that we can fully understand how people have come to hold such beliefs without granting that they contain any truth.

HA is more centrally concerned with the justification for postulating a metaphysical world offered by the existence of things taken to be of the highest value in the human world. Nietzsche's strategy here gives the book its name: to show that these things are "human, all too human," mere sublimations and transformations of things of lower value. Once it is clear that we can explain disinterested contemplation, for instance, as a sublimation of lust and give comparable explanations for other things taken to be of higher value, we show that these things offer no basis for positing a metaphysical world because they can be adequately explained from a purely naturalistic viewpoint.

If these two lines of argument succeed, Nietzsche expects interest in metaphysical questions to die out (*HA* 10). There could be a metaphysical world, he admits. The possibility that truth is simply not accessible from the empirical perspective cannot be ruled out. "We behold all things through the human head and cannot cut this head off; while the question nevertheless remains what of the world would still be there if one had cut it off" (*HA* 9). But although the question about the "thing in itself" therefore remains, Nietzsche's suggestion is that no one would be driven by the thought of discovering its nature (i.e., driven to metaphysics) simply by the question of what things are like apart from our knowledge of them (what the world would be like if we could cut the human head off). That is a purely theoretical problem and is "not very well calculated to bother people overmuch; but all that has hitherto made metaphysical assumptions *valuable, terrible, delightful* to them, all that has begotten these assumptions, is passion, error, and self-deception."

Metaphysics is begotten by error, as we have seen, insofar as it seeks to explain the existence of things (1) that we only erroneously believe to exist, or (2) whose existence we erroneously believe cannot be explained by empirical methods. The role that passion and self-deception play in the acceptance of such errors is suggested by the following passage:

> It is probable the objects of the religious, moral and aesthetic sentiments belong only to the surface of things, while man likes to believe that here at least he is in touch with the world's heart; the reason he deludes himself is that these things produce in him such profound happiness and unhappiness, and thus he here exhibits the same pride as in the case of astrology. For astrology believes that the starry firmament revolves around the fate of man; the moral man, however, supposes that what he has essentially at heart must also constitute the essence and heart of things. (*HA* 4)

In other words, in religion, morality, and art, humans experience certain feelings, the objects of which are the objects of ordinary experience, which counts as the "surface of things" from the viewpoint of both science and metaphysics. But "metaphysical and artistic ages and human beings" (*HA* 3) delude themselves into believing that these feelings are directed towards objects that are closer to the "heart of things"—as when the object of awe or gratitude is taken to be God, or when moral feelings are taken to be bound up with the perception of Platonic forms. The point is that they do not want to think that these value-laden feelings are simply *their* feelings, their reactions to empirical objects. They want some kind of support or validation for these reactions, which they get by taking the feelings to put them in touch with a deeper level of reality, the "heart of things." And they do this by inventing a metaphysical world inaccessible to empirical investigation to house the purported objects of the feelings. This is why the metaphysical world has seemed so important: not for purely theoretical or cognitive reasons, but because it seemed to provide external support for moral, religious, and aesthetic feelings.

This passage suggests that *HA* is committed to value anti-realism, to a denial that moral properties belong to the objective world. It implies that the true objects of moral feelings and of the statements to which they give rise are the naturalistic properties of empirical objects, and not specifically moral properties, such as rightness or wrongness. Indeed, it is hard to see in *HA* the resources for recognizing such moral properties as constituents of the objective world. The general point, as we have already indicated, is that Nietzsche takes the "constituents of the objective world" to be only those objects and properties accessible through perception or the empirical methods of the sciences, and he certainly has no resources (unlike some twentieth-century naturalists)[3] for seeing how moral properties could be among those. *HA* takes the positing of

---

[3] See Miller (2004: 138–42) for an account of these options. Our suggestion is not that any of these would be congenial to Nietzsche, but only that he could have had little inkling of them, hence that we can rule them out as anything that would have kept his naturalism from leading him to anti-realism about moral values.

specifically moral or ethical properties to be cognitively superfluous; it thus endorses anti-realism about moral value.

Leiter is therefore correct to count Nietzsche as a value anti-realist, at least in *HA*. Anyone denying that later Nietzsche is a value anti-realist must assume the burden of showing that and why he changed his mind on this issue. In the next section, we turn to the question whether his anti-realism has any implications for the normative question of moral objectivity, i.e., any implications concerning whether his own values are deserving of acceptance by others.

2. The Cognitivism of *Human, All Too Human*

To answer our question concerning the relationship between anti-realism and moral objectivity, it seems important to consider Nietzsche's view of moral discourse. What does he think is going on when we say of particular actions, for instance, that they are right or wrong, and that particular persons are virtuous or vicious? Turning our attention from metaphysics to semantics seems necessary given that the issue of moral objectivity is a question of whether moral statements are objective and therefore worthy of our acceptance, a question it is difficult to answer without considering whether such statements make genuine claims attributing moral properties to things (actions and persons) or are instead to be understood simply as expressions of attitudes. We sympathize with Leiter's suggestion that we should not expect Nietzsche to offer us a semantics for moral discourse and that a number of different accounts seem compatible with Nietzsche's claims about morality. That said, there are reasons for interpreting *Human, All Too Human* as committed to an "error theory" of morality according to which moral discourse involves the making of genuine but false claims about moral properties.

As we have indicated, Nietzsche admits in *HA* that the empirical world *may* be only the appearance of the thing-in-itself (and therefore, in Schopenhauer's terms, "only representation"). He nevertheless counts it as the "real nature of the world" because it is the only world of any cognitive or theoretical interest once we recognize that any metaphysical world is cognitively superfluous (*HA* 10, 29; see Clark 1998: 47–9; 1990: ch. 4). There is a second world that plays a major role in *HA*, namely, the value-laden world of our practical concerns. But instead of taking this world to point us towards a higher or "true" world, as Plato did, Nietzsche dubs it "the world as representation (as error)" (*HA* 29). Now to say that the value-laden world is the "world . . . as error" is to take it to be the object of erroneous beliefs. The error involved seems to be the postulation of normative properties, and Nietzsche's story about this postulation presupposes that moral claims make genuine claims, attributing to things normative properties that do not actually exist.

Nietzsche's view, as we saw in section 1, is that humans respond to the world with feelings and concerns for which they want external support and this leads them to posit objects of these concerns that could in fact exist only in a nonempirical world. So we are, for instance, appalled by violence and concerned to banish it from the world, whereas we respond positively to acts of charity and are concerned to promote them. Wanting external support for these feelings and concerns, we attribute normative properties such as goodness and evil to the empirical actions we classify as charitable or violent, properties for which there is no room in an empirical world. This is no problem for those belonging to metaphysical ages. In fact, it is an advantage because it makes it possible to suggest that the objects in question have properties that include them in the "heart of things." Moral claims are validated, therefore, as expressing knowledge of a "higher" or "deeper" world than the ordinary empirical world. But in an age of methodological naturalism, it becomes a disadvantage that moral properties have no place in the empirical world. It suggests that the moral person is in touch not with a higher world, but with a lower one, a world of illusion, one that has been invented in order to make moral claims appear to be validated. *HA*'s view therefore seems to be that the real world, the world disclosed by science, does not contain value (normative properties), although the passions and errors of human beings make it appear to contain such properties. In doing so, they construct a second world alongside of the world revealed to us by science. This merely apparent value-laden world is the "world . . . as error."

So it is hardly surprising that Nietzsche ends Part I of *HA* (which contains all of the sections we have been considering) by asking whether "our philosophy [will] not thus become a tragedy?" The issue is whether "truth [does] not become inimical to life, to the better man," and "whether death would not be preferable" to being obliged to "consciously reside in untruth" (*HA* 34). Nietzsche's answer is that it is possible to love life in full view of the truth exposed by his philosophy if one can achieve a "much simpler and emotionally purer life [in which] the old motives of violent desire . . . would gradually grow weaker under the influence of purifying knowledge. In the end one would live among human beings and with oneself as in *nature*, without praising, blaming, contending, gazing contentedly, as though at a spectacle, upon many things for which one formerly felt only fear" (*HA* 34).[4]

Such an (admittedly rare) person is one "from whom the ordinary fetters of life have fallen to such an extent that he continues to live only to know better." He achieves what Nietzsche calls "practical world affirmation" in the face of his

---

[4] The passage continues: "One would be free of emphasis, and no longer prodded by the thought that one is only nature or more than nature. . . . A man from whom the ordinary fetters of life have fallen to such an extent that he continues to live only to know better must rather, without envy or vexation, be able to forego much, indeed almost everything upon which other men place value. He is happy to communicate his joy in his condition, and he *has*, perhaps, nothing else to communicate" (*HA* 34).

"logical world denial" (*HA* 29)—that is, he finds satisfaction and perhaps even joy in living even though he denies that anything is of value. The crucial point here is that what allows this person to avoid the need to "reside consciously in untruth" is his abstention from value claims. This conclusion of Part I of *HA* thus adds further support to our claim that Nietzsche is committed to something very much like Mackie's "error theory" of moral value and its presupposed cognitivist account of moral discourse. Nietzsche's position is that a commitment to truth requires one to abstain from moral claims, and this clearly presupposes that moral claims make genuine claims that are in fact false.

Leiter therefore appears to be correct in thinking that Nietzsche denies moral objectivity at the same time that he embraces anti-realism about moral properties. Since moral claims are all erroneous, how could anyone's be worthy of acceptance by others? In fact Nietzsche goes further. He denies that one's moral claims are worthy of acceptance by oneself. That is surely what he commits himself to when he portrays his "knower" and "better man" as living without making value judgments. But note that this doesn't follow directly from his anti-realism, his denial that moral properties belong to the objective world, but from the combination of such anti-realism with a cognitive account of moral discourse. Nietzsche might continue to hold to his anti-realism regarding moral properties and yet come to a quite different understanding concerning moral objectivity if he gave up his cognitivist assumptions concerning moral discourse. In section 3, we consider evidence that he did just that.

Before turning to this evidence, we need to add that there is another factor perhaps even more directly relevant to Nietzsche's view of moral objectivity in *HA*, namely, his claim that all evaluations are "unjust." Nietzsche stresses this point in the passages that immediately precede his presentation of the "better man" as one who abstains from evaluation. All belief in the value of life "rests on false thinking" and is therefore "unjust" (*HA* 32); all inclination and aversion at the root of value claims involve "unjust assessments" (*HA* 33). The basis for this claim appears to be that our judgments of value always focus on one aspect of things at the expense of other aspects which we forget or ignore; evaluation is based not on a pure knowing of the matter to be evaluated but on a very interested and thoroughly partisan view of it. Valuing is thus directed by the will, not the intellect; the "colored" world of our concerns is a projection not simply of our errors but also of our passions, where passions are understood as partial, as wearing "party colors," "taking sides," being "for and against" (*HA* 371). For Nietzsche, then, even if they did not refer to a cognitively superfluous world, value claims would still not be justified or worthy of acceptance by others, because they represent a partisan's view of things and are not objective. Leiter is right, therefore, about the Nietzsche of *HA*: he does regard moral discourse as a matter of giving one's "idiosyncratic opinion from [one's] idiosyncratic evaluative perspective," even though such discourse is presented so as to give the impression that it "ought to command *our* attention and assent."

3. The Non-cognitivism of *The Gay Science*

No one doubts that Nietzsche's later and greater works differ substantially from *HA*. In particular, no one would claim that Nietzsche continued to adhere to the ideal of the "knower" and "better man" that he presents in *HA* 34. Indeed, it is that ideal of knowing that he has Zarathustra mock as "immaculate perception" in *Thus Spoke Zarathustra* (*Z* II:15). Because that ideal was bound up with his denial that moral judgments are objective, the question is whether the change in his view has implications for Nietzsche's position on the possibility of normative objectivity for value claims.

We begin our attempt to answer this question with Clark's view that *The Gay Science* represents a major shift in Nietzsche's thinking about values. Clark characterizes the shift from *HA* to *GS* as follows:

> In *Human, All too Human*, Nietzsche divided Schopenhauer's "world as representation" into two parts, the disenchanted empirical world revealed by science and the enchanted or value-laden world of our practical concerns. He called the latter "world as representation (as error)." In *The Gay Science*, he still makes a distinction between the two worlds, but now he celebrates the second world as a human creation, rather than looking down on it as an error. (Clark 1998b: 68; paper 12 in this volume)

Why this should be so? What changes in Nietzsche's thinking allowed him to celebrate in *GS* the world that *HA* dubs "the world as representation (as error)"? The answer is evidently not that he came to accept value realism in *GS*; Nietzsche's commitment to value anti-realism in that work seems evident. In a passage Leiter cites as endorsing value anti-realism, for instance, Nietzsche writes: "Whatever has value in our world now does not have value in itself, according to its nature—nature is always value-less, but it has been given value at some time, as a present—and it is *we* who gave and bestowed it. Only we have created the world *that concerns human beings*" (*GS* 301). If Nietzsche continues to endorse value anti-realism, how is the change to be explained? One possibility is that it might be explained by a shift in Nietzsche's understanding of the status of moral discourse. As stated above, we agree with Leiter that we can hardly expect Nietzsche to have a clearly worked out position on the semantics of moral discourse. Yet it is hardly unreasonable to suppose that Nietzsche might have had thoughts about the function of moral discourse, and that some such thoughts might have led to a change in his position. It therefore seems reasonable to look for suggestions of the view of moral discourse his work tends towards, one that he presumably would have developed if he had been working in the light of the distinctions and possibilities recognized within contemporary metaethics. Indeed, we have already done that insofar as we found an "error theory" at work in *HA*. Admittedly, Nietzsche never says that statements such as "murder is wrong" should be understood as the expression of a belief that a normative property attaches to all actions that count as instances of "murder," but that such a property does not in fact exist. Yet, that is an obvious reading of what he was assuming when he labeled the world of our moral concerns "the world as representation (as error)" (*HA* 29). And one possibility is that he came to rethink that assumption and recognize something akin to a non-cognitivist account of moral discourse. This would explain why the Nietzsche of *GS* no longer considers the world of our moral concerns erroneous as he did in *HA*: not because he now takes value claims to be capable of truth, but because he thinks they are neither true nor false. The point would be that they function to express not a cognitive state, a belief, but a non-cognitive state, such as emotion. This is pretty much the account Clark offers (Clark 1998b; paper 12).

Nietzsche's reflections on artists in *GS* provides support for a non-cognitivist reading. Consider *GS* 299, which begins with a question and a statement: "What means do we have for making things beautiful, attractive, and desirable when they are not? And in themselves I think they never are!" Nietzsche is clearly not talking about "things in themselves" here. The assumption behind his question is that if considered merely as they are in nature, in terms of their naturalistic properties, things are not "beautiful, attractive, and desirable." This obviously cannot mean that they do not provoke desire or attraction. So the question and the assumption behind it must concern normative properties rather than naturalistic ones. Nietzsche is asking how to make things *worthy* of aesthetic appreciation and desire. This interpretation of *GS* 299 fits well with the part of *GS* 301 quoted above, which claims that "nature is always value-less, but it has been given value at some time, as a present." Nietzsche's question in *GS* 299 concerns precisely how to confer the "present" of value on nature.

That *GS* continues to maintain the anti-realism we found in *HA* makes sense of the presupposition of this question, namely, that in themselves things are never "beautiful, attractive, and desirable." This means that from the viewpoint of science, which determines the "real nature of the world" (*HA* 29), things do not possess normative properties that would make them worthy of aesthetic appreciation or desire. But unless Nietzsche's metaethical view underwent some change between *HA* and *GS*, it is difficult to make sense of the question itself. In particular, if Nietzsche still accepts the error theory of *HA*, that question could only concern how to make things *appear* to be beautiful and desirable when in fact they are not. Yet the question clearly concerns how we can make things *be* beautiful and desirable, worthy of aesthetic appreciation and desire. This suggests that Nietzsche is backing away from the error theory of *HA*. As we interpreted that theory, it applies to statements attributing both aesthetic and ethical value to things. Interpreting this passage in the light of *HA* suggests—and our section 4 will confirm it—that, contrary to appearances, Nietzsche's question in *GS* 299 concerns how to create not only aesthetic but also ethical value, how to make things worthy of appreciation from the viewpoints of both aesthetics and ethics.

Our interpretation of Nietzsche's apparent answer takes off from the section's title: "What one should learn from artists." What one should learn evidently is how to confer on nature the "present" of value by changing people's perceptions of, and therefore reactions to, natural things. Nietzsche first suggests that "we have something to learn from physicians, when for example they dilute something bitter or add wine and sugar to the mixing bowl." The physician makes the medicine attractive—or at least more attractive—by changing how it affects our taste buds and thus how we react to it. From what Nietzsche goes on to say, the artist does something similar. The general point seems to be that the artist induces in us certain reactions to things by manipulating our perspectives on them, for instance, by getting us to look at things from a distance "until there is much in them that one no longer sees and much that the eye must *add in order to see them at all*," or "extracted from their context," or "through colored glass or in light of the sunset." *GS* 7 implies that the passions constitute "all that has given color to existence." Accordingly, looking at things "through colored glass" would be seeing them through the "lens" of one's passions. So artists can make things beautiful and desirable by portraying them in ways that evoke certain passions, which then color one's view of them. Clark has argued that "color" functions throughout *HA* and *GS* as a metaphor for value (Clark 1998b: 68 ff; paper 12 in this volume). In that case, the obvious conclusion to draw here is that artists show us something about how to create values by showing us how to evoke non-cognitive reactions, such as preferences and attitudes.

This gives us strong reason to conclude that Nietzsche's metaethical position in *GS* is the basically Humean one that values are projections of passions and feelings. That is, we take ourselves to be talking about what has value—what is beautiful and desirable and not merely desired—precisely when we mix our own reactions with the object, seeing it in terms that are borrowed from our own reactions to it. Nietzsche's use of color imagery in *GS* can easily remind one of the famous passage in which Hume distinguishes the offices of reason and taste:

> The former conveys the knowledge of truth and falsehood; the latter gives the sentiment of beauty and deformity, vice and virtue. The one discovers objects as they really stand in nature, without addition or diminution; the other has a productive capacity; and gilding and staining all natural objects with the colors borrowed from internal sentiment raises, in a manner, a new creation. (Hume 1975b: 294)

Hume's metaphor of "gilding" even appears, more or less explicitly, in *GS* 139. Entitled "The Color of the Passions," it contrasts those like St. Paul, who have "an evil eye for the passions" and therefore aim at their annihilation, with the Greeks, who "directed their ideal tendency precisely towards the passions and loved and elevated, gilded [*vergoldet*] and deified them." In the latter case, the passions "evidently made them feel happier, but also purer and more god-like," whereas those in the former group know of the passions only "what is dirty, disfiguring, and heartbreaking." The passions themselves thus come to be valued—as opposed to merely lived or perhaps sought—through the projection of feelings and passions. Seeing them from the perspective of love "gilds" them, bestowing on them attractive colors borrowed from our own positive feelings of love and happiness, whereas an "evil eye" stains the passions, projecting negative feelings onto them. Looking at the passions through the lens of unhappiness and disappointment, it finds in them only those qualities that produce these feelings.

We can thus explain why Nietzsche celebrates as a creation in *GS* what he decries as an error in *HA*, then, by supposing that he comes to think of ethical discourse as expressing not the cognitive state of belief, but such non-cognitive states as preferences, attitudes, emotions, and sentiments of approval and disapproval. This would allow Nietzsche to leave behind the error theory of *HA* by rejecting the cognitivism about value discourse that it presupposed. In itself, however, this would do nothing to show that ethical discourse isn't a subjective affair in which individuals express their own personal preferences. We turn now to arguing that the non-cognitivism of *GS* is more complicated than we have so far suggested, and that the expression of moral claims can be objective.

4. Value Creation and Reasons in *The Gay Science*

We begin by returning to Nietzsche's claim that value is something that *"we"* create and bestow on nature as a "present": "Whatever has value in our world now does not have value in itself, according to its nature—nature is always value-less, but it has been given value at some time, as a present—and it is *we* who gave and bestowed it. Only we have created the world *that concerns human being*" (*GS* 301). This might be taken to suggest that Nietzsche's way of getting over the error theory of *HA* is to reiterate its implicit claim that nature itself lacks normative properties, but to insist that through the act of valuing, human beings bestow normative properties (goodness, rightness, etc.) on things, persons, or states of affairs hitherto lacking them. This is how Richardson evidently interprets the above passage: "there are values only in and by our valuing them" (Richardson 2004: 109). Since Richardson definitely does not take Nietzsche to be a non-cognitivist, the position he attributes to him amounts to the claim that things come to have normative properties they otherwise lack in and through our acts of valuing them. This is evidently the view Bernard Reginster calls "normative subjectivism," which is a denial of "normative objectivism," the view that the source of the normative authority of values is to be found outside "the particular inclinations that make up an individual's will" (Reginster 2006: 58).

If this is what value creation entails, however, Nietzsche's position seems implausible: the goodness and badness of things does not seem to be conferred on them by the valuings of human beings. Murder's wrongness, for example, is due to the fact that it is the intentional killing of an innocent, that it causes pain and suffering, etc. Murder's wrongness is not dependent on anyone considering it wrong. But this implies the falsity of normative subjectivism, as presented above. Unless it can accommodate intuitions like these and so avoid normative subjectivism, Nietzsche's view of value creation seems implausible.

Before considering alternatives to this reading of *GS* 301, we pause to consider an objection. It may seem that the need to accommodate such intuitions is a feature that distinguishes what Leiter calls "morality in the pejorative sense" (MPS), thus that the kind of morality Nietzsche rejects is precisely one in which the possession of normative properties (e.g., an action's being good) cannot be recognized as dependent on the valuings—beliefs or attitudes—of human beings. But this will not get around the problem. There is no doubt that Nietzsche recognizes certain virtues: e.g., loyalty, honesty, courage. But it is no more plausible that courage is good or admirable because people admire it than that murder is wrong because people disapprove of it. Recall that our project is to determine whether Nietzsche does and can consistently claim that his elevation of his own values over those of MPS reflects anything more than his "idiosyncratic opinion from his idiosyncratic evaluative perspective" (Leiter 2002: 137). Following Leiter, we have treated this as a question concerning Nietzsche's metaethical position, and we have traced that position from the error-theoretic claim of *HA* that all valuations, that is, all attributions of normative properties, are based on "false thinking" to the non-cognitivism of *GS*. But one factor that makes non-cognitivism implausible to many is its apparent implication that values are dependent on the contingent affective responses of human beings. Is there a way of interpreting Nietzsche's metaethical position without taking it to have this implication?

Nadeem Hussain (2007) and Bernard Reginster (2006) offer "fictionalism" as a response. The fictionalist reading avoids attributing to Nietzsche the normative subjectivism found problematic above by taking Nietzsche to accept that to be valuable, a thing must be so "objectively," i.e., "independent of contingent feelings and inclinations or contingent beliefs about value that agents have" (Reginster 2006: 89). It further holds, however, that nothing is objectively valuable. Fictionalism thus combines a "*cognitivist* semantics for value judgments"—it takes value judgments to express beliefs about the objective properties of things rather than affective states—and an "*anti-realist* metaphysics of value" (Reginster 2006: 85–6). In these respects it is fully in accord with Nietzsche's position in *HA*. How, then, does it differ from that book's error theory, which we claim *GS* overcomes? The answer is that it does not overcome the error theory; the fictionalist accepts that nothing *really* is valuable. The "gaiety" of *GS* is to be explained not by Nietzsche's overcoming of the error theory, as we claim, but by his discovery of a new strategy for dealing with what Reginster calls the "nihilistic disorientation" brought about by its acceptance. Instead of resorting to *HA*'s fantasy of pure knowers who can live without valuing (*HA* 32–4), Nietzsche now advocates that we "avert [nihilism] by engaging in make-believe in objective values, or imagining that there are such values" (Reginster 2006: 85), even though he believes this is false. The fictionalist Nietzsche claims that we "create" values in the sense that he exhorts us to engage in such "*make-believe.*"

Although some philosophers have recently defended fictionalism (Joyce 2001), we admit to not finding it a very plausible ethical position.[5] So although Hussain and Reginster offer subtle defenses of interpreting Nietzsche as a fictionalist, we consider it worthwhile to pursue our alternative view that Nietzsche was able to overcome the error theory of *HA* by accepting a non-cognitivist account of moral discourse.[6] To strengthen our account, it would be especially helpful to have an alternative account of *GS* 301's claim that "we" give and bestow value on nature, which Hussain and Reginster take as a central piece of evidence for the fictionalist interpretation. We seem to face a dilemma here: given that Nietzsche endorses talk of values and value creation in *GS*, either Nietzsche is a cognitivist and so a fictionalist or he is a non-cognitivist and a normative subjectivist. On our account, the dilemma posed here is false. The non-cognitivism Nietzsche endorses in *GS* has the resources to overcome normative subjectivism and to endorse normative objectivism: the view that things are objectively valuable, that their value does not depend on our attitudes toward them.

Although we will be able to make good on this claim only in the final section of this essay, we begin here to fill out this alternative non-cognitivism by challenging the widespread assumption that the "we" identified in *GS* 301 as creating values are human beings in general. Attention to the context provided by the rest of the passage shows beyond any serious doubt that "we" are instead the "contemplative ones" of its title who are characterized in its first line as

---

[5] See Blackburn (2005) and Hussain (2004) for arguments that support reservations about the fictionalist approach to ethics.

[6] One reason to consider the fictionalist account of Nietzsche's metaethics implausible is that it is difficult to see how it could cohere with the importance he accords to the will to truth. In *HA* 34 he asks, in relation to this very question about the erroneousness of values, whether death "would not be preferable" to being obliged to "consciously reside in untruth?" The burden of our account in this essay is to show that he came to recognize that valuing does not require one to "reside in untruth." The burden of the fictionalist account must be to show that he overcame his commitment to not residing in untruth. One strategy for defending the fictionalist account would be to argue that Nietzsche was able to overcome his commitment to truth enough to affirm values, even though they are fictions, because of his commitment to the value of art. One problem with such a strategy is that it would seem to have Nietzsche reverting too much to the stand on art present in his earlier works. Our book on *Beyond Good and Evil* (Clark and Dudrick 2012) argues that Nietzsche's later philosophy is designed to give full satisfaction to the will to truth, and we do not see this as compatible with the fictionalist option.

"higher human beings." The point of the passage is to rebut the self-misunderstanding of "the higher human being," who "can never shake off a delusion. He fancies that he is a spectator and listener who has been placed before the great visual and acoustic spectacle that is life; he calls his own nature *contemplative* and overlooks that he himself is the poet who keeps creating this life" (*GS* 301). That he "calls his own nature *contemplative*" means that he takes his defining activity to be an essentially cognitive pursuit, a matter of *representing* or *describing* what is already there. Nietzsche's point is clearly that the "contemplative" has this wrong, that he actually creates the world he takes himself to be merely contemplating. Now what exactly is this world or life that the higher human being actually creates? It is "the whole eternally growing world of valuations, colors, accents, perspectives, scales, affirmations, and negations." So Nietzsche's point is that it is the higher human beings, not human beings in general, who create values or the world that can be said to contain normative properties (of both the aesthetic and ethical variety). The next line of the passage makes explicit the contrast between the higher human and other humans: "The poem that we have invented is continually studied by the so-called practical human beings (our actors) who learn their roles and translate everything into flesh and actuality, into the everyday." Given this contrast between "we" and "practical human beings," "we" clearly does not refer to humans in general, but to the higher humans with whom Nietzsche here identifies himself. In that case, the same must be true when Nietzsche continues:

> Whatever has *value* in our world now does not have value in itself, according to its nature—nature is always value-less, but has been *given* value at some time, as a present—and it was we who gave and bestowed it. Only we have created the world *that concerns human beings*!—But precisely this knowledge we lack, and when we occasionally catch it for a fleeting moment we always forget it again almost immediately; we fail to recognize our best power and underestimate ourselves, the contemplatives, just a little. We are *neither as proud nor as happy* as we might be. (*GS* 301)

The "contemplatives" are not as proud as they might be because they fail to recognize that they themselves—and not the so called practical or active human beings—are really the creative ones. In considering their nature contemplative, they underestimate themselves by failing to recognize *not* that human beings in general create values, but that they themselves, *unlike other human beings*, do so. And they create "whatever has *value* in our world." So even though Nietzsche does not specifically mention ethical value in the passage, he is certainly claiming that it is created by these contemplatives. It is precisely because they create ethical value that "the poem that [they] have invented is continually studied" by other humans who learn from it "their roles and translate everything into actuality." This claim makes little sense unless he is taking the so-called contemplatives to be the creators of ethical value.

But now we are left with the question of *how* exactly higher human beings create ethical value. *GS* 301 is evidently not interested in telling us, but only in correcting the self-understanding of the creators. We think it offers us a small clue, however, insofar as it refers to them as "thinking-feeling [or: thinking-sensing] ones," and tells us that "what distinguishes the higher human being from the lower is that the former see and hear immeasurably more, and see and hear thoughtfully" (*GS* 301). So even though the point of the passage is that the creators of value mistake their defining activity as a merely cognitive pursuit, a matter of *representing* or *describing* what is already there, Nietzsche seems to think that there is at least a grain of truth in the creator's self-understanding. If he denies that value creation is purely cognitive activity, he also implies that thought or cognition plays an essential role in it.

What is this "thinking" component? The answer begins to come into focus when we recognize that the value creators of *GS* 301 are or include the "ethical teachers" who are also called "*teachers of the purpose of existence*" in the title of *GS* 1. On reflection, it should be obvious that these religious leaders and philosophers of *GS* 1 are included among the self-described "contemplatives" of *GS* 301. The connection doesn't strike one immediately because Nietzsche praises the latter as "higher human beings" whereas he seems highly critical of the former. For all his criticism of these "ethical teachers," however—and he does say, e.g., that their "ethical systems hitherto have been so foolish and contrary to nature that humanity would have perished from every one had it gained power over humanity"—he also calls them "heroes on this stage." And by the end of *GS* 1, it is clear that he identifies with them, saying "We, too, have our time!" What is it, then, that Nietzsche finds so important about these teachers? The answer, it seems, is what in fact results from their activity: "Life and I and you and all of us became *interesting* to ourselves once again for a while." We suggest that this is Nietzsche's way of saying that with the advent of these "ethical teachers," human life appears as bearing *value*. Nietzsche includes himself and his "brothers" among them precisely because these teachers are the original value creators of *GS* 301.

We can therefore hope to gain some insight into how Nietzsche thinks the "contemplatives" of *GS* 301 create values by considering how he characterizes the defining activity of the teachers of *GS* 1. He tells us that each of them "shouts" such things as "Life is worth living," and "There is something behind life, beneath it; beware!" But they do not simply shout or proclaim; they offer *reasons*, saying things like "Life *ought* to be loved, *because*—! Man *ought* to advance himself and his neighbor, *because*—" And they are arguably "teachers" only because they do so. So creating values seems to have something to do with giving reasons.

We therefore take reason-giving as central to Nietzsche's understanding of value creation and ethical discourse. Now, before we examine the implications of this fact, we must allow that there are several aspects of the passage that make it appear that Nietzsche does not hold the activity of giving reasons in high regard; in fact, these aspects make it seem as if his purpose here is precisely to *debunk* reason-giving. We shall discuss briefly three such aspects of *GS* 1 and then offer an alternative to interpreting them as debunking. First, after describing the teachers' activity of reason-giving, Nietzsche says "the ethical teacher makes his appearance as the teacher of the purpose of existence in order that what happens necessarily and always, by itself and without purpose, shall henceforth seem to be done for a purpose and strike man as reason and an ultimate commandment." The teachers' proclamation of purpose is intended to make all events in the natural world ("what happens necessarily and always") appear to be purposeful, done for a reason. The first reason to think that Nietzsche is debunking the activity of reason-giving is that the teachers who introduce it do so in order to advocate a teleological view of the natural world, one that we know Nietzsche clearly and rightly rejects, based on the achievements of modern science.

A second apparently debunking point is Nietzsche's claim that the teaching of reasons and purposes has altered human nature such that man has become a "fantastic animal": "Man has gradually become a fantastic animal that must fulfill one condition of existence more than any other animal: man *must* from time to time believe that he knows *why* he exists; his race cannot thrive without a periodic trust in life—without faith in the *reason in life*!" (*GS* 1). So evidently all the teachers' attempts to satisfy the need they have created in man lead to false beliefs (e.g., that man's purpose is to serve God). It may therefore seem that Nietzsche thinks reason-giving leads man to become a "fantastic animal" in the sense that he needs such metaphysical fantasies in order to exist.

Third, Nietzsche claims that in their effort to make "what happens" seem to be done for a reason, these teachers invent "a second, different existence and takes by means of his new mechanics the old, ordinary existence off its old, ordinary hinges" (*GS* 1). This "second . . . existence" would appear to be a metaphysical world, like that of Plato's Forms, or some version of a supernatural world, which we know from *HA* that Nietzsche rejects as cognitively superfluous.

These suggestions of *GS* 1 to the contrary notwithstanding, it is evident that Nietzsche's attitude toward the activity of reason-giving introduced by the teachers of *GS* 1 cannot be wholly negative. Consider the very next section, *GS* 2: *Intellectual conscience*. There Nietzsche tells us that "*the great majority lacks an intellectual conscience.*"

> I mean: *to the great majority* it is not contemptible to believe this or that and to live accordingly *without* first becoming aware of the most certain reasons pro and con, and without even troubling themselves about such reasons afterwards: the most gifted men and noblest women still belong to this "great majority."

The passage makes clear that Nietzsche does consider it "*contemptible*" to lack an intellectual conscience; his fullest respect goes only to those who live in accord with beliefs that have been formed or confirmed through an examination of the reasons for and against. He cannot, therefore, regard reason-giving as having been debunked by the considerations of *GS* 1.

This opens the way for our contention that Nietzsche regards the teaching of reasons and purposes as making a contribution to which he and his kind (the "thinking-feeling ones" of *GS* 301) are heir. We take the key claims of *GS* 1 to be that the capacity to consider reasons for and against attitudes, beliefs, or actions—and particularly non-prudential reasons—and to act on these reason is essential to being human, and that it is the teachers of the value of existence that firmly established this capacity among human beings. To exercise this capacity is to partake in a "faith" introduced by these teachers: the faith that there are reasons to do things and that there are events that happen for such reasons. It is, however, a refined version of this faith, since it significantly narrows the range of such events: the teachers held that all events are like this, while Nietzsche holds this to be true only of a subset of events, namely, actions undertaken for non-prudential reasons.[7] So Nietzsche criticizes the teachers' practice of reason-giving when he presents it as the attempt to make all events in the natural world ("what happens necessarily and always") appear to be purposeful, done for a reason—the first "debunking" aspect discussed above. He, of course, denies the teleological view of nature, according to which *everything* happens for a reason, indeed is *done* for a reason. But that is perfectly consistent with recognizing that these teachers achieved something great by establishing the practice of ethical reason-giving among human beings, thereby making it possible for things to be done for non-prudential reasons.

It is the work of these teachers, then, that firmly establishes the capacity of human beings to think and act in terms of non-prudential reasons. This suggests an alternative to our debunking interpretation of Nietzsche's claim that these teachers have caused man to "become a fantastic animal": with the institution of reason-giving, human beings can engage in behavior that cannot be fully understood in non-teleological, purely causal terms.[8] Because Nietzsche holds that the natural world *can* be fully understood in such terms, this makes human beings "fantastic." It also makes human actions part of a world other than the natural world, "a second existence." This helps explain the third debunking aspect of the passage, the claim that the teacher of reasons and

---

[7] Nietzsche clearly doesn't think that it was religious teachers who introduced prudential reasons into human consciousness. For evidence of this, consider both the opening sections of *GM* II on punishment, and the related account of the beginning of reliance on consciousness and prudential reasons in *GM* II:16. Thus, if it is the case, as we have been arguing, that Nietzsche thinks these teachers introduced a practice of reason-giving, it has to be the practice of offering and thinking in terms of non-prudential reasons.

[8] See Clark and Dudrick (2005).

purposes invents "a second, different existence and takes by means of his new mechanics the old, ordinary existence off its old, ordinary hinges." This world is not a metaphysical world, as was supposed above, but a "space of reasons," in contrast with the natural world, which is a "space of causes."[9] Although human actions certainly exist in the latter space, they can also be located in relation to the space of reasons. When the teachers institute the practice of reason giving, the "old existence" (i.e., the space of causes) is "lifted off its old hinges" into the "second existence" (i.e., the space of reasons), where it now operates according to a "new mechanics," insofar as events in the natural world can now be accurately described and explained in reference to reasons.

Before we use this interpretation of *GS* 1 to draw conclusions about how Nietzsche thinks the "contemplative ones" of *GS* 301 create values, it will be helpful to make explicit two distinctions in the use of "value" or "values." First, we can use the terms in a descriptive or a normative sense. "Value" is used in a descriptive sense when one talks about values *without* endorsing them. When one refers to "John's values" or "the values of the Enlightenment," the term is being used in the descriptive sense; it does not commit one to endorsing the values in questions. But if John says that he considers justice a value, he would normally be understood as endorsing the value of justice, as claiming that justice is valuable or good, hence as using the term in the normative sense. Second, John Richardson helpfully brings out that there are two ways one can use "value" in the descriptive sense. Nietzsche wants to study but not to endorse, for instance, Christian values. But "'Christian values' could refer either to such *goods* as relief from suffering, or to the attitudes [involved in] valuing such goods" (Richardson 2004: 71). So in studying values, Nietzsche studies both "the act or activity of *valuing* some content—positing it as good"—and "the *valued*, the content so posited."[10] The former could be more clearly termed a "valuing" or an "assessment," so that "a value" in the descriptive sense would be reserved, as we shall use it here, for the latter, thus for objects or contents posited as valuable, that is, posited as values in the normative sense. These distinctions help to make sense of Nietzsche's otherwise puzzling claim to be investigating "*the value of these values*," "*der Werth dieser Werthe*" (*GM* P:6). While the plural "Werthe" is used in a descriptive sense, and to refer to objects valued (not to the act of valuing), the singular "Werth" is used in a normative sense. These distinctions make clear that "the issue for [Nietzsche]" is whether

---

[9] The distinction between the space of causes and the space of reasons is made explicitly in the twentieth century by Wilfrid Sellars. We think Nietzsche picked up the distinction, though not by these names, from African Spir (Spir 1877). See the essay cited in the previous note for information about Spir and evidence of his influence on Nietzsche regarding this and other issues.

[10] Richardson points out that Nietzsche normally uses words built on "schätzen" to refer to the former, whereas he uses "Werthe" to refer to the latter, "'the thing that is valued, but as valued" (Richardson 2004: 72).

things that have been *posited* as good *are* good (*GM* P:5), thus that his concerns are both descriptive and normative.

We can now argue that Nietzsche holds that values are created in both the descriptive and the normative sense. We interpret Nietzsche's claim that "genuine philosophers" create values (*BGE* 211) in the descriptive sense. These philosophers create values, as Nietzsche himself does in his own writings, by inducing people to posit things as valuable. They do this in part by inducing in people new affective responses to things. This helps us to see why Nietzsche thinks that "we"—presumably the creators of values of *GS* 301—"should learn from artists" (*GS* 299). We saw in section 3 that Nietzsche takes artists to provide perspectives on things that lead us to react to them in particular ways. In doing so, artists influence our affects, our dispositions to feel in particular ways about those things. This means that artists are proficient in some of the skills involved in creating values (in the descriptive sense). To create new values in this sense, one has to lead others to have dispositions to feel towards things in certain ways and to act accordingly. Yet, this is not sufficient, as we have inferred from *GS* 1 and contrary to what we suggested in section 3. To create values in this descriptive sense one must induce people not only to develop dispositions to act and react to things in certain ways, but also to take these ways of acting and feeling to be justified, to be supported by reasons. Nietzsche does this in his own writings by offering new *interpretations* of the dispositions he induces in people (to which he seduces them), ones designed to induce people to regard these dispositions as justified.

But this descriptive sense of creating values does not seem to capture the sense of "creation" in the passage from which we have repeatedly quoted the following: "Whatever has *value* in the present world has it not in itself, according to its nature—nature is always value-less—but rather has been given, granted value at some time, and *we* were the givers and granters!" (*GS* 301). Here the claim seems to be not simply that the creators of values have induced others to take things to be valuable, but above all, that they have made things valuable, bestowed upon them their normative properties. We have already said that this would be highly problematic if it meant that they have, for instance, made murder wrong or friendship good. The link we have established between *GS* 301 and *GS* 1 and our reading of the latter allows us to formulate an alternative to both the subjectivist and the fictionalist interpretation of the passage: namely, that by instituting practices of non-prudential reason-giving, the "teachers of the purpose of existence" bring into existence the space of reasons, and that it is only this space that makes it possible for anything to be a bearer of normative properties, e.g., to be good or bad, right or wrong. The position we are thus attributing to Nietzsche is a plausible one, given the following (we think plausible) assumptions: first, that to value something—as opposed to merely desiring it—is to accept that there is *reason* to take certain actions and attitudes towards it (for instance, to approve or disapprove of it, and to do or refrain from doing it); second, that there are reasons (i.e., reasons exist) *only* for beings who can appreciate reasons—in the case under consideration, non-prudential reasons. So the teachers of the value of existence create values in the sense that, by instituting the practice of non-prudential reason-giving, they help create beings who can consider and appreciate reasons. And this makes it possible for there to *be* reasons and therefore values.

We can now say how our reading of "value creation" can allow Nietzsche to avoid the kind of subjectivism that would take the goodness of loyalty, for instance, to be conferred upon it by the valuing of human beings, without taking values to be fictions. The "present" that the "contemplatives" of *GS* 301 bestow on an otherwise value-less nature is simply that of covering it with—reconfiguring it as—a space of reasons. On this interpretation, Nietzsche's commitment to value creation in the normative sense is perfectly compatible with claiming that once this space of reasons comes into existence, the normative properties there discerned are determined not by the contemplatives or by anyone else, but rather by what reasons there are to act and feel in certain ways. If this is the correct interpretation of Nietzsche's claim, in making possible the space of reasons the contemplatives of *GS* 301 "create the world *that concerns human beings*," the world of value, even though they do not determine which things in that world bear which normative properties.

It may seem that we have now turned Nietzsche into a cognitivist and value realist along the lines of Thomas Nagel or John McDowell. If value claims are claims about what there is reason to do or feel, and what there is reason to do or feel depends on the constitution of the space of reasons, it sounds as if value claims should be understood as *expressing beliefs* about the space of reasons, beliefs made true or false by the facts concerning what we have reason to do or feel. But this would leave us with a highly implausible interpretation of Nietzsche's metaethics. Recall that our major reason for interpreting Nietzsche as a non-cognitivist in *GS* is that it explains how he overcome *HA*'s ideal of abstaining from value judgments and arrived at the "gaiety" of *The Gay Science*. It is just not plausible that he did this instead by deciding that there really hadn't been any problem about values to begin with, that recognizing that value claims are claims about reasons solved all of the problems that led him to the error-theoretic view of *HA*. It was his naturalism that led Nietzsche to the error theory we found in *HA*, and it is not plausible that he concluded that naturalism posed no problems for moral objectivity once we recognize moral claims as claims about reasons. Consider Jerry Fodor's challenge to John McDowell, who endorses such a view: "Having situated . . . the ethical . . . outside the realm of law [in the space of reasons] McDowell needs to face the embarrassing question how, by any natural process, do we ever manage to get at it?" (Fodor 1995: 11, quoted in Miller 2004: 258). In other words, the cognitivist-Nietzsche (if he is not a fictionalist) would have to be able to explain what capacities we, as natural beings, have developed that allow us to have accurate beliefs about this space of reasons that floats free of the merely natural space of causes. It is difficult to see how he could answer this question short of espousing a full-blown Platonism, which we know he rejects. Fortunately, there is an obvious alternative to the realism endorsed by McDowell and Nagel that accords with the emphasis we have argued Nietzsche puts on the connection between value and reasons, namely, to suppose that Nietzsche would endorse a non-cognitivist account of taking something to be a reason. To take something to be of (non-prudential) value, on the view we are attributing to Nietzsche, is to take it that there are reasons (i.e., it is rational) to feel and act towards it in certain ways. On a non-cognitivist account of the type offered by Allan Gibbard, such claims about reasons are to be understood as expressing a non-cognitive mental state. "To say that X is rational is not to ascribe a property to X, to utter a truth-conditional statement about X; rather, it is to *express acceptance* of a system of norms which permits X" (Miller 2004: 96). So the emphasis we take Nietzsche to place on the connection between values and reasons is perfectly consistent with taking him to hold that when we make claims about reasons (and so about values) we are not expressing beliefs; rather, we are expressing a commitment to a system of norms that sanctions some set of reactions and actions.

We do find some evidence that points to a non-cognitivist account of reason-giving in *GS* 1. In particular, Nietzsche says about the activity of reason-giving that a drive "erupts from time to time as reason and passion of mind; it is then surrounded by a resplendent retinue of reasons and tries with all its might to make us forget that fundamentally it is drive, instinct, stupidity, lack of reasons" (*GS* 1). Initially this might appear to be just another aspect of the passage that debunks reason-giving. In advocating reason-giving, the "teachers of the value of existence" evidently teach human beings to offer what they take to be a reason or justification for seeking what is already the object of a drive they have. So drives do all the work; reasons seem epiphenomenal at best. However, as we have already argued, Nietzsche's view cannot involve a debunking of reasons, given the contempt he expresses in the very next section of *GS* towards those who do not "consider it contemptible to believe this or that and to live accordingly without first having given themselves an account of the most certain reasons pro and con, and without even troubling themselves about such reasons afterwards" (*GS* 2). Nietzsche is certainly claiming that in instituting practices of reason-giving, the "teachers of the value of existence" teach human beings to offer what they take to be a reason or justification for seeking what is already the object of a drive they have. Love of life is already there, as "drive, instinct, stupidity, lack of reasons." But if Nietzsche's emphasis on this point is not meant to debunk reasons, as we have argued it is not, the obvious alternative is that it is meant to deny a cognitivist account of what it is to take something to be a reason. His claim is that when a person takes something to be a reason, a drive is erupting "as reason and passion of mind," thereby surrounding itself "with a resplendent retinue of reasons" and attempting to make us forget its affective nature (*GS* 1). It is difficult to see what this could mean if it is not that taking oneself to have a reason is not a matter of representing the world in a certain way, of claiming to be in touch with something beyond the natural world, even a space of reasons, but is instead, at least first and foremost, an expression of some aspect of the person's affective nature, in Nietzsche's language, of the drives or instincts. It is the manifestation in consciousness or language of the activity of such drives. Nietzsche's suggestion in *GS* 1 that drives underlie reason-giving can thus be read as debunking not the practice of reason-giving, but the cognitivist understanding of that practice as expressing, first and foremost, beliefs or representations of the world.

This non-cognitivist reading fits well with what we said above about Nietzsche's views concerning the role of the artist in value creation (*GS* 299, e.g.). If value claims are expressions of commitments, then value creation (in the descriptive sense) will require the ability to modify people's dispositions to feel and to act—an ability found in artists. Now, for a claim to express a commitment and not just a preference—i.e., for the claim to be about what is valuable—it must express a disposition the person regards as justified, as supported by reasons. The non-cognitivist reading helps make clear how philosophers might learn from artists not just how to change dispositions, but also how to induce people to take themselves to have reason to feel and act in accord with a disposition. The key here is to see that to be a valuer in a descriptive sense, one need only to regard oneself as justified, one need not have considered the "reasons pro and con" concerning the disposition in question. If the latter were a requirement, having an intellectual conscience would be a requirement for being a valuer *at all*. Nietzsche's claims about the rarity of intellectual conscience and his claim about the advent of values in religious and moral hucksterism shows that he must deny this. Intellectual conscience, Nietzsche thinks, is something that most valuers *lack*: he regards being *thoughtful* about the "thinking" component of values as a goal or ideal, not a necessary condition. What, then, *is* involved in taking a disposition to be justified, supported by reasons? It involves the feeling of acting in accord with one's "conscience," as described in *GS* 335. The one who takes herself to act in accord with *values* and not just desires "listens" to her conscience when she judges "This is right." It is this (largely inchoate) feeling of being justified that is the key to having a value (in the descriptive sense)—as opposed to a mere set of desires or dispositions. Now, in *GS* 335, Nietzsche tells us that the judgment "This is right' has a prehistory in your drives." This fits nicely with what he says about the role of the drives in *GS* 1, which we used above as evidence for Nietzsche's non-cognitivism: i.e., that when a person takes herself to have a reason, a drive is surrounding itself "with a resplendent retinue of reasons." It is important that what the drive surrounds itself with allows the person to feel justified; thus, the *resplendence* of this finery is as important as its being composed of *reasons*.

5. Normative Objectivity

Nietzsche's new philosophers would no doubt suffer the same fate as the poets in Plato's republic. And one need not be a Platonist to wonder whether there is something underhanded about Nietzsche's proposal. If philosophers are to promote values, we expect them to offer arguments—we don't expect philosophy to have a direct effect on our affects, much less for a philosopher to *seek* this effect. This puts the issue with which this essay is concerned, that of the objectivity of values, in a new light. Recall that Leiter asks whether Nietzsche is "doing anything more than giving his idiosyncratic opinion from his idiosyncratic evaluative perspective. . . . Is there, in short, anything about Nietzsche's evaluation of morality that ought to command *our* attention and assent?" (Leiter 2002: 137). On the account we've given, Nietzsche does more than "offer" his evaluations—insofar as he seeks to create values, he attempts to *change* people's affects, *without necessarily letting them know what he is doing.* Who does Nietzsche think he is? What gives him to the right to promote his values by trying to change people's affects, while (at least sometimes) intentionally concealing this fact? How can he do this in good conscience? Moreover, does Nietzsche even see that there is an issue to be confronted here?

Nietzsche's description of this task in BGE 211 only sharpens the challenge; he tells us that "*True [eigentlichen] philosophers . . . are commanders and law givers*: they say "thus it *shall* be!," it is they who determine the Wherefore and Whither of mankind . . . they reach for the future with creative hand, and everything that is or has been becomes for them a means, an instrument, a hammer" (*BGE* 211). We take the value creation with which Nietzsche is concerned in this passage to be of the descriptive variety distinguished in our previous section; it is a matter of inducing people through various non-philosophical (and certainly non-argumentative) means to adopt certain values, thus to make certain commitments. In particular, it seems that the task of Nietzsche's new philosophers is the same as that of the old-style contemplatives. What he wants from these philosophers is what he himself starts to provide—an interpretation of ethical practices, practices of judging and acting, which reconceives their value[11]—and one that they hope will influence other people in a way that, at least sometimes, bypasses their rational faculties. But what gives philosophers the right to create values in this way?

If Nietzsche were a cognitivist and realist, he might have the makings of a response; the value creation he advocates could be seen as belonging to the Platonic tradition of noble lying, a matter of bringing people who lack

---

[11] A major point here is that the old-style "'contemplatives'" offered ascetic interpretations of the value of such ethical practices, whereas Nietzschean philosophers will offer non-ascetic interpretations, ones that do not devalue the natural world. See the end of Clark (1998a) for a brief account of what this amounts to.

the intellectual power to do it on their own to make the correct judgments regarding the ontologically objective value properties of things—even if they do not do so for the right reasons. But what can a non-cognitivist and anti-realist say in his defense? In this section, we will argue that Nietzsche has a plausible response to this challenge; in fact, we find in his later works a conception of objectivity that is meant precisely to show how philosophers can be justified in creating values. This begins to become apparent when we see that Nietzsche links objectivity to *justice*. In *HA*, Nietzsche denied the possibility of objectivity in ethics in part because he insists that making ethical evaluations is always unjust (*HA* 32–3). In his later works, he comes to endorse the possibility of objectivity in ethics precisely because he thinks value claims can express commitments taken up *justly*. It is, we'll argue, Nietzsche's commitment to justice that makes him a philosopher and not simply an artist: his intellectual conscience requires him to seek to become "aware of the most certain reasons pro and con" when he engages in value creation. His having done so makes him justified in thinking that what he values is valuable "objectively," i.e., "independent of contingent feelings and inclinations or contingent beliefs about value" that he happens to have (Reginster 2006: 89).

The link we suggest between objectivity and justice in Nietzsche's thought may seem implausible, given his well-known assertion that "objectivity and justice have nothing to do with each other" (*UM* II:6). But this appears in an early essay (1874) in which Nietzsche was still operating under the influence of Schopenhauer's idea of objectivity. Following Schopenhauer, Nietzsche took objectivity to be a matter of aesthetic contemplation, and therefore to have nothing to do with the active judging he associated with justice. But this Schopenhauerian conception of objectivity is precisely what Nietzsche rejects in his defense of perspectivism in *GM* III:12.

Denouncing Schopenhauer's conception, Nietzsche claims that one should think of objectivity "not as 'disinterested contemplation' (which is a non-concept and an absurdity), but rather as the capacity to have one's pro and contra *in one's power* and to shift them in and out, so that one knows how to make precisely the difference in perspectives and affective interpretations useful for knowledge. . . . There is *only* a perspectival seeing, only a perspectival 'knowing'; and the more affects we allow to speak about a matter, the more eyes, different eyes, we know how to bring to bear on the same matter, the more complete will our concept of this matter, our 'objectivity' be" (*GM* III:12).

Nietzsche was originally drawn to the contemplative or "mirror" conception of objectivity, presumably because an "interested" perspective would seem to make one's view of an object reflect the peculiarities of one's own subjectivity rather than revealing the object's own features, its "objective" features. Some still take Nietzsche's defense of the perspectival character of knowledge as designed to deny that knowledge can ever be objective. But this is clearly what the passage rejects. Nietzsche denies that the affects that constitute perspectives keep us from grasping the objective features of things; instead they serve as our very access to these features (objective properties or facts). To try to free intellect from affect, Nietzsche goes on to suggest, is to "castrate the intellect." So it would seem that Reginster is correct that for Nietzsche perspectives are "conditions of possibility, rather than limitations" (Reginster 2006: 84). But this doesn't seem quite right either. In fact, while an interest or affect gives the intellect the only access it has to the objective features of things, by focusing the intellect's attention on them and pushing it to register them as important, the affect also limits the intellect to what can be known from the particular perspective that it constitutes. Affects light up certain features of the matter under consideration by hiding others from view. Nietzsche's new conception of objectivity is designed to address this problem. If the perspectives that give us our only access to the objective features of things also hide some of these features from view, the solution is not to try to avoid the influence of affect, but to bring different affective perspectives to bear on the matter. This is his recipe for increasing our "concept of the matter, our 'objectivity'"—our grasp of the objective features of the matter.

Nietzsche's focus in this passage is clearly on knowing rather than valuing. He exhorts us not to be ungrateful, "particularly as knowers," to traditional philosophy's penchant for reversing "familiar perspectives and valuations" because it constitutes training for the intellect's "future 'objectivity,'" which is a matter of being able to bring different perspectives to bear on a matter in the service of knowledge. But his use of the phrase "particularly as knowers" raises the question of what other role Nietzsche's philosophers are to assume in which they might need the training provided by traditional philosophy's reversal of familiar perspectives and valuations. What about in their role as creators of values? We will argue that Nietzsche does consider the conception of objectivity defended in the passage we have been interpreting to be relevant to this task.

We begin by noting that *GM* III:12 is clearly meant as a response to *HA*'s conception of objectivity, one that (as we saw above) does have implications for valuations. As we saw in section 2, *HA* advocated a "simpler and emotionally purer life [in which] the old motives of violent desire . . . would gradually grow weaker under the influence of purifying knowledge. In the end one would live among human beings and with oneself as in *nature*, without praising, blaming, contending, gazing contentedly, as though at a spectacle, upon many things for which one formerly felt only fear" (*HA* 34). And indeed, although he did not use the metaphor then, it was precisely the *perspectival* character of valuing (e.g., "praising, blaming," etc.) that led the Nietzsche of *HA* to insist that all valuation is unjust. That is, Nietzsche saw valuation as unjust because he took it to be rooted in affects—in inclinations and aversions—and so to be based on a partial view of things. Now, *GM*'s perspectivism certainly affirms *HA*'s understanding of valuation as rooted in affects and so as partial—why, then should we think that *GM* would not conclude that valuation cannot be objective and, so, is unjust? Doesn't affirming the "inescapability of contingent perspectives" deny Nietzsche (or anyone else) "a point of view from which he could establish the objective standing of any value" (Reginster 2006: 83)?

To see how *GM* modifies *HA*'s position on the objectivity of values, it's helpful to consider the (1886) preface to *HA*. Echoing *GM* III:12, Nietzsche here tells us how the affects can be harnessed and used so as to make one's perspective more comprehensive, and so, more objective. But this time he is writing of values rather than knowledge. The context for the passage we quote is Nietzsche's question as to why the "free spirit" must turn against his earlier values and virtues (as Nietzsche himself turned against the values and virtues of *The Birth of Tragedy* in *Human, All Too Human*). The answer he tells us the free spirit hears is the following:

> You must become master of yourself and master of your own virtues as well. Previously, they were your masters; but they should simply be tools among your other tools. You must acquire power over your For and Against and learn how to take them out and hang them back up according to your higher aim. You must learn how to grasp the perspectival element in every valuation—the displacement, the distortion, and seeming teleology of horizons and everything else that pertains to perspectivism; and also how much stupidity there is in opposed values and the whole intellectual loss that must be paid for every For and Against. You must learn to grasp the *necessary* injustice in every For and Against; injustice as inseparable from life, life itself as conditioned by perspective and its injustice. Above all, you must see with your own eyes where injustice is always the greatest: namely, where life has developed in the smallest, narrowest, neediest, most preliminary ways and yet still cannot avoid taking *itself* as the purpose and measure of things, and, out of love for its own preservation, secretly and meanly and ceaselessly crumbling away and putting into question all that is higher, greater, richer—you must see with your own eyes the problem of establishing *rank ordering* and how power and right and comprehensiveness of perspective grow up into the heights together. (*HA* P: 6)

This passage provides the link between Nietzsche's understanding of the possibility of ethical objectivity in *HA* and *GM*. In both books he holds that valuations are made from perspectives constituted by affects. Unlike *HA* and like the later (1886) preface to *HA*, however, *GM* holds that this fact does not imply the impossibility of objectivity; it holds, rather, that one is *more* just—and so more objective—to the extent that one's value judgments express commitments that are taken up when one has seen things from different perspectives.

We can see Nietzsche developing the connection between objectivity and justice in *GM*'s discussion of Dühring's conception of justice. Nietzsche rejects

Dühring's proposition that "the homeland of justice is to be sought on the ground of reactive feeling," in particular, of resentment at being injured, claiming that the reverse is actually the case, that "the *last ground* to be conquered by the spirit of justice is that of the reactive feelings! If it really happens that the just man remains just even towards those who injure him (and not merely cold, moderate, distant: being just is always a positive way of behaving), if the high, clear objectivity—that sees as deeply as it does generously—of the just eye, the *judging* eye, does not cloud even under the assault of personal injury, derision, accusation, well, that is a piece of perfection and highest mastery on earth (GM II:11). On Nietzsche's view, then, justice is "in the long run the opposite of what all revenge wants, which sees only the viewpoint of the injured one, allows only it to count—from now on, the eye is trained for an ever *more impersonal* appraisal of deeds, even the eye of the injured one himself (although this last of all, as was mentioned at the start)" (*GM* II:11). In this context, the just person is one who no longer evaluates actions from the narrowly personal perspective to which we are all at least initially inclined, but appraises it from a general perspective, one that sounds like Hume's "common point of view." Training in "*impersonal* appraisal of deeds" is thus the beginning of objectivity.

Nietzsche regards the training in objectivity that begins in the sphere of social justice as something that is carried to a much higher level in philosophical training, and seeing this is crucial as a response to the challenge with which we began this section. *BGE* 211 tells us that as "preconditions" for the task of creating values, thus of being "*commanders and law givers*," the education of a philosopher requires that he has had perhaps to be "critic and skeptic and dogmatist and historian and, moreover, poet and collector and traveler and guesser of riddles and moralist and seer and 'free spirit' and practically everything, in order to run through the range of human values and value feelings and *be able* to gaze with many eyes and consciences from the heights into every distance, from the depths up to every height, from the corner onto every expanse" (*BGE* 211). The "preconditions" for creating values, then, are the different stages of the process whereby the philosopher actually inhabits quite opposed perspectives, e.g., those of the dogmatist, the skeptic, and the critical philosopher, because precisely this is necessary to "run through the range of human values and value feelings" and "consciences" that have stood the test of serious philosophical examination. Although it may not be clear which and how many different perspectives Nietzsche's ideal philosopher would have to inhabit or take seriously to engage in this process, it does seem clear that Nietzsche regards the process as essential for anyone to be worthy of the task of creating values. *BGE* 219 connects this process to justice; after describing what is in effect the same process described in the quotation above, it tells us that the "lofty spirituality" of the one who is "empowered to maintain the *order of rank* in the world" (i.e., the philosopher who has a right to create values) is the "spiritualization of justice." Such "spiritualization" is a matter of bringing to bear on the appraisal of value systems one's training in the "impersonal appraisal of deeds," which was gained in the sphere of social justice, even to the point of turning that training against one's own favored system.

Our interpretation has the surprising consequence that Nietzsche's understanding of objectivity is similar to the one that has been attributed to Thomas Nagel. Nagel's conception of the objective point of view has been described as the viewpoint at which one arrives—or at least that one successively approximates—as one detaches oneself from one's own personal perspective and takes up an impersonal one. Now if this impersonal perspective were a matter of contemplating the world "without interest," Nietzsche would certainly deny that anything would be recognized as valuable from it. Nagel seems to agree, for he claims that "when we take up the objective standpoint, the problem is not that values seem to disappear but that there seem to be too many of them, coming from every life and drowning out those that arise from our own" (Nagel 1989: 147).

This conception of "the objective standpoint" seems close to the conception of objectivity we found in *GM*. As Sigrún Svavarsdóttir (2001) explains it, to occupy Nagel's impersonal viewpoint, we have to be able to see our own viewpoint as just one perspective among others. However, the point is not merely to realize that we could value other things than we actually do, but to come to "appreciate this 'from the inside,'" to "appreciate *what it is like* to see value in all sorts of activities and qualities we would not count among our values." For Nietzsche, we can put slightly differently what it is to appreciate other value perspectives "from the inside": it is to bring into focus the features of objects that give rise to affective responses that involve or lead to a different appraisal of them than one's own. To the extent one does this, one is more objective in holding the values that one does. For both Nagel and Nietzsche, then, to appreciate other value perspectives "from the inside" is to understand what those who occupy these perspectives take to be *reasons* for the judgments made from them. To do so is not simply to take note of them; it is to think and feel what it is like to consider the reasons in question *as reasons*. Having done so, she will have become "aware of the most certain reasons pro and con" for her own values, and will thus be able to affirm them in good "intellectual conscience" (*GS* 2; *GS* 335).

This comparison with Nagel may seem once again to place us in danger of committing Nietzsche to a version of cognitivism. In fact, however, there may be reasons to think that it is Nagel's cognitivism that the comparison renders dubious. Svavarsdóttir tells us that

> Nagel's claim that there are objective values should not be understood as the claim that there are evaluative properties that are objectively understandable or whose instantiations will be recognized from the objective standpoint. Rather, it should be understood as the claim that we

will continue to value certain things—that is, have values—after going through the process of detachment. These would be the attitudes of valuing that all rational evaluators could share and are approximately described as objective: "It is beliefs *and attitudes* that are objective in the primary sense" (*Nowhere*, 4; italics mine). It is only in a derivative sense that we speak of their objects as objective values. (Svavarsdóttir 2001: 167)

The sentence that Svavarsdóttir quotes from Nagel's *The View from Nowhere* nicely captures what is at issue for the non-cognitivist Nietzsche in discussions of objectivity: if value claims are to be understood as expressions of commitments—i.e., of dispositions to act and react which one regards as justified—then the question of the objectivity of values is ultimately a question about those commitments. Whether some values are objective, then, will have to do not with the relationship between claims and things in the world that they purport to represent, but with the relationship of the person to her commitments.

To put the point differently, to ask whether a person's values are objective is to ask about the norms according to which the person has decided what norms to commit herself to. Allan Gibbard's model of objectivity provides a plausible model on which to understand Nietzsche's view. According to Gibbard,

A person who treats his normative judgments as objective has an epistemic story, and the story cannot center on him; it cannot treat him specially, just as himself and for no other reason. Or, more likely, the person acts as if there were such a story, even if he cannot find it. An eligible story will say what constitutes good conditions for judgment, and anyone in those conditions will count as a good judge. (Gibbard 1990: 181–2)

The "epistemic story" in question here is, of course, a normative one: it expresses one's commitment to a set of higher-order norms for making normative judgments and attempts to show that the person's normative judgments meet them. To judge a person's normative judgments to be objective is to express one's commitment to the higher-order norms inherent in the story and to judge that that person's judgments met them.

This is how Nietzsche is able to avoid normative subjectivism, the view that the value of things depends on the particular feelings and inclinations persons happen to have toward them. On the view we attribute to him, to say that a judgment is objective—determined by the weight of reasons rather than by something idiosyncratic to the person—is to express one's commitment to certain norms for good judging and one's belief that the person making the judgment satisfies them. In his perspectivism, Nietzsche puts forward an "epistemic story" which offers such norms for good judging. On this view, objectivity is a matter of degree: a person's value judgments are more or less objective to the extent that they reflect a process in which she has taken up and inhabited evaluative perspectives other than her own.

But there is no guarantee that objectivity will lead inexorably to convergence of opinion—i.e., no reason to think that there is one set of values that even ideal judges will agree on. It's helpful to contrast ethics with science here, since objectivity in science *does* guarantee convergence in opinion, at least ideally. Nietzsche would, on our reading, agree with Bernard Williams' claim that "the best explanation of the [hoped for] convergence [in science] involves the idea that the answer represents how things are." It is less clear that he would agree with Williams that "in the area of the ethical, at least at a high level of generality, there is no such coherent hope" (Williams 1985: 136). Because it is not primarily a matter of saying how things are, but of expressing a commitment to norms, Nietzsche cannot appeal to the way things are to guarantee a convergence of opinion in ethics. Yet, it is possible that the virtues required to go through the process of inhabiting many different value perspectives would lead to a convergence of opinion among the best judges, and we see no reason for denying that it is at least coherent to *hope* that it would, even if there is no guarantee.

It might be objected that, on the view we've attributed to Nietzsche, there *is* reason to deny the coherence of such a hope for convergence. For even if I have taken up alternative evaluative perspectives, I must ultimately judge what I have seen from them from the perspective of *my own commitments*, and so, according to the standards of my own values. While seeing the matter from the viewpoint of different sets of interests and affects may give me a fuller conception of the matter, I'll still have to invoke *my* values in making my eventual judgment. But if everyone who undertakes such a process of occupying different perspectives ends by judging the matter from their original perspective, how is convergence even a possibility? And that seems to raise an even more basic problem: if the process *doesn't* offer the hope of convergence among all who have taken the process to its ideal limit, why think that it increases objectivity at all?

Nietzsche has resources to respond to both challenges. To the first, he can respond that to deem incoherent the hope that the best judges will come to agree is based on a shallow understanding of the exercise in perspectivism. For it assumes that the one who seeks objectivity by inhabiting different evaluative perspectives is unchanged by this process. When Nietzsche says that a person has become "aware of the most certain reasons pro and con" he is not saying that she has simply rehearsed the considerations that she counts for and against some claim; he is saying, rather, that she has seen the matter from the perspective of affects other than her own, allowing these affects to "light up" those aspects of the situation that the perspective leads its occupants to regard as relevant. Even if she does not ultimately share the assessment of the aspects brought to the fore in the other perspective, she is at least likely to come to see them as relevant in a way she hitherto had not. Further, there is certainly no reason to think that one who has gone through the whole process would simply revert to her original perspective at the end of it. Nietzsche undoubtedly thinks of the process as an alternative to the way of "purifying" affect of its partiality that he proposed in *HA*. There the idea was that affects would "grow weaker under the influence of purifying knowledge" (*HA* 34). Although later Nietzsche is no longer interested in affects becoming weaker, it makes sense that he would think that affects are "purified"—their partiality decreased—to the extent that they are the ones that survive a process in which one has truly seen and accepted the world from the perspective of different affects.

To the second challenge, Nietzsche can respond that having inhabited different perspectives increases objectivity, even if it doesn't guarantee convergence of opinion, because it increases fairness. At the very least, allowing different affects to light up different aspects of a situation helps to ensure that one's evaluations aren't based on irrelevant considerations but on those aspects of the situation that are pertinent to the matter at hand. This response may strike us as unsatisfying: aren't questions about what is "irrelevant" or "pertinent" themselves normative ones? And if so, doesn't citing them in an explanation of what makes for objectivity beg the question against the one who challenges Nietzsche's position? Certainly, such a response begs the question against one who criticizes Nietzsche for failing to offer a value-neutral standard or perspective from which to make judgments about values. But as we saw above, this is no problem for Nietzsche: it should be no surprise that no measure of objectivity can be had from a value-neutral perspective, since he holds that *no* values show up from such a perspective. Objectivity is, for Nietzsche, a normative concept—it is among the values that he endorses. Now if someone objects to Nietzsche's conception not on the grounds that it is normative, but on the grounds that there is a better way to achieve objectivity—one other than identification with others' evaluative perspectives—then Nietzsche can and quite possibly should take it seriously. He will try to understand the reasons in favor of this alternative; he'll try to see it as do those who endorse it; and he'll reconsider his own conception of objectivity in light of what he learns. And he'll do this precisely because it is what his understanding of and commitment to objectivity requires of him.[12]

Finally, we want to suggest that it is no objection to Nietzsche's position that it is very difficult, if not impossible, to take leave of one's own evaluative perspective and to inhabit others. Nietzsche can grant this claim; in fact, he can insist on it: it is precisely this difficulty that makes the objectivity required of those who would create values such a rare quality. For Nietzsche, value creation involves seeking to change others' dispositions by means other than the

---

[12] See Blackburn (1999).

rational and argumentative ones of traditional philosophy. Given this understanding of his task, Nietzsche is concerned about objectivity not because he thinks he must justify his position to others, but because he must satisfy his own intellectual conscience. He can create values in good intellectual conscience only because, having inhabited many different evaluative perspectives, he deems himself to have achieved a very serious degree of objectivity.

{ PART II }

Politics

{ 6 }

Bloom and Nietzsche

That Nietzsche plays a central role in Allan Bloom's *The Closing of the American Mind* (1987) is beyond doubt. Whatever else in this book may be fuzzy and ill-defined, it is clear that Bloom defines his own position in opposition to Nietzsche's. My concern here is to determine the nature of that opposition. I will argue that Bloom's view of it is different from what his book originally suggests and that he offers one view for the people but a quite different one for the philosopher. In the interest of suggesting that we reject both of these views of Nietzsche, I will then offer what I believe would be Nietzsche's quite different view of the Bloom–Nietzsche opposition.

Nietzsche appears as the philosophical villain of Bloom's piece. We are told repeatedly that Nietzsche attacks, rejects, abandons, and sacrifices reason, replacing it with a call to war, chaos, and self-assertion (pp. 197–207). Even if Bloom refrained—which he does not (e.g., p. 221)—from suggesting that it led to the Nazis, his characterization of Nietzsche's thought would be sufficient to convince many readers that any movement heavily influenced by it should be fought at all costs.

On Bloom's account, one such movement is directed towards reform of the university by the inclusion of minority voices in the curriculum, and a greater openness to cultures other than our own. Bloom traces this American reform movement to Nietzsche's rejection of reason. Since he is very careless in his use of the word "reason," it is difficult to be sure that I am interpreting him correctly here. Bloom never says exactly what "reason" is, or explains the sense in which Nietzsche rejects it. But he seems to mean that Nietzsche denies that our faculty for reasoning can, all by itself, determine what is valuable. In other words, there are no truths in the realm of value that are independent of what human beings want. Bloom says of the view he attributes to Nietzsche: we "do not love a thing because it is good, it is good because we love it" (p. 197). Since values depend on our will, on what human beings want, we are creators of values rather than discoverers of the good. According to

Bloom, this Nietzschean position leads to cultural relativism—to the claim that any culture's values are as good as any other. Far from celebrating such relativism, Bloom thinks, Nietzsche rejected it and spent his life fighting it. However, since he had already rejected reason as a source of values, he contributed to what he wanted to fight—and to much worse—for that left him with no solution for nihilism except decisions of the will, value commitments, and the hope of a charismatic leader which Bloom claims Weber later developed from Nietzschean premises.

Bloom believes that we have absorbed both sides of Nietzsche's thought from the German intellectuals who brought to American shores the thought of those heavily influenced by Nietzsche, especially Freud and Weber. What we absorbed, he claims, was a watered-down Nietzscheanism, one which did not notice "the darker side of Freud and Weber, let alone the Nietzsche-Heidegger extremism lying somewhere beneath the surface" (p. 150). Nihilism was veiled by (and Continental angst transformed into) an "I'm o.k., you're o.k." American optimism. The disastrous result, Bloom contends, is that our students are relativists, as are most of their teachers (pp. 25–6). They sympathize with attacks on cultural imperialism because relativism has destroyed their faith in their own culture's values. According to Bloom, they also show great respect for those who are willing to use force to accomplish curricular reform. How are we to explain this? If no values are better than any others, whence comes this insistence on respecting other people's values? For Bloom, this is just the other side of Nietzsche's philosophy: his emphasis on value commitment as the only way to fill the void left by reason's flight from the scene of values (p. 201). We respect commitment, any commitment, because we have learned from Nietzsche that we have no recourse to reason, and that only commitment can save us from nihilism and disintegration.

I find Bloom's attempt to trace this movement to Nietzsche far-fetched. But I do not doubt its effectiveness for convincing many readers that no further argument is needed against opening up the curriculum, or in favor of faith in old-fashioned American values. Viewed in this light, Bloom appears to differ from Nietzsche in his insistence that there is a purely rational foundation for values. To counteract Nietzsche's corruption of American youth, Bloom calls us to return to the thought of our true forefathers—the Enlightenment philosophers such as John Locke—to affirm that the values upon which America was founded are based in reason; that all men are equal; that they have equal rights; and that democracy exists to serve the common good.

But this account of the difference between Bloom and Nietzsche is, I believe, mere facade and deception. A quite different picture emerges if we consider the history of philosophy and of the university Bloom offers very late in his book under the title "From Socrates' *Apology* to Heidegger's *Rektoratsrede*." Bloom concludes this section with the claim that the contemplation of Socrates is the most urgent academic task (p. 312). He believes that the university exists to make possible the life led by Socrates, the philosophical life; but that, as the case of Socrates shows, this life is in danger. "The events of Socrates' life, the problem he faced, represent what the philosopher as such must face," according to Bloom (p. 265).

The survival problem of philosophy, on Bloom's account, stems from the fact that only the philosopher is able to face up to the truth about life—the fact of death—which Bloom equates with the truth that there is no cosmic support for what we care about (p. 277). The people deal with the problem of death by believing in divine beings who offer the kind of cosmic support for what humans care about that the philosopher insists does not exist. The philosopher's lack of belief fills the people with the moral indignation that led to Socrates' execution. In denying what humans most need to believe in—the existence of the gods—Socrates brought down upon himself the people's wrath. From then on, goes Bloom's story, a major philosophical concern was to protect the life of philosophy. The ancient philosophers thus invented the "truth party": its name was political science. Its purpose was to figure out and say the kinds of things that needed to be said to protect the life of philosophy (pp. 275–6).

To protect the pursuit of truth, in short, the philosopher is required to lie—to engage in what Bloom calls "a gentle art of deception." The philosopher "loves the truth," he says, "That is an intellectual virtue. He does not love to tell the truth. That is a moral virtue" (p. 279). Philosophers would prefer to tell the truth if they could, but their survival depends on deception. According to Bloom, Socrates is quite obviously insincere in the *Apology* when he pretends belief in the gods and argues for the philosopher as good citizen. Aristotle is more persuasive, but no less deceptive, when he spends most of his *Ethics* speaking about the noble deeds that are the gentleman's specialty, not the philosopher's. Aristotle largely clarifies what the aristocrats practice; but he makes slight changes that point towards philosophy, to make it seem that philosophy is the ally of the aristocrat. According to Bloom, the practical policies of all philosophers have been the same, despite their great theoretical differences: "They practiced an art of writing that appealed to the prevailing moral taste of the regime in which they found themselves, but which could lead some astute readers outside of it into the Elysian Fields in which philosophers meet to talk" (p. 283).

At the risk of revealing my own lack of astuteness here, I must admit my difficulty in seeing how the conversations of these philosophers can avoid boredom, given Bloom's further insistence that their "inner teachings may be to all intents and purposes the same," despite the great differences in the form and content of their writings (p. 283). The "inner teachings," if I understand Bloom correctly, reduce to the claim that deception is necessary to protect the only thing philosophers really care about: the philosophical life, the Socratic life devoted to pursuing truth rather than possessing it. All of the great philosophical doctrines—the claims to metaphysical knowledge that Nietzsche exposed and criticized—are thus merely different attempts to deceive the powers that be into leaving philosophers alone to pursue the Socratic life.

Bloom interprets the Enlightenment philosophers who gave America its original political philosophy in the same way. Liberal democracy or bourgeois society was invented, he tells us, by a small group of men who wanted to protect reason (p. 293), that is, the Socratic life. In the time of the Enlightenment, philosophers changed allegiance from the aristocratic to the democratic party. They saw that they could protect their own freedom to live the philosophical life by inventing human equality, the rights of man, and the idea that democracy served the common good. "The philosophers, however, had no illusions about democracy," we are told. "They knew they were substituting one misunderstanding for another" (p. 289). For Bloom thinks these philosophers actually believed what he himself asserts, that "the real community of man . . . is the community of those who seek the truth," and that this is the "only real friendship, the only real common good" (p. 381). In other words, the old-fashioned American values Bloom originally portrays Nietzsche as threatening have no objective foundation or basis in reason after all. They are given the appearance of having such a foundation only by the philosophers' deception, which is directed towards protecting their own way of life.

If this is correct, Bloom's real disagreement with Nietzsche is not over reason's ability to provide a foundation for values, for Bloom agrees with him that reason cannot do this. On Bloom's account, the only thing the philosopher really values is the philosophical life; and it is difficult to believe that Bloom thinks this valuation is based on reason alone. It would be based on reason alone, according to the account of Bloom I have already given, only if philosophers loved philosophy because they perceived it to possess a goodness that is independent of their desires or preferences. But Bloom's description of philosophical experience leaves no doubt that the philosopher loves philosophy because of his desires and pleasures—because "his soul finds rest therein" (Bloom quotes from Maimonides), because of the intense pleasure it gives him to use his faculties and solve problems, and because it affords him pride, "more complete than that of any conqueror, for he surveys and possesses all" (p. 210).

The last quotation may produce some confusion, since it implies that the philosopher possesses enormous knowledge, whereas I have presented Bloom's philosopher in Socratic terms, as loving truth, but not claiming to possess it. This problem can be resolved by realizing that it is only as a natural scientist that Bloom's philosopher possesses knowledge. Bloom counts Thales as a *knower* because of his ability to predict an eclipse. He counts him as a *philosopher* because he is liberated from myth, i.e., from belief in the gods. This ability to live without the gods is what defines the philosophical life for Bloom. Only philosophers can live without the illusion of cosmic support for what we care about (p. 285). This again suggests that Bloom finds no foundation for the value of what he cares about—the life of philosophy—except the preferences of those who care about it.

We need not conclude from this, however, that Bloom thinks the philosophical life is no better than any other. He does in fact claim that only the philosophical life can, without contradiction, be affirmed as an end (p. 271). But he gives not a clue about how he would argue for this claim. The position on the value of the philosophical life suggested by his text is somewhat different: that it alone can be affirmed as valuable without deception. That is, only philosophers—those who devote their lives to pursuit of truth—can continue to value their lives in full knowledge of the fact that its value depends solely on their desires. To value their non-philosophical ways of life, on the other hand, the people need to believe in the gods: that is, they need to believe the lie that there is cosmic support for their way of life (p. 277).

If this is correct, then Bloom believes that Nietzsche told the truth when he denied that human values are based on reason, and also when he insisted that the gods do not exist, and that therefore human lives cannot have the value most of us believe them to have. Bloom seems to think that philosophers have always known these truths, but have kept quiet about them so they could manipulate the people's beliefs about the gods and values for the purpose of protecting the philosophical way of life. Bloom's real complaint against Nietzsche is that he blew the whistle on the whole philosophical tradition of lying to protect the philosophical life. This is why he claims that Nietzsche's virtue was not love of truth—i.e., love of philosophy, of the life devoted to truth—but intellectual honesty, the moral virtue of telling the truth, which Bloom insists has no place in the university, but only gets in the way (p. 261).

It would be unfair, however, to suggest that Bloom sets up Nietzsche as corruptor of America's youth simply because he spoke the truth. On my interpretation, Bloom has a second problem with Nietzsche: namely, that Nietzsche does not affirm the gulf Bloom finds between the philosophical life and any other kind of life, a gulf which would allow the philosophical life to escape unscathed from Nietzsche's critique of human values. For Bloom, the fact that Nietzsche does not give the philosophical life special status makes him a nihilist. If no other life can be honestly valued, and the philosophical life is no different from any other, then no life—the philosophical life included—can be honestly valued. We can now see a sense in which Bloom can honestly say that Nietzsche's sacrifice of reason leads to nihilism. For Bloom often uses the word "reason" as interchangeable with "philosophy." So Nietzsche sacrifices reason in the sense of denying a special value status to the philosophical life. And if he also shared Bloom's nihilism regarding lives not devoted to the pursuit of truth, he would have to admit that no kind of human life has value.

I see no reason to believe that Nietzsche does share Bloom's nihilism. The non-philosophical nobles of the first essay of the *Genealogy*, for instance, affirm the value of their lives; and Nietzsche does not seem to think they need the gods in order to do this. True, they have their gods; but Nietzsche seems to think they need them largely to express gratitude for their lives.

Nietzsche certainly does deny that reason alone can provide the basis for values. But this gives him plenty of philosophical company, and gives us no more reason to accuse Nietzsche of nihilism or relativism than so to accuse Hume and Hobbes. Nihilism can be found in Nietzsche's early works—for instance, *Human, All Too Human*. Loss of faith in the philosopher's ability, on the basis of reason alone, to know what we should value may well have led to Nietzsche's conclusion here that we need illusion in order to value life (*HA* 32). But this is not Nietzsche's contribution to the history of philosophy. It is the kind of conclusion his later works diagnose rather than endorse.

He subsequently diagnosed this particular move—the inference to nihilism from pure reason's inability to found our values—as a philosophical expression of the ascetic ideal, which is the priestly view that the life of self-denial is the highest human life. According to Nietzsche, this idealization of self-denial deprives human life of any intrinsic value, of any value as an end. It implies that life can have value only as a means, and indeed only as a means to its own negation. But Nietzsche denies that the end to which the ascetic makes life a means has any positive content. Such an end or goal is merely a negation—though it may be a disguised negation—of human life. Nietzsche therefore interprets the ascetic ideal as a nihilistic will directed against life in an act of imaginary or spiritual revenge. The idealization of self-denial, with its devaluation of human life, constitutes a spiritualized version of burning one's opponent in effigy, in which one's opponent is life itself.

Nietzsche interprets traditional or metaphysical philosophy as an expression of the ascetic ideal, I believe, because he thinks it depends on the assumption that the things of the highest value—knowledge, truth, virtue, philosophy—cannot depend on features of ordinary human life, such as the senses or desires. Knowledge had to be a priori, truth had to be correspondence to things in themselves, and values had to be based on reason alone, Nietzsche suggests, in order to keep what philosophers valued safe from contamination by what they did not value: the things of the natural world, of ordinary human life. Nietzsche would therefore diagnose Bloom's idea that nihilism follows from the denial that values can be founded on reason alone as a sign of Bloom's own commitment to the ascetic ideal.

Indeed, there is reason to believe that Nietzsche would find an even closer relation between Bloom and the ascetic ideal. I suggest that he would consider Bloom a more cynical version of those he discusses in the third treatise of the *Genealogy of Morality*, and calls the latest expression of the ascetic ideal. The thinkers who fit this description believe they are free from the ascetic ideal, for they have given up all its trappings: God, the other world, praise for virtues of denial. But they have done so, Nietzsche claims, because of their will to truth—because they consider truth more important than anything else: and precisely *that* is the latest expression of the ascetic ideal. This picture fits Bloom's philosophy perfectly. The philosopher, he claims, "only enjoys thinking and loves the truth. He therefore cannot be disabused. He cherishes no illusion that can crumble" (p. 277).

Nietzsche's response would be that if the philosopher loves the truth this much, there is still an illusion that can crumble: the illusion that there is no faith or value commitment here except to truth. Bloom's philosopher's commitment, he would say, is still to the ascetic ideal. He values the pursuit of truth because he sees in it a denial or negation of natural or ordinary human life.

Consider again what philosophical knowledge as such is for Bloom. It is knowledge that the gods do not exist, that there is no cosmic support for what we care about. What was most important to Thales, he suggests, was not his ability to predict the eclipse, but "seeing that the poetic or mythical accounts of the eclipses are false" (p. 271). Now how can this kind of knowledge be considered the point of human life? How can it be that for the sake of which human life is worth living? Nietzsche has an answer: as in the case of earlier versions of the ascetic ideal, the point of Bloom's valuation of philosophy is precisely to accord human life value only as a means to its own negation. Philosophy has no positive content for Bloom: it is pure negation of what he thinks ordinary humans believe, and need to believe. Bloom's philosopher cannot therefore value philosophy for its own sake. Behind Bloom's view of philosophy and its importance, his elitism, and his disdain for ordinary human life, Nietzsche would see not the self-affirmation of philosophy, but the nihilistic will of the ascetic ideal once again taking its revenge against life.

This is not to say that Nietzsche rejects the value of philosophy or the commitment to truth. He differs from Bloom on this issue insofar as he wants philosophy and truth to serve life—and he thinks that we therefore need to create a new ideal for philosophers. Truth itself cannot give us this ideal, but truths are certainly highly relevant to determining what ideal we need. Bloom's response to Nietzsche's call for a new ideal is to resort to scare tactics. He implies that philosophy can serve life only if it is co-opted for political purposes, as in the case of the Nazis.

I have been suggesting that Nietzsche can answer this charge by diagnosing Bloom's own position as an expression of the nihilistic ascetic ideal. It is not as if we have a choice: to pursue knowledge for its own sake or in the service of some foreign ideal. Nietzsche's claim (in the Third Essay of the *Genealogy*) is that the commitment to truth will always serve such an ideal in any case. The only question is whether we will invent a new ideal for the sake of which to live out our commitment to truth or remain stuck with the old ideal, the ascetic ideal.

I do not know if Nietzsche is right about this; but I take the example of Bloom as one small bit of evidence that he may be. In any case, I find this Nietzschean response to Bloom much more convincing than Bloom's scare tactics in relation to Nietzsche. If we must choose between creating a new ideal for both philosophers and non-philosophers or sitting back in our philosophical corners plotting strategies to protect our hides, Nietzsche's call for a new ideal does not sound so bad.

{ 7 }

Nietzsche's Misogyny

I want to begin by saying something about how I came to write this paper. I originally agreed to write it for a session of the North American Nietzsche Society on Nietzsche and Feminism, not because I knew what I wanted to say on the topic, but because I thought I should have something to say. I have been thinking and writing very sympathetically about Nietzsche for many years, during all of which I have considered myself a feminist. Yet many other people seem to believe that a Nietzschean feminist is a contradiction in terms—or at least close to that. Surely, I thought, I should be able to say something about why I do not.

At that point, however, I think my Nietzschean unconscious took over and asked: but why defend yourself if you can attack instead? Or that at least is how one might be tempted to interpret the question that seized me to begin exploring in this paper. It was not: how can I be a Nietzschean and a feminist? but rather: why hasn't a feminist form of Nietzsche's philosophy been developed in the Anglo-American academic, and especially the philosophical, world?

The two thinkers of the last century who rival Nietzsche in importance and scope—namely, Marx and Freud—have given rise to Anglo-American forms of Feminism. Why hasn't Nietzsche? It is hardly plausible that Nietzsche offers feminists nothing on a par with Freud's account of gender or Marx's account of the role of economic factors. Surely power and empowerment, of which Nietzsche is the great theorist, are extremely important concerns to feminists. And his analysis of resentment should be useful to feminists for understanding much of what has been said and done against women.

I do not want to deny that individual feminists have shown an interest in Nietzsche, sometimes even signs of his influence on them, nor that Nietzschean forms of feminism have been developed by French feminists and others working under the influence of French post-structuralism. But among feminists working in the Anglo-American philosophical tradition, there seems to be no widespread interest in Nietzsche's work—nothing comparable, for instance, to the interest in Nietzsche one now finds among those doing ethics in that tradition, and certainly no general recognition of Nietzsche as a resource for feminist analysis.

I had hoped to use this paper to run through a number of possible explanations for this state of affairs until I arrived at the one I still consider most promising: that Nietzsche is a self-proclaimed immoralist whereas feminism seems to be an essentially moral position. However, I never got that far; for I was waylaid by the interesting material that emerged when I began looking at the first explanation that occurred to me, namely, that perhaps Anglo-American feminists have been too put off by Nietzsche's misogyny to take his thought seriously. And that is how I found myself writing a paper on Nietzsche's misogyny.

This came as somewhat of a surprise, for I have always taken Nietzsche's misogyny for granted, but never considered it very important or interesting. After all, misogyny distinguishes Nietzsche from few other male writers of his time, and in contrast to, for instance, Freud's phallocentric prejudices masquerading as science, Nietzsche's misogynistic comments have probably done little actual harm to women. His nasty comments about women have always seemed to me a reflection not of his basic ideas, but of his understandable, if human, all-too-human need for revenge against Lou Salomé. And Nietzsche himself gives us the theoretical resources to understand them in this way.

On the other hand, some interpreters claim to find a connection between Nietzsche's misogyny and some of his other ideas—his celebration of the will to power, for instance—and I myself have always been bothered by his most vitriolic comments on women, the so-called "truths about woman as such" Nietzsche puts forward in the closing sections of *Beyond Good and Evil*'s Part VII. The "Seven Little Sayings on Woman" of *BGE* 237[1] seem tastelessly, almost obscenely, nasty. These include, "How the longest boredom flees, when a man comes crawling on his knees." And "Science and old age at length give weak virtue, too, some strength." Even worse is the insult of section 238 that woman is to be conceived of as "a possession, as property that can be locked, as something predestined for service and achieving her perfection in that." Nietzsche also seems to express contempt for feminism throughout these sections on woman, and to present anti-feminism as central to his thought. So I decided to use this paper as an opportunity to finally look carefully at this material, to see how bad, and how connected to his other ideas, it really is.

What I discovered is that I had underestimated Nietzsche—certainly not for the first time—and that the misogyny of Part VII of *BGE* is not the simple and straightforward matter it appears to be. I will not be able to examine here the range of passages I would have to consider to make a claim about Nietzsche's

---

[1] I follow Kaufmann's translations of both *BGE* and *GM*, but have made several changes based on the Colli-Montinari *Studienausgabe: Friedrich Nietzsche* (Berlin: de Gruyter, 1980). See the following note for one such case.

misogyny as such. Confining myself to *Beyond Good and Evil* VII, I shall argue that the misogyny exhibited there is on the level of sentiment, *not belief*, and that it is used by Nietzsche to illustrate points he is trying to make about philosophy and the will to truth. I also want to suggest—though I will not have time to present the full argument—that we interpret *BGE* VII's comments on feminism not as a rejection of feminism, but as a challenge to feminists to exhibit virtues comparable to what Nietzsche exhibits in dealing with his misogyny.

Part VII of *Beyond Good and Evil* is titled "Our Virtues." "Our virtues?" it begins.

> It is probable that we, too, still have our virtues, although in all fairness they will not be the simpleminded and foursquare virtues for which we hold our grandfathers in honor—and at arm's length. We Europeans of the day after tomorrow, we first-born of the twentieth century—with all our dangerous curiosity, our multiplicity and art of disguises, our mellow, and, as it were, sweetened cruelty in spirit and senses—*if* we should have virtues, we shall presumably have only virtues that have learned to get along best with our most secret and cordial inclinations, with our most ardent needs. Well, then, let us look for them in our labyrinths—where as is well known, all sorts of things lose themselves, all sorts of things are lost for good.

Part VII thus sets out to search for *our* virtues—Nietzsche's, of course, and the philosophers to whom the book is addressed—the same ones who are asked in its first section: "*What* is it in us that wants truth?"

This question—probably the leading question of *Beyond Good and Evil*—does not receive its full answer until the sections immediately preceding the statement of Nietzsche's "truths" about "woman as such" at the end of Part VII. If we wish to understand these so-called "truths" in their context, it should occur to us that their placement is very strange unless they are intimately connected to what Nietzsche is trying to tell us about both virtue and the will to truth, and that perhaps, as I want to suggest, his "truths" about woman constitute a labyrinth in which we are meant to find the threads of Nietzsche's own virtue.

Beyond Good and Evil 227 leaves little doubt as to what Nietzsche considers "our" main virtue. Honesty, he says, is the "virtue from which we cannot get away, we free spirits," and he calls upon us to "work on it with all our malice and love and not weary of 'perfecting' ourselves in *our* virtue, the only one left us," so that its splendor may "one day remain spread out like a gilded blue mocking evening light over this aging culture and its musty and gloomy seriousness."

So I began to wonder if Nietzsche's truths about "woman as such" could be designed to illustrate for us the virtue of honesty. He certainly seems to be attempting honesty when he prefaces them with the well-known warning that "these are after all only—*my* truths." However, it is unclear exactly what this is supposed to mean. If Nietzsche claims that his comments about woman are true, he can't sensibly claim that they are true only for him. So the warning that these are "only *my* truths" may be Nietzsche's way of disclaiming the belief that his misogynistic comments are true. I think we find a great deal of evidence for this interpretive hypothesis if we look at the warning's immediate context. On the issue of man and woman, Nietzsche writes,

> a thinker cannot relearn but only finish learning, only discover ultimately how this is "settled in him." At times we find certain solutions of problems that inspire strong faith in *us*; some call them henceforth *their* "convictions." Later—we see them as only steps to self-knowledge, sign-posts to the problem we *are*—rather to the great stupidity we are, to our spiritual *fatum*, to what is *unteachable* very 'down deep.' (*BGE* 231)

This is immediately followed by the warning in question:

> After this abundant civility that I have just evidenced in relation to myself I shall perhaps be permitted more readily to state a few truths about "woman as such"—assuming that it is known from the outset how very much these are after all only—*my* truths.

In other words, that these are "only [his] truths" should already be clear to us from the comments that evidence Nietzsche's "abundant civility" in relation to himself. Those comments told us that what thinkers have to say about man and woman merely express their convictions, and that convictions express the "great stupidity" they are, and are only "steps to self-knowledge, sign-posts to the problem [they] are." Nietzsche thus admits in effect that his so-called "truths" about woman as such are really expressions of the great stupidity he is, and are therefore more likely to produce self-knowledge—if understood and analyzed appropriately—than knowledge of the world (in this case, of women).

At the very least, Nietzsche is letting us know that he is not claiming that his comments on woman are true. Some interpreters may find nothing puzzling in this, for they think that Nietzsche denies that any beliefs are true. But I have argued at length elsewhere that Nietzsche overcame this kind of nihilism in his later works (Clark 1990: 63–125) and I can find no other basis he would have for denying that making an assertion involves putting it forward as true. So I am left with the puzzle of what his point could be when he makes assertions about woman after letting us know that he does not consider them true.

I start with the observation that Nietzsche would be able to use these assertions to express his feelings towards woman—for instance, his anger and resentment—even if he does not consider them true. The use of assertions we do not believe in an attempt to hurt those we love or are dependent upon is hardly uncommon among human beings, especially when in particularly childish moods. This suggests a way to make sense of Nietzsche's "Seven Little Sayings on Woman," which seem so unlike anything else he wrote and have always reminded me of children calling each other names and sticking out their tongues at each other. That, I now see, suits them perfectly to play the role of easily recognized expressions of resentment.

Who could fail to recognize the resentment in, for instance: "How the longest boredom flees, when a man comes crawling on his knees"? And since these "little sayings" do not even have the grammatical form of assertions about woman, it is clear that we cannot simply read them as Nietzsche's beliefs about woman. Instead, we must arrive at these beliefs through a process of interpretation which requires us to consider what his point is in reciting for us these sayings about woman. (It is not even clear whose "little sayings" they are; they might be simply common sayings that *BGE* 237 in effect quotes.)[2] Nietzsche's "Little Sayings on Woman" can therefore serve to warn us that his "truths" about "woman as such," the ones that do have the form of assertions about woman, also require interpretation, and that they might also be expressions of resentment disguised as beliefs. Nietzsche's "truths" about woman might serve to exhibit for us (and to express) his misogynistic feelings, even though he is honest enough to admit that the assertions these feelings inspire are not really true.

I would find this strategy for interpreting Nietzsche's misogynistic comments problematic—because too open to abuse—if it required us to deny that Nietzsche means or believes what he actually says about women. But I think the interpretation I have suggested can be reformulated so that it avoids this problem. It requires only that we read Nietzsche very carefully and distinguish what he actually asserts from what the reader is likely to conclude (erroneously) from his assertions.

When Nietzsche asserts that woman does not *want* truth, that "her great art is the lie, her highest concern is mere appearance and beauty" (BGE 232), for instance, most readers will assume he means that women do not want truth. In fact, however, he is writing not about women, but about "woman as such," which he also calls "the eternal feminine." He is referring to the feminine

---

[2] That Nietzsche is in effect quoting sayings about women is suggested by the fact that unlike other sections of the book, *BGE* 237 is given a title (namely, "Seven Little Sayings on Woman"). I owe this observation to Peter Burgard, who also pointed out to me that Kaufmann's translation of *Sprüchlein* as "epigram" (rather than "little saying") does not adequately capture the diminutive form of the original. Because of the association of Nietzsche himself with "epigrams," Kaufmann's translation also makes it easier to assume that the point of these sayings is to express Nietzsche's own beliefs. I do not find it plausible, however, that Nietzsche is simply quoting these sayings from the surrounding culture without any suggestion that he accepts them too, because not making it clear that he is simply quoting such nasty sayings sets up a presumption that he accepts them. We can explain why Nietzsche would set up this presumption, while at the same time leaving clues that we cannot interpret his sayings as straightforward expressions of his own beliefs, if we interpret them instead as expressions of his feelings.

essence, a social construction that individual women need not exemplify. The German that Kaufmann translates as "woman as such" is *"das Weib an sich"* or woman in herself (or itself). Given *BGE*'s central claim that *das Ding an sich* (*BGE* 16) is a contradiction in terms, Nietzsche's use of the phrase *"das Weib an sich"* cannot be accidental. He is probably suggesting that our idea of the "eternal feminine" also involves a contradiction in terms and therefore that no woman could really exemplify it. But I must leave this consideration for another time. In any case, though we might want to disagree with Nietzsche about what the common understanding of femininity involves, once we see that his truths about woman as such are about this construction rather than about individual women—especially if he thinks it involves a contradiction in terms—it is difficult to read them as either misogynistic or anti-feminist.

BGE 238's claim that woman must be conceived as a possession is a slightly more complicated matter. Nietzsche actually claims that this is how woman must always be thought of by any man who has "depth, in his spirit as well as in his desires, and also that depth of benevolence that is capable of severity and hardness and is often confused with them." It seems to me clear that he is talking about how such a man must think of individual women insofar as he thinks of them as exemplifications of *das Weib an sich*, of the eternal feminine. This has no implications for how Nietzsche must think of *women* given his skepticism about such essences.

But why does Nietzsche think that a man of depth and benevolence must think of woman as a possession? Contrary to some interpretations of this passage (e.g., Schutte 1984: 162, 178–80), I find no evidence in it, nor in any section of *BGE* VII, that Nietzsche thinks a patriarchal structure is necessary for the existence of higher culture.[3] He does say it is worth pondering how necessary and even humanly desirable it was that the Greeks became more severe against woman as "their culture increased along with the extent of their power" (*Kraft*). I think the emphasis here is on the increase in the ability of males to use force against women.

This passage begins by calling "shallow" those who deny "the most abysmal antagonism" between man and woman, and the necessity of an "eternally hostile tension." I take the claim to be that such eternal hostility exists between men and women insofar as they see themselves as embodiments of the eternal masculine and feminine. So it makes sense for Nietzsche to say that a man of depth and benevolence must think of embodiments of the eternal feminine as

---

[3] In fact, he suggests early in Part VII (*BGE* 223) that given our "historical sense" and consequent willingness to dissect history to study the "costumes" of culture—i.e., the "moralities, articles of faith, tastes in arts, and religion"—perhaps nothing today has any future except our laughter. Among the "articles of faith" which have been dissected by those with a "historical sense" and which Nietzsche here suggests may have no future must certainly be included the naturalness and justice of a patriarchal structure.

property, if Nietzsche thinks, as I assume he does, that this would be the best protection available to those cast in the role of the eternal feminine against the worst abuses of male hostility and power. He may be wrong about this, of course, but he neither says nor implies that women should accept for themselves the status of property. Therefore, I do not see his claim here as anti-feminist.

In fact, if we read Part VII carefully, we will see that nothing in it asserts or entails that women should not seek their own enlightenment and emancipation from traditional sex roles and power structures. Nietzsche's most explicit claim against such attempts is that they involve a "corruption of the instincts" (*BGE* 233) and a loss of "the sense for the ground on which one is most certain of victory" (*BGE* 239). Readers can be expected to conclude from such claims that Nietzsche is against the emancipation of women, and that he thinks he has reason to be.

But careful readers of Part VII will find that its earlier sections give grounds for making exactly parallel arguments against those who seek truth, and that Nietzsche nevertheless encourages their search. I will consider his claims about the will to truth in some detail in order to exhibit the parallel I have suggested that Nietzsche sets up between truth-seekers and feminists, and to answer another question I am sure many will wish to pose. This question is: why, if I am at all right about his actual assertions, did Nietzsche go out of his way to make his comments on woman in these passages appear misogynist and anti-feminist?

The two sections immediately preceding *BGE* 231's warning that these are "only *my* truths" finally answer the book's initial question: *what* is it in us that wants truth? *BGE* 229 tells us that "almost everything we call 'higher culture' is based on the spiritualization of cruelty, on its becoming more profound: this is my proposition." When applied to those who seek knowledge, this proposition becomes the claim that "any insistence on profundity and thoroughness" in matters of knowledge, i.e., any will to truth, "is a violation, a desire to hurt the basic will of the spirit which unceasingly strives for the apparent and superficial."

BGE 230 seeks to clarify this claim. It presents the desire for theoretical knowledge as an expression of the will to power.[4] The theoretician originally wants not truth, but to "appropriate the foreign," to "assimilate the new to the old, to simplify the manifold and to overlook or repulse whatever is totally contradictory." What is wanted, Nietzsche summarizes, is growth, "or, more precisely, the feeling of growth, the feeling of increased power." While intellectual appropriation may happen upon truth, it is too easily satisfied with a sense of mastery to exhibit a will to truth, i.e., an "insistence on profundity and thoroughness" in matters of knowledge. So it should be no surprise that Nietzsche

---

[4] See Clark (1990: 205–44) for my interpretation of Nietzsche's claims about the will to power.

thinks the will that leads to theorizing is served by an apparently opposite drive, which produces "a suddenly erupting decision in favor of ignorance, a satisfaction with the dark, with the limiting horizons, a Yea and Amen to ignorance—all of which is necessary in proportion to a spirit's power to appropriate, its 'digestive capacity.'"

But, then, to repeat Nietzsche's original question: if philosophers can be so easily satisfied with the dark and the superficial, what in them wants truth? The answer, given in *BGE* 231, is that it is their cruelty, their will to power turned against itself. To develop a will to truth, Nietzsche is claiming, the spirit has to deprive itself of what it most wants: a sense of power or mastery of the world. It has to discipline itself to give up what it wants to believe—because of the sense of power belief would give—for the sake of what it has reason to believe.

In so disciplining itself, according to Nietzsche's theory, the spirit still gets a sense of mastery, but it is mastery of the self rather than of the world.

But if the basic will of the spirit aims at mastery of the world (which I take to be equivalent to the non-self), how can it give that up for the sake of mastery of itself? I think Nietzsche's answer is that it can do so only if it interprets its power over self as power over the world. He claims, most explicitly in his *GM*, that the will to truth is the latest expression of the ascetic ideal, that thinkers have been able to commit themselves to giving up what they want to believe for the sake of what they have reason to believe only under the auspices of the ascetic ideal.[5]

The ascetic ideal is a life-devaluing ideal, which gives priests and philosophers a sense of mastering the material and temporal world precisely because it devalues that world, by treating it as a mere instrument or expression of the spiritual and eternal world with which contemplative types identify. According to Nietzsche's story, however, this same ideal finally forbids itself the "lie involved" in belief in God, in metaphysics and in any spiritual or eternal world, thus leaving us with what *BGE* 230 calls the "strange and insane task" of translating human beings back into nature, of interpreting their activities, virtues, and value in completely naturalistic terms. Part VII carries out this task in its account of honesty as an expression of cruelty.

Nietzsche calls "insane" the task of understanding philosophers and their honesty in naturalistic terms, I think, because he believes that the will to power was able to become a will to truth only insofar as honesty or truthfulness was interpreted in ascetic terms, as the overcoming of nature. The naturalistic interpretation of honesty to which truthfulness itself leads therefore involves the "insane" task of undercutting its own psychological support or attacking the ground on which it has been standing.

---

[5] See Clark (1990: 159–203), for my account of Nietzsche's claims concerning the ascetic ideal.

Truthful philosophers are therefore in a position even worse than the one Nietzsche ascribes to feminists, that of abandoning the ground on which they are most sure of victory. Philosophers probably abandoned the ground on which they were most sure of victory, on Nietzsche's view, when they abandoned God and metaphysics. And now he expects them to admit that their truthfulness is just a matter of their willingness to be cruel to themselves. This surely involves at least as much corruption of the instincts that have protected and furthered the interest of contemplative types—whom Nietzsche describes in *GM* (III:10) as originally living under a tremendous "*oppression of valuation*"—as feminism involves a corruption of the instincts that have protected and furthered the interests of those forced to play the role of the "eternal feminine."

Yet, far from encouraging us to abandon our truthfulness, Nietzsche calls on us to perfect it, in the passage on "our virtue" I quoted earlier. But how can we perfect our honesty without the support of the ascetic ideal? I have elsewhere interpreted Nietzsche's *Genealogy* as claiming that we need a new ideal for our truthfulness to serve (Clark 1990: 193–203). Some of the thinking behind Nietzsche's claim is revealed by *BGE* 227, the passage on "our virtue." Here Nietzsche suggests that, to get the help we will need in maintaining and perfecting the virtue of honesty, we dispatch to the assistance of our honesty "whatever we have in us of devilry . . . our subtlest, most disguised, most spiritual will to power and overcoming of the world . . . let us come to the assistance of our 'gods' with our 'devils.'" In other words, honesty needs the support of a sense of power over the world, and perfecting it therefore requires new sources for the sense of power philosophers previously acquired from devaluing the world under the influence of the ascetic ideal.

One way of achieving a sense of power discussed in *BGE* 230 is the "by no means unproblematic readiness of the spirit to deceive other spirits and to dissimulate in front of them." In this, Nietzsche writes, "the spirit enjoys the multiplicity and craftiness of its masks, it also enjoys the feeling of its security behind them: after all, it is surely its Protean arts that defend and conceal it best." If the interpretation I have offered is on the right track, Nietzsche must think of himself as employing precisely this strategy when he conceals from us what he is actually asserting about women and feminism—while leaving it fully accessible to the careful reader. Nietzsche thus illustrates for us what it means to bring our "devils" to the support of our "gods," and thus the kind of support he thinks the will to truth will need once we completely abandon the ascetic ideal.

In playing this game of concealment, Nietzsche is not, or not only, having fun at the expense of women and feminists. Misogyny is a particularly good issue with which to illustrate *BGE*'s claim about the future of our honesty, our will to truth. By expressing misogynistic sentiments, Nietzsche shows us that he has an interest in believing things about women that would justify those sentiments. What would justify such sentiments is precisely his "truths" about "woman as such," if they were truths about women. We can therefore interpret Nietzsche's comments about "woman as such" in Part VII of *BGE* as overcoming what he would like to believe about women, out of his commitment to truth.

If this interpretation is correct, Nietzsche's comments on "woman as such" *exhibit* his honesty at work more clearly than anything else in *BGE*, because nothing else shows us so clearly the conflict between what he would like to believe and what he knows he has reason to believe. So Nietzsche can bring out here, more vividly than he could otherwise, the issue of what allows him to be honest, to overcome his desire to believe, given his rejection of the ascetic ideal, all moral posturing, and all ascetic conceptions of virtue. This is, I think, the major role of play in Nietzsche—not a substitute for truth, as post-modernists sometimes seem to think, but an activity that supports truthfulness in its non-ascetic reincarnation that Nietzsche here attempts to promote. Play can also function as a sublimation of resentment, which Nietzsche also exhibits here.

In conclusion, let me make clear that I am not saying that Nietzsche is a feminist, or denying that he had problems with nineteenth-century feminism and would have them with contemporary feminism. The issue for him would still be, as *BGE* 232 suggests, whether women really want enlightenment about themselves, whether we can will it. This means: whether we are willing to understand ourselves and our virtues in completely naturalistic terms and to promote feminism without the help of the ascetic ideal and what Nietzsche calls "moral word tinsels" (*BGE* 230). Whether or not Nietzsche is anti-feminist ultimately comes down to whether a feminism beyond good and evil can and will be developed.[6] This is an issue for the future. But feminists interested in this possibility could do worse than to look both seriously and with a sense of humor at Nietzsche's attempt to turn resentment into laughter in *Beyond Good and Evil* VII.

---

[6] One attempt in that direction is Wendy Brown, "Feminist Hesitations, Postmodern Exposures," *differences: A Journal of Feminist Cultural Studies* 3, no. 1 (1990): 63–84. Others are surely possible, e.g., ones that do not depend on a post-modernist critique of truth.

{ 8 }

On Queering Nietzsche

Originally presented to the Society for Gay and Lesbian Philosophy in 1997, this paper was a response to papers by Kevin Hill and Tamsin Lorraine. Their papers raised complicated issues: how to "queer" Nietzsche, how to understand him, whether the tradition of postmodern French Nietzscheans is helpful to gays and lesbians, and/or helpful for understanding Nietzsche. In my paper, I respond to these issues and doing so leads me to say things about Nietzsche's relation to homosexuality that I had not quite seen before and that, as far as I know, had not been discussed by others. Two relatively common views of Nietzsche in relation to homosexuality are that he was anti-gay and that he was gay. In this paper I argue against both views (or, in the case of the latter view, at least that we lack sufficient evidence).

Let me begin with what was for me the most basic issue, concerning the very idea of "queering Nietzsche." I began considering how to do it without a clear idea of what it meant. My first stab at its meaning, and I think this coincides with Kevin Hill's understanding (Hill 1997), is that it is a matter of looking at Nietzsche's work in a way that makes it of particular interest to gays, lesbians, bi- and transsexuals, or to thinkers interested in issues that are of particular concern to these groups. On the one hand, showing that Nietzsche was gay would be one way, though not the only or even the main way, to do this. On the other hand, however, whether Nietzsche was gay might be considered completely irrelevant. Eve Sedgwick's (1990) pioneering attempt to queer Nietzsche in *The Epistemology of the Closet*, for instance, does not seem so much about Nietzsche's own sexuality, but about the character of his ideas. Sedgwick thinks that his writings do something with sexuality that should be of particular interest to what Tamsin Lorraine (1997) calls "queer subjects"—which I understand as subjects who do not perceive or understand their own sexuality in culturally standard ways. Nietzsche might have to be a "queer subject" to write about sexuality in this way, but that does not mean that he was gay. In any case, the more I thought about this issue, the more I came to think of queering Nietzsche as a matter of revealing or getting at ideas that show him to be a queer subject, and/or that show his ideas to be of particular interest to other queer subjects, to those who do not think about their own sexuality, or sexuality in general, in "straight" or mainstream ways. (It must be admitted, however, that what is considered "mainstream" has certainly changed since I wrote this paper.) I think this is probably in line with how Tamsin Lorraine and Eve Sedgwick understand the project. I am less sure that it is in line with Kevin Hill's understanding.

Certainly both Hill and Lorraine agree with Sedgwick's general approach to queering Nietzsche in the sense that they both focus on the character of his ideas and not on whether Nietzsche was gay. But they offer quite contrasting views of why Nietzsche's ideas should be of particular interest to gays and other queers. To Hill, it is because Nietzsche shows us the dangers of the closet. Many of the problematic features of Nietzsche's work can be explained, Hill thinks, if we take him to be a closeted homosexual extracting revenge from his society for the fact that his sexual orientation could not be received with respect. Tamsin Lorraine, in contrast, finds Nietzsche of more positive interest because she thinks his idea of eternal recurrence gives us a way of conceiving of, and perhaps suggestions for embodying, queer subjectivity. In particular, I take it, she thinks that eternal recurrence gives us a way of overcoming resentment and other strategies of passive/reactive living and becoming active, creative livers of our own lives. There is undoubtedly something to this, but I must admit that I do not understand well Lorraine's suggestions concerning how Nietzsche's ideas are particularly helpful to queers, probably because of something I share with Kevin Hill: a belief in the faultiness of the major ideas of the postmodern French Nietzscheans whose ideas form the background of her paper. Hill and I aren't in complete agreement, however. We agree that the views associated with Nietzsche by way of postmodernists are faulty, but he is much more willing to ascribe these ideas to Nietzsche than I am.[1] In fact, even though

---

[1] Consider, for example, the first two paragraphs of Hill's paper:
"In this paper, I will argue that Nietzsche's view of culture, communication and language is flawed. This view, in turn, has inspired various postmodern *aporiae*, the problem of shared standards, of cross-cultural norms, of intercultural understanding, the situatedness of Reason and its context-dependent, interest-relative, power-laden character. While Nietzsche's account of the perspectival character of the cognitive capacities and practices that generate these difficulties is roughly right, he often (though not always) draws skeptical conclusions from them that depend upon a faulty conception of communication. Nietzsche seems committed to the claim that communication between significantly different perspectives, and hence negotiation between significantly different kinds of agents and communities (which will often have very divergent interests) is for all practical purposes impossible. I believe that the genealogy of this claim is Nietzsche's own unwillingness to communicate clearly or to reveal even to himself those aspects of his own being namely, his sexual orientation that he justifiably believed could not be received with respect by his own community. *Ressentiment* over his fate served then as the affective foundation for his analytic of power. If critique and genealogy undermine the cognitive and affective

I share many of Hill's background assumptions about both Nietzsche and philosophy, I found that I could agree with very little of his paper. I found myself more in agreement with Tamsin Lorraine—at least with her title idea that Nietzsche is in flight from Oedipal masculinity—even though our background assumptions and basic orientations in philosophy seem to have little in common. So what we have here may be a test case for communication across philosophical cultures, one kind of cultural difference with which Nietzsche was particularly concerned. But I am not sure how to conduct the test. So I have concentrated here on what is much easier: trying to get at my disagreements with Hill, whose background assumptions I largely share. I will come back to Lorraine's paper at the end in the hopes of getting at where we can see commonalities and differences, stemming from what I believe to be our very different cultures.

Was Nietzsche Gay?

Kevin Hill claims that he was, whereas I have no idea. I am not even sure what Hill is claiming. That Nietzsche wanted to have sex with men? Hill's account of Nietzsche's interaction with Ludwig von Scheffler may be evidence of that.[2] However, I assume, perhaps in my Freudian naïveté, that all men want, at least at some time or other, to have sex with other men. So to say that Nietzsche was gay must be to say something more, probably either that he wanted, whatever he might have thought, to have sex with men to the exclusion of, or at least in preference to, sex with women, or that he chose to identify himself

---

presuppositions of Nietzsche's claims about objectivity and equality, the way remains open to renew modernism rather than transcend it."

"Furthermore, our democratic interests are in tension with Nietzsche's ethical perfectionism and his esoterism. These latter, Nietzsche thinks, are in some sense demanded by the human condition, in the same way that a bourgeois economist might claim that exploitation is demanded by the human condition—to which Marx replies that this is the human condition under a certain regime which might be abolished. Similarly, Nietzsche's understanding of the human condition, I believe, presupposes a certain regime which might be abolished, but whose abolition he can't really envision, because he has internalized it. Nietzsche's attitude toward drives, instincts, etc., to wit, that they should neither be extirpated nor indulged, but sublimated through a project of self-perfection and self-overcoming, derives, I believe, from his having had homosexual desires whose social stigma he had partially internalized and partially repudiated. Nietzsche's conception of self-overcoming seems to involve both an element of asceticism (thus endorsing the stigma) as well as a repudiation of stigma (being 'beyond'). Hence it seems to him that the chaos of drives itself cries out for sublimation, self-fashioning, self-overcoming. But if we contrast a drive which is not stigmatized, or which is only partially stigmatized (eating, for example) then the whole sense of there being a deep problem involved with the human condition which requires something radical be done with/to the self looks questionable; what should I do with the fact that I periodically have to eat? I eat. Simple as that." (reprinted with Hill's permission).

[2] Hill infers Nietzsche's homosexuality from von Scheffler's account of a meeting with Nietzsche. See, for example, Gilman (1987: 71–5). See also Köhler (2002) for an argument that Nietzsche was homosexual.

with those with such exclusive or preferential desires. In claiming that Nietzsche was gay, Hill is not making a claim about Nietzsche's sexual/political self-identification, so I assume the claim is about his exclusive or preferential sexual desire for men. Perhaps something weaker would do for his purposes, however: that Nietzsche wanted to have sex with men, that this was an important part of his psycho-sexual make-up, and that because he couldn't admit his desires to himself, he acted out his conflicts in his philosophy, being drawn to philosophical views concerning communication and legislation of values that both reflected his unconscious perception of his situation and gave him consolation for it.

The main point I would make about this is that, as I think he would agree, Kevin Hill has not provided much in the way of evidence that Nietzsche's sexual desire was exclusively or preferentially directed towards men, or even that such desire played a large role in his psychic economy. Even if the von Scheffler incidents show that he wanted to have sex with a male student—which I doubt—it surely does not tell us very much about Nietzsche's sexuality. Not, I hasten to add, that I would be surprised if it turned out that Nietzsche was gay. That speculation seems, at the very least, a more plausible explanation for the relative absence in Nietzsche's life of romantic relations with women than the one we find in Ronald Hayman's biography: that Nietzsche's "sexual drive must have been abnormally low" (1980: 64).

If Nietzsche Was Gay, Did He Lack Knowledge of This?

My serious disagreement with Hill begins with this second question: assuming for the sake of argument that Nietzsche was gay, even in the weaker sense that sexual desire for men played an important part in his psycho-sexual make-up, is it likely that he did not know it? Whereas Hill finds this plausible, I do not. Freud may not have been right about very much, at least not very much that he didn't take from Nietzsche, but I think he was right about Nietzsche's incomparable self-knowledge, which he considered, according to his biographer Ernest Jones, a greater self-knowledge than any man who had ever lived or was ever likely to live (Jones 1955: 385). Or as Eve Sedgwick puts it in more contemporary terms: "one never does well to bet the mortgage money" on Nietzsche's self-ignorance (1990: 155)—warnings against blithely pitting our own self-knowledge, much less our knowledge of Nietzsche, against his self-knowledge.

I am not denying Hill's claim that we can learn something about Nietzsche's sexuality from his writings. In fact, Nietzsche pretty clearly invites us to do just that. According to *Beyond Good and Evil* 75, "the degree and kind of a human being's sexuality reaches up into the pinnacle of his [or her] spirit." Since his writings are the most obvious expression of Nietzsche's spirit, this really is an invitation to ask: what kind and degree of sexuality is present and/or exhibited in Nietzsche's writings, and, specifically, in *Beyond Good and Evil*? This book begins with, and is plausibly seen as set up on the basis of, a sexual metaphor. "Supposing truth is a female," it begins: "what? Are there not good grounds for the suspicion that philosophers, insofar as they were dogmatists, have been very inexpert about women? That the gruesome seriousness, the clumsy obtrusiveness with which they have usually approached truth so far have been inept and inapt methods for winning a female's heart?" In other words, philosophers so far have been "clumsy lovers" (Pippin 2001), and Nietzsche thinks he knows better how to win a female's heart. This means, of course, that he knows better how to approach truth. Nietzsche might have dropped his opening metaphor here, and proceeded to show philosophers how to approach truth without any reference to females. But he doesn't. The whole book is permeated with this metaphor of seduction: his exhibition of how to approach truth is interwoven throughout with a development of this metaphor of how to win a female's heart. If we keep in mind the claim of *BGE* 75 that the "degree and kind of a human being's sexuality reaches up into the ultimate pinnacle of his spirit," it is hard to avoid the idea that in showing us how to win a female's heart, the book aims to exhibit the degree and kind of Nietzsche's sexuality.

Of course, the whole thing could just be heterosexual bravado, designed to protect himself from knowledge of his real sexual desire. One factor that makes this seem implausible to me is what Nietzsche actually wrote about homosexuality. If he really were the J. Edgar Hoover of philosophers, it seems to me very unlikely that he could have written about Greek homosexuality in the way he did. Consider from one of Nietzsche's early works, *Human, All Too Human*, a passage called "A culture of Men" (in the sense of "males"):

> Greek culture of the classical era was a culture of men. As regards women, Pericles says it all in his funeral oration: they are at their best when men talk about them as little as possible.—The erotic relationship of the men with the youths was, to a degree we can no longer comprehend, the sole and necessary presupposition of all male education (somewhat in the way in which with us all higher education was for a long time introduced to women only through love-affairs and marriage); all the practical idealism of the Hellenic nature threw itself upon this relationship, and young people have probably never since been treated with so much attention and kindness or so completely with a view towards enhancing their best qualities as they were in the sixth and fifth century—in accordance with Hölderlin's fine maxim "for the mortal gives of his best when loving." The greater the regard paid to this relationship the less was paid to social intercourse with women: considerations of child-bearing and sensual pleasure—that was all that counted; there was no spiritual intercourse, not even an actual love affair. (*HA* 259)

This passage exhibits a matter of fact and sympathetic attitude towards Greek male homosexuality: Nietzsche sees its benefits but also, at least to some degree, has a sense of its cost: the exclusion of women from culture, the relegation of woman to mere nature. Of course, those who assume that Nietzsche was a misogynist, as I do not (see Clark 1994b, paper 7 in this volume), will assume that he considers the exclusion of woman an advantage. In that case, however, the passage still serves my purpose here: to indicate that Nietzsche did not write about homosexuality the way one would expect from one unaware of his own desires. The most important point I gather from this passage is that Nietzsche does not see any essential opposition between hetero- and homosexuality, that he does not view male homosexuality as a particular kind of sexuality, much less a deviant kind. Rather there is male sexuality, which is by nature (I am assuming Nietzsche thinks) directed towards females, but which by culture can be directed towards either men or women, depending on what is done to idealize one or the other, to make them seem higher, brighter, worthy of desire for something other than simply sensual pleasure. This passage suggests how far Nietzsche is from thinking of sexuality (or any other drive, for that matter) as a brute biological drive that culture can do nothing with, except possibly to set up dams, as Kevin Hill claims.

Consider also from one of Nietzsche's final works, *Twilight of the Idols*, Nietzsche's use of Plato to critique Schopenhauer's view of beauty as "the redeemer from the focal point of the will, from sexuality"—as "the negation of the drive towards procreation."

> Queer saint! Somebody seems to be contradicting you; I fear it is nature. To what end is there any such thing as beauty in tone, color, fragrance, or rhythmic movement in nature? What is it that beauty evokes? Fortunately, a philosopher contradicts him too. No lesser authority than the divine Plato (so Schopenhauer himself calls him) maintains a far different proposition: that all beauty incites to procreation, that just this is the *proprium* of its effect, from the most sensual up to the most spiritual.
>
> Plato goes further. He says with an innocence possible only for a Greek, not a "Christian," that there would be no Platonic philosophy at all if there were not such beautiful youths in Athens. It is only their sight that transposes the philosopher's soul into an erotic trance, leaving it no peace until it lowers the seed of all exalted things into such beautiful soil. One does not trust one's ears, even if one should trust Plato. At least one guesses that they philosophized differently in Athens, especially in public. (*TI* IX:22–3)

Again, this does not sound like a closeted homosexual to me, but more like a person who is aware of his own feelings and is not threatened by them.

Are Nietzsche's Philosophical Doctrines Plausibly Interpreted as an Expression of Closeted Homosexuality?

This is the third and most important question about which Kevin Hill and I disagree—the most important from the viewpoint of Nietzsche scholarship. Indeed, Hill claims that "Nietzsche's sexuality would be of no more than biographical interest were it not for its profound influence on his thought." The major issues here concern what Nietzsche's doctrines actually are. Although these issues are too complicated to go into in much depth here, I want at least to sketch an alternative to Hill's often compelling picture and to give some indication of how I would argue for this alternative. In Hill's picture, which is based especially on *BGE* 268 and *GS* 354, Nietzsche believed that we have a knowledge of ourselves—of our "unique, ineffable sensory flow"—that we cannot communicate to others. Understanding, communication, and negotiation is possible between people who share the same inner experience, but not between those who occupy significantly different perspectives. People who are more alike have the advantage in making themselves understood, whereas the "more select, subtle, strange" are at a great disadvantage and often fail to survive their isolation. To survive, they need masks. The higher spirit does not write to communicate, but to hide himself, the point being evidently to avoid the pollution of contact with the common culture. But this higher spirit, especially Nietzsche's philosopher, is not content to avoid contact with the lower culture; he also insists on sitting in judgment on it and legislating its values. Those liberated from the common culture, Hill says, "can demand and impose new conventions, new artifices, new values, with which to shape and reshape the recalcitrant community they have left behind" (Hill 1997: 13). Their legislation of values is an act of "unfettered creativity," an "arbitrary act of will, because to accept any prior order guiding one's will is to submit to the will of others, to have not yet fully cast off one's chains."

If Nietzsche did hold the philosophical positions Hill attributes to him—and if we had independent reason to view him as a closeted homosexual—I would find it plausible that these doctrines were an expression of and consolation for his closeted state. But I have a very different view of Nietzsche's philosophical doctrines. In my alternative picture of Nietzsche, there is no ineffable knowledge, no impossibility of communicating across perspectives, no possibility of leaving a common culture behind, no casting off of chains, no unfettered creativity, and no arbitrary imposition of the philosopher's will.

I would begin filling in and defending this picture by arguing that only Nietzsche's first work, *The Birth of Tragedy*, involves a commitment to any kind of ineffable knowledge. Hill's claim to the contrary is based on *Gay Science* 354, from Nietzsche's later writings, which he interprets as placing self-knowledge or consciousness "into distinct tension not only with the needs of the community, but with communication itself," and suggests that Nietzsche draws skeptical conclusions about what can be communicated by way of "the dubious claim that self-knowledge would involve the right sort of appreciation of our sense impressions." I agree with Hill that such a claim is dubious at best. It is opposed by a major line of thought, with which I am in agreement, that runs from Hegel's critique of sense-certainty to Wittgenstein's private language argument. However, I take Nietzsche's views in this passage to be completely in accord with, indeed an expression of, the Hegel to Wittgenstein line of thought. True, the passage commits Nietzsche to sense impressions that we can't *say* anything about; but we can't *know* anything about them either—*except* on the basis of "physiology and the history of animals," as the same passage tells us, thus from a third-person point of view. What we can't know from a first person point of view, nor therefore attempt to communicate, may nevertheless affect us: our body processes and reacts to sensory stimuli, as in subliminal perception, without these entering into consciousness. Consciousness, self-knowledge, language, and communication—these all go together according to *GS* 354: "Consciousness does not really belong to our individual existence." Instead, "consciousness is really only a net of connection between human beings [*ein Verbindungsnetz zwischen Mensch und Mensch*]"—one of Nietzsche's great images, I think.

One factor encouraging Hill's assumption that Nietzsche cares about the individual's "unique, ineffable sensory flow" is Kaufmann's translation of *Empfindung* as "sensation" in the passage on "commonness [*Gemeinheit*]," which Hill quoted (*BGE* 268). If we translate it as "feeling" instead—and this translation choice is at least as possible—the passage makes much more sense. Human beings of the same people understand one another better than those of another people, "even if they employ the same language," not because they have the same sensations—what sense would that make?—but because their similar conditions of life lead them to have similar feelings, and thus to use the same words for the same species of "inner experience." Nietzsche's use of "inner" here may be misleading, but I think his point makes sense and is probably true—misunderstandings are bound to occur, even if people use the same words for the same publicly observable objects, if these words and objects are "colored" by different emotions. Pop psychology on problems of communication between men and women (some of it very bad in the details and implications) attempts to drive home this point (see e.g. Gray 1992).

Later in the same passage Nietzsche writes: "Which group of feelings [Kaufmann: sensations] within a soul is aroused, expresses itself, and issues commands most quickly, is decisive for the whole order of rank of its values and practically determines its table of goods," thus revealing something of the soul's "structure." Again, Kaufmann's translation of *Empfindung* as "sensation" reduces one's chances of making sense of Nietzsche's claim. It is surely one's recurring feelings or emotions, not one's private sensations, that Nietzsche thinks determine one's values and reveal the structure of one's soul. The development towards the herd-like and common, of which Hill makes so much, is thus a development towards similar feelings and values.

But what is so bad about that? Hill sees Nietzsche as privileging our individual existence over our social existence. I certainly agree that Nietzsche values individualized human beings over those made from the exact same mold, those who live as if the worse fate in the world is that of being different. I take it that is part of what Tamsin Lorraine finds attractive in Nietzsche for queer subjects. But Nietzsche did not consider individualized forms of existence possible except against the backdrop of a common culture. Far from being filth, as Hill claims, common culture is for Nietzsche the essential prerequisite for the development of anything of value. The "greatest danger," he tells us, in *Gay Science* 76,

> is the eruption of madness—which means the eruption of arbitrariness in feeling, seeing, hearing, the enjoyment of the mind's lack of discipline, the joy in human unreason. . . . And man's greatest labor has so far has been to reach agreement about very many things and submit to a law of agreement—regardless of whether these things are true or false. This is the discipline of the mind that mankind has received; but the contrary impulses are still so powerful that at bottom we cannot speak of the future of mankind with much confidence.

Contrary to what Hill suggests, I doubt that the impulses Nietzsche is thinking of here are sexual ones. But I also find it difficult to deny, given the violence of human history, that there is a set of impulses that needs organizing, namely, aggressive ones. I take this to be Nietzsche's view. That he also recognized that when sex is combined with cruelty, it can yield a "real 'witches brew'" (BT 2), does not support Hill's criticism of Nietzsche on drives (n. 1 above).

Returning now to the passage under consideration, *GS* 76, we see that Nietzsche is explicit here about only one expression of the "enjoyment of the mind's lack of discipline": "Precisely the most select spirits bristle at this universal binding force," he writes, "the explorers of truth above all. Continually this faith, as *everybody's* faith, arouses disgust and a new lust in subtler minds." Those who so bristle are plausibly thought to be engaged in a higher or sublimated expression of the will to power. But it is a "need of the first rank," he concludes *GS* 76, that "the faithful of the great shared faith stay together and continue their dance. . . . We others are the exception and the danger—and we need eternally to be defended.—Well, there actually are things to be said in favor of the exception, *provided that it never wants to become the rule*" (*GS* 76).

There is much to be said about this passage that I must leave for another occasion. But I want to point out that it does not take for granted the value of the exception. Instead, it presents common ways of seeing and judging as a necessity of the first rank for any human community. The exception is what needs to be justified. One thing Nietzsche elsewhere puts forward in favor or justification of the exception is that its different emotions and values give it access to truths that remain hidden from others. This is a major implication of Nietzsche's perspectivism, his claim that all knowing is perspectival, which is explicitly directed against the idea of objectivity as disinterested knowing, knowing uninfluenced by willing and feeling (*GM* III:12). Stripped of its visual metaphor, perspectivism amounts to the claim that all knowing is "interested," rooted in affect or will. I originally misinterpreted it, I should point out for those familiar with my work, because I took it to be an a priori claim rather than an empirical one (Clark 1990: ch. 5). I now see it as based on the application of evolutionary theory to human cognitive capacities. Evolutionary advantage is conferred not by attention to any and all features of reality, but by selective attention—at first, at least, to factors most relevant to human survival and reproduction. And it is precisely affect, I take Nietzsche to be claiming—interest, emotion, feeling, passion—that turns the mind in a particular direction, focusing its attention on certain features of reality and pushing it to register them as important. Perspectivism is thus a metaphorical formulation of the claim that knowledge is acquired only by means of the focus and interest supplied by affect (see Clark 1998b: 73–8, paper 12: 245–49 in this volume).

So interpreted, perspectivism has no skeptical implications. Its point is not that there are different truths from different perspectives, or that perspectives constitute their objects, but only that different affects call our attention to or reveal different features of reality. But since we are talking about actual, "objective" features of reality, one can continue to recognize their existence and take them into account even when one is no longer in the grip of whatever affect allowed one to notice them in the first place. And one can also, at least sometimes, move other people to recognize their existence even when they do not share one's original affect, if for instance they have an interest in taking you seriously or in being fair to people with other experiences or perspectives. This, I take it, is much of why minority perspectives are important in science and other disciplines. Occupants of these perspectives are likely to notice things others will not, and, given conditions of equal power and respect, will often be able to bring others to see what they would not have noticed on their own. This may not sound like Nietzsche to many. I can only say that I arrived at it by thinking through Nietzsche's perspectivism along with his commitment to science and his understanding of science as an essentially democratic enterprise. I take Nietzsche's well-known claim about the need for "more eyes, different eyes" (*GM* III:12) as a claim about science as a whole and not about the individual researcher or research program, which he sees as usually serving knowledge best by remaining stuck in some particular "nook," a particular affective stance or perspective.

But there is no doubt that Nietzsche thinks the philosopher must be able to view things with more and different eyes. And this, I think, has to do with his problematic-seeming claim about philosophers legislating values (*BGE* 211). I see his claim as rooted in his metaethical position, one he got from Hume by way of Schopenhauer (Clark 1998b, Clark and Dudrick 2007; papers 12 and 5 in this volume). It follows from this view that values cannot *simply* be chosen or legislated. We can't just decide to regard something—characteristics, persons, ways of life—as valuable or not; they do and must present themselves to us as valuable, to be loved, furthered, cared for, etc. But what explains why they present themselves as having the kind of value we perceive in them, according to both Hume and Nietzsche, is our feelings, which "color" the world according to Nietzsche's frequent metaphor, "gilding or staining" it, according to Hume's (Clark 1998b: 62–9, paper 12: 235–41 in this volume). Certain features are highlighted at the expense of others and the world is given a certain "feel." Values thus present themselves as "in the world," but what explains why they so present themselves is that the world appears to us in ways that are "colored" by our emotions and feelings. For Nietzsche, however, unlike Hume, there is no fixed, ahistorical human nature that determines our feelings. Whatever is "given" through our original nature,[3] according to Nietzsche, is taken over and transformed by all the interpretations or symbolic systems written over it, which encourage and transform feelings and therefore structures of souls and values. So decisions have to be made. This, I think, is the kind of "legislation of values" Nietzsche wants philosophers to be engaged in. They are not to sit in judgment on common culture, telling it what to do—how would they possibly get the power to be anything other than laughable in that pose?—but to offer affective interpretations, ones that embody and encourage certain feelings, states of soul, and virtues. The priests did it the last time around; they gave new interpretations to ways of life and states of soul that were already there, but did not experience this as "legislation" because they believed they took their directives from "on high." They did not do what Nietzsche expects new philosophers to do, to stand on their own two feet and commit themselves to values without thinking of them as being handed down by any "authority." But what gives philosophers a right to make such a commitment? I think Nietzsche's answer is: the long training in objectivity they have undergone.

Nietzsche's story of the development of objectivity is itself a long one, beginning with learning to give precedence to the common point of view over the individual's (see *GM* II; Clark and Dudrick 2007, reprinted in this volume). The historically realized versions of the common point of view do not involve "true objectivity" however, as Kevin Hill has stressed, but are interpretations or constructions imposed from the viewpoint of some particular set of interests. But this does not mean that true objectivity, or at least progress towards it, is impossible for Nietzsche. That progress, he thinks, begins from the philosophers,

---

[3] This original nature is called "first nature" and contrasted with "second nature" in *UM* II:3. This "first nature" is not simply the nature we are born with, our biological nature, but that nature as it is affected by early models and training. For Nietzsche says that even our "first nature was once a second nature, and that every victorious second nature will become a first nature."

indeed the ascetic philosophers, "see[ing] differently . . . for once" (*GM* III:12) and proceeds through a long process of philosophical training—in skepticism and overcoming of common-sense points of view—to the kind of work we find in Nietzsche's own writing, which I take to involve a tremendous commitment to and training in objectivity. This "true objectivity" he understands as the ability to move in and out of perspectives, to really take on strange and uncustomary perspectives, to actually experience the world from the viewpoint of very different affects, without being locked into them. But let me stress that Nietzsche is not envisioning new philosophers as handing down principles of right. Such principles must emerge from the common culture, in our case, from a democratic culture. Nietzsche's concern is the development of certain feelings and virtues. Is he going to impose them on anyone? Not exactly. The idea is to use certain affects in such a way as to draw people, to seduce them into his writings, where they may be induced to take on a discipline which eventually leads to changed affect and an appreciation of the virtues and values Nietzsche seeks to promote. To Hill's question (in reference to Nietzsche's reference to "dancing in chains" in *HA* II/2:140; cf. *BGE* 226): "Why do we need 'chains'?" Because the things of the highest value require tremendous discipline and long training. Why does Nietzsche need masks instead of just addressing us directly? Because we don't yet have the training and discipline necessary to appreciate the virtues and values he promotes. If he addressed us directly, we would never get there. But everything he is doing and saying is there in plain sight—to appreciate that we simply have to become people who can see and hear it. This is not closeted homosexuality. This is Plato—or something Nietzsche could have learned from Plato.

Or so at least I see it. There is of course much more to say on these issues, but I hope to have given some indication of how one can read the aspects of Nietzsche's philosophy that Kevin Hill interprets as an expression of and consolation for Nietzsche's closeted homosexuality without so taking them, but in such a way that Nietzsche's being queer might well have a lot to do with their genesis.

But Was Nietzsche Queer?

In conclusion I want to say a few words about this. I take it that he was in the sense that Tamsin Lorraine's title specifies, that he *was* in flight from "oedipal masculinity." Although I am not at all sure how she understands this, it makes sense to me to interpret oedipal masculinity, the phenomenon Freud's account of the Oedipus complex was designed to understand, as first and foremost a matter of defining the masculine or male over against and in opposition to the feminine or female: to be a "man" is to have to a high degree just those qualities that are the opposite of those that are perceived as characterizing women. It seems to me that the heterosexual fantasy of seduction that Nietzsche plays out in *Beyond Good and Evil* is above all an attempt to "deconstruct" this version of masculinity, by showing that the higher forms (and especially the highest) of the masculinity that begins by being set over against the feminine eventually and essentially incorporates its apparent opposite. Nietzsche identifies with women enough and loves women enough that I was tempted to claim that if he was in the closet, he was actually a closeted lesbian.

But here is what bothers me about Tamsin Lorraine's suggestions concerning Nietzsche's flight from the form of masculinity we now see. I do not see how Deleuze's mechanistic talk of desiring machines and intensities can be helpful for such flight. It seems to me more an expression of than a flight from oedipal masculinity. It is a picture of sex and life which seems to withdraw from it all the passion, warmth, color, value, and significance that comes from the projection of affect or feeling. And this seems to me prototypical of the masculinity that defines itself in opposition to the feminine, as does Deleuze's (1983) influential dichotomy between active and reactive with which Lorraine is operating here. I agree that in some important sense Nietzsche thinks we are "desiring machines." We understand ourselves, he says, to the extent that we understand ourselves mechanistically (*A* 14).[4] Further, in line with the Humean position I have attributed to him, reason cannot rule the will. What ultimately determines the will and sits in judgment over it can only be the will itself, its actions and reactions, its desires and feelings. I believe that Nietzsche recognizes higher or more developed forms of desire and feeling, but what counts as higher and more developed is again determined by desire and feeling. So all of this is in line with the talk of desiring machines that Tamsin Lorraine takes over from Deleuze. But for Nietzsche, the view that I have just attributed to him comes from a theoretical point of view. It does not give us the world as it appears from a practical point of view, the viewpoint from which we care about things and live our lives, including, I would hope, our sex lives. The world we care about is a world full of significance and value which are projections of our feelings. Perhaps the problem that makes Deleuze seem attractive to Lorraine is that previous interpretations and values have not been advantageous to queers. But for Nietzsche the solution cannot be to abstain from value and significance, contrary to what Tamsin's Deleuzean conception would seem to require of us. We may have to destroy old values and significances, but, as Nietzsche says in *The Gay Science* 58, we can destroy "only as creators." To simply wipe value and significance from our picture of the world, as is done by the Deleuzean picture of us as "desiring machines," is simply to destroy, and for Nietzsche that means: actually accepting the old values. But that is the beginning of a very different—though certainly related—part of the story I have been sketching here.

---

[4] I did not yet see at the time I wrote this that, for later Nietzsche, the mechanistic view is a completely third-person view. The color, warmth, value, and significance to which I refer here is not available from that viewpoint, but only from the first- and second-person viewpoint, which is the basis for Nietzsche's later metaphysics, the object of my concern in papers 13 and 14.

{ 9 }

Nietzsche's Antidemocratic Rhetoric

Despite great lack of agreement concerning most other aspects of his thought, a near consensus has emerged over the last decade concerning Nietzsche's later political philosophy, namely, that it is (to put it mildly) radically antidemocratic. This consensus stands in opposition to Walter Kaufmann's long influential "existentialist" interpretation of Nietzsche as an essentially nonpolitical, even an antipolitical, thinker who was concerned with the individual and not the group. Recent interpreters, especially those who have written extensively and/or influentially on Nietzsche's political philosophy—for instance, Keith Ansell-Pearson (1994), Bruce Detwiler (1990), Lawrence Hatab (1995), Richard Rorty (1989), and Mark Warren (1998)[1]—reject Kaufmann's attempt to save Nietzsche from his seemingly obvious antidemocratic statements. In this paper, I begin challenging what I take to be the near-consensus view embraced by these authors. I argue that, contrary to appearances, Nietzsche is not committed to an antidemocratic politics. I believe, in fact, that a stronger thesis can be defended, namely, that Nietzsche is committed to democracy—not simply, as several interpreters have already argued, that his principles commit him to democracy, but that he himself recognizes that they do. Although I shall not be able to argue for the stronger thesis here, I want to at least mention that I base my hopes for doing so eventually on Nietzsche's commitment to science and his explicit and repeated recognition of science as an essentially democratic enterprise.

The weaker position I will argue for here is that Nietzsche is *not* committed to an aristocratic political system, which seems difficult enough to defend. My paper focuses on *Beyond Good and Evil*, Nietzsche's most problematic work in terms both of how difficult it makes my task and of how much it makes him seem to be a philosopher with whom I would not wish to be associated. It is a

---

[1] For a more recent addition to this group and a vociferous critic of Nietzsche's antidemocratic views, see Geoff Waite, *Nietzsche's Corps/e* (Durham, NC: Duke University Press, 1996).

key work of Nietzsche's mature philosophy and undoubtedly one of his masterpieces; yet, it seems to support a truly obnoxious, indeed despicable, aristocratic attitude and politics, and to have nothing but contempt for democracy and the majority of people, which it seems ready to have reduced to "incomplete human beings" for the sake of some higher type. In this paper, I begin the task of looking at this most disturbing aspect of Nietzsche's philosophy—a task I would have put off even longer than I have were it not for the impetus provided by the Spindel Conference—to see if there is anything in it that a philosopher ought to take seriously and learn from.

The Standard View and its Basis

The first section of this paper sets out what I take to be the near-consensus or standard view of Nietzsche's later political philosophy, which I will construct largely from the passages of *Beyond Good and Evil* that support it. These passages suggest that Nietzsche sees nothing good about democracy, that he is disgusted by and completely contemptuous of the liberal-democratic order that has progressively taken over Europe under the influence of "modern ideas," in particular, the idea of human equality. Such ideas have given rise to a completely mediocre culture because "they make men small, cowardly, and hedonistic" (*TI* IX:38). As a consequence, modern human beings are not a pleasant sight: They want above all else comfort and safety; they want to avoid above all else the discomfort and danger of being alone, of standing alone, especially in their value judgments. Nietzsche is therefore led, as Detwiler puts it, to "a thoroughgoing repudiation of the dominant social ideals of modernity" (Detwiler: 190). Because modern ideas (that is, liberal-democratic ideals) have led to a complete decay of both the political order and the human type (*BGE* 203), Nietzsche places his hopes for turning things around in a new aristocratic order. For all enhancements of the human type, he says, are the work of an aristocratic society, a society that recognizes a difference in rank between human beings, hence does not accept the "modern" idea of equality (*BGE* 257).

Despite the good work he claims they do, Nietzsche seems to be under no delusions about aristocrats. The ones he describes in the final part of *Beyond Good and Evil* (titled "What is Noble?") take over a society and rule it through compulsion and violence (*BGE* 257). Members of "a good and healthy aristocracy," he claims, necessarily "accept with good conscience the sacrifice of untold human beings, who, *for its sake*, must be reduced and lowered to incomplete human beings, to slaves, to instruments. Their fundamental faith has to be that society must not exist for society's sake but only as the foundation and scaffolding on which a choice type of being is able to raise itself to its higher tasks and higher state of being—comparable to those sun-seeking vines of Java . . . that . . . enclasp an oak tree with their tendrils until eventually, high above but supported by it, they can unfold their crowns in the open light and display their happiness" (*BGE* 258).[2]

How nice for them!—or so we may want to say. But if we are philosophers, we will have the comfort, or the further distress, of realizing that in this case, the "them" is supposed to be us, or at least some of us. The new aristocracy Nietzsche envisions is evidently to be peopled by those he calls "new philosophers," who are evidently to form, or at least to be part of, a "new caste to rule Europe," a phrase Nietzsche uses twice in *Beyond Good and Evil*, the first time in the midst of his discussion of new philosophers (*BGE* 208). He has already told us that we have "no choice," we who agree with him concerning the poverty of liberal-democratic culture, except to turn to such new philosophers who will devote themselves to revaluing "eternal values," the values that have led to a democratic order (*BGE* 203). Nietzsche brings out the antidemocratic and aristocratic leanings of his "new philosophers" particularly in his discussion of the relationship between philosophy and scholarship. "The scholar's declaration of independence, his emancipation from philosophy," he claims, "is one of the more refined effects of the democratic order and disorder . . . 'freedom from all rulers!' that is what the instinct of the rabble wants in this case too" (*BGE* 204). Scholars and scientists, it seems, are no longer inclined to believe in philosophy's "ruling task" in relation to them. Nietzsche thinks there is good reason for this, namely, that "science is flourishing today and her good conscience is written all over her face," whereas the modern development of philosophy has gradually reduced it to the theory of knowledge, a timid "doctrine of abstinence." Philosophy is left, that is, with the task of providing an analysis or justification of what is achieved elsewhere, in science or scholarship, the realm to which philosophy now assigns the task of acquiring knowledge. According to Nietzsche, this "is philosophy in its last throes. How could such a philosophy *rule!*"

Although one may well wonder what kind of posturing is going on here, it seems clear that Nietzsche's "new philosophers" will understand that, as philosophers, their task is to rule. Rule whom? Well, apparently, at least the scholar, in fact "the *ideal* scholar in whom the scientific instinct, after thousands of total and semi-failures, for once blossoms and blooms to the end." Nietzsche regards this ideally "objective person" as a precious instrument, indeed as "one of the most precious instruments there is," certainly one that deserves "care and

---

[2] I have generally followed Walter Kaufmann's translations of both *Beyond Good and Evil* (New York: Random House [Vintage], 1966) and *The Gay Science* (New York: Random House [Vintage], 1974), but have made some changes. In particular, I have used forms of "rule" to translate all forms of "herrschen" because of the importance of keeping in mind that Nietzsche is using versions of the same word in all of these cases. Versions of "rule" seemed natural in more contexts than versions of "master," "lord," or "dominion," even though one of these other terms may seem more appropriate in certain individual contexts.

honor." But he warns us not to follow the contemporary trend of taking this objective person for the goal of humanity, its "redemption and transfiguration." The scholar or scientist is "no goal . . . no complementary man in whom the *rest* of existence is justified . . . much less a beginning, a begetting and first cause, [something] tough, powerful, self-reliant that wants to rule." Because he is merely an instrument, this objective person, the one whose job it is to acquire knowledge, is also "something of a slave though certainly the most sublime kind of slave, but in himself nothing." Which is to say that "he belongs in the hands of one more powerful" (*BGE* 207).

This more powerful one is, no doubt, the philosopher. And what is the "ruling" task of philosophy? Nietzsche leaves no doubt. Genuine philosophers are *"commanders and legislators":* their task as philosophers is to create and legislate values (*BGE* 211). If we consider this claim about the task of philosophy in the light of Nietzsche's insistence that any enhancement of the human type depends upon the existence of an aristocracy and his hope for a "caste to rule Europe," it is not difficult to see why proponents of the standard view see in *Beyond Good and Evil* the hope that a group of philosopher-aristocrats will eventually bring about a revaluation of the values of the modern democratic-liberal order by imposing their own new values on the larger society in which they will live—through force and violence, if necessary. Philosophers, that is, are to rule not only scholars or scientists—presumably by providing an account of the goals of science, the values it is to serve—but everyone else as well, presumably by imposing on them the philosophers' account of the goals of human life, the values it is to serve (cf. *BGE* 211).

Initial Questions Concerning the Standard View

In this section, I raise initial questions concerning the standard view that *Beyond Good and Evil* looks forward to the existence of "new philosophers" who, as the value-legislators of a projected "new caste to rule Europe," will impose their own (aristocratic) values on society. The realization of such a hope seems so far-fetched that we should at least pause to consider whether it is really what Nietzsche has in mind—especially in a book that emphasizes "the difference between the exoteric and the esoteric, formerly known to philosophers . . . wherever one believed in an order of rank and *not* in equality and equal rights" (*BGE* 30).[3] After all, the ineptness of philosophers at worldly

---

[3] Waite takes account of Nietzsche's distinction between the esoteric and exoteric meaning of a text, but thinks that what I have called the "standard interpretation" is the esoteric meaning of Nietzsche's text. Since that interpretation seems to be the most obvious interpretation of the text and not one that calls for any particular subtlety of interpretation, it seems to me much more plausible to consider it the exoteric meaning. I would put forward the interpretation I offer later in this paper as a more plausible candidate for the esoteric meaning of *BGE*.

tasks is the stuff of legend. Of course, if philosophers are to create or "legislate" values, that is, to determine the goals of human life, the values to be served by it, it will make sense to think of them as "rulers" in a metaphorical sense.[4]

My issue with the standard view is whether Nietzsche wants those who "rule" in this sense to rule in the literal sense, i.e., to have political power. Philosophers clearly have no political power in our world nor much chance of gaining it. How could they possibly get into a position to impose their values on the larger society? Well, the details are far from clear, but recent interpreters of Nietzsche's later political philosophy assume that he looks forward to some combination of philosophy and political power, perhaps on the model of the ancient Brahmins who chose the kings but kept out of direct politics themselves. The idea seems to be for philosophers to determine the values in accord with which the society is to operate, and for nonphilosopher rulers, the political rulers, to make sure that the people accept and follow these values, in part at least by setting up the institutions of the society in accord with them. Now, I must admit that I find no plausibility whatsoever in this idea: the vision of philosophers dominating people by imposing their values on them, either directly or by means of a political elite, strikes me as too silly for words. If philosophers themselves are to rule in the most literal sense, they would hardly have enough time to be philosophers; much less enough of the "*freedom above things*" (*GS* 107) or the "refined neutrality" of conscience (*BGE* 25) that Nietzsche believes is necessary for their task. Even if philosophers choose only those who would rule (the "kings") and perhaps the institutions, time and freedom would have to be sacrificed perhaps almost as much as in the first case. I am not at all sure it would take less time to rule than to find the people suitable for ruling. Then there is the important question as to what the philosophers would have to offer those in political power to get them to rule in the name of their values. There are next to no details on these questions anywhere that I know of in what Nietzsche wrote, and certainly not in his books. Is there really a strong basis for attributing this view to him?

---

[4] As Nietzsche makes clear in GS 301, the "contemplatives" who appear to be mere spectators of life are really the "poet[s] who keep creating this life." Philosophers and religious thinkers can be said to "create this life" because they "continually fashion something that wasn't there before: the whole eternally growing world of valuations, colors, accents, perspectives, scales, affirmations, and negations." Nietzsche adds that the "poem" created by the so-called contemplatives is "continually studied by the so-called practical human beings (our actors) who learn their roles and translate everything into flesh and actuality." Nietzsche's point is that those who make the world go round are not, contrary to appearances, the so-called actors, the movers and shakers, but rather the contemplatives who have created the value-laden world we live in. For, Nietzsche goes on to say, "whatever has *value* in our world now does not have value in itself . . . but has been given value at some time, as a present—and it is *we* [the contemplatives: the philosophers and religious thinkers] who gave and bestowed it. Only we have created the world *that concerns human beings!*"

There is certainly a basis for doing so. The view in question may well be the most obvious political position to attribute to Nietzsche on the basis of *Beyond Good and Evil*. "Most obvious" does not mean "best," or even "justified" or "adequate," however. In fact, there is much of the standard view to which Nietzsche does not explicitly commit himself in *Beyond Good and Evil*. For instance, this book does not say that the philosophers of the future will or should have political power. It does not say that philosophers are to impose their values on the people. Nor does it say that the political structure of the future should be an aristocracy, or that enhancements of the human type require an aristocratic political structure.

I would sum up what *Beyond Good and Evil* does explicitly say on these issues in five points:

1. Democratic values have helped create a culture of mediocrity and triviality, a world in which both political organization and human beings have decayed (*BGE* 203).
2. Those who have faith in what can still be made of human beings, i.e., a commitment to the enhancement of the human type, have no choice but to turn towards new philosophers who will legislate new values (*BGE* 203).
3. Genuine philosophers are "commanders and legislators" in the sense that they determine the goals of human life, hence the values it is to serve and realize (*BGE* 211).
4. All enhancements of the human type are the work of an aristocratic society, a society that believes in an order of rank, takes its own form of existence to be the *telos* of society, and is willing to have other human beings reduced to incomplete human beings, i.e., to instruments and slaves, for its sake (*BGE* 257–258).
5. The "European problem" is a serious matter for Nietzsche, and he understands this problem as "the cultivation of a caste to rule Europe" (*BGE* 251).

Now these five claims have been put together by interpreters to form the doctrine that philosophers should have direct or indirect political power in an aristocracy that will impose their values on the populace, if necessary, through compulsion and violence. My first point is that those who think this is the doctrine of *Beyond Good and Evil* cannot simply read it off what Nietzsche says in the book; it must be *read into* what he says. In itself, this is not a problem. I assume that all important interpretation involves reading something into what an author explicitly says. What justifies doing so, at least in the case of a philosophical text, is that it makes the most sense of what the author explicitly says, that it gives at least as good an explanation of why the author said what he said as any available alternative. In this case, it is assumed that Nietzsche's commitment to the standard view makes the best sense of his actually saying the things

I have summed up under my five points. And to a point, I agree. For instance, it makes little sense for Nietzsche to say what he does say unless he favors attempting to enhance the human type in the face of the decay brought about by a democratic order, believes it is at least possible that this can be accomplished by philosophers who legislate new values, and believes that there is no alternative that has a better chance of success.[5]

But having conceded this much to the usual reading of *Beyond Good and Evil*, I am left with a major question: namely, does Nietzsche believe that enhancing the human type depends on the existence of an aristocratically organized political system, a system conceived, as one commentator puts it, "along the lines of a pyramid in which each social group is assigned privileges and duties appropriate to its social role" (Ansell-Pearson: 41)? And if by "legislating values," philosophers will thereby be part of "new caste to rule Europe," need we conceive their "rule" as involving force and violence, as a matter of imposing their will on a resisting populace?

I begin with the point that although Nietzsche claims that enhancements of the human type are always the work of an aristocratic society, he does not say that this requires aristocratic political institutions. He in fact says nothing at all in *Beyond Good and Evil* about the kind of political organization or institutions (of the larger society) that are required for the enhancements with which he is concerned. He does claim that the democratic movement is "a form of the decay of political organization" (*BGE* 203). I suspect that readers often take it for granted that Nietzsche regards this decay as something bad because he mentions it in the same breath with another form of decay that he clearly does regard as something bad, the "decay, namely, the diminution, of the human being," which he says "make[s] him mediocre and lower[s] his value" (*BGE* 203). In fact, Nietzsche does not say that the "decay of political organization" is a bad thing. Although he undoubtedly thinks its decay reduces the value of political organization for some purposes, what he actually says is perfectly compatible with believing that this decay makes possible things of even higher value, e.g., the development of individuality. I suggest that Nietzsche believes that the enhancement of the human type with which he is concerned depends upon the development of individuality and that he recognizes that such development is made possible by a weakening of political organization (see, e.g., *GS* 23 and *GS* 356). The claim that democracy represents the decay of political organization therefore gives me no reason to concede that Nietzsche is against democratic

---

[5] In opposition, for instance, to Conway's 1997 claim that in his post—Zarathustrian works (which include *Beyond Good and Evil*), Nietzsche views human beings and human society as so decadent that he sees no hope of "turning things around." His hope, according to Conway, is to train a group of philosophers who will keep his message alive to be used once a nondecadent (and presumably nondemocratic) era emerges.

political institutions or in favor of aristocratic ones. In fact, the claim is perfectly compatible with believing (as I think Nietzsche does, although I cannot argue that here) that the "decay" of the political order brought about by the development of democratic institutions has made possible the very aristocratic society that Nietzsche wants to encourage, that of his "new philosophers."

Although Nietzsche clearly claims that enhancements of the human type will always be the work of an "aristocratic society," he does not characterize such a society in political terms or say that its existence depends on aristocratic political institutions. Instead, he characterizes it in terms of its underlying value orientation, as "a society that believes in the long ladder of an order of rank and differences in value between man and man, and needs slavery in some sense or other." A group of philosophers should therefore be able to form an aristocratic society in Nietzsche's sense by sharing such a value orientation, one that posits their own form of existence as the *telos* or highest good achieved by society, even if the larger society in which they live is governed by democratic political institutions. To be sure, Nietzsche claims that "slavery" will be needed by the aristocratic society he regards as a precondition for any enhancement of the human type. But he says "slavery in some sense or other," which makes clear that he has refrained from specifying the sense of "slavery" involved. In fact, scholars and scientists form the only group Nietzsche picks out as deserving the status of "slaves" in relation to philosophers. Surely, Nietzsche's point is not that scholars should be "slaves" of philosophers in the literal (i.e., social and political) sense. In *Gay Science* 18, Nietzsche tells us that the ancient philosophers thought of all nonphilosophers as slaves, but makes more explicit (though still not fully so) that he is using the term "metaphorically," to characterize one who lacks true independence or freedom. I suggest that he uses "slave" in the same sense in *Beyond Good and Evil*, the difference being that the later text leaves it more up to the reader to figure out for herself that he is using the term in a metaphorical sense.[6] In the same way, I suggest, this book leaves it to the reader to determine for herself whether Nietzsche considers aristocratic political institutions necessary for the enhancement of the human type. How is she to do that? My suggestion is that she should begin by seeking to determine Nietzsche's reasons for claiming that an aristocratic society is necessary if the human type is to be enhanced and whether, given these reasons, it makes sense for him to think that such enhancement depends upon the existence of an aristocratic political system.

---

[6] Why would he do this? It fits with the distinction he draws early in the book between the exoteric and the esoteric and his accompanying claim that "our highest insights must—and should sound like follies and sometimes like crimes when they are heard without permission by those who are not predisposed and predestined for them" (*BGE* 30).

Nietzsche's Reasons for Supporting an Aristocratic Society

Those who hold the near-consensus view I am contesting here seem to have a strong basis for thinking that Nietzsche believes in the necessity of aristocratic political institutions. But that is because they find the reasons Nietzsche gives in support of aristocratic society not in *Beyond Good and Evil*, but in works of his earliest period, particularly "Schopenhauer as Educator" (1874) and "The Greek State" (1871–1872), the latter an essay Nietzsche himself did not choose to publish. "Schopenhauer as Educator" is infamous for its perfectionism: its claim that the goal of culture is the production of the genius (that is, of the highest human types), and that "humanity should work ceaselessly towards producing great individuals—this and only this should be its task" (*UM* III:6).[7] To the objection that it "seems absurd that one human being should exist for the sake of another," Nietzsche responds scornfully that the modern world's only alternative is for the individual to exist for the sake of the majority, "as if it were less absurd to have the numbers decide where it is a matter of value and significance! For surely the question is: How can your life, the life of the individual obtain the highest value, the deepest significance? How is it least wasted? Surely only by living for the benefit of the rarest and most valuable exemplars, not for the benefit of the majority, that is, for the benefit of those who, taken as individuals, are the least valuable exemplars." Although the sentiment involved here is certainly "antidemocratic" in some important sense, Nietzsche's claim does not immediately entail commitment to the antidemocratic view that political life should be organized to benefit or promote the existence of the most valuable human beings. A contemporary liberal might hold that the most valuable life is the religious or the artistic life, and that other types of lives have their greatest value through the contributions they may make to the religious or artistic life, and yet still might hold that political life should be organized so that individuals have the maximum freedom possible to have and act on their own conception of what makes a life valuable. Nietzsche's position in "Schopenhauer as Educator" is somewhat difficult to reconcile with democratic liberalism, however, for he appears to hold that nothing has value except the higher forms of human life. This is because we find underlying this work, and indeed all of the works of Nietzsche's early period, a view Nietzsche derived by slight transformation from Schopenhauer's philosophy: that natural existence has no intrinsic value, that only by acquiring a "second nature" through culture can human existence come to be worthy of any respect whatsoever, for otherwise it is nothing more than a slavish and worthless struggle for existence and subservience to animal needs. It is not easy to reconcile this view with a commitment

---

[7] I use Richard T. Grey's translation of "Schopenhauer as Educator" in *Unfashionable Observations*. However, following the argument of Conant 2002, I have used "exemplars" rather than "specimens" for "Exemplare."

to liberal or democratic practices unless one believes that these practices are a good way to ensure the existence and flourishing of culture and thus of higher human types. But Nietzsche seems to have believed the opposite, namely, that democracy can only be disastrous for higher culture.

The clearest statement of this view is found in "The Greek State." "In order that there be a broad, deep, fertile soil for the development of art," which he equates with higher culture, Nietzsche claims that "the overwhelming majority has to be slavishly subjected to life's necessity in the service of the minority, *beyond* the measure that is necessary for the individual. At their expense, through their extra work, that privileged class is to be removed from the struggle for existence, in order to produce and satisfy a new world of necessities." Therefore "we must learn to identify as a cruel-sounding truth the fact that *slavery belongs to the essence of a culture*."[8]

Nietzsche's position in this early essay seems to be that human life has value or deserves respect only because of the higher or cultured individuals to which it gives rise. But the culture that makes such valuable exemplars possible depends on the existence of a leisure class and therefore on the majority doing more work than is needed to support its members. Because they would never do this extra work willingly, and in fact will never willingly take on any of the responsibilities that make political life possible, nondemocratic institutions that will force them to do these things are necessary.[9] Those who subscribe to the standard view assume that the same argument provides the basis for Nietzsche's claim in *BGE* that enhancements of the human type are always the work of an aristocratic society. I grant that later Nietzsche continues to believe (1) that the ultimate value or *telos* of human society lies in the higher type of human being it makes possible and (2) that an aristocracy is necessary if this higher type is to be produced. But I deny that he continues to base these beliefs on the early argument (specifically the one found in "The Greek State") he gives in defense of aristocracy.

My reasons for this denial are two-fold. First, nothing like Nietzsche's earlier *argument* in defense of aristocracy is actually found in *BGE*. Proponents of

---

[8] "The Greek State" is translated by Carol Diethe in On *the Genealogy of Morality*, edited by Keith Ansell-Pearson (Cambridge: Cambridge University Press, 1994), 176–186.

[9] Consider as evidence the following passage from "The Greek State": "*This truth* [that '*slavery belongs to the essence of a culture*'] is the vulture that gnaws at the liver of the Promethean promoter of culture. The misery of men living a life of toil has to be increased to make the production of the world of art possible for a small number of Olympian men. Here we find the source of that hatred which has been nourished by the Communists and Socialists as well as their paler descendants, the white race of 'Liberals' of every age, against the arts, but also against classical antiquity. If culture were really left to the discretion of the people, if inescapable powers, which are law and restraint to the individual, did not rule, then the glorification of spiritual poverty and the iconoclastic destruction of the claims of art would be *more* than the revolt of the oppressed masses against drone-like individuals: it would be the cry of compassion tearing down the walls of culture; the urge for justice, for equal sharing of pain would swamp all other ideas" (Diethe translation, 178–179).

the standard view read the same *argument* into this book only because they find in it no other reason Nietzsche would have had for putting forward the same *claim* in favor of aristocracy. I will, however, provide an alternative account of Nietzsche's later defense of aristocracy later in this paper. Second, in the works of his middle period, Nietzsche had already given up one of the central premises of his early argument for aristocracy. *Human, All Too Human*, the work that begins Nietzsche's middle period, clearly rejects his earlier claim that a high culture is incompatible with democratic political institutions. Although he continues to see many downsides to the democratic movement (especially the demand for rights without a concomitant deepening of the commitment to responsibilities, and a tendency towards "leveling" which he considers disadvantageous to higher culture), he presents himself as reconciled to the modern political understanding, according to which the "the purpose of all politics is to make life as endurable for as many as possible," hence that "these many-as-possible are entitled to determine what they understand by an endurable life" (HA 438).[10] He does not object to this idea of politics as directed towards ensuring an endurable life for as many as possible and upholding the individual's right to self-determination in such matters, as long as it is not insisted that everything must be "politics in this sense," which means as long as the few have the right to believe that the goal of human life lies outside of the "happiness of the many." In other words, Nietzsche has no objection to democratic political institutions as long as they are compatible with "aristocratic values"—as long as they allow the few to posit the goal of human life in something beyond that to which the majority can relate. Further, in *The Wanderer and his Shadow*, published as the second part of the second volume of *Human, All Too Human*, Nietzsche makes clear that he considers the democratization of Europe "irresistible" and that he sees in this a major upside for the higher culture in which the "few" see the goal and value of human life. Democratization, he says, makes it "impossible for the fruitful fields of culture again to be destroyed overnight by wild and senseless torrents. It erects strong dams and protective walls against barbarians, against pestilence, against *physical and spiritual enslavement*," and will make possible, after several centuries, the cultivation of a higher culture and a higher type of human being than previous cultures have produced (*HA* II/2:275). Thus Nietzsche evidently continues to believe that the ultimate value of society lies in the higher type of human being it makes possible. But he no longer argues that this is the view everyone should take because he no longer holds that democratic institutions serve only to undermine the higher culture that makes the higher type possible. In abandoning the latter claim, Nietzsche rejects a crucial part of his early argument in defense of aristocracy.

---

[10] *Human, All-Too-Human*, translated by R. J. Hollingdale (Cambridge: Cambridge University Press, 1986).

According to the standard view, however, Nietzsche soon gave up his hope for democracy: *Human, All Too Human* was a mere phase that Nietzsche went through before returning to his early antidemocratic views. There is certainly no direct evidence for this interpretation: Later Nietzsche never says that he is rejecting the political views of *Human, All Too Human* and returning to an earlier view. The only basis for accepting it is the assumption that it makes the most sense of what Nietzsche actually says in his later works, particularly in BGE. But does it? If we consider the actual reason given in this work for the claim that enhancements of the human type are always the work of an aristocratic society, we see that it differs substantially from the reason given in his early works. What Nietzsche explicitly says is the following:

> Every enhancement of the human type has been the work of an aristocratic society—and it will be again and again—a society that believes in the long ladder of the order of rank and differences of value between human beings, and that needs slavery in some sense or other. Without that *pathos of distance* that grows out of the ingrained difference between strata—when the ruling caste looks afar and looks down upon subjects and instruments and just as constantly practices obedience and command, keeping down and keeping at a distance—that other, more mysterious pathos could not have grown up either, the craving for an ever new widening of distances within the soul itself, the development of ever higher, rarer, further, wider-spanning, more comprehensive states—in brief, the enhancement of the human type, the continual self-overcoming of the human, to take a moral formula in a sense that goes beyond morality. (*BGE* 257)

There is nothing here about how the majority must be forced to work if a leisure class is to exist. Instead Nietzsche claims that (1) only a society that believes that there are differences in rank or value between human beings will give rise to the craving for higher states of soul, and (2) without such a craving, these higher states, the realization of which constitute the enhancement of the human type, will not be achieved. My interpretation may seem to ignore a crucial point: that the aristocratic society Nietzsche describes in the passage quoted above does not merely *believe* in an order of rank, but enforces that belief through a set of political institutions that make it a "ruling caste [that] constantly . . . looks down upon subjects and instruments." In the context, this certainly sounds like a call for an oppressive political aristocracy; it does not seem plausible that Nietzsche is here using "ruling caste" simply in a metaphorical sense. However, if we read what he actually says very carefully, we can distinguish his description of *actual historical aristocracies* from his description of the (let us call it) *ideal aristocratic society* that Nietzsche believes is necessary for the enhancement of the human type. The latter is defined in the first sentence quoted above merely in terms of a *belief* in differences in rank and value;

the second sentence claims that without the existence of a ruling caste that looks down on subjects, the higher states of soul, the realization of which constitutes the elevation or enhancement of the human type, would never have come into existence. This is similar to the main argument of the first essay of Nietzsche's *Genealogy:* that the idea of goodness or superiority of soul originally developed out of the idea of political superiority. This claim from *Genealogy* concerns the historical prerequisites for our current idea of goodness; it is not a claim about what must be present now if we are to have an idea of goodness. Likewise, I believe, in the case of the claim from *Beyond Good and Evil* that we are considering. A ruling caste that provided a constant *experience* of the difference in rank between human beings originally made possible not only the idea of but also the striving for higher states of soul. However, this is not to say that such a (political) ruling caste is necessary if such striving is to exist now.

What *is* necessary, according to the interpretation I have already offered, is a society that believes that there are differences in value among human beings. The problem with democracy, I take Nietzsche to be saying, is that it rejects this part of the aristocratic belief system, and thereby undermines the craving for higher states of soul. How exactly does it do this?

In my attempt to get at the answer Nietzsche suggests to this question, I am indebted to Lawrence Hatab's recent critique of Nietzsche's aristocraticism, with which I have considerable sympathy and to which I shall return. What I find helpful at this point is something I think Hatab gets dead wrong. According to Hatab, Nietzsche's "assault on egalitarianism" follows from the belief that "most people [in a democratic society] are not capable of honoring excellence and success" (Hatab: 114). Hatab proceeds to argue against Nietzsche's aristocraticism on the grounds that "democratic societies have never collapsed into egalitarian mush—consider how readily we affirm many unequal power relations in milieus such as the military, the professions, and education, and how prone we are to idolize talent in various arenas." In other words, Hatab thinks that Nietzsche's complaint against democracy is that it produces equality, and he therefore takes the obvious fact that our democratic society has not produced equality as evidence that Nietzsche's worry is unfounded. In fact, however, Nietzsche denies that democracy produces equality. Hatab himself quotes Nietzsche's claim in *Gay Science* 18—"we are accustomed to the *doctrine* of equality, though not to equality itself"—to show that Nietzsche exaggerates the deleterious effect of egalitarianism. I would be astonished, however, if Nietzsche could really be consoled or reassured about democracy by considering our idolization of athletes, movie stars, and other entertainment specialists, or our appreciation of almost all of the qualities that give one a chance of having one's name added to the list of the rich and famous. Nietzsche's problem with democracy is not that it destroys the appreciation of or desire for success or excellence, I suggest, but that it *debases our standards for what constitutes success and excellence*, making them crude, plebeian, and even barbaric.

In a democracy, I take Nietzsche to be claiming, standards for success become common or democratic, as those of American society certainly are now: Just about everyone can have some of what constitutes success. In alphabetical order: fame, money, pleasure, power, sex. The successful just have more of it. And we have little shared idea of excellence beyond such success. This point was brought home to me once by an interview I saw with someone who had succeeded in amassing a large fortune at a very early age. When asked what had motivated him to work so hard to make money, he replied, in what struck me as all sincerity and innocence, that he had always been driven by a passionate desire to achieve excellence. It seemed that it had simply never occurred to him that there could be any measure of excellence or success other than money.

This is anecdotal, of course, and there are certainly various forms of achievement and success recognized in our democratic society. It is becoming increasingly difficult for anything to be regarded as an achievement, however, unless it brings the achiever more of what we can all have: e.g., money or the "feeling" that television commentators are always asking various winners to share with us. So even though most of us will never win an important sporting event, for instance, every attempt will be made to allow us to share in "how it feels" to win each of them, which, of course, will turn out to sound not very different from what we have felt on various occasions, usually even pretty ordinary. This is not at all to say that democracy thereby discourages the desire to win—or that it makes us really want to be equal. It obviously doesn't, and I see no evidence that Nietzsche thinks it does. The desire to achieve, to be a winner, is very strong; it is just that the measure of winning, of achieving excellence, is common, is reduced to increments of the lowest common denominator, of what everyone can relate to without having to change any fundamental aspect of their character. What is missing is any room for the idea that there are higher states of *soul*, virtues or excellences of character, ones that are not mere increments of that to which everyone can already relate. It was not always this way. Under the influence of religion, human beings have traditionally believed in "higher human beings," in human beings who have achieved a level of spirituality or virtue of which most people are not capable. In the discourse of our now more democratic culture, on the other hand, virtue has only a minor presence. And there is certainly nothing in this discourse to challenge and stir the soul, to induce a craving for higher virtues or degrees of virtue. This is, I think Nietzsche would say, because the only virtues about which we talk are the old, tired virtues, virtues interpreted under the auspices of the old ideal, hence ones of which we assume everyone is already capable. But "what can be common," says Nietzsche, "always has little value" (*BGE* 43)—which is to say that what we perceive as ordinary cannot inspire us to extraordinary passion or effort. And without such passion and effort, Nietzsche very plausibly claims, no enhancement of the human type, no new level of spiritual achievement, will be possible.

Democratic Political Institutions versus Democratic Values

Suppose Nietzsche's claim is as I have suggested: that democracy discourages the desire for, hence the development of, higher states of soul, higher spiritual states, higher virtues. We then need to ask: Are democratic political institutions—by which I mean institutions that treat persons as equals, as bearers of equal liberty or equal basic rights—plausibly seen as the problem, as standing in the way of such desire and development? Here, I agree with Hatab's argument in *A Nietzschean Defense of Democracy* that the problems Nietzsche sees with democracy are due not to democratic institutions, but to the values that are traditionally taken as the justification for such institutions, in particular, the value of equality. Arguing "that democracy can be sustained without its traditional banner of human equality," Hatab grants that democracy requires that all citizens have equal rights, thus "that they all have the same access to and fair treatment by the legal system, that they all have the same opportunity for political participation, and that all voices count the same in elections (one person, one vote)." But he denies that these "functional or procedural parities," as he terms them, imply or depend upon a belief in "any kind of substantive or intrinsic equality" (Hatab: 57).

I completely agree with Hatab that a commitment to democratic institutions need not depend on a belief that human beings are of equal worth. This is certainly not a new point as far as political philosophy goes, for it is a major component of Liberalism in the version defended, for instance, by John Rawls. Already in *A Theory of Justice* (and the change in Rawls's view that leads to *Political Liberalism* simply allows him to hold to this point more consistently), Rawls argues that a commitment to equal liberty or equal basic rights for all persons in one's society (and thus to what I am calling "democratic institutions") does not require one to accept that these persons of are equal value. According to his contract doctrine, Rawls argues, "the equal liberty of citizens does not presuppose that the ends of different persons have the same value, nor that their freedom and well-being is of the same worth" (Rawls 1971: 329). Hatab's use of this point in Nietzsche scholarship—to argue that we can accept Nietzsche's objections to democracy and equality without giving up either in the political sense—is new. Unlike Hatab, however, I believe that Nietzsche would actually agree with it, that *Beyond Good and Evil* is written in cognizance of the distinction between democratic political institutions and democratic values, and that Nietzsche sees his commitment to aristocratic values as compatible with the acceptance and approval of democratic political institutions. I would formulate his "compatibilist" position as a claim that commitment to a democratic political system is compatible with an aristocratic ethical outlook, an outlook defined by the belief that some human beings are of greater value than others.

This characterization of the compatibility between democratic institutions and aristocratic values is one Hatab clearly wishes to avoid, and his implicit arguments against it are instructive. He argues that Nietzsche's version of aristocraticism "seems to apportion excellence and mediocrity in such clean and categorical terms: higher and lower 'types,' the creators and the herd, and so on, suggesting clear delineations between a few great individuals and a mass of lowly, inept sheep" (Hatab: 115). The problem, Hatab thinks, is that Nietzsche emphasizes only one kind of excellence—the excellence of cultural creators, such as artists and philosophers—and seems to "ignore or conceal a much wider range of excellences and apportionment." But there are many sorts of excellence, Hatab protests. Although he is better at philosophy, his auto mechanic has much greater excellence when it comes to fixing machines. Surely this is correct, but how could Nietzsche disagree? As Hatab's own quotations demonstrate, in *Human, All Too Human*, Nietzsche clearly recognizes different kinds of excellence and even characterizes "civilized circumstances" as ones in which "everyone feels himself to be superior to everyone else in at least *one* thing" (*HA* 509). And *The Gay Science* expresses his gratitude to artists for teaching us "to esteem the hero concealed in everyday characters" (*GS* 78). I do not see any reason to think that Nietzsche later abandoned these views. I grant that Hatab is in fundamental disagreement with Nietzsche's aristocraticism, but I believe that he has failed to put his finger on the source of the disagreement. It is not that Nietzsche denies that everyday characters can embody many excellences, but that he denies that such characters can, at least without significant transformation, embody the *highest* human excellences.

Although Hatab does not directly address this view, it clearly runs counter to his democratic sensibilities. He defends these sensibilities on what he considers Nietzschean grounds (albeit ones he does not believe Nietzsche recognized) by appealing to Nietzsche's rejection of the metaphysical self, which he thinks requires us to "limit the recognition of excellence to praising contingent performances rather than 'persons.'" If "we take Nietzsche's lead" and reject metaphysical or essentialist conceptions of selfhood, he claims, "we can go a long way toward resolving the egalitarian-aristocratic debate. . . . People can be ranked in all sorts of contexts in terms of better and worse performances, without any *essential* ranking of persons." We can make a democratic gesture, Hatab thinks, by saying that no one is essentially superior to anyone else, that no one is a better person, and make an aristocratic gesture by making "comparative judgments in appropriate settings. . . . Artists, thinkers, leaders, athletes, laborers, and so on across the social spectrum, all can have their excellences, both within and between domains, and the recognition will continually fluctuate within and between domains—on a given day, in a given context, for example, a good locksmith is far superior to the President of the United States" (Hatab: 117).

True enough, who could deny it?—especially in current circumstances![11] But notice that these circumstances are not really relevant, given Hatab's presentation

---

[11] Namely, impeachment proceedings to remove the President of the United States, Bill Clinton, from office.

of the issue, for one kind of excellence that does not come into Hatab's account is excellence of character, i.e., virtue in the traditional sense (virtues of the person, rather than of the mechanic, locksmith, or president). His argument is basically that since, in Nietzsche's own words, there is no "being [i.e., no self or person] behind doing" (*GM* I:13), there are no virtues or excellences of the self or person, hence no higher virtues of the self or person.

But this appeal to Nietzsche's denial of the metaphysical self distorts its point. To deny that there is a "being behind doing" is to deny the existence of a soul or self that is the spontaneous or uncaused cause of all of its actions. Such a self is "metaphysical" in the sense that it could only exist outside of the nexus of time, space, and causality. But denying the existence of such a self does not prevent Nietzsche from talking repeatedly about souls and their characteristics. For instance, from *BGE* 268: "The group of feelings that is aroused, expresses itself, and issues commands in a soul most quickly, is decisive for the whole order of rank of its values and ultimately determines its table of goods. The values of a human being betray something of the *structure* of its soul." In *BGE*, I suggest, Nietzsche is attempting to show us something of the structure of his soul. Of course, that soul can only be known through its actions, but these actions—i.e., what Nietzsche says in this book—reveal the characteristics, dispositions, structure of his soul, hence its values and virtues. The point of exhibiting these characteristics is not to show that he is better at philosophizing than others, but rather to exhibit to us the higher states of soul that are exhibited in his philosophizing. And these states involve characteristics of the person, such as justice and generosity, rather than mere characteristics of the philosopher, such as being good at various dialectical moves.[12]

---

[12] Is there an argument to be made against Nietzsche here on the grounds that he is willing to include among enhancements of the human type only enhancements of the soul and not of the body? For instance, doesn't the fact that our best athletes are now at a very different level from where they were at the beginning of the modern Olympics, a little over a century ago, constitute an enhancement of the human type? I think that Nietzsche can grant this without giving up his commitment to aristocratic values. For surely the enhancement of human athleticism depended on the existence of an aristocratic society, as Nietzsche defines that, in relation to athletics: that is, "a society that believes in a long ladder of the order of rank, and differences in value between man and man"—as athletic competitors, of course. Think of the long order of rank for tennis players, for instance.

Does this contradict my argument against Hatab that standards for excellence in a democratic society become common? Not at all. I find it quite plausible that the fact that athletes are now our prime symbol of excellence and achievement shows the plebeian character of the kinds of achievement our democratic society cares about—I say this as a devoted sports fan, by the way. Everyone can understand athletic talent and the virtues involved in developing it, and the vast majority can relate to what goes on in this arena—especially now that women are no longer virtually excluded from it. None of this is to deny that it is an arena, thus that it involves ranking and the recognition of differences in value. So Nietzsche can admit that these rankings do pick out differences in value or excellence without giving up his insistence that the highest excellences are beyond the experience and therefore the reach of most human beings, at least as they are presently constituted.

What is interesting about Hatab's argument, I suggest, is that its use of Nietzsche in its attempt to do without egalitarianism exhibits precisely the tendency of democratic society that Nietzsche believes encourages mediocrity and "leveling": Within a democratic culture, there is a resistance to the idea of anyone being superior to anyone else—as a person. We can cheerfully admit that we are not equal in the sense that our talents differ, and that some of us are far superior to others at doing all sorts of things (locksmithing, making money, thinking, philosophizing, being president). What we resist is the idea that some of us are superior persons, superior as persons. Hatab would reject two of the traditional ideas used to defend our resistance to the idea of such superiority: the metaphysical idea of an equal personhood lurking behind all of our various differences and inequalities, and the moral idea that, whatever our differences, each of us has an equal opportunity to achieve what is of the highest value. Hatab defends our resistance instead by denying that we can judge the worth of persons at all. I think Nietzsche would diagnose this as merely a different strategy with the same end and the same result: Each of these strategies defends our egalitarian prejudice against the possibility of higher human beings, and thereby directs our desire for excellence towards those goods to which everyone can relate.

Hatab sees it differently. He presents himself as sympathetic to "egalitarian rhetoric" when it is "pitted against aristocratic estimations of human worth in terms of class, lineage, or other designations that fix people into stratified categories that hold firm from the ground up and throughout the temporal span," such as race, gender, and sexual preference, I take it. He thinks that the postmodern idea of selfhood, which he derives from Nietzsche, "can address this same issue without swinging to an egalitarian extreme. From a postmodern perspective, achievements, even great achievements, would not translate into any notion of a superior 'person' or someone who is closer to the 'truth' or the 'good.' With a decentered self, we can talk of performances rather than 'natures.' There is no unified essence in the light of which we might be tempted or prompted to sum people up, close the book on them, or presume to measure them in some fundamental way" (Hatab: 118). Notice two assumptions behind Hatab's argument. The first is that if we make any such "stratifying" judgments, we are buying into the "aristocratic" estimations of human worth in terms of class, lineage, race, gender, or the like. But this is simply not so. No such prejudices are required even to sum up a person, close the book on them, or judge them in a fundamental way, three very different things to do, by the way—and therefore in need of different justifications—much less to say that one person is closer to truth or goodness than another.[13] The second assumption is that there

---

[13] I can sum a person up without closing the book on him if I think he can change, and I can judge him in some "fundamental way," that is, in terms of what I take to be most fundamental to being a good or superior person, and can even close the book on him, without this having anything to do with class, lineage, race, ethnic group, gender, or sexual identity. Likewise when it comes to issues concerning truth and goodness.

are only two ways to avoid such prejudices: the "egalitarian extreme" of claiming that persons are of equal worth or Hatab's postmodernist position that we should not judge the worth of persons at all, but only their "contingent performances." This is clearly false, since Liberalism in many of its versions, including Rawls's, avoids both substantive egalitarianism and the denial that one can judge the worth of persons. It therefore seems to me fair to suggest that Hatab's argument actually expresses the same egalitarian prejudice I have been discussing. In the name of protecting the goodness of persons from arbitrary assignment, Hatab's postmodernism is willing to junk the whole idea of a good person (not to mention the idea of truth). Ultimately, he suggests that only by limiting the evaluation of human beings to "contingent performances" can we make sure that "no person can be essentially devalued to the point of being excluded from the political order because of the presumption of some kind of fundamental, unalterable inferiority" (Hatab: 119).

For Hatab, in other words, to make sure that no one is excluded, we must give up the whole idea of a good or superior person. But this violates Hatab's own basic insight—that a commitment to democratic institutions, to institutions that embody a commitment to treating people as equals, does not commit one to a substantive egalitarianism, to a belief that people are of equal value—and suggests that the democratic prejudice in favor of equality is influencing him unawares. I cannot see how he could otherwise find it plausible, given his basic insight, that if anyone can be a superior person, then some people can be excluded from political participation. I suspect that the real problem to which he is responding is one he cannot acknowledge without admitting that he believes in the equal worth of persons: the problem that if anyone can be a superior person, then others can be excluded—from being superior persons.

Conclusion

Let me summarize briefly the interpretation of *Beyond Good and Evil* I draw from the foregoing train of thought. If we read the book carefully in the light of the relevant distinctions, I have been arguing, we need not interpret it as expressing a commitment to aristocratic political institutions or a rejection of democratic ones. It certainly exhibits a commitment to aristocratic values: to the view that some human beings are of higher value than others. They are of higher value not because of birth or class, however, much less because of race or sexual orientation. Nietzsche's claim is that they are of higher value because they realize higher states of soul, even though most people—at least in their natural/current state—cannot relate to these states and will therefore be unable to recognize their value. Nietzsche does not claim that most people should recognize the higher value of these states, much less that they should regard them as the *telos* of society. He claims only that those who actually realize these states must regard themselves as the *telos* of society, the highest good made possible by social organization.

I understand his argument in these terms: To have much of a conception of such higher states requires significant experience and training, and therefore one will be unable to achieve these states unless she has developed a craving for doing so, a craving that depends on a perception of their higher value. Such a craving could never have developed, Nietzsche claims, without an aristocratic political system. Such institutions were once necessary, I believe he thinks, because only they could have given very crude human beings the experience or perception of differences in rank and value among human beings. Does Nietzsche think that aristocratic political institutions have remained necessary for such experience? I think not. *Beyond Good and Evil* does not say that they remain necessary, and Nietzsche certainly recognized, for instance, that the major religions have all provided human beings with the experience of higher human beings. Of course, the experience of religious persons as higher types is increasingly impossible in the modern world, i.e., in the modern West. But that is precisely because this world has developed under the influence of what Nietzsche considers the peasant revolt led by Luther against the "'higher human being' and the rule of the 'higher human being,' as it was conceived of by the Church" (*GS* 358). Nietzsche regards "modern ideas," the liberal-democratic ideas he holds responsible for the degeneration of both political organization and the human type, as further developments of the same impulse. After conceding Luther's role in "having prepared and favored what we today revere as 'modern science,'" he ends the passage of *The Gay Science* I have been quoting with the claim that "'modern ideas' also belong to the peasant rebellion of the north against the colder, more ambiguous and mistrustful spirit of the south that built its greatest monument in the Christian Church. . . . A Church is above all a structure for ruling that secures the highest rank for the *more spiritual* human beings and that *believes* in the power of spirituality to the extent of forbidding itself the use of all the cruder instruments of force; and on this score alone the Church is under all circumstances a *nobler* institution than the state" (*GS* 358). This kind of nobility is what democratic sensibilities oppose and work against, and this opposition is the ground of Nietzsche's criticism of these sensibilities. I have been arguing that Nietzsche need not be interpreted as advocating political inequality in *Beyond Good and Evil*. But he clearly does advocate the recognition of personal inequality—precisely because such recognition opens up the possibility of securing "the highest rank for the *more spiritual* human beings."[14]

---

[14] Many thanks to Jon Mandle and Ed Witherspoon for very helpful comments on an earlier draft of this paper, to the organizers of the Spindel conference, Jackie Scott in particular, for inducing me to begin working on this material, and to Todd Franklin and Allen Wood, who provided great help as commentators on two different versions of the paper.

{ 10 }

The Good of Community
(co-authored with Monique Wonderly)

Nietzsche is often read as an extreme individualist whose only concern is the flourishing of exceptional individuals. Proponents of this reading typically hold either that Nietzsche is indifferent to society and the vast majority of those who constitute it or that he regards society as valuable only insofar as it is a means for the production of exceptional individuals. Julian Young cites Walter Kaufmann and Alexander Nehamas as exemplars of the first kind of individualist reading of Nietzsche and Brian Leiter and Keith Ansell-Pearson as exemplars of the second. Young has written two books devoted to rejecting these interpretations. According to Young, "Nietzsche's fundamental concern, his highest value, lies with the flourishing of community" (2006: 2). On his view, Nietzsche is not only concerned with society as a whole but holds that its interests actually *take precedence over* those of the individual. On the face of it, this is an implausible interpretation of Nietzsche, for there is nothing more apparent in his work than the high value he places on individuality and especially on individuality of the highest kind. Young grants that Nietzsche values exceptional individuals, but argues that he does so only because they play an essential role in the community. We will argue against this claim here. While we applaud Young for highlighting the often-neglected fact that the community does have import for Nietzsche, we part ways with him insofar as his view commits Nietzsche to what is essentially a *conservative* political position. We defend the more traditional and more liberal view that the good of community, the source of its value, concerns the things of value that it makes possible. The greatest of these objects of value, we take Nietzsche to claim, is true individuality and, especially, the exceptional individual, one who exhibits the highest form of individuality. In the final section, we suggest that Nietzsche's view might nevertheless be able to accommodate a richer notion of community value than is commonly supposed—one that, in important respects, is similar to the value that he attributes to the exceptional individual.

Young's Argument

Young aims to establish, then, that Nietzsche values above all else the flourishing of the whole community, in opposition to the traditional view that he cares most about the individual, and in particular, the exceptional individual. Young approaches this task by going through Nietzsche's books in chronological order and noting how *each* of them, in one manner or another, exhibits a concern with the community. Even where Nietzsche does not employ the term *community* (*das Gemeinwesen*), Young finds support for his communitarian reading in Nietzsche's use of terms such as *Volk* or people, *culture*, and *humanity (or species)*.[1] According to this reading, a community flourishes only when its members share an ethos or ideal. Young's Nietzsche is not simply a communitarian, however, but a *religious* communitarian; he takes communal flourishing to be both undergirded and partially constituted by a unifying ethos that is provided by religious myth and promoted by religious festivals.

Young's reading is most plausible in regard to *The Birth of Tragedy*. Setting out in his first book to diagnose the malaise he sensed in modern culture, Nietzsche locates its source in a scientific culture that destroys myth. "Without myth," he claims, "all cultures lose their healthy, creative, natural energy; only a horizon surrounded by myths encloses and unifies a cultural movement." Absent such a horizon, there is only a "wilderness of thought, morals, and action" (*BT* 23). Nietzsche is clearly using *horizon* here in a metaphorical sense. What a culture needs is not a limit beyond which its members cannot see, but rather a limit on the choices they can even recognize, on ways of feeling, thinking, and acting they can even consider. And myth helps to establish such a horizon, presumably, by celebrating the community's way of doing things, marking it as *the way*. So Young seems correct to take from this passage both a definition of community as "a common enterprise shaped by a shared conception of the good life" and the suggestion that if such a conception is not surrounded by myths, community disintegrates. A society thus becomes fragmented and empty, and "communally and individually, life becomes meaningless" (2006: 32). *BT* is only Nietzsche's first book, of course, and he abandoned many of the views expressed therein in subsequent writings. So the onus is on Young to persuade us that Nietzsche never abandoned his religious communitarianism.

In *Human, All Too Human*, he finds support for his communitarian reading in Nietzsche's claim that "the branch of a people [*Volk*] that preserves itself best is the one in which most men have, as a consequence of sharing habitual and undiscussable principles . . . a living sense of community" and that this involves learning the "subordination of the individual" (*HA* 224). In a later

---

[1] See, for example, Young's (2006) use of "society" on p. 4, "Volk" on pp. 4, 27, 139, "culture" on pp. 27, 32, and "global community" on pp. 87, 124, and 123.

addition to the same work, "The Wanderer and His Shadow," Nietzsche expresses hope for the flourishing of a *global* community when he talks about "that distant state of things in which the good Europeans will come into possession of their great task: the direction and supervision of the total culture of the earth [*gesamten Erdkultur*]" (*HA* II/2:87). Young sees this passage as evidence that "Nietzsche's highest value is global community" (2006: 81). Asking what it is "that makes Nietzsche so keen on global community," Young thinks the answer is "the obvious one that only through the consequent demilitarization [discussed in *HA* II/2:284] can there come into being an age when everyone has transcended animal aggression and can genuinely say [quoting from Nietzsche here]: 'peace all around me and goodwill to all things closest to me.'" Young interprets the following lines from the final aphorism of *HA* as claiming that "Christianity said this too early": "The time has, it seems, still *not yet come* when *all* men are to share the experience of those shepherds who saw the heaven brighten above them and heard the words: 'on earth peace, good will towards men.' —It is still *the age of the individual*" (*HA* II/2:350). Young adds that the final line here is "a difficult remark for the 'individualist' interpreter to accommodate" (2006: 82).

We can think of at least two promising paths down which the individualist interpreter might try to accommodate it. The first would be to insist that the individuals about whom Nietzsche is here worried are those still filled with "animal aggression," and not the exceptional individual he values. The latter has overcome animal aggression and lives "only to know" (*HA* 34), whereas the former (because he encourages a militaristic culture) is indeed detrimental to the kind of community that is most conducive to producing Nietzsche's exceptional individual. The second path would start by noting that *HA* is an early work in which Nietzsche is still very much under the influence of Schopenhauer and therefore Christianity. To make his case, therefore, Young needs to supply evidence from Nietzsche's later works. And this, of course, he tries to do. For instance, he also finds passages in *The Gay Science* that seem to support the value of the community over that of the individual. In *GS* 55, Nietzsche goes so far as to note that previously "it was rarity . . . that made noble," but that "this standard involved an unfair judgment concerning everything usual, near, and indispensable—in short, that which most preserves the species and was the *rule* among men hitherto: all this was slandered . . . in favor of the exceptions" (*GS* 55). Nietzsche concludes this aphorism with the thought that "the ultimate form and refinement [of] noblemindedness" might be to "become the advocate of the rule." As Young reads this: "Given that the 'rule' genuinely promotes the health of the community . . . nobility consists precisely in *commitment to and defense of* the ethos of one's community rather than in opposition to it" (2006: 91). That, however, might be going too far; for it is not clear how such a commitment would fit Nietzsche's understanding of nobility in this book, which is a matter of "feeling heat in things that feel cold to everyone else" (*GS* 55). So it makes most sense to think of the noble-minded person as defending not the community ethos itself, but the type of person slandered by thinkers from Socrates on, who takes that ethos for granted, for whom it constitutes the "horizon" of *BT* and the "undiscussable principles" of *HA*. In any case, Nietzsche is certainly engaged in that kind of defense in *GS* 76, according to which "humanity's greatest labor so far has been to reach agreement about many things and to submit to a *law of agreement*—regardless of whether they are true or false. This is the discipline of the head that has preserved humanity—but the counter-drives are still so powerful" that it is difficult to speak of humanity's future with confidence. Nietzsche locates "the greatest danger that has hovered over and still hovers over humanity" in "the outbreak of madness," by which he means the joy in breaking free of this "discipline of the head," in departing from the common faith. He finds the tendency towards such lack of discipline not in the "slow spirit," who exhibits the "virtuous stupidity" he considers an "exigency of the first order," but among the "select spirits" with whom he identifies. Therefore, Nietzsche concludes, "*We others are the exception and the danger*—we stand eternally in need of defense!—Now there is something to be said for the exception, *provided it never wants to become the rule*" (*GS* 76).

It is difficult to see why those who interpret Nietzsche as an (exceptional) individualist should have problems with these passages from *GS*. For instance, Brian Leiter's interpretation of Nietzsche's critique of morality (in the narrow or "pejorative" sense) stresses the importance of culture: Nietzsche's problem with morality is that it produces a culture that is unfit for producing higher types of humans. It would seem that Leiter's interpretation can accommodate with ease all of the aforementioned passages that Young adduces in support of his view. For all of Nietzsche's concern for culture, it still might be valuable only because and insofar as it is suitable for producing higher types. According to Young, however, this suggestion gets things precisely back to front (2006: 2).

Young argues that for Nietzsche, the higher or exceptional individual is "valuable only as a means to the flourishing of the social organism in its totality" (2006: 135). Much of his evidence for this claim concerns the communal roles and responsibilities that Nietzsche attributes to members of the higher types. In *HA*, for example, Nietzsche tells us that the "deviant natures," which serve to subvert the status quo, are vital to societal progress in that they inoculate the community with something new, enabling its evolution (*HA* I:224). Young thinks a similar story is told in *GS*, but now with more stress, as in passages we have quoted, on the necessity of a community "rule." In *BGE*, Nietzsche describes the "true philosophers" as the "commanders and legislators of values" and they are to "determine the 'where to?' and 'what for?' of people" (*BGE* 211). Presumably, if members of a higher type are endowed with the task of creating and legislating values for a people, they are *responsible* for others in the community. Young adduces similar claims from *Twilight of the Idols* in support of this picture. He suggests that the "exceptional person" bears an "extraordinary weight of social responsibility" on his shoulders, and that the demand that such a leader has a "conscience," as expressed in *TI* I:37, 40, is clearly the demand that he has a "social conscience"—that he accept the responsibility not just for his own flourishing but for the flourishing of the community as a whole (2006: 165). The role of exceptional individuals, then, is to apply their special abilities toward the improvement of their community. Furthermore, such individuals must take this role very seriously because, according to Young, Nietzsche holds that "individuals only truly flourish, *when their own highest commitment is to the flourishing of the community as a whole*, that is, their highest personal goal is the communal good" (2006: 2, Young's italics).

Indeed, many, if not all, of the individuals for whom Nietzsche expresses admiration in his work are those who made substantial contributions to culture and community. Young points out that Nietzsche praised Wagner, at least in part, for his effort to revive the "Volk" through his music. Similarly, he argues that Nietzsche admired Goethe and Napoleon for embodying virtues reminiscent of earlier ages—virtues that promoted higher culture (2006: 76, 100). Nietzsche also regarded himself as a member of the "exceptional type," presumably as a "philosopher of the future," whose role is to create new values.[2] But granting that Nietzsche's exceptional individuals all have roles in the production of culture, and that perhaps this has not been brought out sufficiently in individualist interpretations, it simply does not follow that this is the *only* source of their value. In the next section, we look at some passages that suggest strongly that Nietzsche does not think so.

Problems for Young's Account

We begin with the second two essays of *Untimely Meditations*. Young finds in the first of these, the essay on history (*UM* II), "a sophisticated theory of cultural ... 'health,'" according to which the three types of history serve life "provided that they interact in the right way." The "right way" is for monumental history to inspire cultural change and for antiquarian history to put "a break on the wilder uses of the 'monument,'" thus helping to "ensure that cultural change ... takes the shape of reform rather than 'revolution.'" Finally, the role of critical history is to counteract "the ossifying effects of pure antiquarianism," thereby creating "the ground on which alone effective monuments can be constructed" (2006: 39). Young presents this theory as "important to the argument of [his] book" for two reasons: first, because it "stayed with Nietzsche all his life" (later developments being "refinements rather than rejections"), and

---

[2] According to Young, Nietzsche recognized that he was an exceptional individual, but lamented his destiny as a "free spirit" and longed for community (2006: 79–80).

second, because the theory "reveals the communitarian heart of Nietzsche's thinking, that his overriding concern is for 'people' or 'culture.'" Taken together, these two points have as a consequence that Nietzsche's "later concern for the production of exceptional individuals must derive from a conception of them as, in some way, promoters of communal 'health'" (2006: 39).

We raise two objections. First, Young ignores the extent of Nietzsche's concern with individuals in this essay. Nietzsche begins his discussion of the three kinds of history by discussing the kind of individual for whom each is appropriate: monumental history for the "human being who wants to create something great" and "needs exemplars, teachers and comforters," which he cannot find among his contemporaries; antiquarian history for those who wish to remain within the realm of the "habitual and time-honored"; critical history for "those who are oppressed by the affliction of the present and wish to throw off this burden" (*UM* II:2). Nietzsche's point is that the three kinds of history serve "life" when used by the appropriate type of individual. In the hands of other kinds of individuals, it may be deadly. The passages we have quoted are from the same section of the essay in which Young claims to find a "sophisticated theory of cultural 'health.'" Such a theory may also be present in that section, but we are not sure that it is and it is certainly not obvious. The overwhelming impression created by this (second) section of the essay is that Nietzsche is concerned with how history (hence culture) serves the interest of individuals in leading meaningful lives. The individuals, it seems, are the end, culture or community, the means.

Further, this impression is confirmed—and this is our second objection—by a later and very famous passage in the essay, which Young does not mention. Here Nietzsche argues, against Hegelians, that "the goal of humankind cannot possibly be found in its end stage, but only in its highest specimens [or exemplars]" (*UM* II:9). In this passage, Nietzsche expresses longing for

> a time in which we will no longer pay attention to the masses, but once again only to individuals, who form a kind of bridge over the turbulent stream of becoming. Individuals do not further a process, rather they live timelessly and simultaneously, thanks to history, which permits such a combination; they live in the republic of geniuses of which Schopenhauer once spoke. One giant calls to another across the desolate expanses of time, and this lofty dialogue between spirits continues, undisturbed by the wanton, noisy chattering of the dwarfs that crawl about beneath them. The task of history is to be their mediator and thereby continually to incite and lend strength to the production of greatness.

So, yes, Nietzsche is concerned with culture in the second *Untimely Meditation*. But it seems abundantly clear that he regards the task of culture (here exemplified by history, and especially monumental history) to be the production of great individuals.

The third *UM*, "Schopenhauer as Educator," makes the same impression. Young admits as much, claiming that it "contains some of the most extreme statements of what *appears* to be Nietzsche's 'aristocratic individualism.'" Because such statements also appear to contradict his main thesis, Young considers it important to try "to put these remarks in their proper context" (2006: 43). Although Young does not mention it, one such remark is Nietzsche's explicit claim that "the aim of all culture" is the "production of genius" (*UM* III:3). The same point (but without the explicit reference to culture) is made later in a passage, and Young does quote it, namely, that "humanity should work ceaselessly towards producing great individuals—this and only this should be its task" (*UM* III:6). After commenting that "this certainly looks like elitism of the most radical sort," Young attempts to put the remark into its "proper context" by calling attention to what Nietzsche says immediately thereafter:

> one would like to apply to society and its goals something that can be learnt from observation of any species of the animal or plant world: that the only thing that matters is the superior individual specimen [or exemplar] . . . that, when a species has arrived at its limits and is about to go over into a higher species, the goal of its evolution lies, not in the mass of its specimens and their well-being . . . but rather in those apparently scattered and chance existences which favorable conditions have here and there produced. (*UM* III:6)

The point, as we understand it, is that given how nature operates, it is not as strange as it may seem to claim, as Nietzsche does, that the task of culture is to produce great individuals and that the lives of those who cannot become great will "obtain the highest value, the deepest significance" by "living for the sake of the rarest and most valuable exemplars." Young sees it differently. Asking us to "reflect upon this Darwinian analogy," he notes that "the evolution of a species is evolution of a *total species*—not the consequence-less evolution of a couple of finer-than-usual exemplars."

> What happens of course is that the "random mutations"—a term I shall take over to apply to Nietzsche's exceptional individuals —adapt better and breed whereas those that do not tend to die out before reproducing. So gradually the characteristics of the "higher" (more adaptive) type becomes the rule of the species rather than the exception. Later on, as we shall see, Nietzsche expresses considerable interest in eugenics. So it is possible that it is already in his mind as part of "preparing within and around oneself" for the redemption of culture—though there is no explicit mention of "breeding" in the third Meditation itself. What the biological analogy strongly suggests, however, is that the appearance of the great individual *is not an end in itself but rather a means to the redemptive evolutions of the social totality* (*UM* III:6). (2006: 49)

There are many problems with this, including the gratuitous reference to eugenics (which is not justified by other passages in the book cited in the Index under "eugenics") and the apparent interpretation of the "Darwinian analogy" in too literal a fashion. But the most important problem is the assumed either/or of the final line. Young does not explain, here or elsewhere in either book under consideration, why exceptional individuals cannot be *both* ends in themselves and means to the redemption of the community. No doubt, SE presents great individuals as means to the redemption of the community. It is only through them, by means of them, that the community is redeemed. They therefore have instrumental value in relation to the community. Perhaps Young reasons that if individuals have instrumental value in relation to the community, then the community itself must have intrinsic value. But even if this is so, it does not follow that individuals cannot be valuable in themselves. In fact, it seems that the community is redeemed through individuals precisely because they are intrinsically valuable and that it is only in giving rise to them that the community achieves something of true value.

To see this, consider the identity of these great individuals: Nietzsche calls them "those true human beings, those no-longer-animals, the philosophers, artists, and saints" (*UM* III:5), because they are the only ones who have "elevated their gaze above the horizon of the animal." Here is Nietzsche's description of animal life in the same section of the essay:

> It is truly a harsh punishment to live in the manner of an animal, subject to hunger and desires, and yet without arriving at any insight into the nature of this life, and we can conceive of no harsher fate than that of the beast of prey, who is driven through the desert by its gnawing torment, is seldom satisfied, and this only in such a way that this satisfaction turns into agony in the flesh-tearing struggle with other beasts, or from nauseating greediness and oversatiation. To cling so blindly and madly to life, for no higher reward, far from knowing that one is punished or why one is punished in this way, but instead to thirst with the inanity of a horrible desire for just this punishment as though it were happiness—that is what it means to be an animal. And if all of nature presses onward toward the human being, then in doing so it makes evident that he is necessary for its *salvation from animal existence* and that in him, finally, *existence holds before itself a mirror in which life no longer appears senseless* but appears, rather, in its metaphysical meaningfulness. (*UM* III:5) (our italics)

So animal existence is senseless, without value or meaning. It needs salvation for this very reason and it is redeemed precisely insofar as it finally gives rise to beings who transcend animality and are therefore of value. Further, Nietzsche says that the description he has just given of animal life is "the way it is for all of us" most of the time: "usually we do not transcend animality, we ourselves are those creatures who seem to suffer senselessly." Communal life, in particular, as Nietzsche goes on to describe it, is "just a continuation of animality." It is only in the philosopher, the artist, and the saint that animality is transcended and nature achieves salvation.³ Nature "has arrived at its goal, arrived at the place where it realizes that it has staked too much on the game of living and becoming" (*UM* III:5).

Admittedly, in SE Nietzsche is looking at nature and therefore the community through the lens of what he later called the ascetic ideal. Nature has no value, and the only way to give it value—to redeem it—is to make it into a means to its transcendence, to its opposite. We in no way suggest that this is Nietzsche's later view of things. We have discussed the two *Untimely Meditations* to counter Young's claim that it exhibits a communitarianism about which Nietzsche never changed his mind, and therefore that his later praise of exceptional individuals should be assumed to be praise for what these individuals contribute to the community. Our claim is that when he wrote *UM*, great individuals redeemed the community precisely by being intrinsically valuable, which nature and a natural community are not. We think this sets up a presumption in favor of interpreting Nietzsche's later emphasis on exceptional individuals as due to his continuing belief in their intrinsic value.⁴

One passage from the later works that suggests this, seeming to contradict Young's claim that Nietzsche regards exceptional individuals as valuable *only* insofar as they contribute to communal flourishing, is *Beyond Good and Evil* 258:

> But the essential feature of a good, healthy aristocracy is that it does *not* feel itself to be a function (whether of the monarchy or of the community) but instead feels itself to be their *meaning* and highest justification—and therefore that it accepts with good conscience the sacrifice of countless people who *for its sake* [*um ihretwillen*] have to be pushed down and reduced to incomplete human beings, into slaves, into tools. Its fundamental belief must always be that society may not exist for the sake of society, but only as the substructure and framework for raising an exceptional type of being up to its higher duty and to a higher state of *being*. In the same way, the sun-seeking, Javanese climbing plant called the sipo matador will wrap its arms around an oak tree so often and for such a

---

³ In particular, "nature ultimately needs the saint, whose ego has entirely melted away and whose life of suffering is no longer—or almost no longer—felt individually, but only as the deepest feeling of equality, communion, and oneness with all living things; the saint in whom that miracle of transformation occurs that the game of becoming never hits upon, that ultimate and supreme becoming human towards which all of nature presses and drives onward for its own salvation."

⁴ Note that much has been written contesting both the notion of intrinsic value and its distinction from instrumental value. See, for example, Korsgaard 1983. By use of these terms, we mean only to suggest the following basic ideas: An object has intrinsic value if it is valuable in itself or for its own sake. An object is instrumentally valuable insofar as it is a means to something else of value (Zimmerman 2002).

long time that finally, high above the oak, although still supported by it, the plant will be able to unfold its highest crown of foliage and show its happiness in the full, clear light. (*BGE* 258)

In this passage, rather than portraying the higher type as an instrument for the betterment of the community, Nietzsche seems instead to portray the community as an instrument for the existence of the higher type. More accurately, he says that the higher type must view the community in such a light, feeling itself to be the community's "*meaning* and highest justification."

One option for Young might be to say that we have confused members of the aristocracy with Nietzsche's higher or exceptional human beings. But Young cannot take this option because he thinks Nietzsche is committed to aristocracy as the ideal form of society, so long as it is an aristocracy of a spiritual kind. In fact, he thinks that "Nietzsche's 'ideal' for the future is the rebirth of something resembling the hierarchical structure of the medieval church, the rebirth of a society unified by the discipline of a common ethos, the discipline expounded and given effect through respect for the spiritual authority of those who occupy the role once occupied by the priests" (2006: 99). Young goes on to assure us that the message of these new priests will be naturalistic and life-affirming. But *BGE* 258 remains a problem for him. His new priests are going to be members of an aristocracy, and section 258 implies that they must therefore think of themselves as the "*meaning* and highest justification" of the community. Young's actual response is to suggest that taking this as Nietzsche's own belief "is inconsistent with almost everything else Nietzsche has told us about social elites." We have already provided evidence from the *Untimely Meditations*, on which much of Young's case depends, that this is not the case. But Young says that the purported inconsistency "provides a motive for reading BGE 258 in something other than the standard way" (2006: 135).[5] It is not difficult to find a way to do this, he claims, correctly noting that Nietzsche does not assert in his own voice that any member of an aristocracy *is* the "meaning and justification" of the community, but only that the aristocracy must *view* itself as such. But even if Nietzsche means only to assent to the latter claim, Young's view would still have trouble accommodating it, given his recognition that Nietzsche looks forward to an aristocracy of exceptional individuals. These individuals would have to embrace a lie, and not just any lie but a lie that, on Young's account, would prevent them from *truly flourishing*. Recall that Young takes Nietzsche to hold that "individuals only truly flourish, *when their own highest commitment is to the flourishing of the community as a whole*, that is, their highest personal goal is the communal good" (2006: 2, Young's italics). So Young cannot have it both ways: (1) that Nietzsche does not himself believe what he claims aristocrats

---

[5] He actually begins by presenting the standard reading of the passage as claiming that all that matters to Nietzsche is the "production of a couple of Goethes per millennium . . . *nothing else* has any value to him." This is a caricature, but we cannot deal with that now.

must believe and (2) that Nietzsche believes in an aristocracy of exceptional individuals, of which, of course, he would be a member.

In his search for a reading that is consistent with his communitarian interpretation, Young resorts to the claim that in speaking of what aristocracies must believe Nietzsche means only to *survey the past*, "noting that in healthy aristocracies, the aristocrats have a sublime arrogance, which when it collapses, leads to the decay . . . of society" (2006: 135). But this claim is quite dubious, for two reasons. First, there is nothing to signal or in any way indicate that Nietzsche is speaking only about the past in *BGE* 258 when he says that "every good and healthy aristocracy must feel itself to be the meaning and justification of the community." Furthermore, this passage echoes remarks in the preceding section, where Nietzsche writes, "Every enhancement so far in the type 'man' has been the work of an aristocratic society—and *that is how it will be, again and again*" (*BGE* 257, our italics). Nietzsche goes on to make explicit what he means by an "aristocratic society": "a society that believes in a long scale of orders of rank and differences of worth between man and man and needs slavery in some sense or other." We leave the slavery issue for the footnotes[6] to concentrate on the fact that Nietzsche makes perfectly clear here that every past and future enhancement of the type man will be the work of a society that believes in differences in worth between human beings.[7] When he then goes on in the next passage to say that members of a good and healthy aristocracy—so the ones on the top of the order of rank—must see themselves as the meaning and justification of the community, the obvious implication is that the aristocrats who will be responsible for any future enhancements of the type man must so see themselves.

As one of us has argued previously, Nietzsche thinks that only a society that believes that there are differences in rank or value between human beings will give rise to the craving for higher states of soul—the realization of which constitutes the enhancement of the human type (Clark 1999: 130; paper 9, this volume). Exceptional individuals, those who have achieved higher states of soul, should therefore regard themselves as the *telos* of society, or "the highest good made possible by social organization" (ibid. 137). Reading Nietzsche thusly in no way

---

[6] An unreflective reading of this passage is likely to encourage a disturbing and misguided interpretation of Nietzsche's view. As one of us notes in a previous work (Clark 1999: 125–6; paper 9, this volume), when Nietzsche writes of an aristocratic society, he refers not to a governmental institution, but to a society that believes in "an order of rank and differences in value between human beings"—and this is wholly consistent with, for example, a democratic political structure. Likewise, the term "slave" is not used literally here, as indicated by Nietzsche's more qualified phrase "slavery in some sense" in the preceding section. In fact, in other passages he extends the term *slave* even to scholars and scientists (see, for example, *HA* 283; *GS* 17). So his use of the term clearly does not commit him to the view that any group should be forced into servitude to ensure the flourishing of the exceptional type.

[7] This does not seem to be consistent with Young's interpretation. He claims that as individuals, Nietzsche values equally members of the herd and exceptional individuals. If he values the latter more, it is just because there are fewer of them.

commits him to the view that the community must be suppressed and spent for the advantages of the individual, but only that it is a prerequisite for having the value structure that *constitutes* exceptional individuals that they regard themselves as exemplifying the highest value that can come from a society.

An Alternative View

As we've said, Young claims that Nietzsche values exceptional individuals only because and insofar as they contribute to communal welfare, while his highest object of value is the flourishing of the community as a whole. In this section, our aim is twofold. First, we argue that Young's view represents an impoverished conception of the value that Nietzsche places on the exceptional individual. Second, while putting to the side the question as to whether communal flourishing is Nietzsche's highest value, we attempt to elucidate the nature of the value that he attributes to the community. We are concerned to show not merely *that* Nietzsche regards the community as valuable, but also to give an account of *why* he so regards it. We emerge with an alternative to Young's account of Nietzsche's suggested value relationship between the exceptional individual and society as a whole.

On Young's account, Nietzsche views the exceptional individual as instrumentally valuable. Let us assume his account is true. The exceptional individual then derives his value, at least in part, from his contribution to (and capacity to contribute to) another object of value, namely the community as a whole. In the preceding section, we presented evidence that that this cannot be the *sole* source of the exceptional individual's value. Nietzsche's exceptional individual is no *mere* instrument of his community, but rather its "meaning and highest justification." Nietzsche explicitly states that we "misunderstand great human beings" if we "look at them from the pathetic perspective of public utility" (*TI*, Skirmishes: 50). Similarly, the value or good of the community lies, at least in part, in its ability to produce and support exceptional individuals. Yet, Nietzsche's view may admit of an interpretation that can accommodate the possibility that the exceptional individual and the community each have instrumental value for the other, while still retaining their respective intrinsic value.[8]

---

[8] While it may appear suspect to attribute both *intrinsic* and *instrumental* value to an object, this is not as strange as it may seem. Harry Frankfurt, for example, noted, "It is a mistake to presume that the value of a means is exhausted by the value of the ends . . . certain kinds of activity—such as productive work—are inherently valuable not simply in addition to being instrumentally valuable but precisely because of their instrumental value" (1999: 177–8). See Korsgaard (1983) and Dorsey (2012) for more on this point. Importantly, however, not much hangs on the terminology that one prefers to employ here. Our aim in this section is to articulate a plausible view of how Nietzsche might regard the relationship between communal value and the value of the exceptional individual, one on which the community is no *mere* instrument for the production of exceptional individuals, though its value *is* integrally connected to said production.

It is noteworthy that just as he takes Nietzsche to regard exceptional individuals as only instrumentally valuable, Young attributes a similar status to art. Claiming that "Nietzsche values neither art nor philosophy for its own sake," his point is that they have value only insofar as they "create *important, socially beneficial*, art" or philosophy (2010: 426). Young cites *BGE* 208's discussion of "L'art pour l'art" in support of his claim (2010: 406). While Nietzsche certainly does denounce "art for art's sake" in this passage, he does not, pace Young, deny that art can hold value without contributing to communal flourishing. His intended meaning is made clearer in *TI*, where he again criticizes the notion of "L'art pour l'art," now specifying the object of his ridicule as "art that is altogether purposeless, aimless, and senseless." Works of art are inherently purposive; they are expressions, *communications*, of their creators. What "all art" does, Nietzsche suggests, is to "praise," "glorify," "choose," and "prefer." And this is no accident, he adds, but "the very presupposition of the artist's ability" (*TI* IX:24). In other words, the "purpose of art" is to express and communicate the artist's values.[9] Nietzsche calls "art for art's sake" a form of "nihilism" not because it denies that art need be socially beneficial, but because it denies that art has any purpose at all (*BGE* 208). His point is not that art must do something beyond being art in order to have value, much less that the value of art is contingent upon its contribution to communal flourishing, but rather that all genuine art is, by its nature, inherently purposive in the aforementioned sense.

A proponent of Young's view might argue that the communication of values that is art's purpose is meant to serve the community. After all, Nietzsche goes on to say that art "strengthens or weakens certain valuations," presumably, those of its audience. At a minimum, the success of the communication depends on proper reception by the community. Therefore, it may seem, art's very purpose betrays its instrumental value in relation to the community. But it is far from obvious that the communication of values *must* aim at the betterment of society.[10] Also, while it is clear that art typically does have instrumental value for the community, we have already denied the basis for inferring from this that art is not valuable in itself. After all, objects are sometimes bearers of both intrinsic and instrumental value.[11]

A natural corollary of Young's view that Nietzsche's *highest object of value* is the flourishing of the community would seem to be that Nietzsche regards the community as intrinsically valuable, or valuable for its own sake.[12]

---

[9] Young acknowledges that *TI* IX:24, along with other passages, implies that for Nietzsche, art is necessarily purposive (1992: 128; 2010: 508).

[10] Nietzsche, for example, expressly denies that the purpose of art must be "improving man," and he characterizes the tragedian, not as aiming to communicate to the masses, but as presenting his "drink of sweetest cruelty" to the "heroic man" alone (*TI* IX:24).

[11] For discussions which suggest art as a candidate for possessing both intrinsic and instrumental value, see Davies (2006) and Guest (2002).

[12] Young might deny this, arguing that his view implies that Nietzsche regards "communal flourishing" rather than the community itself as intrinsically valuable. But if Nietzsche did not view the community as valuable for its own sake, then it is difficult to see why *its* flourishing as opposed to the flourishing of any other entity would be Nietzsche's *highest* object of value.

Nietzsche surely would not deny, however, that the community, like good art, is purposive. In fact, as we argued in the previous section, he suggests that at the very least, one purpose, or *telos*, of the community is the exceptional individual. Yet, we cannot infer from the fact that one role of the community is to produce and support exceptional individuals, that the community has *only* instrumental value. On our reading of Nietzsche, just as art and the exceptional individual are both purposive and intrinsically valuable, the community might possess this pair of attributes as well.

Some of the best evidence that Nietzsche regards the community as valuable for its own sake appears in *The Antichrist's* discussion of the splendor and fall of the Roman Empire.[13] There, Nietzsche describes the Roman Empire as "the most magnificent form of organization ever to be achieved under difficult conditions, compared to which everything before or after has just been patched together, botched, and dilettantish" (*A* 58). It is reasonable to suspect that this "most remarkable artwork in the great style," such that "nothing like it has been built to this day" and that "nobody has even dreamed of building on this scale, from the standpoint of eternity," might have had intrinsic value on Nietzsche's view, and furthermore, a value that superseded that of any single individual therein.

In expressing his admiration for the Ancient Roman Empire, Nietzsche emphasizes various aspects of the *form* or *structure* of the community. He views the Roman Empire as a "tremendous structure" and as an example of "great

---

[13] We take it that some of the best support for Young's communitarian reading of Nietzsche comes from his discussion of this passage. The Roman Empire certainly did have an exalted upper-class, the "higher individuals" were neither divorced from their community, nor did they view it as a mere instrument for their own promotion; rather, Rome's higher type seemed to place a different sort of value on their community, deeming themselves responsible for its flourishing. Nietzsche describes these individuals as "those valuable, those masculine-noble natures that saw Rome's business as their own business, their own seriousness, their own pride" (*A* 58). Yet, the Empire, which should have stood "more enduring than bronze" would eventually fall to what Nietzsche refers to as "The Chandala Revenge" (*A* 58). On Young's account, Nietzsche means to analogize the conditions that led to the fall of the Roman Empire to a "design flaw" in the Lawbook of Manu (2006: 185; 2010: 513). The Law of Manu was a form of Indian religious legislation, the goal of which was to "eternalize the supreme condition for a thriving life, a great organization of society" (*A* 58). This code recognized and mandated a strict caste-order. The highest classes consisted of priests and warriors, while the lowest, the Chandala, were "untouchables" who were relegated to the worst and most neglected areas of society and forced to live in filth. Some might interpret Nietzsche as unequivocally endorsing the hierarchical class structure of Manu as an exemplary model, but to interpret him in this way is to miss the point of his noting the "Chandala Revenge" which weakened, and eventually broke, the glory of Rome. According to Young, Nietzsche means not to commend Manu's caste system, but rather to admonish against the creation of a persecuted underclass. The gross mistreatment of the lower individuals in any society lays the foundations for "ressentiment" and the eventual decay of the community entire. It was the creation of such a "Chandala" underclass that ultimately led to Rome's decline (Young 2006: 514). While Young's interpretation may not be the standard reading of *A* 58, we largely agree with the view as he presents it. It is also worth noting that Brian Leiter (2002) and Thomas Brobjer (1998) have also argued that Nietzsche takes a negative stance toward the Law of Manu.

architecture," explicitly identifying it as a work of art (*A* 58). Likewise, Nietzsche's condemnation of "L'art pour l'art" notwithstanding, he does seem to express praise for art's formal elements. In *BGE* 254, for example, he refers to artistic "devotion to form" as a "mark of cultural superiority." Recall that Nietzsche's object of criticism is the idea that art is purposeless. The form of an artwork can both ground its intrinsic value and help to facilitate the fulfillment of the artwork's purpose. Formalist theories of art, for example, often hold that "possession of significant form" is a necessary condition for an object to be considered art and that art has "the exhibition of form as its special or peculiar province of value" (Carroll 1999: 110). Also, consider Jose Bermudez and Sebastian Gardner's description of art's *expressive form*. They write, "A work of art's expressive form is the contribution its formal features make to its expressive capacity, understanding expression in a broad sense on which abstract ideas and ethical perspectives can be expressed no less than emotions and feelings" (Bermudez and Gardner 2003: 7–8).[14] Just as the structure or form of art might facilitate its purpose—the expression of the artist's values—the structure or form of the community might facilitate its own purpose, which on our account, is the production of goods, the highest good being the exceptional individual.[15] Nietzsche's identification of the Ancient Roman Empire as a work of art seems particularly difficult for Young's view to accommodate if he wants to maintain that the former, but not the latter, is valuable for its own sake.

If Nietzsche does view the (well-formed) community as valuable in itself, we would like to suggest that it is in virtue of its form, of the nature of its internal hierarchal structure. For Nietzsche, it might be that a community is successful or exemplary when it is structured by a ranked order of disparate components that manage to function harmoniously and productively. A perfectly structured community is, for Nietzsche, a work of art—one that promotes the flourishing of its inhabitants and importantly, produces other valuable objects. Interestingly, Nietzsche draws parallels between the structure of a community and the structure of the individual's soul.

Consider Nietzsche's description of the state in *The Genealogy of Morality* as "a ruling structure that *lives*, in which parts and functions are delimited and related to one another, in which nothing at all finds a place that has not first had placed into it a 'meaning' with respect to the whole" (*GM* II:17). Clark and Dudrick argue that Nietzsche here refers to the "*form* of the state," the "parts and functions" of which are analogous to the hierarchical order of drives that constitute the structure of the soul (2012: 294). Nietzsche indicates that the

---

[14] In *The Will to Power* 818, Nietzsche suggests that in the case of art, form is content: "One is an artist at the cost of regarding that which all non-artists call 'form' as content, as 'the matter itself.' To be sure, then one belongs in a topsy-turvy world: for henceforth content becomes something merely formal—our life included."

[15] Nietzsche's view might be that in order to count as art, an object must communicate values *by means of its formal properties*.

structure of one's soul both exemplifies his values and determines his status as a lower or higher type of individual. He writes, "The group of feelings that is aroused, expresses itself, and issues commands in a soul most quickly, is decisive for the whole order of rank of its values and ultimately determines its table of goods. The values of a human being betray something of the structure of its soul" (*BGE* 268). Earlier in *BGE*, Nietzsche writes,

> our body is, after all, only a society constructed out of many souls—. *L'effet c'est moi*: what happens here is what happens in every well-constructed and happy community: the ruling class identifies itself with [i.e., takes credit for] the successes of the community. (*BGE* 19) (bracketed material ours)

This passage makes explicit that Nietzsche means to analogize the individual's hierarchal psychic structure to the internal structure of a community.

Young also recognizes such an analogy in Nietzsche's work, stating that just as Plato argued "that state and soul are structurally the same" standing in relation to each other as "macrocosm to microcosm," Nietzsche holds a similar view (2006: 161–2). While there are parallels between the views of Nietzsche and Plato in this regard, it is important to note that there are also significant differences. Plato's *Republic* offers a political ideal, a vision of society wherein philosopher kings rule over a populous arranged in a pyramidal structure. Young suggests that this closely resembles Nietzsche's own view (2006: 132). We would deny this. While Nietzsche certainly endorses a societal hierarchy, he does so only in the sense that his ideal society would recognize some individuals as better or "higher" than others. This recognition in no way implies regarding exceptional individuals as political sovereigns. Yet they are exemplars of superior modes of being, and the recognition that there are such superior modes of being is what induces the craving for higher states of soul (Clark 1999: 130, 138; paper 9 in this volume)). This may be important both for potential exceptional individuals and for exemplars of lower types who will never achieve the "exceptional" status, but who can nonetheless strive to live better lives. We take the latter to be the point of the particularly elitist-sounding section of "Schopenhauer as Educator" (*UM* III:6). To be sure, Nietzsche's exceptional individual is a leader and a legislator of *values* (*BGE* 211), but it is far less clear that he is, or ought to be, a legislator of political ordinances or codes of conduct. On our view, Nietzsche does not argue for any particular type of political system.[16] We agree with Young, however, that Nietzsche wants "both in the microcosm of the soul and the macrocosm of human society at large . . . 'unity in multiplicity,'" which Nietzsche identifies with human greatness (2006: 214).

---

[16] Leiter (2002) states that Nietzsche "has no political philosophy in the conventional sense of theory of the state and its legitimacy" (296). This, however, is a widely contested claim. For more on the debate regarding Nietzsche's political orientation, see Sluga (2014) and Clark (1999; paper 9 in this volume).

On one promising interpretation, Nietzsche identifies the value of an individual with the structure of his soul. The exceptional individual is valuable for his own sake, and indeed has his status as "exceptional," in virtue of the harmonious and productive functioning of the elements of his internal hierarchical structure. If this is the case, then it is reasonable to suspect that for Nietzsche, the well-formed community might also be intrinsically valuable for the very same reason, namely its superior internal hierarchical structure, which is such that its parts function harmoniously and productively for some end.

For Nietzsche, then, (one source of) the value of the community as a whole and that of the individual might depend on the nature of their respective internal hierarchical structures, and notably this is not unrelated to their respective instrumental value for one another. For it is the internal organization of the community that enables it to support and produce its highest good—the exceptional individual; likewise, it is the well-structured soul of the exceptional individual that enables him to make such substantial contributions to his community.[17] Young claims that the flourishing of the community as a whole is Nietzsche's highest object of value, but he does not explain *why* it is that Nietzsche would place such value on the flourishing of the community as a whole. Why would he regard the community as more important than the individuals, especially the higher individuals, who inhabit it? We have denied that he does. But we have suggested an account that can accommodate the view that the community has a kind of intrinsic value, in addition to its instrumental value for producing exceptional individuals, and can explain why Nietzsche regards the community as intrinsically valuable in terms of what it shares with exceptional individuals.

---

[17] Note that this view of what grounds the intrinsic value of the exceptional individual and the community needn't commit one to a particular view of how to *quantify* or *compare* such value across entities; e.g., to a method of weighing the value of the exceptional individual versus that of the community. Thanks to John Richardson for raising this possibility in discussion.

{ PART III }

Metaphysics

{ 11 }

Deconstructing *The Birth of Tragedy*

In a mystifying passage in section 18 of *The Birth of Tragedy,* Nietzsche classifies the Dionysian as a stage of illusion, on a par, as far as truth goes, with the Apollonian and the Socratic. Since, as I shall attempt to show, he thereby contradicts the book's core conception, it is easy to sympathize with Wilcox's suggestion that we are faced here with "one of Nietzsche's careless mistakes, a slip on his part" (Wilcox 1974: 109). On the other hand, recent deconstructive approaches have taught us to suspect that "mistakes" of this magnitude cannot be mere slips. Something of deeper importance must be going on when a thinker of Nietzsche's stature is led into such a contradiction. One virtue of Paul de Man's deconstruction of *The Birth of Tragedy* is that it allows us to see a deeper significance in this contradiction than straightforward analytical approaches have discovered. To many, however, the cost of this advantage—de Man's claims about truth, language, and philosophy, and his denial of a development in Nietzsche's position after *The Birth of Tragedy*—will seem too high. In this paper, I will argue that we need not pay this price in order to benefit from de Man's insight that Nietzsche's self-contradiction is not a mere mistake. After explaining what the contradiction is, I will examine de Man's deconstructive analysis of how it arises, and then argue that a more traditional approach can offer a better account of what led Nietzsche into it.

In his first book, Nietzsche used the terms "Apollonian," "Dionysian," and "Socratic" to denote three different "redemptive strategies," i.e., ways of overcoming the terror and horror of existence, of affirming life or finding it worth living.[1] For followers of Socrates, the belief that being is knowable, hence correctable, makes life affirmable. In the other two cases, art plays this redemptive role. Apollonian art throws a veil of beauty over the empirical world; it makes life seem worth living by transforming and glorifying individuals involved in it. Dionysian art, on the other hand, glorifies neither individuals nor any other

---

[1] For a detailed discussion of redemptive strategies in *The Birth of Tragedy,* see McGinn 1975.

aspect of the empirical world. It either by-passes the empirical world altogether—as in music—or destroys individuals—as in tragedy. Redemption is gained through identification with something that is more important than individuals, something that remains powerful while the individual is destroyed.

Walter Kaufmann's efforts to the contrary notwithstanding, it is difficult to resist the impression that Nietzsche values the artistic strategies more highly than the Socratic. While its stated aim is to explain the origin of tragedy, the book's philosophical aim is to establish the priority of aesthetic values: to show that art is of greater value than science, and aesthetic values more important than "scholarly" ones. Again, pace Kaufmann, the Dionysian seems to be the preferred of the aesthetic strategies. This impression is confirmed by Nietzsche's later comment about *The Birth of Tragedy:* "Indeed, what is Dionysian? This book contains an answer: one 'who knows' is talking, the initiate and disciple of his god" (*BT* P 4).[2] Although Nietzsche presents Apollo as an equal partner in the origin of tragedy—the words, characters, and action are Apollonian—the feature he considers most important—the redemption tragedy provides, the affirmation of life despite its horrors—is Dionysian.

When we ask for the basis of Nietzsche's apparent value hierarchy—his basis for valuing the Dionysian over the Apollonian, and both of these over the Socratic—the answer seems to lie in the comparative truthfulness of the strategies. Dionysus represents redemption in full knowledge of the truth, Apollo combines truth with illusion, whereas the Socratic mode of redemption is based completely on illusion. Nietzsche identifies Socrates as the god of the theoretical person who is motivated to search for truth by the "profound illusion that first saw the light of day in the person of Socrates: the unshakable faith that thought, using the thread of causality, can penetrate the deepest abysses of being, and that thought is capable not only of knowing being but even of correcting it" (*BT* 15).[3] The illusion of the Socratic, Nietzsche makes clear a few sections later, has been exposed by "the extraordinary courage and wisdom of Kant and Schopenhauer," who have "diagnosed for the first time the illusory notion which pretends to be able to fathom the inner nature of things with the aid of causality," and who have "gained the victory over the optimism concealed in the nature of logic" (*BT* 18). Nietzsche takes the Socratic form of redemption to depend on a false belief, the belief that we can discover the ultimate truth about things through rational inquiry. His judgment as to the falsity of this belief (and the illusory nature of the Socratic) depends on his acceptance of the Schopenhauerian claim that the world accessible to us through sense experience and theory (ordinary, non-mystical modes of knowledge) is mere appearance, a distortion of reality as it is in itself.

---

[2] Translations are from Walter Kaufmann's edition of *The Birth of Tragedy* (*BT*), with minor changes based on the Colli-Montinari *Gesamtausgabe*.

[3] Nietzsche seems to treat "the thread of causality" as equivalent to "the thread of logic," something much easier to associate with Socrates.

In itself, according to Schopenhauer, the world is blind, striving will, involving no plurality or individuation. It appears to the subject of sense experience and theoretical knowledge as a world of individuals caught up in a network of spatial, temporal, and causal relations only because the subject of such knowledge is an instrument of will, and its object is therefore organized for it in terms of causal, temporal, and spatial structures which make possible willing guided by knowledge.[4] Socratic knowledge is illusory, then, in the sense that it presents the world to us only as it appears through the distorting veil of time, space, and causality.

Nietzsche also identifies Apollo with illusion—as "the ruler over the beautiful illusion of the inner world of phantasy" (*BT* 1), whose highest effect is the triumph over "an abysmal and terrifying view of the world and the keenest susceptibility to suffering through recourse to the most forceful and pleasant illusions" (*BT* 3). The Apollonian makes life appear justified by transforming and glorifying it, thus veiling or withdrawing from view the reality of empirical existence (*BT* 3). It nevertheless possesses a "higher truth" and "perfection" than "the incompletely intelligible everyday world" (*BT* 1). Nietzsche's basis is, once again, the acceptance (and transformation) of Schopenhauer's philosophy. Nietzsche considers the dream, the natural counterpart of Apollonian art, more real than empirical life because, as the mere appearance of a mere appearance, it is a "higher appeasement of the primordial desire for mere appearance" (*BT* 4), which is responsible for the existence of the empirical world.[5] The Apollonian attitude—that beauty or the transfiguration of life is more important than empirical reality—is in touch with the truth about the empirical world, that it is only appearance and not the reality the Socratic person takes it to be.

But only Dionysian art gives access to the ultimate truth, i.e., to the world as it is in itself, the reality lying beyond the empirical world. As Nietzsche contrasts Apollo and Dionysus:

Apollo overcomes the suffering of the individual *by* the radiant glorification of the eternity of the phenomenon; here beauty triumphs over the suffering inherent in life; pain is obliterated *by* lies from the features of nature. In Dionysian art and its tragic symbolism the same nature cries to us in its true, undissembled voice: "Be as I am! Amid the ceaseless flux of phenomena, the eternally creative primordial mother, eternally impelling to existence, eternally finding satisfaction in this change of phenomena."

---

[4] This understanding of Schopenhauer's view of the ultimate significance of the a priori forms of time, space, and causality is suggested by section 34 of the first volume of *The World as Will and Representation,* in which he claims that the final goal of knowledge structured by these forms is to relate things to one's own will.

[5] Nietzsche transforms Schopenhauer's will into an "artist-god" who frees himself from the contradictions in his soul by creating the empirical world: "The world-at every moment the attained salvation of God, as the eternally changing, eternally new vision of the most deeply afflicted, discordant, and contradictory being who can find salvation only through *illusion* [*im Scheine*]" (*BT* P 5). The empirical world thus appeases the creator's desire for Apollonian art and must itself be illusory.

>Dionysian art, too, wishes to convince us of the eternal joy of existence; only we are to seek this joy not in phenomena, but behind them. We are to recognize that all that comes into being must be ready for a sorrowful end; we are forced to look into the terrors of individual existence—yet we are not to become rigid with fear: a metaphysical comfort tears us momentarily from the bustle of the changing figures. We are really for a moment primordial being itself, feeling its raging desire for existence and joy in existence; the struggle, the pain, the destruction of phenomena now appear necessary to us in view of the excess of countless forms of existence which force and push one another into life, in view of the exuberant fertility of the universal will. (*BT* 16–17)

Nietzsche's basis for believing that Dionysian art puts us in touch with the true voice of nature is again found in Schopenhauer. In what Nietzsche calls Apollonian art, Schopenhauer believes the intellect is released from subservience to the will and therefore from the distorting influence of the forms of time, space, and causality. Art can therefore give us a truth inaccessible to science or theory: it can make present to us the eternal essences, the Platonic forms, of the world at the different levels of its articulation for the subject. But precisely because this still takes place within the confines of the subject/object relation, this gives us the world only as it appears to the subject, not as it is in itself. But if the subject/object relation is itself a distorting influence which reduces the object to the status of appearance, the only solution is the dissolution of that relation.

And this is precisely how Nietzsche describes Dionysian experience: we become one with reality itself, which, following Schopenhauer, he calls "will." There is no longer any separation of subject and object to distort the truth. This interpretation is supported by Nietzsche's earlier claim (*BT* 5) that "all our knowledge of art is basically quite illusory, because as knowing beings we are not one and identical with that being which, as the sole author and spectator of this comedy of art, prepares a perpetual entertainment for itself. Only insofar as the genius in the act of artistic creation coalesces with this primordial artist of the world [Nietzsche's reinterpretation of Schopenhauer's will], does he know anything of the eternal essence of art; for in that state he is . . . at once subject and object, at once poet, actor, and spectator."

Tragedy is also Apollonian, but only by virtue of elements of illusion which act to veil, thereby making more bearable, the Dionysian truth. The truth revealed in tragedy—the horror of individual existence and the underlying oneness of all being—is identified solely with Dionysus. The tragic story is the attempt to put into words, to articulate in terms of individual characters and actions, the Dionysian vision of the chorus. But Dionysian wisdom is not adequately expressed by these Apollonian devices. Language itself is inadequate for disclosing the truth (*BT* 6, 17), and can at most point the way to the Dionysian experience in which truth is fully present.

Consider now the problematic passage from section 18:

> It is an eternal phenomenon: the insatiable will always finds a way to detain its creatures in life and compel them to live on, by means of an illusion spread over things. One is chained by the Socratic love of knowledge and the delusion of being able thereby to heal the eternal wound of existence; another is ensnared by art's seductive veil of beauty fluttering before his eyes; still another by the metaphysical comfort that beneath the whirl of phenomena eternal life flows on indestructibly—to say nothing of the more vulgar and almost more powerful illusions which the will always has at hand. These three stages of illusion are actually designed only for the more nobly formed natures.

Nietzsche is apparently saying that the "metaphysical consolation" involved in the Dionysian experience of tragedy is just another illusion which seduces us to go on living. In that case, however, he loses his argument for the priority of aesthetic values.[6] If there is no access to a truth beyond the empirical, he cannot even consider art more truthful than theory on the grounds that it at least recognizes the illusoriness of empirical reality. But, within the parameters of *The Birth of Tragedy*, only Dionysian experience can provide the required access to transcendent truth. How could Nietzsche fail to see that the classification of Dionysian experience as illusory undercuts his whole argument?

Yet, he undermines his own argument in even more obvious ways. He proclaims the inadequacy of language for expressing the truth, yet presents himself as offering us the truth—in language, of course. On the basis of a theory (Schopenhauer's, or his own variation on it), he presents himself as knowing that only art, and not theory, can provide true knowledge. The straightforward or analytical response to such contradictions at the heart of *The Birth of Tragedy* is that they reveal the book's incoherence and explain why Nietzsche spent so much of his later work rejecting it. To the deconstructionist, on the other hand, it is by means of such contradictions that *The Birth of Tragedy* accomplishes its aim: namely, the deconstruction or subversion of its own logocentrism.

Used by Derrida to denote the valuation of speech over writing, "logocentrism" normally has the wider meaning captured by John Searle: "roughly the concern with truth, rationality, logic and 'the word' that marks the Western philosophical tradition."[7] It is taken to involve a set of value priorities typical

---

[6] If art is not more truthful than theory, Nietzsche has no basis for considering it more life-affirming either. The Socratic also compels us to go on living, and, from what Nietzsche says in section 15, is apparently more important for the preservation of life than is art. Within the confines of the argument of *BT*, it is only insofar as art is considered more truthful than theory that it can be said to affirm life more fully.

[7] John Searle, "The Word Turned Upside Down," review of On *Deconstruction: Theory and Criticism after Structuralism*, by Jonathan Culler, *New York Review of Books*, October 27, 1983, p. 74.

of Western philosophers and intellectuals: the value of truth over illusion, of science over art, of logic over rhetoric, of literal language over figurative, of the spoken over the written word. Since this is close to what Nietzsche means by the "Socratic," *The Birth of Tragedy* would seem to involve an argument against logocentrism. As a straightforward argument against the Socratic; however, it is self-contradictory in the ways I have indicated. Indeed, all arguments against the Socratic or logocentric would seem to be self-defeating. How can one argue against the possibility of truth, the validity of logic, the importance of argument without presupposing that against which one is arguing? While the philosopher may smile at this point, assured that his values are immune to criticism, de Man claims that Nietzsche's text undermines these values from within, by showing that logocentrism leads to self-contradiction.

Despite its apparent anti-logocentrism, de Man places *The Birth of Tragedy* squarely in the logocentric tradition because it gives priority to voice (or "speech," language as immediately present) over language as representational or graphic ("writing"), because its value reversals are in the service of what de Man takes to be the core of logocentrism: "the claim that truth can be made present to man" (88).[8] This claim is put into question, according to de Man, by the conflict between Nietzsche's theory and rhetorical praxis—between the theory that truth is present only in Dionysian experience, and the narrator's non-Dionysian presentation of this theory as the truth. Instead of yielding a mere cancellation or negation, this contradiction between theory and practice is supposed to leave a residue of meaning which can be translated into a statement having to do with the limits of textual authority (99): i.e., the limits of its own access to truth. The text cannot make this statement—at least not without reducing itself to nonsense. The point seems to be that it can exhibit what it cannot sensibly assert. Since its own theory that truth is present in Dionysian experience can only be expressed by a rhetorical praxis inconsistent with that theory, we are here shown something about the limits of textual authority or access to truth which cannot simply be asserted in the text. It does surface in the text, de Man believes, in somewhat veiled form, in "enigmatic" statements which "cannot be integrated within the value-pattern of the main argument" (99). This is how he interprets section 18. In classifying the Dionysian as a stage of illusion, Nietzsche is in effect admitting that the author who is speaking in the name of the god Dionysus does not possess the truth. If he had made this admission more directly, it would have been impossible for the text to unfold the "fallacy" (102) of claiming to possess truth.

One of the attractive features of de Man's interpretation is that it makes *The Birth of Tragedy* into a work of art. The text seems to aspire to a truth which de Man calls "referential": literal correspondence to an external reality. But when read in this referential mode, it contradicts itself, thereby subverting its own

---

[8] Numbers in the text correspond to pages in de Man 1979.

claim to such truth. In thereby showing what it cannot sensibly or literally say, it is like a work of literature, which may exhibit reality and truth to us, even though its sentences do not correspond in any literal way to external reality. This is why de Man takes *The Birth of Tragedy* to support the view that literature is "the model of truth to which philosophy aspires," and that philosophy is an "endless reflection of its own destruction at the hands of literature" (115). On his interpretation, the central criticism of *The Birth of Tragedy* can be answered: namely, if its point is that only art conveys truth, why didn't Nietzsche create a work of art? The deconstructionist answer is that this is precisely what he so brilliantly did, while at the same time subverting or deconstructing the dichotomy between art and theory.

Yet the question remains as to why a deconstructive interpretation of *The Birth of Tragedy* should be accepted. Granted that Nietzsche's theory and practice are at odds, why not interpret this, in traditional terms, as the sign of an inadequate theory of truth which Nietzsche tried to overcome? Rather than a case of logocentrism deconstructing itself, why isn't it just a bad argument against logocentrism?

The best answer I can find in de Man's text is that the nature of language is such that logocentrism—particularly, the claim to possess truth—always undermines itself. De Man believes that Nietzsche is "in the grip of a powerful assumption about language, an assumption that is bound to control his conceptual and rhetorical discourse whether the author is aware of it or not" (87), "bound to control all the movements of the work" (89). This assumption—that all language is figural and cannot therefore express literal truth—is made explicit and, according to de Man, is demonstrated deconstructively in Nietzsche's essay "Truth and Lies in the Non-Moral Sense." However, if statements that contradict Nietzsche's logocentric claims follow directly from a demonstrable assumption about the nature of language, then language itself is such that logocentrism leads to its own contradiction, and de Man has every reason to interpret *The Birth of Tragedy* as an instance of this deconstructive pattern. His interpretation could be challenged by arguing against the assumption that language is incapable of expressing truth. I will ignore that issue and challenge the interpretation by arguing that this assumption does not dictate the contradictions of section 18.

De Man argues that Dionysian experience belongs either to "the domain of the text" (i.e., is essentially linguistic) or to "nature." He rejects the second alternative on the grounds that the Dionysian would then be "forever and radically separated from any form of art," since no bridge connects nature to its representation (100).[9] Dionysian experience must therefore be essentially

---

[9] See Corngold 1983 for a discussion of de Man's own errors in the translation of the passage from which he draws this argument.

linguistic. But given the assumption that language cannot express the truth, it must also be illusory, as section 18 claims.

Unfortunately, de Man offers only an inadequate reason for denying that Dionysian experience could be non-linguistic. Of course, art cannot state the truth present in ineffable experience, but Nietzsche's reason for associating Dionysus with art is not that such art states Dionysian truth, but that it induces in us a certain state in which we are able to experience that truth, a state in which the subject/object relation which distorts the truth collapses. Nietzsche's denial that language can adequately capture the essence of things may require him to admit that "Dionysus" is an inadequate name for the experience in question, just as "will" is an inadequate name for the "in itself." But, contrary to de Man (100–101), this does not rule out the possibility that the experience that we, however inadequately, call "Dionysian," does capture the essence of things, even if it cannot gain linguistic expression without distortion. The only assumption concerning language that would force Nietzsche to deny that Dionysian experience makes truth present is a denial that truth or experience can be ineffable or non-linguistic. However reasonable this assumption may be, there is no evidence that Nietzsche is making it, or that de Man wants to attribute it to him. I therefore find no reason to believe that the admission of the illusory nature of the Dionysian is controlled by Nietzsche's assumptions about language.

What, then, does push Nietzsche to the self-contradiction of section 18? To support my answer to this question, it is helpful to consider another puzzling line which occurs a few lines after Nietzsche implies that the Dionysian is illusory:

> All that we call culture is made up of such stimulants; and, according to the proportion of the ingredients, we have either a dominantly *Socratic* or *artistic* or *tragic* culture; or, if historical exemplifications are permitted, there is either an Alexandrian or a Hellenic or a Buddhistic culture. (*BT* 18)

The implication that Buddhism exemplifies tragic culture has always been considered incomprehensible since Nietzsche otherwise interprets tragedy as the highest means of affirming life, and as a remedy against longing for the negation of the will which he associates with Buddhism (*BT* 7). Again, it seems implausible that this is merely a "slip": how could Nietzsche possibly equate Buddhism with the affirmation of life, or forget he was interpreting tragedy as affirming it? On the other hand, I see no way of accounting for it in terms of anything Nietzsche believed about language.

I believe that we can account for both of the apparent lapses in section 18 as the surfacing of a conflict about the value of life to which the whole of *The Birth of Tragedy* gives expression, and which infects the very concept of the Dionysian. In the later preface to the work, Nietzsche writes that he used the term "Dionysus" to name the "instinct that spoke in favor of life and discovered for itself a fundamentally opposite doctrine and valuation of life" than that of Christian morality (*BT* P:5). If Dionysus functioned as the god of the affirmation of life, however, he was also the god of truth. In itself, this is no problem. The greatest affirmation of life must be the one that admits the most truth, since one can affirm only as much life as one will admit to exist.[10] The problem is that Nietzsche regards as the truth not simply Schopenhauer's metaphysical doctrine of the world as will, but, more importantly, the conclusion Schopenhauer drew from it, that life is not worth living. Nietzsche translates this into the "terrible wisdom of Silenus" (*BT* 3–4) and Hamlet's "horrible truth" (*BT* 7). I propose that in *The Birth of Tragedy*, Nietzsche is accepting this "truth," but is attempting to avoid the conclusion Schopenhauer drew from it: that the ascetic life is the highest life, that only negation of the will brings redemption. Nietzsche's alternative to asceticism is art—that "only as an *aesthetic phenomenon* is existence and life eternally justified" (*BT* 5). As de Man points out, this famous line is "an indictment of existence rather than a panegyric of art" (93). What he doesn't seem to realize is that this is sufficient to explain why the Dionysian must be identified with illusion: if life is not worth living, no art can redeem except through illusion. Given what Nietzsche takes the truth to be, Dionysus cannot represent both truth and the affirmation of life.

Section 18 lays bare the concept's contradictory nature. First we see what happens when one fully identifies Dionysus with the affirmation of life: it must be considered illusory: on a par, as far as truth goes, with the Apollonian and Socratic. The other side then receives its due: that Dionysus represents the truth. In that case, it must be associated with the rejection of the value of life, with the negation of the will, as it is when Nietzsche equates the tragic, whose truth is Dionysian, with the Buddhist.

If this is correct, section 18 provides no evidence for an ironic or deconstructive reading of *The Birth of Tragedy*. Instead it gives evidence against the claim de Man needs to defend such a reading, namely, that "all the movements of the work" are controlled by assumptions about language (89). Nietzsche's assumptions about values are more important than, and probably control, his assumptions about language. What surfaces in section 18 is the conflict between his acceptance of Schopenhauer's values and his desire to reject them (in terms of the *Genealogy*, between the ascetic ideal, which is responsible for both indictments of existence and metaphysics, and the life-affirming ethic Nietzsche would later develop). The book's major contradictions are an expression of, and an unsuccessful attempt to resolve, this

---

[10] This follows the argument in Wilcox: 190.

ambivalence. Assumptions about language provide no shortcut or special access to understanding the value commitments of a text, and the door is left open for believing that old-fashioned Socratic strategies—which always interpret contradiction as something to be overcome—provide the necessary and appropriate means for such understanding.[11]

---

[11] I would like to thank students and faculty of the English Department of Columbia University for their comments on the original version of this paper, especially Stanley Fish, who tried (unsuccessfully I'm sure he believes) to teach me what deconstruction is, and Susan Fox, who suggested the title.

{ 12 }

On Knowledge, Truth, and Value
Nietzsche's Debt to Schopenhauer and the Development of his Empiricism

Nietzsche expresses his debt to Schopenhauer very clearly—Schopenhauer is his "great teacher," his "first and only educator" (*GM* P:5; *HA* II/P:1).[1] He is less clear concerning what his philosophy owes to Schopenhauer. He counts "Schopenhauer as Educator" in his essay of that title not because of any doctrine he accepted, but because Schopenhauer provided him with a model of the philosophical life; and the passage about his "great teacher" tells us not what he learned from Schopenhauer, but only that he arrived at his own view of morality by engaging in a struggle with Schopenhauer's values. At first, he tells us, his problem with Schopenhauer's values was only an "isolated matter, a lone question mark" about the value of compassion; but because he stuck with this issue and learned to ask more questions about it, a whole "new vista" opened up for him, one that eventually led to his revaluation of values. One might well think that Nietzsche considers Schopenhauer important to his development simply because he was able to learn from his teacher's mistakes and see them as symptoms of something larger, rather than because of anything Schopenhauer got right which Nietzsche therefore incorporated into his own philosophy.

In this essay I will argue that a much more substantial connection exists between Nietzsche's philosophy and Schopenhauer's, that on issues concerning truth and knowledge Nietzsche derived his own views fairly directly from Schopenhauer, and that he himself tells us that this is so. To this end I will focus on drawing out and substantiating the implications of one passage, *The Gay Science* 99. Entitled "Schopenhauer's Followers," it actually says nothing explicit

---

[1] The translation of *GM* is by Clark and Swensen. I have used Hollingdale's translation of *HA* and Kaufmann's translation (sometimes with Hollingdale) of the other books by Nietzsche quoted in this essay. I often make minor, and sometimes substantial, revisions in these translations, usually for the sake of preserving consistency of word choice or phrasing across books and sections.

about Nietzsche's debt to Schopenhauer, but I consider that its main concern. According to my reading of this passage, Nietzsche locates his debt to Schopenhauer in matters of substance, and the similarity between his own philosophy and Schopenhauer's not where it is often found—in the relationship between Schopenhauer's will and Nietzsche's metaphysical-sounding doctrine of the will to power—but rather in the empiricist tendencies of both philosophies. It follows from my interpretation that one has little hope of understanding Nietzsche's thought and development on issues concerning truth and knowledge unless one understands it as deeply tied into Schopenhauer's thought. Among the benefits of doing so is a counter to temptations to say many of the things that are often taken for granted about Nietzsche—e.g. that he regards truth as perspectival and views science as "only a perspective."

GS 99 begins by claiming that one can observe in the case of Schopenhauer's German followers the process that occurs when barbarians come into contact with a higher culture, namely, that "the lower culture always accepts first of all the vices, weaknesses, and excesses of the higher and only then, on that basis, feels a certain attraction to it and eventually, by way of the vices and weaknesses it has acquired, also accepts some of the overflow of what really has value in the higher culture." Nietzsche goes on to list what he implies "really has value" in Schopenhauer: "his sense for hard facts, his good will for clarity and reason, which so often makes him appear so English and un-German," his intellectual conscience, his cleanliness in matters of religion, and his "immortal doctrines of the intellectuality of intuition, of the *a priori* nature of the causal law, of the instrumental character of the intellect and the unfreedom of the will." None of this, Nietzsche claims, enchanted Schopenhauer's German followers, who were drawn instead to his "mystical embarrassments and subterfuges in those places where the factual thinker allowed himself to be seduced and corrupted by the vain urge to be the unriddler of the world." In other words, they were attracted not by the empiricist or "factual thinker" Nietzsche takes Schopenhauer to be, but by the metaphysician or "unriddler of the world." Among the embarrassments of the latter Schopenhauer Nietzsche includes: his doctrine of the one will as the inner nature of the world, the denial of individuality (the claim that it belongs only to appearance), his "ecstatic reveries about genius," and the "nonsense" about how compassion breaks through the principle of individuation and is the source of all morality—"these and other such *excesses* and vices of the philosopher are always accepted first of all and turned into articles of faith: for vices and excesses are aped most easily and require no long training."

After setting out this thesis, Nietzsche proceeds to illustrate it with the case of Wagner, who he says misinterpreted his own characters and the philosophy implicit in his most characteristic works when he began to read Schopenhauer's doctrines into them and to apply to himself the categories of "will," "genius," and "compassion." Schopenhauer cast a "spell" over Wagner, which blinded him not only to other philosophies that might have suited his art better, but "even to science itself," so that more and more his art presented itself "as a companion piece and completion [*Ergänzung*] of Schopenhauer's philosophy," explicitly renouncing "the loftier ambition of becoming a companion piece and completion of human knowledge and science."

An interesting fact about *GS* 99 is that Nietzsche illustrates only the first part of his thesis: that his German followers initially accepted only the vices and weaknesses of Schopenhauer's higher culture. Nothing is done to illustrate its second part: that the vices eventually led to an appreciation and acceptance of what was truly of value in that culture. Nor does he provide any basis for believing that he thinks the second part was true of Wagner, or any indication of another Schopenhauerian follower of whom it might be true.

It is hardly plausible that Nietzsche simply failed to realize that he was illustrating only half, and clearly the less interesting half, of his thesis. The obvious explanation is that he is encouraging the reader to think about another German follower of Schopenhauer: Nietzsche himself. The reasonable inference to draw from the passage is that Nietzsche includes himself among those who were "initially fascinated and seduced by [Schopenhauer] like barbarians." In fact, as I shall argue, a number of the Schopenhauerian doctrines listed as "mystical embarrassments and subterfuges" are ones found in *The Birth of Tragedy*. The implication of the passage is that these embarrassing features of Nietzsche's first book eventually helped him to acquire what "really has value" in Schopenhauer, those aspects of his philosophy that make him a "factual thinker" rather than a metaphysician. We would therefore expect Nietzsche's early work to be caught up in Schopenhauer's metaphysical subterfuges, hence blind both to science and to what would otherwise be its philosophy, so that it presents itself as a "companion piece and completion of Schopenhauer's philosophy," in contrast to his later work, which should reflect an appreciation and acquisition of Schopenhauer's empiricist tendencies and "the loftier ambition of becoming a companion piece and completion of human knowledge and science."

Are these implications of *GS* 99 plausible in the light of the actual development of Nietzsche's views? This chapter attempts to show that they are, that the passage fits the actual development of Nietzsche's views concerning truth and knowledge and can be further illuminated by a consideration of that development. Sections 1 and 2 provide an account of that development from *The Birth of Tragedy* to *Human, All Too Human* that accords with the standard view that Nietzsche went from being a follower of Schopenhauer in the former to being a "positivist" in the latter. However, I call Nietzsche an "empiricist" rather than a "positivist" because the latter is now a term of abuse and I do not believe Nietzsche's empiricist doctrines are so easily dismissed. Further, I claim that he became an empiricist precisely *as* a follower of Schopenhauer and that he remained one to the end. In Section 3 I give interpretations of *The Gay Science* and of Nietzsche's perspectivism which are at odds with most accounts of Nietzsche's later works, including much of my own previous interpretation.

1. A Barbarian in Contact with Schopenhauer's Higher Culture: Early Nietzsche on Truth and Knowledge

Nietzsche's writings on truth have generated interest in recent years, and have exerted great influence, especially on so-called postmodernists. Indeed postmodernists such as Richard Rorty trace the genealogy of their skepticism about truth above all to Nietzsche (Rorty 1989: 10). In particular, Nietzsche's early essay "On Truth and Lies in the Non-Moral Sense" (1873) seems to offer an extended defense of postmodernist skepticism, summed up in the well-known charge that "truths are illusions" (TL 84; 880–1).[2] Nietzsche makes clear elsewhere in the essay that this charge does not apply to tautologies, the only non-empirical truths he recognizes. "Truths are illusions" is therefore a slogan for skepticism regarding empirical truths, for a denial that even the best-confirmed empirical truths are really true. Postmodernists tend to sympathize with this denial and to interpret Nietzsche's later claims about truth as extensions of and variations on it, so that his later perspectivism, for instance, is interpreted as implying that truth is relative to one's perspective. And this provides major encouragement for the view that Nietzsche considers science at best "only a perspective." I believe we can plausibly arrive at a very different view of Nietzsche's position on truth and science if we examine the development of his thought under the guidance of *GS* 99.

Although I agree that Nietzsche's position in "Truth and Lies" is an early version of postmodernist skepticism, I deny that his later works, and in particular his mature perspectivism, offer support for postmodernist denials of knowledge and truth. I have elsewhere offered a detailed account of Nietzsche's development that supports this judgment and this chapter will both supplement and revise that account. Particularly important is my argument for the claim from which I begin here: that Nietzsche's skepticism about empirical truth in "Truth and Lies" is based on Schopenhauer's account of the empirical world as only appearance or phenomenon, not the thing in itself (Clark 1990: 63–94). Nietzsche thus calls empirical truths "illusions" precisely because he believes that even the best-confirmed empirical theories inform us only about the appearance of things, never about the thing in itself. If this is correct, Nietzsche's skepticism in "Truth and Lies" is plausibly interpreted as serving the same critique of modern Western culture to which he devoted his first book, published the previous year. In *BT*, Nietzsche presents modern culture as superficial and

---

[2] I cite TL by the page of Breazeale's translation, followed by the page number in *KSA*, volume 1.

deeply unsatisfying compared to the culture of the ancient Greeks, diagnosing this dissatisfaction as due to the fact that modern culture values science above all else, whereas Presocratic Greece gave priority to art and myth. Nietzsche argues against the modern valuation of science by arguing against what he takes to be its presupposition: that science gives us truth, whereas art does not. His argument makes use of two major components of Schopenhauer's philosophy, its account of the distinction between appearance and thing in itself and its theory of art.

According to Schopenhauer, the world in itself is blind will or willing, involving no plurality or individuality. The empirical world of individuals exists only as a representation, and its spatial, temporal, and causal structure, which makes plurality and individuality possible, is derived not from the nature of the world as it exists independently of consciousness, but only from the nature of the subject whose representation that world is. That subject or intellect comes into existence to serve the will, and its perception and knowledge are therefore organized in terms of structures that relate objects to the will. "The intellect is not originally destined to enlighten us on the nature of things, but only to show us their relations in reference to our will" (*WWR* II, ch. 17: 176). It follows that science, whose knowledge is always in terms of these structures, is not "pure" knowledge of the world as it is in itself, but a knowledge of objects in terms that relate them to each other and ultimately to the will. These structures—time, space, and causality—belong not to the true "kernel" of the world, but only to its "outer shell," to its necessary appearance to a subject that is in the service of the will.

"Pure" knowledge is possible, according to Schopenhauer, only if one can contemplate the object without being directed by the will, and this he thinks happens in genuine aesthetic experience: "Knowledge tears itself free from the service of the will precisely by the subject's ceasing to be merely individual, and being now a pure will-less subject of knowledge" (*WWR* I, §34: 178–9). The object is freed from the framework of time, space, and causality as the intellect becomes a pure mirror of the object:

> We forget our individuality, our will, and continue to exist only as pure subject, as clear mirror of the object, so that it is as though the object alone existed without anyone to perceive it, and thus we are no longer able to separate the perceiver from the perception, but the two have become one, since the entire consciousness is filled and occupied by a single image of perception.

The object of the subject freed from service to the will is perceived as it is *in itself*, that is, as it is apart from its relations to other objects or to the will. It is nevertheless still appearance or phenomenon rather than the thing in itself because it is still an *object* for a subject—it is only "as though" there were no one there to perceive the object—and Schopenhauer thinks this entails that the object is a representation, something that exists only in relation to a subject rather than in itself. In other words, no *object* could be the thing in itself. Only because we have immediate access to our own willing without thereby objectifying it (without making it into a mere object for a subject) do we have, in this one case, Schopenhauer thinks, access to the thing in itself, to that which has reality in itself and is not merely a representation.[3]

Schopenhauer interprets the objects of most aesthetic experience as "the eternal Ideas" (in what he takes to be the Platonic sense), "the persistent, essential forms of the world and of all its phenomena" at the different levels at which the will objectifies itself for the pure subject (*WWR* I, §36: 186).[4] Music differs from the other arts because it is a direct copy of the thing in itself, the will's objectification for the pure subject without the mediation of the Ideas, hence of the empirical world.

In *The Birth of Tragedy*, Nietzsche takes over Schopenhauer's distinction between appearance and thing in itself, arguing that science, as Kant and Schopenhauer had shown, confines us to the world of appearance and never takes us beyond it to the thing that appears (*BT* 18).[5] Therefore, as Schopenhauer had argued, science cannot provide the intelligibility it seeks. Nietzsche uses Schopenhauer's theory of art to distinguish Apollonian from Dionysian art, and argues that both types give access to a kind of truth from which science is excluded. Schopenhauer's interpretation of the non-musical arts provides a basis for his account of Apollonian art—which Nietzsche claims makes possible contemplation of a "higher truth" and "perfection" than can be found in the "incompletely intelligible everyday world," i.e. than ordinary perception of empirical objects could ever yield (*BT* 1)—whereas Schopenhauer's account of music supplies his model for Dionysian art, which Nietzsche presents as able to provide direct access to the thing in itself because it eludes the subject-object form of knowledge (*BT* 5, 16). Schopenhauer's distinction between appearance and thing in itself, the basis for the doctrines listed as Schopenhauer's "mystical embarrassments and subterfuges" in *GS* 99, thus gave Nietzsche a basis for thinking that art yields metaphysical truth—Dionysian art, the truth about the

---

[3] That the will is known immediately without being made into an object, hence a representation, is clear from *WWR* II, ch. 18: 196–7. But Schopenhauer also qualifies the claim here by acknowledging that one of the forms of the representation or object, that of time, is already involved in our "immediate" or non-objectifying knowledge of our willing. Nietzsche rejects Schopenhauer's claim that the "I will" is known immediately, as I discuss in section 3.

[4] Schopenhauer claims that each of the arts (except for music) makes manifest the inner nature of the empirical world, revealing its nature as will. The different grades of the will's objectification are distinguished in terms of the clarity each brings to the nature of the will: architecture corresponds to the will's objectification at its lowest level of clarity, as inorganic nature, whereas tragedy corresponds to its objectification in human beings, the level at which its nature is most clear.

[5] The basis for the sentence that follows is Schopenhauer's claims about science, which I discuss at the end of section 2.

reality that underlies the empirical world; Apollonian art, the pure truth or essence of empirical objects—whereas science is forever caught in the illusion of getting at truth when it only reveals the laws that relate appearances to each other.

A major objection to this interpretation might be raised on the basis of Nietzsche's notes "On Schopenhauer" of 1868, for they indicate that he already had serious objections to Schopenhauer's system four years prior to the publication of *The Birth of Tragedy*.[6] However, Nietzsche's main objection concerns Schopenhauer's claim to have *knowledge* of the thing in itself, and I will argue that *The Birth of Tragedy* is plausibly seen as an attempt to resolve this problem in a way that is compatible with the spirit of Schopenhauer's philosophy and with the appropriation of as much of it as Nietzsche needs for the purpose of revaluing art over science.

In 1868, Nietzsche's major problem with Schopenhauer's system was that the thing in itself is placed "wholly outside the sphere of cognition" by the way in which Schopenhauer distinguishes it from appearance. According to Schopenhauer, writes Nietzsche, the thing in itself is "wholly distinct from its appearance and entirely free from all the forms of appearance which it enters into when it does appear, forms which therefore concern only its objectivity and are alien to it itself. Even the most general form of all representation, that of an object for a subject, does not concern it." So when Schopenhauer claimed that the thing in itself was will, he was necessarily borrowing its predicates from the world of appearance, decking out a "totally obscure, inconceivable X" in "brightly colored clothes, with predicates drawn from a world alien to it, the world of appearance" (OS 3). The logical proofs for the will as thing in itself completely fail, according to Nietzsche, and Schopenhauer is able to put the will "in place of the Kantian X... only with the aid of a poetic intuition" (OS 2).

None of this suggests that Nietzsche questioned Schopenhauer's right to distinguish the phenomenal or empirical world from the thing in itself, where the latter is understood as the underlying reality of the world, or that he rejected Schopenhauer's claim that the subject-object form of knowledge precludes knowledge of this underlying reality, confining us in a circle of appearance and representation. In fact, he explains Schopenhauer's failure to recognize the problem in his claim to knowledge of the thing in itself by saying that he did not want to "feel what was obscure and contradictory in the region where individuality gives out" (OS, introd). This suggests that he accepts Schopenhauer's claim that there is "a region where individuality gives out" (because individuality is completely a function of the subject's necessary structure as servant to the will and therefore cannot belong to the thing in itself) and believes that Schopenhauer simply found it too discomforting to think we could have no knowledge of it.

---

[6] Nietzsche's notes are translated by Christopher Janaway as "On Schopenhauer" in Janaway 1998: 258–265.

I suggest therefore that Nietzsche accepted Schopenhauer's distinction between appearance and thing in itself, where the latter is understood as the true reality lying behind or underneath appearance, but concluded that this reality was unknowable and that any attempt to say something about it was bound to be on the order of a "poetic intuition" that borrowed its descriptions from the world of appearance. *The Birth of Tragedy* is then plausibly viewed as an attempt to save Schopenhauer's metaphysics by showing how to avoid Schopenhauer's own inconsistency.[7] Nietzsche's account of tragedy as the expression of Dionysian wisdom in Apollonian images admits in effect that any description of the thing in itself must be derived from the phenomenal world, the only world to which we have linguistic or conceptual access. However, Nietzsche claims that tragedy begins with a kind of non-conceptual, non-linguistic experience, in which the artist becomes one with the realm beyond individuality and description, the thing in itself. Although this experience of the thing in itself is incommunicable, it gives rise to a vision which the artist expresses in language and images that are able to induce in spectators the same pre-linguistic and incommunicable experience of the thing in itself. I therefore see *The Birth of Tragedy* as an attempt to save Schopenhauer's metaphysics by reinterpreting the will as the poetic expression of a non-conceptual *experience* of the thing in itself. Although the philosophical poet's words can only gesture towards the experience, as it were, and are unable to say literally what it is like, at their best they are able to induce the same experience in others. His redoing of Schopenhauer's metaphysics along these lines is presumably what Nietzsche called the "artists' metaphysics in the [book's] background," and what convinced him that art represents "the highest task and the truly metaphysical activity of this life" (*BT*, "Attempt at a Self-Criticism," 2; *BT*, "preface to Richard Wagner").

But he had solved one problem for Schopenhauer's metaphysics at the cost of another. For if an experience cannot be put into words, how can one possibly know that something has induced the same, or even a similar, experience, much less that it was an experience of the thing in itself? By the time Nietzsche wrote "Truth and Lies," in any case, he had clearly abandoned the view that art or experience gives access to metaphysical truth. He now denies that we have any access whatsoever to the nature of the thing in itself, which becomes the

---

[7] It is perhaps even clearer that *BT* attempts to fix a second major difficulty with Schopenhauer's system: namely, Schopenhauer's attempt to make knowledge intelligible given his claim that knowledge does not belong to the thing in itself. The problem, as Nietzsche recognizes in OS 4 is that Schopenhauer claims that the intellect comes into existence to serve the will, and only at that point brings the whole world of appearances into existence. But he also claims that the need for the intellect arises only because there is a plurality of wills and therefore struggles over the means of satisfaction, such as food. In *BT*, Nietzsche responds to this problem by making the thing in itself into an artist god. Intellect therefore belongs to the thing in itself and it becomes intelligible, in a way that it cannot be for Schopenhauer, why the world of appearance comes into existence: as a work of art (an Apollonian vision) that relieves the primal being from the pain of its contradiction.

unknowable and mysterious *X* that appears first as a nerve impulse, then as an image, and finally as a linguistic expression (TL 83; 879). Although he relinquishes the claim that art gives access to metaphysical truth, he abandons neither the aim of showing that art is superior to science nor the strategy of presenting art as more truthful than science. Art is more truthful, he now claims, not because it gives access to a truth that science cannot reach, but because it does not claim to give truth, because it fully owns up to its nature as appearance and illusion. Science or empirical knowledge, on the other hand, pretends that its illusions are truth. When we talk of physical things we think we are talking about the things themselves, when in fact we are only talking about our own representations, which in no way correspond to the original entity, the thing in itself that underlies all appearance. Thus, "all the material within and with which the man of truth, the scientist and the philosopher, later works and builds, if not derived from the never-never land, is at least not derived from the essence of things" (ibid.).[8] This is the point of Nietzsche's claim that "truths are illusions we have forgotten are illusions," which should therefore be seen as an attempt to redeploy against the modern valuation of science the same strategy used in *The Birth of Tragedy*, but without the backing of any version, even a "poetic" one, of Schopenhauer's metaphysics of the will.

But Nietzsche's new position has difficulties of its own. We can make sense of a denial that empirical truths are really true within the framework of *The Birth of Tragedy* because it claims that we can *experience* the underlying metaphysical reality to which empirical truth fails to correspond. "Truth and Lie," in contrast, allows absolutely no access to the thing in itself. How then can one possibly know that empirical truth fails to correspond to it? Nietzsche recognizes this problem in one case, namely, his claim that "even our contrast between individual and species is something anthropomorphic and does not originate in the essence of things." He quickly adds that "we should not presume to claim that this contrast does not correspond to the essence of things: that would of course be a dogmatic assertion and, as such, would be just as indemonstrable as its opposite" (TL 83–4; 880). Although Nietzsche does not acknowledge it, this move involves a major change in his position. He is no longer claiming that "truths are illusions" (that empirical truths fail to correspond to the thing in itself), but rather that we can't know whether or not they are illusions. But the latter claim would not serve his purposes very well: he is out to deflate modern culture's valuation of scientific and theoretical knowledge, and a mere denial of certainty would not give him what he needs.[9] So he

---

[8] The use of the plural verb form in Breazeale's translation obscures the fact that Nietzsche is here equating "the man of truth" with "the scientist and the philosopher," as Nietzsche indicates by using the singular verb form.

[9] There is no obvious reason, and Nietzsche certainly adduces none, for thinking that science needs to claim certainty for its truths.

proceeds to adopt, without acknowledging the change, yet a third position: that the very idea of correspondence to the thing in itself, of "an adequate expression of the object in the subject," is a "contradictory impossibility" (TL 86; 884). If correspondence to the thing in itself (explicitly equated with "the pure truth") is a contradiction in terms, Nietzsche's claim that empirical truths *fail* to correspond to the thing in itself eludes the charge of dogmatism. The problem is that this solution completely undermines the whole strategy for revaluing art relative to science. If the kind of truth science cannot have is a contradiction in terms, how in the world could the value of science be bound up with the claim to possess it? We can't really want or have any use for a contradiction in terms; so how can there be any reason to think that science claims to possess it, or to consider art more truthful than science because it admits it does not? Failure to correspond to the thing in itself can be used to devalue empirical truths only if such correspondence is at least conceivable, but that would make Nietzsche's position once again vulnerable to the charge of dogmatism. Therefore, as I have argued elsewhere, "Truth and Lies"'s denial of truth is based on an unstable amalgamation of three mutually incompatible positions: the "Kantian" position that the "pure" truth is conceivable but unavailable to human beings, the "agnostic" position that we simply cannot know whether our truths match the "pure" truth, and the "neo-Kantian" position that such truth is unavailable precisely because it is inconceivable (Clark 1990: 90–3).

2. Appropriating "What Really Has Value" in Schopenhauer: The Empiricism of *Human, All Too Human*

In *Human, All Too Human* (1878) Nietzsche turns his back on the whole project of establishing art's superiority to science, claiming that the "mark of a higher culture" is "to value the little unpretentious truths found by means of rigorous method," i.e. by science, "more highly than the errors of metaphysical and artistic ages and human beings that blind us and make us happy" (*HA* 3). He reverses himself on the value of science by adopting the "agnostic" position of "Truth and Lie." "It is true," he says, "there might be a metaphysical world," meaning that the true nature of reality (the thing in itself) might differ from its empirical character. For "we behold all things through the human head and cannot cut this head off; while the question nonetheless remains what of the world would still be there if one had cut it off" (*HA* 9).[10] Stripped of its

---

[10] Schopenhauer uses the same image at *PP* II, §28, 37n.: "If I behold some object such as a view and think to myself that, if at this moment my head were chopped off, I know that the object would still be there unmoved and undisturbed, then this implies fundamentally and at bottom that I too would still exist."

metaphors, the argument is that we can only know things as they appear to us, and therefore cannot know that they do not differ from how they appear. This is similar to the argument Schopenhauer offers for the conclusion that empirical knowledge fails to give us knowledge of the thing in itself, the difference being that Nietzsche is clear that the very argument that sets up the possibility of a metaphysical world also precludes any possible knowledge of it, and therefore any possibility of knowing whether the empirical world differs from the thing in itself or coincides with it. This forecloses the possibility left open by his notes on Schopenhauer ten years earlier, that aesthetic experience of the thing in itself could provide a basis for recognizing that the empirical world fails to correspond to it.

This means, in effect, that Nietzsche has downgraded his earlier charge that empirical truths are illusions to the claim that they *may* be illusions. He does not make this change explicit, however, because he no longer believes it matters: if empirical truths are illusions, he thinks we are deprived only of a truth that is of absolutely no use to us. Knowledge of it would be "the most useless of all knowledge: more useless even than knowledge of the chemical composition of water must be to the sailor in danger of shipwreck" (*HA* 9). Nietzsche thus rejects the metaphysical knowledge he had once sought from art as of no earthly use.

He argues for the uselessness of metaphysical knowledge by offering a genealogy of the belief in a metaphysical or non-empirical world.[11] Human beings received their first idea of a "second world" from dreams, he claims, and later thinkers exploited the idea to explain the existence of things that seemed to have no place in the empirical world, for instance, permanent things (substance), free will, and things of a "higher" value than the normal residents of the empirical world. When thinkers failed to find a way of explaining how such things could be part of the world accessible to empirical methods, they concluded that these methods were themselves faulty, and that the real world is accessible only to non-empirical methods. The empirical world was thereby taken to be a mere appearance or distortion of a second world, which was thereby constituted as the "true" one. This non-empirical world was then posited as the source of things of "higher" value—such as rationality, logic, disinterested contemplation, and altruism—whose existence seemed inexplicable in empirical terms.

The major project of *Human, All Too Human* is to induce skepticism concerning the metaphysical world by showing it to be cognitively superfluous.[12]

---

[11] That this might be better called an "anti-empirical world" is suggested by Nietzsche's implied claim in *GS* 99 that Wagner's blindness to science was due to a hatred of science.

[12] *HA* 21 tells us that inducing skepticism about metaphysics can be as effective as "directly refuting" it.

Nietzsche employs two main strategies to this end. In some cases he argues that beliefs that led thinkers to posit a non-empirical world—e.g. the beliefs in free will and in permanent substances—arise from mistakes that have occurred "in the course of the overall evolution of organic being" and which we have therefore inherited as part of our cognitive make-up. Nietzsche assumes that it is already clear to his readers that these beliefs are contradicted by the "disclosed nature of the world," the world as disclosed by modern science (*HA* 10, 29). His contribution is to remove any remaining tendency to think there must nevertheless be some truth in them (how otherwise explain why they are so commonly believed?) by showing that we can fully understand why the beliefs arose without assuming they contain any truth.

Nietzsche is more centrally concerned with the justification for metaphysics offered by the existence of things regarded as of higher value than the typical residents of the empirical world. His strategy here gives his book its name: to show that these things are "human, all too human," mere sublimations and transformations of things of lower value. Once it is clear that we can explain disinterested contemplation, for instance, as a sublimation of lust, and give a parallel explanation for all other things of so-called "higher" value, we show that these things offer no basis for positing a metaphysical world.

If these two lines of argument succeed, Nietzsche expects interest in the purely theoretical problem of the thing in itself and appearance to die out (*HA* 10), and perhaps to be recognized as worth a "Homeric laugh": for "it appeared to be so much, indeed everything, and is actually empty, that is to say, empty of significance" (*HA* 16). No one is driven to metaphysics by the question of what things are like apart from our knowledge of them (in the metaphorical terms quoted earlier: what the world would be like if we could cut the human head off). That is a purely theoretical problem and is "not very well calculated to bother people overmuch; but all that has hitherto made metaphysical assumptions *valuable, terrible, delightful* to them, all that has begotten these assumptions, is passion, error, and self-deception" (*HA* 9).

Metaphysics is inspired by error insofar as it aims to explain the existence of things (1) that we erroneously believe to exist, or (2) that we erroneously believe cannot be explained by empirical methods. The role of passion and self-deception in inspiring metaphysics is suggested by the following passage:

> It is probable that the objects of religious, moral and aesthetic feeling [*Empfindens*] belong only to the surface of things, while man likes to believe that here at least he is in touch with the world's heart; the reason he deludes himself is that these things produce in him such profound happiness and unhappiness, and thus he here exhibits the same pride as in the case of astrology. For astrology believes the starry firmament revolves

around the fate of man; the moral man, however, supposes that what he has essentially at heart must also constitute the essence and heart of things. (*HA* 4) [13]

Religion, morality, and art involve responding to the world with certain sentiments or feelings, the objects of which are probably features of the empirical world, which the metaphysician considers only the "surface of things." "Metaphysical and artistic ages and human beings" (*HA* 3) do not see it this way, however; they take the object of their feelings to be entities that could only exist in a metaphysical world. This is why the metaphysical world has seemed so important: the distinction between appearances and the thing in itself, the fact that the empirical world is or might not be the way things are in themselves, seemed important only because it provided a space that could be furnished with objects of our sentiments, invented objects of moral, religious, and aesthetic feeling.

A later passage in *HA* suggests a similar diagnosis of Nietzsche's early view of art. If we accept the "metaphysical presupposition" that the visible world is "only appearance," he writes, "then art would come to stand quite close to the real world . . . art would represent the uniform, the types and prototypes of nature" (*HA* 222). In other words, the metaphysician does not think of aesthetic feeling as a merely human response to natural objects, but takes it to be bound up with the perception of "higher" objects, "the types and prototypes of nature" (the Platonic Ideas or essences in terms of which *The Birth of Tragedy* interpreted Apollonian art). But even if he denies the existence of such "types and prototypes" (as Nietzsche did in "Truth and Lie"), the passage implies, the idea of the empirical world as mere appearance can still allow the metaphysician to believe that aesthetic feeling is more than a human response, that it somehow brings one closer to the true nature of reality. Nietzsche now rejects this view, holding that aesthetic feeling, like moral and religious sentiment, is to be explained as a merely human reaction to natural features of the world and gives us no basis whatsoever for positing a metaphysical world.

Using as our guide *GS* 99, the passage from which I began, we can see *HA* as related to Schopenhauer in the following way. Nietzsche was seduced by Schopenhauer's metaphysical system, his account of the distinction between appearance and the thing in itself, because it provided support for what he cared about: aesthetic experience. That aesthetic feeling touched the world's

---

[13] Hollingdale usually translates *Empfinden* and *Empfindung* as "sensation," as he does in this passage, although he is sometimes forced to use "feeling" instead (e.g., *HA* 16), as I do here and throughout. Kaufmann also switches back and forth between the two words. I have not found that "sensation" is a required translation in any of the passages I quote or that it makes better sense than "feeling" does. On the other hand, "feeling" often seems to make more sense of the passage ("sentiment" would do as well), as it does in *HA* 4. The consistent use of "feeling" can make it seem that existing translations have suppressed the extent of Nietzsche's interest in feelings.

heart meant that his concerns were woven into the world itself, that the world cared about what he cared about. But this blinded him to science, i.e. to the cognitive value of science. He could not see what he sees in *HA*: that science gives us our only access to truth (apart from perception, on which it is based), the only truth that could be of any real concern to us.

In thus relinquishing his earlier attempt to devalue science, Nietzsche becomes an empiricist. For his rejection of metaphysics amounts to the claim that if there is a metaphysical world, a truth that differs from empirical truth, we have no way of knowing either that it is or what it is. But that leaves empirical knowledge as the only kind of human knowledge. Of course, any current empirical theory might be false, but the reasons for thinking so will be empirical reasons; *HA* denies that there is any external standpoint from which to undertake a cognitive critique of empirical knowledge.

By classifying Nietzsche as an empiricist, I am not attributing to him a full-blown epistemology, but only a broad orientation on issues concerning knowledge. He is certainly not an empiricist in the sense that he accepts a classical empiricist account of the origin of ideas, for he believes that some aspects of our ideas are not derived from experience but are inherited from ancestors whose chances of survival and reproduction they enhanced. But this makes them "prior to experience" only in terms of their origin, not in terms of their justification. Nietzsche's view of justification in *HA* does not seem either verificationist or foundationalist (hence he should not be classed with twentieth-century positivists) but it does place him with the empiricists against the rationalists and Kantians. For he accepts what he later formulates as the claim that "all evidence of truth comes only from the senses" (*BGE* 134). Whatever the origin of our knowledge, none of it is justified independently of experience, i.e. is immune to revision on the basis of experience. The only exceptions Nietzsche allows are mathematics and logic, which, as a good empiricist, he claims are "formal science(s)" or "sign-conventions" in which "reality is not encountered at all, not even as a problem"—that is, which simply make no claims about reality (*TI* III:3).[14] He is thus an empiricist in the sense of denying that there are any synthetic a priori truths—substantive truths, as opposed to the formal truths of logic and mathematics, that are justified independently of experience. And he is consistent enough not to make an exception of his own claims. The non-metaphysical, historical version of philosophy he aims to be practicing in *Human, All Too Human* is, he claims, "no longer to be separated from natural science," meaning that his claims about

---

[14] This is actually Nietzsche's later formulation of his position. In *Nietzsche on Truth and Philosophy* (103–5, 122), I claimed that in *HA* and *GS* Nietzsche holds that logic falsifies reality, but that he overcame this in his later works. I now doubt that he ever believed that logic actually falsifies reality; *HA* 11 and *GS* 111 can seem to be making such a claim, but may mean only that logic could never have got off the ground without the benefit of false beliefs (in permanent things, for instance).

knowledge and its a priori components, for instance, are themselves intended as empirical claims (*HA* 1).

Because empiricism is one of the most "English"[15] of all philosophical doctrines, Nietzsche's conversion to it in *Human, All Too Human* goes a long way towards explaining one of the implications I drew from *Gay Science* 99: that Nietzsche eventually acquired the aspects of Schopenhauer's work that make him seem "so English and un-German." This point gains further support if we recognize that *Human, All Too Human* also involves the acceptance of two other doctrines that are associated with Hume, namely, naturalism and value anti-realism.

The naturalism of *Human, All Too Human* is closely tied to its empiricism; it is a commitment to viewing whatever we can know anything about as part of the natural world, the world perceived by the senses and described by the sciences. This means, in particular, a commitment to explaining everything about human beings in a way that connects it to other parts of nature, most likely as a development from traits found among other animal species. Nietzsche gives his naturalism its most striking formulation in *Beyond Good and Evil* 230:

> To translate man back into nature; to become master over the many vain and overly enthusiastic interpretations and connotations that have so far been scrawled and painted over the eternal basic text of *homo natura*; to see to it that man henceforth stands before man as even today, hardened in the discipline of science, he stands before the *rest* of nature, with intrepid Oedipus eyes and sealed Odysseus ears, deaf to the siren songs of old metaphysical bird catchers who have been piping at him all too long, "you are more, you are higher, you are of a different origin!"—that may be a strange and insane task, but it is a *task*—who would deny that? Why did we choose this insane task? Or, putting it differently: "why have knowledge at all?"

To have *knowledge* of human beings, Nietzsche thus claims, is to fit human beings and their abilities into our understanding of the natural world. And this means that nothing about us will be *sui generis*, in particular, our motives and abilities. We may have motives and abilities that go way beyond anything found elsewhere in nature, but we should be able to see them as in some important sense *continuous* with what else is found there. This is the naturalistic project Nietzsche embarked on in *Human, All Too Human* in his attempts, often very crude, to show that human motives and activities that were thought to be "higher" than merely natural aspects were in fact continuous with them, mere sublimations of the "human, all too human," that is, of the "lower" or merely natural side of humanity.

---

[15] Nietzsche evidently uses "English" as equivalent to "British" since he explicitly classifies Hume, who was Scottish, among "Englishmen" in BGE 252.

Finally, the empiricism and naturalism of *HA* lead Nietzsche to value anti-realism, the position that there is no value in the world, that there are no value facts to which our normative discourse or talk of value corresponds. That this is Nietzsche's position in *HA* seems clear from the fact that he separates out the true character of the world from the world that is of interest to us: values are not part of the former; what belongs to the "true nature of the world" is only what natural science tells us is there. Value anti-realism follows from Nietzsche's empiricism and naturalism, insofar as the natural sciences do not discover normative facts or take them as objects of investigation. The world science discloses to us is thus one stripped of its practical significance: it contains neither normative facts, nor significance or meaning, and is therefore often considered a "disenchanted" world compared to the world of our practical concerns. Color is Nietzsche's favorite metaphor for the difference between the two worlds: unlike the world disclosed by science, the world of our practical concerns is a colored world—bright, significant, and attractive to us.

In *Human, All Too Human*, Nietzsche seems to accept a particular version of anti-realism, namely, an "error theory" of value; for he dubs the colored world of our concerns "the world as representation (as error)" (*HA* 29).[16] He thus divides Schopenhauer's world as representation into two aspects: first, the empirical world disclosed by science, which *may* be only appearance of the thing in itself but can still be treated as "true nature of the world" because it is the only world of any *cognitive* or *theoretical* interest to us, and then the world of our practical concerns, which Nietzsche treats as the world of appearance in the sense of "error." His theory appears to be that the world, valueless in itself, receives an appearance of value through us, in particular, through our errors and passions. We have already seen that Nietzsche believes we respond to the world with feelings and concerns for which we desire an external support; so we invent objects for these feelings that can exist only in a non-empirical world, whence they serve to confirm the importance of our feelings by making them seem to touch the depth of things.[17] Nietzsche clearly sees such inventions as coloring our world. Although art has also colored the world for us, he believes it did so only with the help of the inventions of philosophy and religion. He records his "deep sadness" at having to admit that

> in their highest flights the artists of all ages have raised to heavenly transfiguration precisely those conceptions which we now recognize as false: they are the glorifiers of the religious and philosophical errors of mankind, and they could not have been so without believing in the absolute truth of these errors. If belief in such truth declines in general, if the rainbow-colors at the extreme limits of human knowledge and supposition grow

---

[16] A classic statement of an "error theory" of moral value is found in J. L. Mackie, *Ethics: Inventing Right and Wrong* (London: Penguin Books, 1977), ch. 1.

[17] See *HA* 15 for Nietzsche's critique of this idea of depth.

pale, that species of art can never flourish again which, like the *Divina Commedia*, the pictures of Raphael, the frescoes of Michelangelo, the Gothic cathedrals, presupposes not only a cosmic but also a metaphysical significance in the objects of art. A moving tale will one day be told how there once existed such an art, such an artist's faith. (*HA* 220)

Surprisingly, Nietzsche does not claim merely that religious art will no longer exist, but predicts the "death" of art itself, anticipating the thought and metaphor of his later announcement of the death of God, as in the following description of its "evening twilight":

The artist will soon be regarded as a glorious relic, and we shall bestow upon him, as a marvellous stranger upon whose strength and beauty the happiness of former ages depended, honours such as we do not grant to others of our own kind. The best in us has perhaps been inherited from the feelings of earlier ages to which we hardly any longer have access by direct paths; the sun has already set, but the sky of our life still glows with its light, even though we no longer see it. (*HA* 223; cf. *GS* 125)

The sun has set in that the "higher" objects posited by philosophy and religion do not fit into the world disclosed by science, now recognized as the "true nature of the world." We can hardly understand feelings of earlier ages because we don't have their beliefs, and cannot experience the world in the light cast by objects in which we do not believe. Yet the setting sun leaves some color behind: things in the human world still seem to possess a "higher value" because they have been associated for so long with the higher objects in which we cannot believe. Nietzsche's major project in this book—to drive home the point that things of the human or natural world are only "human, all too human"—therefore seems designed to remove the world's remaining color, its appearance of value.

But does Nietzsche's "philosophy not thus become a tragedy" (*HA* 34)? And "what place still remains for art" (*HA* 222)? Nietzsche's answers to these questions are closely related. To the first, he replies that his philosophy is one of "*logical world-denial*," but can "be united with a practical world-affirmation just as easily as with its opposite." "Logical world-denial" would be a belief that the world contains no value; "practical world-affirmation," a claim that one can, without illusion, find the world to be valuable. To the second he replies that art has already done its job, having taught us, for instance, to "look upon life in all of its forms with interest and pleasure, and to educate our feelings so far that we at last cry [with Goethe]: 'life, however it may be, is good.'" Thus "if art disappeared the intensity and multiplicity of the joy of life it has implanted would still continue to demand satisfaction." Both answers suggest that we can find value in the world or aspects of it without error. But if there is no value in the world how can one find it there without error? The answer of *Human, All*

Too Human concerns the possible "after-effect of knowledge" in certain individual instances:

> a life more purified of affect [*von Affecten reineres Leben*] [in which] the old motives of violent desire . . . would gradually grow weaker under the influence of purifying knowledge [*reinigenden Erkenntniss*]. In the end one would live among human beings and with oneself as in *nature*, without praising, blaming, contending, gazing contentedly, as though at a spectacle, upon many things for which one formerly felt only fear. (*HA* 34)

Such a person ("from whom the ordinary fetters of life have fallen to such an extent that he continues to live only to know better") can without error find joy and value in living because he only *looks* at life and does not make value judgments. He may say that "life is good," but that merely expresses his satisfaction with it; it does not express preference for anything in life over anything else. He follows the model of Schopenhauer's aesthetic contemplator and finds value not in the objects of the contemplative gaze, but rather in the gazing.

But what is erroneous about valuing something other than the spectator's gaze? Granted that projecting objects of sentiments into the metaphysical world involves error, it is not at all clear why valuing need always involve such projection. If the point of the projection is to acquire an external guarantee for what we care about, why couldn't we get over the need for the guarantee and still care, i.e. still find value? Does Nietzsche think that the expression of these sentiments in value discourse necessarily involves error because it always involves saying that value is in the world when in fact (as science shows us) it is not? Perhaps, but I think a different reason lies behind Nietzsche's privileging of the spectator's gaze: that even when valuing does not involve metaphysical projection, it still involves partiality or non-objectivity. This is the point stressed in the passages immediately preceding his idealizing of spectatorship. All inclination and aversion involve "unjust assessments," and all belief in the value of life "rests on false thinking" (*HA* 34, 32). The basis for this claim appears to be that our interests and judgments of value always focus on one aspect of things at the expense of other aspects which we forget or ignore; such valuing is a response not to a pure knowing of the situation but to a very interested and thoroughly partisan view of it. The problem is that in the normal human case, valuing is directed by the will, not the intellect, and is therefore unobjective. The "colored" world of our concerns is a projection therefore not simply of our errors but also of our passions, where passions are understood as partial, as wearing "party colors," "taking sides," being "for and against" (*HA* 371). Objectivity is undermined by the partiality of our sentiments and is only possible for the contemplator of life, not for the participant, the person of action.

Although the "error theory" I have just attributed to Nietzsche is not Humean, the empiricism, naturalism, and value anti-realism of *Human, All Too Human* are very close to Hume's. And it is plausible that Nietzsche owes these

Humean doctrines to Schopenhauer. To begin with, Schopenhauer was a serious admirer of "the great Hume" (*WWR* II, ch. 26:338).[18] He refers to Hume at least thirteen times in *The World as Will and Representation* and claims: "There is more to be learned from each page of David Hume than from the collected philosophical works of Hegel, Herbart, and Schleiermacher taken together" (*WWR* II, ch. 26: 582). More importantly, the Humean doctrines of *Human, All Too Human* are very close to Schopenhauer's own. If he was not quite an empiricist, naturalist, or value anti-realist, he was very close to being all three.

Schopenhauer recognizes that empiricism and naturalism go together and he clearly believes that these doctrines, which he resists, must be accepted if one denies the possibility of metaphysical knowledge. This is because he views natural science (which he often calls "physics," noting that he is using this word "in the widest sense," which he also calls "the sense of the ancients"—*WWR* II, ch. 17:172, 177) as equivalent to systematic knowledge of the phenomenal world, which he equates with both the world of nature and the empirical world. In fact, he makes perfectly evident that perception is the "source of all knowledge" (e.g., *WWR* II, ch. 7:77). Therefore, "a system of physics which asserted that its explanations of things—in the particular from causes and in general from forces—were actually sufficient, and therefore exhausted the inner essence of the world, would be *naturalism* proper" or "pure naturalism"; and "if there were no other entity except those existing by nature, physics would be the first science" (*WWR* II, ch. 17:174–7). Schopenhauer thus holds that in the absence of metaphysical knowledge, natural science would be the only kind of general knowledge we could have, the only kind of knowledge beyond immediate perception. His empiricism about scientific knowledge is clear from his explanation of what "contemporary naturalists" fail to see, who, "captivated" as they are

> entirely by their empiricism, accept nothing but what their eyes see. With this they imagine they arrive at the ultimate ground of things, not suspecting that between the phenomenon and that which manifests itself therein, namely the thing-in-itself, there is a deep gulf, a radical difference. This difference can be cleared up only by the knowledge and accurate delimitation of the subjective element of the phenomenon, and by the insight that the ultimate and most important information about the inner nature of things can be drawn only from self-consciousness. Without all this, we cannot go one step beyond what is given immediately to the senses. (*WWR* II, ch. 17:178)

That science does not take us "a step beyond what is given immediately to the senses" means that it does not reach a different level of intelligibility, but

---

[18] *WWR* II, ch. 26, 338. Schopenhauer also made a serious proposal to translate Hume's works into German. For details, see Bridgwater 1988: 326–9.

is merely a more complete and systematic version of the knowledge given in perception. Metaphysics, on the other hand, does take us to a new level (but only by way of a special kind of "immediate" perception) and in doing so completes physics, which cannot, by itself, really explain anything. Physics "explains phenomena by something still more unknown than are they, namely by laws of nature resting on forces of nature," which Schopenhauer calls "the absolutely inexplicable" (*WWR* II, ch. 17:172, 176). Therefore, "*physics* is unable to stand on its own feet, but needs a *metaphysics* on which to support itself."

To get from Schopenhauer's philosophy to empiricism and naturalism, Nietzsche had only to reject Schopenhauer's claim that metaphysical knowledge is possible and necessary for the intelligibility science seeks. This is the strategy of *Human, All Too Human*. Arguing that Schopenhauer's metaphysics gets its foothold by promising to tell us what things are like *in themselves*, Nietzsche claims that even if it could do that, which it cannot, it would not add to the intelligibility science already supplies. His point is not to deny that scientific explanation always leaves something unexplained—that it ends in contingency (in facts, in the way things are) rather than necessity. This is, of course, a good Humean point which has as its implication that the "most perfect" natural science "only staves off ignorance a little longer." The point is simply that knowing what things are like "in themselves," as Nietzsche thinks Schopenhauer understands that (as Nietzsche himself did in HA 9), will not change that situation one whit.

Schopenhauer's account of the thing in itself seemed to bring added intelligibility, according to Nietzsche's argument, only by seeming to explain the existence of things that could not be explained in empirical terms. But the things in question either do not really exist or can now be explained as sublimations of other parts of the empirical world. Therefore, the thing in itself is no longer needed for intelligibility; its only remaining function is to give assurance that our values have external support. But we have no reason to suppose they do have such support—only self-deception convinces us otherwise. Once honesty wins out, Schopenhauer's philosophy leaves standing only the world of appearance or representation, the empirical or natural world, the world disclosed by the empirical methods of the natural sciences.

Finally, Schopenhauer also gives expression to the core of value antirealism, a third Humean doctrine, in his discussion of the view that

> places man's inner nature in a *soul* that is originally a *knowing*, indeed really an abstract *thinking* entity, and only in consequence thereof a *willing* entity. Such a view . . . regarded will as of a secondary nature, instead of knowledge, which is really secondary. The will was even regarded as an act of thought, and was identified with the judgement, especially by Descartes and Spinoza. (*WWR* I, § 55:292)

From the traditional view that the soul is primary, it follows that one first knows a thing to be good and in consequence wills it, the reverse of Schopenhauer's theory that has us "first *willing* it, and in consequence calling it *good*." The latter view follows from "the whole of [Schopenhauer's] fundamental view": "The will is first and original; knowledge is merely added to it as an instrument belonging to the phenomenon of the will." This could pass as a statement of Hume's basic metaethical position: that "reason is, and ought only to be the slave of the passions" (Hume 1978: 415). According to the traditional view: we will and therefore pursue certain things because of what we believe valuable; values are ultimately objects of reason or knowledge. According to Schopenhauer and Hume, the reverse is the case: we believe certain things valuable because of our emotions and passions; values are ultimately projections of will.

How does the primacy of will or intellect relate to realism, the question concerning whether values are "in the world"? It is the issue behind that question. Reason can have primacy only if it is able to discover normative facts (facts about what is valuable) that constrain the will. But to say there are such normative facts is just to say that values are in the world. Conversely, if the intellect is able to discover normative facts that constrain the will, then reason is not a mere instrument or slave of the will but its ruler. Schopenhauer's doctrine concerning the primacy of will therefore commits him to value anti-realism.[19]

Because the basis for this anti-realism lies in his metaphysics of will, Nietzsche could not in this case arrive at the Humean doctrine simply by rejecting Schopenhauer's metaphysics. What would it be reasonable for a Schopenhauerian to say about the will once he rejects it as the underlying metaphysical reality? Nietzsche says that Schopenhauer's "will" turns out to be "a disaster for science: for this will has been made into a poetic metaphor when it is asserted that all things in nature possess will" (*HA* II/1:5).[20] Stripping will of this metaphorical extension would reduce it to the non-cognitive or affective side of human beings and other animals, the non-cognitive aspect of instinct, desire, impulse, inclination, sentiments, passions, feelings, stances, attitudes.

---

[19] Schopenhauer seems to forget his claim that good always "denotes the *fitness or suitableness of an object to any definite effort of the will*" (*WWR* I, § 65, 360) when he insists that the ultimate good is the overcoming of the will, something achieved by a pure knowing of the world that turns against the will without itself serving any of the will's motives. So he does not remain an anti-realist all the way down as it were.

[20] In this same passage, Nietzsche declares that Schopenhauer's celebrated doctrine of "the primacy of the will over the intellect" is an error. This would count strongly against the interpretation I am offering of Nietzsche's position if he had not qualified it by making clear he means only that "in the sense in which [Schopenhauer] understands [it]," the doctrine is an error. Nietzsche might mean that it is an error simply because Schopenhauer understands the doctrine in metaphysical terms, or he might think that for his "pure knower" value is independent of will. But I do not see evidence that Nietzsche was rejecting the doctrine that in anything but the extreme and exceptional case, will has primacy over intellect when it comes to values.

Schopenhauer's claim regarding the primacy of the will would then be reduced to the claim that in humans and other animals, the cognitive side is ultimately an instrument of the affective side. This in fact seems to be Nietzsche's view, at least by the time he writes *Beyond Good and Evil*,[21] and anti-realism follows from it as surely as from Schopenhauer's metaphysics of the will. The basis Nietzsche would have for the view given his rejection of Schopenhauer's metaphysical answer is that it is the most obvious view of the relation between cognition and affect for a thoroughgoing naturalist to take. In the case of other animals, it seems clear that cognition is a mere instrument that provides information it is useful for the animal to take into account in the pursuit of its ends, which are inscribed in its instincts, passions, emotions. But if human beings are in basic continuity with other animals, as the naturalist claims, then this is also true in the human case. Therefore, Nietzsche must deny that values are "in the world" and accept basic value anti-realism.[22]

By drawing Nietzsche into his philosophical system, Schopenhauer thus led Nietzsche to three empiricist doctrines, ones Schopenhauer himself could not fully accept because of his commitment to metaphysics. Rejecting that commitment leaves Nietzsche as an empiricist, naturalist, and value anti-realist, which is to say, in a "disenchanted" world, the very world whose existence he announces in *The Gay Science*'s declaration that "God is dead." Nietzsche expects God's "shadows" to live on, probably for centuries, and claims that we must vanquish these too, a process he equates with completing the "de-deification" of nature and the "naturalizing" of humanity (*GS* 108–9). This is the process Schopenhauer had already undertaken. In Nietzsche's words: Schopenhauer's philosophy gives us "a horrified look into a de-deified world" (*GS* 357).[23] Schopenhauer had already stripped the world of most of the values the Christian tradition had written into it in an effort to connect the human world to a higher world. Schopenhauer's de-deified picture, in contrast to the traditional one, emphasizes those features of the world that Christianity devalued, what it considered animal, worldly, or merely natural, and de-emphasizes what Christian philosophers considered supernatural, above all, reason and intellect. For Nietzsche, Schopenhauer took "reason" out of the world and put a very stripped-down naturalized version of it back where it belongs, in human beings, where it does serve to distinguish humans from other animals (*WWR* I, §8:36–9).

---

[21] e.g., *BGE* 191: "Reason is merely an instrument."

[22] As I have already argued, however, he does more than that: he also argues that error is always involved in our values, and that does not follow simply from value anti-realism. It does seem to follow from Schopenhauer's doctrine regarding the primacy of the will. Since our values are ultimately an expression of our will rather than our intellect, they partake of the partiality or lack of objectivity that all willing involves. And that is the kind of error I have tried to show Nietzsche thinks is involved in all valuing.

[23] Is Nietzsche suggesting that Schopenhauer is basically a Humean, with the thing in itself and a claim to metaphysical knowledge tacked on as an expression of horror?

Schopenhauer's explanation concerning why philosophers have placed the fundamental nature of human beings in the intellect rather than the will is that they "aimed at presenting man as differing as widely as possible from the animal," and were vaguely aware that "the difference between the two was to be found in the intellect and not in the will" (*WWR* II, ch. 18:199). In other words, the insistence on the primacy of the intellect represents a resistance to naturalism, an insistence on seeing human beings as constituting a radical break with the animal world. Bernard Williams remarks, concerning the currently emerging consensus in favor of a "naturalistic moral psychology," one that understands human beings as part of nature, that no one knows exactly what that involves but that on this problem Nietzsche "can be of great help" (Williams 1995: 67–8). If this is correct, if as the twentieth century comes to an end Nietzsche is already standing there, very close to where we want to go philosophically, it is because Schopenhauer almost got there even earlier. By drawing Nietzsche into his system, Schopenhauer drew him into an empiricist understanding of knowledge and a completely naturalistic understanding of human beings. This is why it seems plausible to accept the suggestion of *Gay Science* 99 that although he was drawn into Schopenhauer's philosophy by its weaknesses and vices—the different aspects of its claim to metaphysical knowledge—Nietzsche eventually absorbed its "higher" culture, the culture of the factual thinker or empiricist, and thereby overcame those aspects that initially attracted him.

3. "Gilding or Staining" the World: The Idea of "Gay Science"

But even if Nietzsche was drawn into empiricism by Schopenhauer, didn't he "get over" it? In particular, didn't he abandon the idea that science discloses the "true nature of the world"? That he did so is the standard picture, and is usually taken to be implied by the standard view that *HA* represents Nietzsche's "positivistic phase." If the account I have given of Schopenhauer's influence is correct, however, it is not plausible that Nietzsche *simply* "got over" his empiricism. Given that influence, he was left with no basis for denying that science discloses the true nature of the world once he rejected metaphysics. There are, no doubt, ways to withdraw from that position, but an argument that Nietzsche did so requires an explanation of the reasons that allowed so radical a change in his thinking. I will examine various ways such a change might have occurred and argue that Nietzsche never discarded his three empiricist doctrines, that the works of his later period involve a more thorough appropriation of Schopenhauer's empiricist culture than he had achieved in *HA* and thereby allow us to understand why Nietzsche regards his philosophy as a "companion piece and completion of human knowledge and science" (*GS* 99).

It is certainly true that Nietzsche revised his view of science after *HA*. Four years later he published *The Gay Science*, which even in its title gives expression to a very different attitude towards science. The question is: what changed? In particular, does Nietzsche's idea of "gay science" require him to give up any of the empiricist doctrines he accepted in *HA*? I cannot see that it does, indeed, that he had any reason to abandon the Humean doctrines of the earlier book.

To begin with, Nietzsche never withdrew that book's rejection of metaphysics. Quite the reverse: he takes a step beyond its agnostic position on the metaphysical world in his later six-stage "History" of that world, now termed the "true world" (*TI*, "How the 'True World' Finally Became a Fable"). The first three stages of Nietzsche's "History" correspond to the Platonic, Christian, and Kantian versions of the metaphysical world, whereas its fourth stage mirrors Nietzsche's own position in *Human, All Too Human*: the "true" world (the world previously thought to be true) is recognized as completely superfluous. The fifth stage represents a further step: the very existence of the "true" world is denied—which indicates that Nietzsche has replaced his earlier claim that "there might be a metaphysical world" with a flat denial that any such world exists.

I have argued elsewhere (Clark 1990: 99–103; 109–117) that this change is due to Nietzsche's revised view of the thing in itself, which he now considers a contradiction in terms, a mere "seduction of words" (*BGE* 16). My argument would have been more plausible, however, if I had stressed that Nietzsche's critique is directed specifically against *Schopenhauer's* concept of the thing in itself—the one he himself had once accepted. Nietzsche concludes that the thing in itself is a contradiction in terms from a critique of the idea of "immediate certainty"—such as Schopenhauer claimed to find in "I will"—and it is difficult to see what this has to do with the Kantian thing in itself. But Nietzsche seems right to connect the intelligibility of Schopenhauer's idea of the thing in itself to "immediate certainty." In the first place, it is clear that Schopenhauer thinks that we can have knowledge of the thing in itself only because we have *immediate* knowledge of our own will. Consider also his claim that "*Kant's greatest merit is the distinction of the phenomenon from the thing-in-itself*, based on the proof that between things and us there always stands the *intellect*, and that on this account they cannot be known according to what they may be in themselves" (*WWR* I, app: 417–18). Here Schopenhauer must be thinking of the thing in itself in terms of what the object would be like if it could only be grasped immediately, i.e. without the intervention of the intellect. Or, as Nietzsche puts it in BGE 16: if only knowledge could behold "its object purely and nakedly as 'thing-in-itself,' without any falsification from the side of either subject or object." Schopenhauer's idea of the thing in itself is that of something that could be known, if at all, only immediately, i.e. without either the subject or the object being affected and therefore changed ("falsified") by the other. Nietzsche is certainly right to consider this idea of "immediate certainty" a contradiction in terms; it really requires a knowing that isn't a knowing, or, in Schopenhauer's own formula, a knowing in which "the object alone [exists] without anyone to perceive it." Once Nietzsche recognizes this contradiction as the image of knowing that allowed him to think he had a concept of the thing in itself (e.g., in HA 9), he also has reason to reject that concept as contradictory, as a mere "seduction of words," and to insist, as he already had in *GS* 54, that he has no concept at all of an essence or "unknown *X*" that is the opposite of "appearance": after all, "what could I say [hence think] about any essence except to name the attributes of its appearance?"

The change in Nietzsche's claim about the metaphysical world cannot give him reason to reject any of the three empiricist doctrines of *Human, All Too Human*. If anything, we should expect the reverse: since we have no idea of the thing in itself, there is no foothold whatsoever for belief in a metaphysical world, and the empirical world is left as the only world of which we have any idea. This is precisely the position we find in the sixth and final stage of Nietzsche's history of the "true world" in *Twilight of the Idols*, which adds to the fifth stage the claim that with the abolition of the "true" world, "*we have also abolished the apparent one.*" In its context, this claim's obvious meaning is that the denial of the "true" world removes all basis for regarding the world that remains, the empirical world, as "merely apparent."

The context is a discussion of philosophers' propensity to devalue empirical knowledge because it is based on the testimony of the senses, in contrast to knowledge based on reason. Nietzsche declares in opposition that "we have science only to the extent that we have decided to accept the testimony of the senses," that "the rest is miscarriage or not yet science," or formal science, such as logic and mathematics, which makes no claim at all about reality (*TI* III:3). He goes on to say that "the reasons for which 'this' world has been characterized as 'apparent' are the very reasons which indicate its reality; any other kind of reality is absolutely indemonstrable (TI III:6)." In other words, the fact that knowledge of the empirical world was based on the testimony of the senses was taken to indicate that it was merely "apparent," whereas Nietzsche claims that this is precisely what indicates its reality. Or, to repeat the terms of *BGE* 134: "all evidence of truth comes only from the senses." Thus Nietzsche did not backtrack from the empiricism of *HA*; apart from formal sciences, which make no claims about reality, all knowledge is empirical, and natural science is simply the general or systematic form of such knowledge.

Nor is it plausible that Nietzsche abandoned naturalism. If anything, it became more definite in his later works, as *BGE* 230 and *A* 13–14 especially suggest. The former, which I quoted earlier, tells us that Nietzsche conceived his very task as that of "translating man back into nature," whereas the latter presents the fact that "we have placed [man] back among the animals" as the upshot of the modern overcoming of the priestly devaluation of science and its methods, the same devaluation Nietzsche himself attempted in his early works.

The only empiricist doctrine it is at all plausible that Nietzsche gave up is value anti-realism. The world of *The Gay Science*, it must be admitted, no longer has the "feel" of a "disenchanted" world;[24] the emphasis on "gay science" already suggests that Nietzsche now views the commitment to science as compatible with a commitment to values. But did he come to think that value, meaning, and significance are part of the world? That depends on what is meant by "the world." Values are certainly part of the world of our practical concerns—part of how we see the world in so far as we care about its contents and are committed to action in it—but that was already the case in *HA*. Are they also part of the world of our theoretical concerns?—i.e. do values belong to the "disclosed nature of the world (*HA* 10)," to the world that is the object of knowledge? I just do not see a plausible story that can be told about how Nietzsche moved from *HA*'s conception of the world as an object of knowledge to one in which value is part of that world. In fact, although Nietzsche is now less blunt about it, *GS* affirms his earlier claim that natural science offers us "the disclosed nature of the world." *GS* 110 claims that "over immense periods of time the intellect produced nothing but errors," some of which proved useful, helped to preserve the species and were therefore "continually inherited." Since he cannot possibly mean to deny that human beings discovered many facts or truths that served their practical interests—about weather, crops, other animals, etc.—Nietzsche's point must be that they discovered "nothing but errors" in their theorizing about the nature of the world. Among these "basic errors" he includes the following "articles of faith": "that there are enduring things; that there are equal things; that there are things, substances, bodies; that a thing is what it appears to be; that our will is free; that what is good for me is also good in itself." Nietzsche thinks we know these are errors because of what science tells us: for instance, that things are constantly changing and that they do not have the qualities they appear to us to have (e.g. color).[25] He claims that the "basic errors" were denied and doubted "only very late," that "it was only very late that truth emerged—as the weakest form of knowledge." What Nietzsche calls "knowledge" (*Erkenntniss*) emerged, that is, in a weak form, with little power behind it. Why? Because we were not prepared to live with it; "our

---

[24] Consider Nietzsche's description of the world in *GS* 339 as "covered by a veil interwoven with gold, a veil of beautiful possibilities, sparkling with promise, resistance, bashfulness, mockery, pity, and seduction."

[25] See *GS* 107, which tells us that science gives us "insight into general untruth and mendaciousness . . . into delusion and error as a condition of the knowing and feeling form of existence [(*eine Bedingung des erkennenden und empfindenden Daseins*])." The untruth, delusion, and error in question here are undoubtedly the inherited "erroneous articles of faith" discussed in *GS* 110. Without these, the knowing and feeling form of existence could not have emerged, as *GS* 110 makes clear. If this is correct, the claim of *GS* 107 does not mean that delusion and error are necessarily involved in human knowledge, as Kaufmann's translation unfortunately suggests, but that knowledge (*Erkenntniss*), in the sense in which Nietzsche uses this word in *GS* 110 (and, I believe, throughout GS), could not have come into existence without error. I interpret *GS* 111 as making a corresponding claim about logic: not that logic necessarily involves us in error, but that it could not have come into existence without error, in particular, the belief in unchanging things.

organism was prepared for the opposite; all our higher functions, sense perception and every kind of feeling worked with those basic errors." Nietzsche proceeds to give a short history of how "the intellectual fight became an occupation, an attraction," whereby

> knowledge became a piece of life itself, and hence a continually growing power—until eventually knowledge collided with those primeval basic errors; two lives, two powers, both in the same human being. A thinker is now that being in whom the impulse for truth and those life-preserving errors clash. . . . Compared to the significance of this fight, everything else is a matter of indifference; the ultimate question about the conditions of life has been posed here. . . . To what extent can truth endure incorporation? That is the question; that is the experiment.

This is the same question Nietzsche had raised in *Human, All Too Human*, asking whether death might not be preferable to being obliged to "consciously remain in untruth" (*HA* 34). His question there, as here, is whether it is possible to live in full view of the truth about the nature of the world revealed to us by science, the disenchanted world. His affirmative answer in *Human, All Too Human* was based on the assumption that one could learn to "live among human beings and with oneself as in *nature*, without praising, blaming, contending, gazing contentedly, as though at a spectacle."

This, I suggest, is what Nietzsche gives up in *The Gay Science*: not value anti-realism, but the "error theory" version of it, the claim that the only honest way to face up to the truth disclosed by science is as non-valuing spectators. He has Zarathustra mock this view of life and knowledge as "immaculate knowledge" (*die unbefleckte Erkenntniss*) (*Z* II:15)[26] and he replaces it in *GS* with one in which the "knower" (*der Erkennende*) belongs to the dance of existence and is one of its "masters of ceremony" (*GS* 54). Here the "knower" is less the scientist engaged in acquiring knowledge than the philosopher committed to science as the ideal of knowing, the philosopher whose basic view of the universe is formed by science: the empiricist, naturalist, and value anti-realist. This is the person whose problem it is to determine whether one can incorporate knowledge, and the message of Nietzsche's "gay science" is that this can and must be done while remaining a participant in life rather than a mere spectator, i.e. while making value judgments. But there is nothing here to suggest that this is because values are already in the world. In fact, Nietzsche quite clearly denies this:

> Whatever now has *value* in our world does not have value in itself, according to its nature—nature is always valueless—but has been *given* value at some time, as a present—and it was *we* who gave it and bestowed it. Only we have created the world *that concerns human beings*.

---

[26] Rendered by Kaufmann as "On Immaculate Perception."

"We" in this passage refers to the "contemplatives" of its title, presumably religious thinkers and philosophers. The contemplative finds it difficult to "shake off a delusion":

> He fancies that he is a *spectator* and *listener* who has been placed before the great visual and acoustic spectacle that is life; he calls his own nature *contemplative* and forgets that he is himself the poet who keeps creating this life. Of course, he is different from the *actor* of this drama, the so-called active type; but he is even less like a mere observer or festive guest in front of the stage. To the poet certainly belongs *vis contemplativa* and the ability to look back upon his work, but at the same time and above all *vis creativa*, which the active human being *lacks*, whatever visual appearances and the faith of all the world may say. It is we, the thinking-feeling ones, who really and continually *make* something that was not there yet: the whole eternally growing world of valuations, colors, accents, perspectives, scales, affirmations, negations (*GS* 301).

In *HA* Nietzsche divided Schopenhauer's "world as representation" into two parts, the disenchanted empirical world revealed by science and the enchanted or value-laden world of our practical concerns. He called the latter the "world as representation (as error)." In *GS* he still makes a distinction between the two worlds, but he now celebrates the second world as a human creation rather than looking down on it as an error. Value is not already in the world, waiting for us to discover it. But there is no necessary error involved in none the less discovering value in the world, finding it there. The only error is at the meta-level: the error of failing to recognize that value can be discovered in the world only because "we" put it there. "Only we have created the world *that concerns human beings*."

Nietzsche identifies the creators of the value-laden world as "wir, die Denkend-Empfindenen," in Kaufmann's translation, "we who think and feel at the same time," or as I translated it above: "we, the thinking- feeling ones."[27] What does feeling have to do with the creation of a world of values? *Gay Science 7* tells us that the passions (*Passionen*) constitute "all that has given color to existence." Here "passion" seems to be a general cover term for whatever belongs to the affective side of human beings.[28] The passage insists that those interested in moral matters must undertake to study "all kinds of passions" in "different ages, peoples, great and small individuals: their whole reason and all their evaluations and illuminations [*Beleuchtungen*] of things must be brought to light." Nietzsche's position thus appears to be the basically Humean one that valuing

---

[27] Compare the formulation of *GS* 107 and see n. 25 above.
[28] The term Nietzsche uses for "passion" in a more narrow sense is *Leidenschaft*, the term translated as "passion" in "The Color of the Passions" (*GS* 139), discussed below.

is an expression of passion (in the wide sense), that values are not in the world until they are put there as projections of sentiment or feeling, of the affective or non-cognitive side of our mental life, the side whose function it is not to gain information about the world, but to determine our responses to the information we receive.

Although we presently have little evidence that Nietzsche actually read Hume, it is almost impossible to believe that *The Gay Science* is not indebted to a reading of the famous passage in which Hume makes the following distinction between the offices of reason and taste (where the latter is identified as "internal taste or feeling, or whatever you please to call it, which distinguishes moral good and evil, and which embraces the one and rejects the other"):

> The former conveys the knowledge of truth and falsehood; the latter gives the sentiment of beauty and deformity, vice and virtue. The one discovers objects as they really stand in nature, without addition or diminution; the other has a productive faculty; and gilding or staining all natural objects with the colors borrowed from internal sentiment raises, in a manner, a new creation. (Hume 1957: app. 1:112)

Nietzsche uses Hume's metaphor of "gilding" in *GS* 139, an aphorism on the passions (*Leidenschaften*), here understood in a narrower sense than above. Entitled "The Color of the Passions," it contrasts St Paul and his like, who have "an evil eye for the passions" and whose idealistic tendency therefore aims at their annihilation, with the Greeks, who "directed their idealistic tendency precisely towards the passions and loved and elevated, gilded [*vergoldet*] and deified them." In the latter case, "passions evidently made them feel happier, but also purer and more godlike," whereas those in the former group know of the passions only "what is dirty, disfiguring and heartbreaking." The passions themselves thus receive their value as a projection of feelings and passions: seeing them from the perspective of love "gilds" them, giving them attractive colors, which are projections of our own positive feelings of love and happiness, whereas an "evil eye" projects negative feelings onto the passions, staining them, and thus finds in them only what corresponds to and produces these feelings.

Thus Nietzsche does not claim that only "contemplatives" have created the value-laden world; that world is first and foremost the creation or projection of human feelings or sentiments. Things do present themselves to us as valuable or not so valuable, but only because they invoke in us certain feelings, feelings that "color" things for us, gilding or staining them, thereby making it seem as if we are simply perceiving or recognizing their value. Nietzsche believes that the feelings with which we respond to things reflect in part an affective nature inherited from ancestors whose reproductive success it furthered. But this is not to deny that beliefs have an effect on feelings and therefore valuing. Consider Nietzsche's description of "the greatest change" (*GS* 152):

> The illumination and the color of all things have changed. We no longer completely understand how the ancients felt about what was most familiar and frequent—for example, the day and waking. ... The same goes for the whole of life, which was illumined by death and its significance; for us "death" means something quite different. All experiences were lighted differently, for a god shone through them. All decisions and perspectives on the remote future, too; for they had oracles and secret portents and believed in prophesy. They felt differently about "truth," for the insane could be accepted back then as its mouthpiece—which makes *us* shudder or laugh.

The colored or value-laden world of the ancients differed from ours because they felt differently about things, and they felt differently because their beliefs differed from ours. What they believed about death was undoubtedly a product of certain facts about it that were accessible to them, e.g. how and when it was likely to befall themselves and those they loved, but also of what they had been taught about it by old-style contemplatives: e.g. that it was a gateway to another life. Such beliefs about death and its significance produced the feelings that colored the ancient world, or at least that revised to some extent the way it had already been colored by our inherited affective dispositions. But now "we knowers," we who have put forward the scientific view of the world as the truth about it, have destroyed the beliefs that established the significance of death and much else. *HA* hoped that our "purifying knowledge" would allow the destroyers of the old beliefs and colors to live as non-valuing spectators by weakening "the old motives of vehement desire" and allowing the emergence of a "life more purified of affect" than now exists. This is a far cry from *GS*, which in effect says that "we knowers" must become "we thinking-feeling ones," those who embody the "knowing and feeling form of existence." Because it is feeling or affect that colors the world with value, the point is that those who have destroyed the old colors must give the world new ones.

Why they are the ones who must do this eventually becomes clear in a passage that contains some of Nietzsche's strongest praise of science. Those who "merely glance at [science] in passing" are said to be

> terrified to see how here the most difficult is demanded and the best is done without praise and decorations. Indeed what one hears [in science] is, as among soldiers, mostly reproaches and harsh rebukes; for doing things well holds as the rule, failure the exception; but here as elsewhere the rule tends to keep quiet. This "severity of science" has the same effect as the forms and good manners of the best society; it frightens the

uninitiated. But whoever is used to it would never want to live anywhere else than in this bright, transparent, vigorous, electrified air. (*GS* 293)[29]

Those who are used to science, Nietzsche claims, "have their full strength" only in this "severe and clear element"—"here they can fly." Elsewhere things "are not pure and airy enough for them," and they suspect that "their best art would rightly profit no one and would give themselves no joy; that half of their lives would slip through their fingers among misunderstandings; that they would be required to exercise a great deal of caution, conceal things, be inhibited." The remainder of the passage makes clear, for those with any doubt, that Nietzsche has been talking about himself, thus that his own "best art" requires for its proper use the scientific view of things.

Why, then, go down into those muddy waters where one has to swim and wade and get one's wings dirty?—No, it is too hard for us to live there: is it our fault that we were born for the air, clean air, we rivals of the beams of light, and that we wish we could ride on ethereal dust specks like these beams—not away from the sun but *toward the sun*! That, however, we cannot do:—thus we want to do what we alone can do: bring light to the earth, be "the light of the earth!" (Ibid).

What "we cannot do" (for reasons my account of perspectivism will shortly make clear) is embody *HA*'s ideal of purity. We cannot live as pure knowers of the world science reveals to us because science itself requires what is impure or "muddy," what always pulls us back to the earth: passion or affect and therefore values. The last point is not made clear in this passage, which is devoted instead to expressing Nietzsche's sympathy with his younger self, whose ideal he now repudiates, as well as the ideal with which he proposes to replace it: to "bring light to the earth, be 'the light of the earth.'" The sense in which "we knowers" *must* color the world is the sense specified here: that "we alone" can do it. But why can only those who flourish in the air of science, that is, who embrace a naturalistic view of things, "bring light to the earth"?[30] I take Nietzsche's point

---

[29] I do not want to suppress the fact that Nietzsche ends the last quoted sentence with a final description of the air in question—"this *manly* air"—nor that this carries out the suggestion at the beginning of the passage that women in particular have the negative attitude towards science it describes, but "unfortunately also many artists." The passage in effect explains why this would be the case with women since it claims science frightens the uninitiated, a position that was clearly forced upon women in Nietzsche's time. What explains the artists' attitude is another matter, and one much closer to Nietzsche's main concerns here, since his ideal for art, as suggested in *GS* 99, is that of being "a companion-piece and completion of human knowledge and science." *GS* 294 when read in conjunction with *GS* 59 suggests one explanation for artists (if we avoid being distracted by the reference to women that occurs in the latter passage as well).

[30] Kaufmann's translation of "was wir einzig können" as "what alone we can do" keeps this question from surfacing by implying that Nietzsche's point is solely about the only thing we can do and not also about what we alone can do. Although his translation may seem to fit the context better, "we alone" is also a possible translation of "wir einzig," and once this is recognized a new line of questioning and interpretation opens up.

to be that science discloses the truth about the world, and that those who ignore or resist that truth will be presenting only a fantasy of the world, rather than lighting up the one that is there. He believes that "hitherto all valuations and ideals were built on *ignorance* of physics or in *contradiction* to it" (*GS* 335), using "physics" in the sense of "natural science," as Schopenhauer often does. Those who built values in that way did not simply color or paint the world, gilding and staining the objects of nature; they painted *over* natural objects, obscuring or denying the truth about them. Both coloring and coloring over fulfill the task Nietzsche notoriously assigns philosophers—the "creation" or legislation of values (*BGE* 211)—but only the former in a way that is compatible with what he says "compels us to physics" and elsewhere calls "our virtue": honesty (*GS* 335; *BGE* 227).

How is the mere "coloring" of objects of nature to be distinguished from painting *over* them? I take the latter to involve making false claims about things, the former to be a matter of presenting them in a certain light, which includes above all "allowing only perspectival views" and therefore emphasizing or focusing on certain features at the expense of others. This and similar techniques "we should learn from artists," Nietzsche tells us, "while being wiser than they are in other matters. For their refined power stops where art stops and life begins; but *we* want to be the poets of our life" (*GS* 299). Artists continually glorify things and states "whose value for human happiness is considered safe and secure"—their "refined power" consists precisely in knowing how to portray such things so as to provoke attraction or repulsion—but they themselves are not the appraisers of the things they gild and stain (*GS* 85).

One might think of Nietzsche's project in terms of Hume's distinction between two species of moral philosophy. Abstruse or scientific philosophy aims at knowledge, at discovering the principles that determine our feelings and "make us approve or blame any particular object, action, or behavior," whereas the aim of popular philosophy is practical; its practitioner is the painter rather than the anatomist of human values. Painting virtue "in the most amiable colors," and "borrowing all helps from poetry and eloquence" to treat their subject in a manner "best fitted to please the imagination, and engage the affections," philosophers of the second type "make us *feel* the difference between vice and virtue; they excite and regulate our sentiments" (Hume 1975b: 1–2). We could say that Nietzsche's later work is devoted to being both the scientific anatomist and the painter of the world of human values, and that he does not think one can really be the former without to some extent being the latter as well. His anatomy of values follows Hume's general approach, as I have in effect been arguing, but its "historical spirit" distinguishes Nietzsche's "physics" or anatomy of values from that of its first practitioners, the "English psychologists" he discusses at the beginning of *Genealogy* (*GM* I:1–2). Above all, Nietzsche is aware of and desirous of understanding "the whole range of values and desiderata to date" (*GS* 382). But he wants to be, and thinks he must be, the painter as well—he must at the very least select and focus our attention on some features rather than others, which will affect our feelings and value judgments (depending in part on which affective dispositions and value orientations we already have).

But he obviously wants to do more than engage in the necessary amount of selectivity. Because the ideal of *Human, All Too Human*—that of being the pure spectator or the presenter of the pure spectacle, of "immaculate knowledge"—is impossible, he has a choice between being the unwilling artist and conveyor of values decided on by others or becoming the willing painter and thus the "poet of our life."[31] Who or what determines how the painter paints, which features of the world to emphasize or veil, gild or stain?[32] Not the anatomist, who only explains why people value what they do, and not the painter, who only gilds or stains things whose value is already assumed. Hume relies for his answer on "our common human nature," but Nietzsche would regard that as a "construction" of certain interests and previous decisions about what is really valuable. These decisions are always made, he claims, by "the rich and the idle" (*GS* 85), where "idle" only makes sense if he means the contemplatives: religious thinkers and philosophers. As an artist of the world of human values, his choice is between painting what has been determined as valuable either by the rich or by a previous breed of contemplative (as he was doing in *HA*) or finding a way to make his own decisions about how to paint things. This is the major project to which I believe the empiricist spirit and intellectual conscience he found in Schopenhauer's philosophy eventually led Nietzsche, and is what makes his later philosophy "a companion-piece and completion of human knowledge and science." But that is the beginning of another long story.

To bring this one to a close, I will discuss briefly a doctrine that seems to constitute a major objection to my interpretation of Nietzsche, namely, his perspectivism. Usually treated as the claim that truth is relative to one's perspective, the perspectivism found in Nietzsche's later work seems to show that he abandoned the empiricism of *HA* and came to recognize science as "only a perspective." According to my own interpretation, he recognized that he could not just be a scientist because science itself requires values. But isn't this perspectivism? And doesn't it show that he could no longer "privilege" science in the way an empiricist does, that the whole distinction between facts and values I have been relying on must be called into question? My answer is that it is perspectivism, but that this doctrine as it appears in Nietzsche's work does not have the implications claimed for it.

---

[31] The refrain that haunts Zarathustra—"only fool, only poet"—indicates that the latter choice was not something Nietzsche could embrace without conflict.

[32] I do not mean to imply that staining or negatively coloring and veiling go together. In fact, one of the major things Nietzsche thinks we learn from artists is how to make things more attractive by veiling them, because what attracts is precisely the desire to unveil.

The main point is that Nietzsche never says that truth is perspectival, only that knowing is. His longest and most important statement of perspectivism—*Genealogy* III:12—makes explicit that he calls knowing "perspectival" to help us guard against conceiving of it as "disinterested contemplation." The latter conception of knowing, he claims, requires us to think (the equivalent of) a complete "absurdity": "an eye that cannot possibly be thought, an eye that must not have any direction, in which the active and interpreting forces through which seeing first becomes seeing-something must be turned off, must be absent." In claiming that "there is only a perspective seeing, only a perspective knowing," Nietzsche rejects the spectator conception he had taken over from Schopenhauer's account of aesthetic contemplation and used in *HA* as a model of knowing (and living) after the acquisition of a scientific world-view. Stripped of its visual metaphor, Nietzsche's perspectivism is the claim that all knowing is "interested," rooted in affect, in the will. But the impossibility of disinterested *knowing* obviously does not follow from the fact that *seeing* is perspectival. What, then, is Nietzsche's basis for this doctrine? It is, I submit, his naturalistic understanding of the intellect, which is very similar to the one he originally derived from Schopenhauer, according to which human cognitive capacities exist because of the evolutionary advantage they confer. No such advantage is conferred by attending to any and all features of reality. Instead, the intellect must be directed to certain features—for instance, those most relevant to human survival and reproduction. And it is precisely affect—interest, emotion, feeling, passion—that turns the mind in a particular direction, focusing its attention on certain features of reality and pushing it to register them as important.[33] Nietzsche's claim is that knowledge is only acquired when the intellect is so pushed and focused; his perspectivism is a metaphorical formulation of this empirical claim about knowledge. We know that seeing cannot be without a direction supplied by the body based on our empirical knowledge of the eye. Likewise, we know that knowing cannot be without a direction supplied by the will based on our empirical knowledge of the intellect.

But if perspectivism is itself an empirical doctrine, it cannot challenge empiricism, or show that science is "only a perspective" in any sense that is incompatible with the claim that science discloses the "actual nature of the world" (*HA* 29).[34] The view that it can show this must be based on the assumption that perspectivism is an a priori doctrine. I myself once interpreted it that way (Clark

---

[33] A contemporary source for this view is Damasio 1994. For a view of emotions very similar to the one I am attributing to Nietzsche, see Robinson 1995: 53–74.

[34] That he recognizes the point I have made in the text seems to me clear from *BGE* 15. A well-marked book in Nietzsche's library contains what I take to be the clear source for *BGE* 15 (Spir 1877, I:135), which makes it even clearer that the argument is the one I have given in the text. Spir, the "distinguished logician" quoted in *HA* 18, influenced a number of the formulations in the first part of *BGE* and is clearly a major source for Nietzsche's knowledge of Hume. For much more on this topic, see Clark and Dudrick 2012.

1990: ch. 5). However, I recognized that, precisely because it was a priori, it had no substantive implications about knowledge: since it only ruled out a conception of knowing that we could recognize a priori as absurd, it did not rule out a kind of knowledge which we could really want or for which we could have any real use. It certainly could not show that truth, hence the nature of the world, is indexed to (depends upon) perspectives. I was never happy about precluding Nietzsche's use of the metaphor of perspective from saying something substantive about knowledge, but, given my interpretation of perspectivism as an a priori doctrine, I could not see how it could be both a substantive thesis about knowledge and a thesis Nietzsche could have reason to accept. Those who believe perspectivism challenges the claim that science discloses the "true nature of the world" must think that both can be true. But it is very difficult to see how, once the depth of Nietzsche's empiricism is recognized. This much at least is clear: perspectivism cannot provide a way of explaining how Nietzsche gave up the empiricism of *HA*; only if he has an independent reason to abandon empiricism could he consistently hold that perspectivism is a substantive a priori truth about knowledge, which is what it has to be to challenge empiricism.

Suppose, then, that it is an empirical thesis about knowledge. How does that allow us to avoid attributing to Nietzsche the claim that truth is perspectival? After all, he claims that the more perspectives we bring to bear on a matter, the more complete our concept of the object, our "objectivity," will be, and "objectivity" here seems to mean the same as "grasp of the objective features of reality," i.e. of truth. Doesn't that mean that complete objectivity or truth depends on viewing an object from all perspectives, that to the extent we do not or cannot do that, we have access only to a partial truth, one in need of completion by other perspectives? Tempting as that interpretation is, it should be resisted. Not to do so is to saddle Nietzsche's perspectivism with endless problems about self-reference, and endless new attempts to avoid them, which is like fiddling while Rome burns. That may seem like fun to some; to me, it seems like frittering away one's time while the real problems go wanting. One way to resist is to admit that every perspective is indeed partial or one-sided, and that it therefore cannot reveal everything there is to know (all of the truths) about any object or matter, but to deny that what it does reveal is any less true, only partially true, or necessarily in need of completion by what can be revealed by other perspectives.

Different affects make different aspects of reality salient and focus our attention on them, so that other features disappear from view—that is why perspectives are partial or "one-sided." But that gives us no basis for denying that our affects give access to truth, that the features to which they call our attention are really there, are "objective" features of the world whether we notice them or not.[35] If our ideal is to know as many features of an object as possible, it will be

---

[35] Nor is it to deny that some perspectives give distorted views of their objects. See Leiter 1994: esp., 343–52.

important to view it from as many different perspectives (sets of affects) as possible. But why should that be our epistemological ideal? It certainly was not Nietzsche's. He suggests that scholars usually serve knowledge by being locked into their own "nook" or perspective, their own set of interests, to such an extent that they usually damage themselves as human beings (*GS* 366).[36] The narrowness of a perspective *by itself* in no way keeps one from discovering truth, though it certainly means that there will be other truths one will be unable to discover. But no truth at all can be discovered without the narrowing of focus that comes with a perspective. That is Nietzsche's point. Whether the truths accessible from one's current perspective need supplementing by other perspectives really depends on what one is trying to find out and what that perspective is. If the perspective is, for instance, the interests and concerns of the typical middle-aged white American male, and the object of investigation is the health of Americans, other perspectives will of course be necessary—not because the middle-aged white American male only sees things that are partially true (or true from his perspective) but because there are too many things that he is likely to ignore or overlook that will become apparent from certain other—fairly obvious—perspectives. Even if some truths are unlikely to be discovered from his own perspective, however, perspectivism gives no reason to deny that he can recognize these truths once they are called to his attention—depending, of course, on his concerns and affects. But the affects that will allow him to recognize the truth when presented by an equal in his profession differ from those that will allow him to discover it himself. All of which is relevant to why science needs democracy, as Nietzsche himself was well aware. Understood as an empirical thesis, perspectivism has precisely that implication. But it in no way implies that science is itself a perspective that needs supplementation from some other form of knowledge.[37] A perspective is a set of affects, whereas science is a practice, and, under democratic circumstances, one that allows and encourages different perspectives to be brought to bear in the service of knowledge.

It follows that perspectives do not constitute their objects, but merely reveal them. But if we have no access to these objects except through our perspectives, how do we know that they are there independently of our perspectives? Because our best empirical theories tell us they are. Of course, these theories too reflect our perspectives, but that is no problem for holding that the objects

---

[36] If knowledge or scholarship often requires being locked into a perspective, the objectivity Nietzsche requires of philosophers involves the reverse: the ability to move from one perspective to another to "have and not have one's affects" (*BGE* 284), hence "to control one's pro and con" (*GM* III:12). But that is because the philosopher's primary task is not the discovery of truth, but the creation of new values (*BGE* 253). See the section entitled "Knowledge" in Clark 1998a for more on this.

[37] *GS* 373 may seem to imply that science does need such supplementation. Read carefully in the light of the interpretation offered in this essay, however, the passage claims only that science cannot provide meaning or value.

known through these perspectives exist quite independently of them (of our affects). Only if we ignore Nietzsche's empiricism will we find a problem here. We have already seen that perspectives do create a world, but it is not the world of nature, whose "true nature" science discloses. It is rather "the world *that concerns human beings*," the colored world that is the projection of our affect onto the first world. This is the world that science needs for its completion. Nietzsche no longer considers this second world an "error" because he now rejects as absurd the spectator ideal of objectivity that had made all valuing seem non-objective and unjust, but he does sometimes call it a "fiction" (BGE 34), which it is when measured against the world disclosed by science.

A critic of my earlier interpretation has cited Nietzsche's claim that "*we want to be the poets of our life*" in opposition to my denial that human knowledge necessarily falsifies (Anderson 1996: 333). To be sure, if we want to *think of ourselves* as the poets or creators of the world that is the object of knowledge, we will have to think of that world as a falsification (though it will be difficult to say of what). But that world, I am claiming, is one Nietzsche thinks we discover rather than create, even though we discover it only by means of our affective perspectives, and it is a delusion to think we created it. It is also a delusion, as Nietzsche tells us, for a poet to think of herself as a mere spectator or discoverer of a life she has actually created. But that is a delusion philosophers will need to worry about avoiding only if they give up trying to be merely anatomists of beliefs and values and also engage with Nietzsche in the other project of his "gay science," that of learning actually "to *be* the poets of our life" (*GS* 299, my emphasis)—of that other world, Hume's "new creation," the world that *concerns* us, the world of values that is the projection of our feelings.[38]

---

[38] This essay owes a great deal to discussion with Simon Blackburn and the other participants in his NEH Seminar "Emotion and Objectivity," especially Christopher Williams and Daniel Jacobson, and to the support and patience of Connie Jones and Christopher Janaway.

{ 13 }

Nietzsche as Anti-metaphysician

Metaphysics aims to establish what there is to know about the world that goes beyond what can be discovered by science. In this sense, Nietzsche himself put forward metaphysical views in his final works. But he is better known for the criticism of metaphysics he began developing in the works of his middle or "positivistic" period. This criticism is specifically directed against "two-world" metaphysics, the kind of metaphysic put forward by Parmenides, Plato, Leibniz, Kant, and Schopenhauer, among others, according to which there is a second world in addition to the empirical world studied by science, and it is the "true" or real world whereas the empirical world is mere "appearance." Although he turns against metaphysics in this sense in the works of his middle period, Nietzsche began his philosophical career as a devotee of Schopenhauer's two-world metaphysics.

Nietzsche's Early Work

Nietzsche's main concern in his early work was the condition of contemporary European culture, which he judged to be inferior to that of the pre-Socratic Greeks. He used Schopenhauer's metaphysics to interpret the achievements of the latter and the falloff of modern culture from its standard. He criticizes modern culture in effect for having become anti-metaphysical, for having accepted that the empirical world is the only one. By following Socrates' preference for the rational and clear over the artistic and mythical, it has come to assume that only science gives us truth. Nietzsche's early work sets out to combat this assumption.

One argument he gives against it in his first book, *The Birth of Tragedy*, is that Kant and Schopenhauer have demonstrated that the empirical world of individuals, the only reality recognized by science, is mere appearance. A second argument is based on Schopenhauer's claim that the deeper truth about existence is that it is will and therefore suffering without end or point. Nietzsche argues that modern culture's blindness to this truth has led it to a shallow optimism. According to *BT*, the Greeks were not shallow optimists. They recognized that the empirical world is mere appearance and that the character of the underlying reality is horrifying and were therefore in effect Schopenhauerian pessimists. Their great art was produced in the attempt to deal with their pessimism, to find a way to affirm life in spite of it. Apollonian art induced affirmation by presenting an idealized version of life, thus by means of a beautifying illusion, but the Dionysian affirmation of tragedy was undertaken in full appreciation of the horrifying character of the underlying reality, i.e., of the Schopenhauerian truth.

Nietzsche probably did not think that "will" captured the literal truth about the thing in itself (or that the Greeks would have thought it did). In unpublished notes written before *BT*, he rejects Schopenhauer's proofs that the thing in itself is will and says that only a "poetic intuition" allowed him to substitute will for the "Kantian X" (OS 2). Nietzsche seems to agree with Kant, claiming that the thing in itself is "wholly outside the sphere of cognition," but thinks that Schopenhauer helps us see that we can nevertheless have a kind of intuitive or pre-linguistic grasp of it, which we can only put into language by describing the thing in itself in terms borrowed from the world of appearance. He thinks that this is what Schopenhauer did when he called the thing in itself "will," and that something similar happened in the case of ancient tragedy: the members of the (originally) dancing, chanting chorus produced in themselves an ecstatic state in which they identified with and thus gained an intuitive grasp of the inner nature of the world, which they expressed in words and images as the "Apollonian dream image" of the play itself. It seems probable that he understands his use of Schopenhauer's metaphysics in the same way, as a translation of his inchoate sense of the thing in itself into the language of appearance.

Nietzsche did not remain satisfied with this "artist's metaphysics" for long. After *BT*, he no longer held that art provides access to a truth that is beyond the grasp of science, although he did try out other ways of defending "the metaphysical significance of culture" (*UM* III:6), the idea that by means of culture human activity becomes "explicable only by the laws of another, higher life" (*UM* III:4). The main suggestion seems to be that we should act as if it is true that we belong to a higher life even though we know it is not. In his essay on history (*UM* II), he urges that history be practiced as art rather than as science, on the grounds that certain scientific doctrines, clearly meaning Darwin's theory of evolution and its implications, are "true, but deadly," apparently fearing that the loss of the myth that humans are more than animals—that they belong to "another, higher life"—will foster a disintegration of culture into "systems of individual egoism, brotherhoods whose purpose will be the rapacious exploitation of non-brothers" (*UM* II:9).

Nietzsche Middle ("Positivistic") Period

In the works of his middle period, Nietzsche turns his back on the attempt to imbue culture with "metaphysical significance." In *Human, All Too Human*, he abandons his polemic against the high value placed on science in modern culture, now taking it as "the mark of a higher culture to value the little unpretentious truths discovered by means of rigorous method more highly than the errors handed down by metaphysical and artistic ages and men, which blind us and make us happy" (*HA* 3). Hereafter he never doubts that science gives us truth. In fact, in the works of his middle period (at least in *HA* and *Daybreak*), *only* science gives us truth, which leaves no room for metaphysics as Nietzsche understands it. He regards philosophy as he now practices it as part of natural science (*HA* 1).

HA aims to induce skepticism about any metaphysical world, thus contributing to the anti-metaphysical modern culture against which Nietzsche directed his first book, by showing that it is cognitively superfluous. He concedes that "there might be a metaphysical world," meaning that the true nature of reality (the thing in itself) might in fact differ from the empirical world studied by science. For "we behold all things through the human head and cannot cut this head off; while the question nonetheless remains what of the world would still be there if one had cut it off" (*HA* 9). We can only know things as they can appear to us, and therefore cannot rule out the "absolute possibility" that they differ from how they appear (and would appear even to idealized human observers). Nietzsche's metaphorical formulation of this point above might also seem to imply that we could know nothing about the metaphysical world even if it does exist. But he does not rely on such an argument in *HA*, presumably because he knows that metaphysicians have always thought that special methods—usually a priori ones, which do not belong merely to the "human head"—provide access to a reality that is inaccessible empirically. So his strategy is to induce skepticism about metaphysical assumptions by arguing that

> passion, error, and self-deception . . . the worst of all methods of acquiring knowledge, not the best of them, have taught belief in them. When one has disclosed these methods as the foundations of all extant religions and metaphysical systems, one has refuted them! Then that possibility still remains over; but one can do absolutely nothing with it, not to speak of letting happiness, salvation and life depend on the gossamer of such a possibility. (*HA* 9)

To make good on this claim, Nietzsche offers a genealogy of philosophers' belief in a metaphysical or non-empirical world. The first idea of a "second world" came from dreams, he claims: primitive human beings thought that in dreaming they were "getting to know a *second real world*" (HA 5). Philosophers later exploited this idea to explain how they could have knowledge of things they recognized they could not know empirically. These things include what "all metaphysics has principally to do with," namely, "substance and freedom of the will" (*HA* 18). Instead of concluding that these things did not exist, metaphysicians claimed that empirical methods were faulty, and that the real world was accessible only to non-empirical methods. The empirical world was thus taken to be a mere appearance or distortion of a second world, which was thereby constituted as the "true" one.

Nietzsche assumes that it is already clear to his readers that the beliefs in substance and free will that led philosophers to posit a metaphysical world are contradicted by the "disclosed nature of the world," the world as disclosed by modern science (*HA* 10, 29). This is because he assumes that substance is unchanging and that free will requires uncaused events, whereas science shows that everything changes and that all events have causes. *HA* aims merely to counteract any remaining tendency to think there must be some truth in these beliefs by showing that we can explain how they arose without assuming that they contain any truth. His explanation seems highly implausible, however. The basic idea is that both beliefs are shared by "everything organic" and that we have inherited them from lower organisms who did not notice change, in the case of substance, or have a grasp of causality, in the case of free will (*HA* 18).

Nietzsche's more interesting concern in *HA* is a second reason philosophers had for positing a metaphysical world, namely, to explain the existence of things they held to possess a higher value than typical occupants of the empirical world—for instance, knowledge, objectivity, art, the virtues. Because metaphysicians assumed that things cannot "originate in their opposite, for instance, rationality in irrationality . . ., disinterested contemplation in covetous desire, living for others in egoism," they could explain the origin of such things only by assuming "for the more highly valued thing a miraculous source in the very kernel and being of the 'thing in itself'" (*HA* 1). Nietzsche's strategy here gives his book its name: to show that these more highly valued things are "human, all too human," mere sublimations and transformations of things of lower value. By showing that we can explain disinterested contemplation as a sublimation of lust, altruistic acts as disguised egoistic ones, etc., he shows that the things of higher value provide no basis for positing a metaphysical world.

If these two lines of argument succeed, Nietzsche expects interest in the purely theoretical problem of the thing in itself and appearance to die out (*HA* 10). Indeed, it may be considered worthy of a "Homeric laugh": for "it appeared to be so much, indeed everything, and is actually empty, that is to say, empty of significance" (*HA* 16). That is, no one is driven to metaphysics by the question of what things are like apart from our knowledge of them (in the terms of his earlier passage: what the world would be like if we could cut the human head off). That is a purely theoretical problem and is "not very well calculated to bother people overmuch; but all that has hitherto made metaphysical assumptions *valuable, terrible, delightful* to them, all that has begotten these assumptions, is passion, error, and self-deception."

Error is involved when a metaphysical world is postulated to explain the existence and knowledge of things that do not in fact exist (substance and free will) or that can be explained by empirical methods (things taken to be of a higher value). Nietzsche evidently takes passion and self-deception to play a role in generating and sustaining the belief in things of a higher value.

> It is probable the objects of the religious, moral and aesthetic sentiments belong only to the surface of things, while man likes to believe that here at least he is in touch with the world's heart; the reason he deludes himself is that these things produce in him such profound happiness and unhappiness, and thus he here exhibits the same pride as in the case of astrology. For astrology believes that the starry firmament revolves around the fate of man; the moral man, however, supposes that what he has essentially at heart must also constitute the essence and heart of things. (*HA* 4)

Although the actual objects of religious, moral, and aesthetic feelings probably belong only to the empirical world, metaphysicians posit other objects for them, ones they situate in the metaphysical world—as when the object of awe is taken to be God instead of the features of the natural world, or when morality is taken to be the perception of Platonic Forms rather than the expression of a "human, all too human" attitude, and the empirical world is thereby taken to be only the "surface of things." They do so in an attempt to convince themselves that their concerns are not theirs alone, that support for them is somehow woven into the fabric of the universe. This is why they concern themselves with questions about "appearance" and the thing in itself: because the latter provides a space that can be furnished with the objects of the moral, religious, and aesthetic feelings, thus seeming to provide external support for them. Note that this explains Nietzsche's own concern with such questions in *BT*: he was seeking external support for the importance of art and of his own aesthetic experience. But this is all illusion and self-deception as far as he is now concerned. *HA* sets out to show that aesthetic, moral, and religious feelings are to be explained as merely human reactions to natural features of the world, hence that "the origin of religion, art and morality" can be "perfectly understood" without invoking a metaphysical world (*HA* 10). Only self-deception remains to motivate metaphysics.

Nietzsche's Final Works

The works of Nietzsche's third and final period show significant changes in his analysis of two-world metaphysics. To begin with, he no longer claims that "there might be a metaphysical world," evidently recognizing the problem with the metaphor that led him to this conclusion in *HA*. In *The Gay Science*, he denies that appearance is to be contrasted with an essence or "unknown X," claiming that we have no conception of the latter except in terms of "the predicates of its appearance" (*GS* 54). He makes the consequence of this explicit in *Beyond Good and Evil*, calling the thing in itself (the "unknown X") a "contradiction in terms" (*BGE* 16). Finally, in *Twilight of the Idols*, he offers a history of "How the 'True World' Finally Became a Fable." This is a six-stage history of metaphysics, including Plato, Christianity, Kant, and the various stages of Nietzsche's criticisms of metaphysics, which ends with the denial that there is any "true" world and a recognition (which was missing, for instance, in *GS*) that the remaining world, the empirical world, can no longer be considered the merely "apparent" world. It is the only demonstrable world, but also the only world of which we have any conception. Why, then, have philosophers thought otherwise? Nietzsche revises and refines his earlier answer and in doing so seems to develop some sympathy with the aims of metaphysics, perhaps recognizing the possibility of a kind of metaphysic that does not conflict with science or reduce the empirical world to mere "appearance."

One change is that he no longer locates the origins of metaphysics' errors in beliefs inherited from lower organisms, but instead, anticipating Wittgenstein, gives language the major role in generating them. He sometimes seems to claim that language itself falsifies reality, as when he holds the subject-predicate structure of Indo-European languages responsible for philosophers' propensity to think that reality itself must consist of ultimate subjects that could never be part of the experienced world: God, the ego or soul, and indivisible atoms of matter. But he is better interpreted as saying of language what he ultimately says of the senses: only what we make of its testimony introduces error (*TI* III:2). Language misleads us into traditional philosophy only if we in effect assume that the grammar of some natural languages offers us a blueprint of reality that is a substitute for and can be used to challenge the adequacy of empirical theories.

Nietzsche tells us that grammar seduced human beings into a "realm of crude fetishism," a primitive "metaphysics of grammar," as soon as they started thinking about what the world in general was like. This metaphysics sees "a doer and a doing everywhere; it believes in will as *the* cause," that is, as the cause of all events we would now explain mechanistically. It also believes "in the ego as being, in the ego as substance, and it projects this faith in the ego-substance upon all things—only thereby does it first *create* the concept of 'thing'," in the sense of substance. When philosophers "very much later" recognized "the sureness, the subjective certainty, in our handling of the categories of reason" and realized that these could not be derived from experience, indeed did not apply to the empirical world, they concluded that it applied instead to a "higher world" in which they had once been at home and to which they now had access "since we have reason" (*TI* III:5). They believed that they possessed "pure reason," that their ability to reason brought with it the ability to reach truth without reliance on empirical data. Nietzsche often refers to the "errors" or "prejudices of reason," but what he thus refers to are the prejudices derived from the "belief in grammar," the implicit assumption that grammar reveals the truth about reality. It is from this assumption that the "categories of reason" were actually derived. Only the primitive "metaphysics of grammar" so derived provided philosophers with a basis for thinking that they grasped the structure of a world (the "true world") that differed from the empirical one.

But metaphysics isn't a matter of innocent confusion or error that philosophers simply fall into (contrary to what *HA* sometimes seems to suggest). Philosophers are willingly seduced by grammar; they exploit it for their own purposes, in particular, to express and defend their own values. This is the more important change in Nietzsche's understanding of metaphysics, the greater emphasis he now gives to the role of values in it. One well-known example of how the "metaphysics of grammar" is exploited to underwrite value conclusions is his account of the "belief in a neutral 'subject' with free choice" in *On the Genealogy of Morality*.

> A quantum of power is just such a quantum of drive, will, effect—more precisely, it is nothing other than this very driving, willing, effecting, and only through the seduction of language (and the basic errors of reason petrified therein), which understands and misunderstands all effecting as conditioned by an effecting something, by a "subject," can it appear otherwise. For just as common people separate the lightning from its flash and take the latter as a doing, as an effect of a subject called lightning, so popular morality also separates strength from the expression of strength as if there were behind the strong an indifferent substratum that is free to express strength. But there is no such substratum; there is no "being" behind the doing, effecting, becoming; the "doer" is simply fabricated into the doing—the doing is everything. (*GM* I:13)

Nietzsche is not denying that there are doers in the sense of persons or agents; he denies only that the doer is a "neutral 'subject'" or "indifferent substratum," something that is the bearer or cause of all its properties, but which is itself distinct from any and all of them, and so is completely free to choose what kind of person to be. Nietzsche's claim is that people are seduced into this belief in a real subject behind "doing" by the necessity of a grammatical subject for every predicate, just as scientists were seduced into positing indivisible atoms. But in the case of the materialistic atom, the empirical evidence eventually overcame the metaphysics of grammar (BGE 12). In the case of the "neutral 'subject,'" things are more difficult because the error was exploited "by the suppressed, hiddenly glowing affects of revenge and hate" to "hold the bird of prey *accountable* for being a bird of prey" and to interpret certain effects of powerlessness—e.g., patience and humbleness—as a "voluntary achievement, something willed, something chosen, a *deed*, a *merit*" (GM I:13).

According to later Nietzsche, two-world metaphysics involves the same kind of exploitation of the errors of reason that one finds in the pre-philosophical notion of free will. Holding "the moral (or immoral) intentions in every philosophy" to be "the real germ of life out of which the entire plain has grown," he suggests that such intentions explain how the "most abstruse metaphysical assertions have actually been arrived at" (*BGE 6*). His most important example is that of the Stoics, who claimed to derive an ethical imperative from nature, when they actually arrived at their view of nature (as following rational laws) by reading their own ethical ideal of self-governance into it (*BGE* 9). Because he claims that all philosophy does what the Stoics did, Nietzsche can't criticize metaphysicians for reading their values into the world (unless he is willing to dispense with all philosophy, which he is not). His objection is twofold: that self-deception keeps metaphysicians from recognizing that their "truths" are actually a matter of reading their values into reality, and that the values their metaphysics reads into reality are those of the ascetic ideal.

The ascetic ideal is the ideal of self-denial shared by most of the major religions. The assumption or value behind the idealizing of self-denial, according to Nietzsche's diagnosis, is that merely natural (earthly) existence has no intrinsic value, that it has value only as a means to something else that is actually its negation (e.g., heaven or nirvana). This life-devaluing ideal infects all the values supported by most religions. Although these values originally came into existence in support of some form of life, the ascetic priest gives them a life-devaluing interpretation. For instance, acts are interpreted as wrong on the grounds that they are selfish or animal, that they affirm natural instincts, and thus become not merely wrong but "sinful." Nietzsche sees traditional ("metaphysical") philosophers as successors to the ascetic priest because they interpret what they value—truth, knowledge, philosophy, virtue—in non-natural terms. He thinks that the assumption of the ascetic ideal lies behind this: that whatever is truly valuable must have a source outside the world of nature, the world accessible to empirical investigation. What ultimately explains the traditional assumption that philosophy must be a priori, and therefore concerned with a metaphysical world, is philosophers' assumption that nothing as valuable as philosophy or truth could be intimately connected to the senses or to the merely natural existence of human beings. Nietzsche therefore understands two-world metaphysics as an act of disguised revenge against life, and his later philosophy aims to provide a life-affirming alternative to it.

The question remains as to whether his later philosophy has room for some other kind of metaphysics, one that would not run afoul of his criticism of the two-world variety. Much is unsettled on this issue, and it must be admitted that what is said here about it will inevitably be more controversial than the claims about Nietzsche's rejection of two-world metaphysics. The notorious doctrine that life and the world are will to power is one reason to take later Nietzsche to leave room for metaphysics, for the doctrine seems clearly metaphysical, a mere variation on Schopenhauer's claim that the world is will. Richardson (1996) made the most successful attempt to work out the details of this doctrine and to argue that it does not conflict with Nietzsche's criticism of metaphysics. But this interpretation is based to a large extent on Nietzsche's unpublished notebooks, a notoriously unreliable basis for interpretations, and, as Richardson (2004) admits, there is no empirical or scientific basis for the doctrine in this unrestricted form. In this form, the doctrine evidently needs an a priori basis, and Nietzsche's criticism of metaphysics makes it difficult to see where he would find a basis for that. Indeed, in *Beyond Good and Evil* §15, he seems to embrace "sensualism" (that is, empiricism) as a "regulative hypothesis," which seems in line with the recent interpretation of Nietzsche as a methodological naturalist, who insists not only that philosophy aim for consistency with what the best science tells us, but also that it follow the methods of the sciences (Leiter 2002). Embracing a doctrine of the will to power on a priori grounds would therefore seem to be inconsistent with his overall philosophical orientation.

However, one problem for interpreting later Nietzsche as a methodological naturalist is his suggestion in the second edition of *The Gay Science* (1887), addressed to "Mr. Mechanic," that a "'scientific' interpretation of the world, as you understand it, might still be the *stupidest* of all possible interpretations of the world," precisely because it would allow no room for its own reality (*GS 373*). Nietzsche's wider point in this passage is that there are certain things that cannot be recognized or understood using only the methods of the natural sciences, e.g., the intellect and its products, agents and their actions, ethical and aesthetic properties. These show up only from a perspective that is constituted by value commitments. Just as one cannot recognize the value of a piece of music from a purely scientific perspective, but only if one is equipped with aesthetic standards from which to judge it, one cannot recognize behavior as constituting an action or as exhibiting thought unless one is equipped with standards for differentiating good from bad, rational from irrational, action and thought. And Mr. Mechanic cannot respond that the "real" world knows nothing of such value properties without admitting that his interpretation of the world has no place in reality, but is just a collection of marks or sounds.

Later Nietzsche thus seems to recognize that there is more to reality than what science can tell us, and this opens the possibility of recognizing metaphysics as a legitimate discipline. One example of the kind of metaphysics this might involve will have to suffice. Consider that if thought and actions can't be recognized from the viewpoint of science, the one who thinks and performs actions—the person—cannot be recognized from that perspective either. But what is a person? Nietzsche's answer is given in *Beyond Good and Evil* in terms of the traditional metaphysical notions of the soul and the will. Of course he rejects the soul as it was conceived by two-world metaphysics—as "indestructible, eternal, indivisible"—but makes explicit that this does not require us to "get rid of 'the soul' itself and thus forgo one of the most venerable of hypotheses," unlike "clumsy naturalists who cannot touch 'the soul' without losing it" (*BGE* 12). Clark and Dudrick (2012) argue that the "venerable" hypothesis referred to is Plato's tripartite soul. Nietzsche wants to revise and refine that hypothesis because he doesn't believe that conceiving reason as a separate part of the soul, as an independent source of motivation and therefore of values, can be squared with what we know of human beings from science, which is that our cognitive faculties always operate in the service of some interest. But he aims to explain the possibility of values, as distinguished from desire or appetite, and thereby to make conceivable weakness of the will. He attempts to do this with the hypothesis that the soul is the "political order of the drives and affects." Briefly put, drives are dispositions to behavior, and their relative strength at any time determines how one behaves at that time. But what gives a human being values, hence a soul, and makes her a person is that her drives also have a political order. Some drives are recognized as having authority to command and be obeyed, and therefore to speak for the whole; as such, they constitute the viewpoint of the person. How such a political order of the drives came about is precisely what Nietzsche attempts to explain in his account of the origin of "bad conscience" in his *Genealogy of Morality*. The upshot is that Nietzsche aims to rehabilitate traditional metaphysical notions on a normative basis. What science can't tell us is precisely what is revealed only from the viewpoint of values. Nietzsche's own notions of the soul and the will are presumably grounded in the value he places on rational and self-governed behavior. If so, this leaves questions about the metaphysics of value that *Nietzsche* scholars have only begun to raise.

{ 14 }

Nietzsche's Philosophical Psychology
Will to Power as Theory of the Soul
(co-authored with David Dudrick)

Julian Young claims that Nietzsche's *Beyond Good and Evil* is "really . . . two books of unequal size, one concerned with 'theoretical philosophy,' the other with 'practical' philosophy, 'ethics' in the very broadest sense of the word. The first is largely, but by no means exclusively, to be found in Part I, the second in the remaining eight parts" (Young 2010: 411). In the course of working on *The Soul of Nietzsche's Beyond Good and Evil* (Clark and Dudrick 2012), we came to appreciate the force of this claim. Our book concentrates on the first part of *BGE* (*BGE* One), which we show to be a deeply interconnected set of variations on traditional philosophical themes. The positions expressed in *BGE* One form not only the theoretical foundation of the book's practical philosophy, as found in its remaining eight parts, but also the theoretical foundation of Nietzsche's later philosophy, the centerpiece of which is Nietzsche's philosophical psychology.

In this paper, we develop our interpretation of that psychology by comparing it to the one offered by Paul Katsafanas in "Nietzsche's Philosophical Psychology" (Katsafanas 2013a).[1] That paper clearly and persuasively sets out the two main options for interpreting Nietzsche's philosophical psychology and develops a new option that seems to combine their advantages while overcoming their disadvantages. Katsfanas's account is similar to our own in several respects: both present Nietzsche's philosophical psychology as foundational to his philosophy, and take the will to power to be central to that psychology. But there are also major differences—ones that perhaps constitute a gulf—between Katsafanas's account of Nietzsche's philosophical psychology and our own.

---

[1] The account of drives Katsafanas offers plays an important role in his account of Nietzschean constitutivism in his *Agency and the Foundations of Ethics: Nietzschean Constitutivism* (Katsafanas 2013b).

Reading Nietzsche

Our first area of disagreement with Katsafanas is over a methodological issue concerning how to read Nietzsche. Katsafanas makes liberal use of the *Nachlass* to develop his reading of Nietzsche's views, and particularly in his account of drives. Because *BGE* 12 offers the hypothesis that the soul is the political order of the drives and affects, the concept of drive must be taken as a central component of Nietzsche's philosophical psychology. Katsafanas therefore devotes much of "Nietzsche's Philosophical Psychology" to an analysis of what Nietzsche takes drives to be. Like John Richardson before him, Katsafanas's account of drives is based largely on one passage from Nietzsche's later works—*BGE* 6—which he then interprets in terms of a number of passages from the *Nachlass* and one or two from Nietzsche's earlier works. Our reading of *BGE* rejects this way of proceeding.

Alexander Nehamas said years ago that interpreters didn't yet know how to read *BGE* as a whole because they were dazzled by the gems—especially the quips, jabs, and one-liners that everyone knows—and thereby blinded to the surrounding material (Nehamas 1998). We add that this blindness also often keeps us from knowing what to make of those gems. Nietzsche told us this himself, at least in effect. Just after finishing *BGE*, he wrote the new preface to *Daybreak*, which includes his well-known request of his readers: "*learn* to read me well!" Reading well, he tells us, is what the "art" embodied in his work teaches: "it teaches to read *well*, that is to say, to read slowly, deeply, looking cautiously before and aft, with reservations, with doors left open, with delicate eyes and fingers" (*D* P:5). An obvious implication is that if we don't pay special attention to the context in which Nietzsche embeds what he says, we are likely to wind up with a distorted view of it. A perhaps less obvious message is that taking account of the context will not come naturally, that we have to *learn* how to do it, and that we can do this only by paying special attention to it and to how Nietzsche writes. We do not mean to deny that the *Nachlass* can ever be helpful, but we do suggest that in general it does more harm than good. Reliance on it works against following Nietzsche's request of his readers for two reasons. First, the *Nachlass* typically provides very little in the way of context. After all, much of it consists of quick notes Nietzsche wrote to himself while out hiking in the Swiss Alps. Second, passages from it are often used to interpret his statements in his published works in lieu of devoting serious attention to the rich context Nietzsche provides for them. Our interpretation of *BGE* tries to abide by Nietzsche's request to *learn* to read him well by trying to make use of all of the information that book gives us if we look "cautiously before and aft" the specific passages we are attempting to interpret.

In doing so, we think we provide support for the idea that this kind of reading is necessary—at least to understand *BGE*—and that it does not come naturally, that our natural responses to the text must often be overcome if we are to see what is going on in it. We argue that Nietzsche wrote *BGE* in view of the distinction between the "exoteric and the esoteric," which he introduces in *BGE* 30 (as recognized formerly among philosophers "wherever one believed in an order of rank and *not* in equality and equal rights"). He deliberately writes in a way that will often make it appear to readers that he believes something quite different from what he actually believes.[2] Our book argues that this is especially true in regard to *BGE*'s claims about the will to power. Contrary to what *BGE* appears to be claiming, the will to power is not part of Nietzsche's understanding of biology, physics, ontology, or even of what a drive is. Drives have a will to power only insofar as they become components of a political order, of the commonwealth that is the human soul. We argue that the teaching or doctrine of the will to power one finds in *BGE* is Nietzsche's theory of the human soul.

We provide the evidence to make this plausible in our 2012 book. Here we will focus on the way we read *BGE* 6 in the context of surrounding material to arrive at an account of Nietzsche's philosophical psychology that differs markedly from the one offered by Paul Katsafanas. As we will see, Katsafanas criticizes a major feature of our account: that the drives that make up the soul are little (proto-) agents or homunculi. We begin by sketching Katsafanas's account of the drives and his criticism of our account.

Katsafanas on Nietzsche's Understanding of Drives

Katsafanas begins his account with the *Oxford English Dictionary*'s definition of a drive as "any internal mechanism which gets an organism moving or sustains its activity in a certain direction, or causes it to pursue a certain satisfaction... *esp.* one of the recognized physiological tensions or conditions of need, such as hunger and thirst" (Katsafanas 2013a: 727). He agrees that hunger and thirst "are indeed what spring to mind when we think of drives" (Katsafanas 2013a: 727) and would perhaps agree with us that the sex drive springs to mind even more readily. On this view, drives are "very basic motivational states, such as urges or cravings," which Katsafanas interprets as "physiological states or mere causal forces" (Katsafanas 2013a: 727). He denies that this captures Nietzsche's understanding of drives, on two grounds. First, he takes *BGE* 12 as evidence that Nietzsche "explicitly *contrasts* his drive psychology with certain 'materialistic' explanations of human behavior" (Katsafanas 2013a: 728). But the term "materialistic" does not occur in this passage—unless he has a different one in mind, he must be referring to *BGE* 12's claim about "'clumsy naturalists,' who can hardly touch the soul without losing it" (*BGE* 12). We will return to

---

[2] His purpose here is to educate readers, at least those who can learn the "art" of reading he is trying to teach. In the conclusion of our 2012 book, we argue that his way of writing is ultimately designed to inculcate certain virtues in those who can learn from it.

this important claim, here simply noting its implication that Nietzsche, unlike a certain kind of naturalist, wishes to retain the soul. The same passage, as we've said, takes the soul to be the political order of the drives and affects. So Katsafanas's reasoning seems to be that Nietzsche's own account of the soul would be an example of a "clumsy" naturalism that loses the soul, if he took drives to be simply "physiological states or mere causal forces." His second objection is that Nietzsche often uses agential language in describing the drives. Drives value, interpret, and adopt perspectives, and Katsafanas takes it to be obvious that "physiological states and urges do not do *that*" (Katsafanas 2013a: 728).

Because persons are the kind of beings who do value, interpret, and adopt perspectives, an alternative interpretation is that the drives are actually agents or little persons: homunculi. And indeed, as we've said, we count among the interpreters who embrace this reading, as does Peter Poellner (2000). Although Katsafanas admits that this reading has the advantage of fitting the agential language Nietzsche uses to describe drives, he claims that there are "compelling philosophical and textual reasons" against it (Katsafanas 2013a: 730). His first objection is that it has unacceptable implications concerning the nature of drives. According to Thiele's interpretation, for instance, drives have "agendas, perspectives, worldviews, and political relations with other drives," each drive having a "will to dominate and exploit its competitors" (Katsafanas 2013a: 730; Thiele 1990: 57–8). Now we agree with this description of drives, insofar as they have entered into the political order that forms the human soul. But according to Katsafanas, if taken literally, to view drives in this way implies that they are aware of, communicate with, and reason with each other, and therefore, that drives are self-conscious (Katsafanas 2013a: 730). But this, he adds, is "scarcely conceivable," perhaps being too polite to call it "absurd" or "ridiculous." We assume that its inconceivability or absurdity has to do with the fact that whatever else they are, drives are part of the natural world. Nietzsche's account of the soul is designed to show that we can retain the soul even as we view human beings completely as products of nature,[3] as members of an animal species that has no supernatural connection or component. But it seems obvious that no naturalistic account of the human soul or person could have it populated with little persons. If this is not what is behind this objection, then it seems to collapse into the second objection.

Katsafanas's second objection is that the homuncular reading deprives Nietzsche's drive psychology of any explanatory power: "it is difficult to see how there could be any theoretical advantage in explaining agency and selfhood by appealing to entities that already possess the properties of full-fledged agents" (Katsafanas 2013a: 728). But, as Katsafanas recognizes, we don't actually think that Nietzsche's homunculi are "full-fledged persons." Although they

---

[3] This is not to rule out that human beings are formed by culture. The contrast term for "natural" here is "supernatural" or "metaphysical," not cultural.

have political relations with other drives, some of which wield authority ("command") and others of which are prepared to accept that authority and therefore obey, the drives that make up the soul are not full-fledged persons on our view. We will return to this below. Katsafanas's third objection to the homuncular reading, his one textual objection, is that it fails to do justice to Nietzsche's "other commitments," in particular, his commitment to offer a revolutionary view of the self. "Nietzsche is not simply claiming that there are *more* selves than we think there are; instead, he is claiming that we have a mistaken conception of selfhood" (Katsafanas 2013a: 731).

Although Katsafanas calls this last criticism a "more fundamental problem for attributing the homuncular view to Nietzsche" (Katsafanas 2013a: 731), it does not seem to be a strong one. Perhaps some proponents of a homuncular reading interpret Nietzsche as claiming *simply* that "there are more selves than we think there are," but Katsafanas offers no evidence that this is the case, and it is certainly not true of our reading. In any case, it is not a problem for homuncular readings as such, but only for claiming that conceiving of the self as containing little selves is, by itself, enough to explain Nietzsche's reconceptualization of the self. So we take the important objections to readings like ours to be, first, that it attributes to drives properties they cannot have insofar as they belong fully to nature and, second, that it lacks explanatory power. Before turning to our answers, we look at Katsafanas's positive account of the drives.

Katsafanas develops his alternative to the homuncular reading by returning to the more usual interpretation of drives as urges or inclinations. His strategy is to see what needs to be added to this reading to account for Nietzsche's use of agentive language in talking about drives. His first move is to treat these urges as dispositions. In other words, drives aren't simply causal forces, but are also dispositions to behave in ways that bring about a certain end. While Katsafanas takes dispositional readings to avoid "the difficulties that plague the homuncular view," he thinks they fail to do justice to Nietzsche's persistent use of agential rhetoric in describing the drives. He asks, for instance, how a mere disposition—such as to scratch my head while thinking—can "be said to evaluate or interpret" (Katsafanas 2013a: 729). Katsafanas takes John Richardson's account of drives to do a better job of accommodating Nietzsche's agential language: a drive is a particular kind of disposition, one that was "selected for a certain result; this result is its individuating goal, which explains its presence and its character" (Richardson 2004: 13; quoted in Katsafanas 2013a: 732). So a disposition to engage in a certain pattern of behavior "aims" at a specific state of affairs (e.g., eating food, having sex), even though no conscious aiming is going on, because this outcome of the behavior explains the presence of that disposition in the organism that has it. As Katsafanas makes clear, this allows Richardson to make good on his denial that Nietzsche attributes consciousness to drives when he describes them as aiming, having a viewpoint, or valuing (Richardson 1996: 38). What he doesn't make clear is that the importance of this to Richardson, at least in his later book, is that by thus "naturalizing ends," we thereby "render valuing something that [Nietzsche's] science (genealogy) can study" (Richardson 2004: 13). For, according to Richardson, "a drive's values are precisely the goals it drives towards," i.e., the outcome that explains the disposition to engage in a pattern of behavior.

Katsafanas offers a compelling criticism of Richardson on this point. He asks us to consider "a typical ascetic" who "regards sexual activity as disvaluable." Such a person, he tells us, "will nonetheless be strongly disposed toward sexual activity"—he will, that is, have a drive whose goal is sexual activity. Katsafanas points out, however, that "we would typically say that the agent does not value sexual activity"—contrary to what Richardson's account implies. He concludes that Richardson's account is problematic precisely because "being disposed as a result of selection toward an E [i.e., having a drive to E] and valuing E can come apart" (Katsafanas 2013a: 732).

Having argued that both the homuncular and the dispositional reading of the drives are problematic, Katsafanas offers his alternative. On his view, drives are a *particular kind* of disposition, one that "induces an affective orientation" (Katsafanas 2013a: 740), and he rightly emphasizes Nietzsche's view that affects are active in "'coloring,' 'gilding,' 'lighting,' and 'staining' the world" (Katsafanas 2013a: 742; cf. Clark 1998b, paper 12 in this volume). He takes this as encouragement to interpret a Nietzschean drive as a disposition that mobilizes such affects. Drives thus "manifest themselves by coloring our view of the world, by generating perceptual saliences, by influencing our emotions and other attitudes, by fostering desires" (Katsafanas 2013a: 743). On Katsafanas's reading, then, drives do not operate by urging us blindly to do things; rather, they lead us to act by influencing our experience of the world. The advantage of this account, he thinks, is that it avoids the problems of the homuncular account—drives are simply dispositions—but yet is able to account for Nietzsche's agentive language in describing drives. Because the drives are simply a certain kind of disposition, Katsafanas thinks that we can transfer Nietzsche's agentive language from the drive to the person, where it (more literally) belongs. Nietzsche can "deny that drives, *considered in isolation*, can reason, evaluate, and interpret, while maintaining that *embodied drives*—drives considered part of a whole organism—can reason, evaluate, and interpret" (Katsafanas 2013a: 744). The point, then, is that the person reasons, interprets and evaluates by virtue of the affective orientations that a drive mobilizes.

But does this solve the problem Katsafanas presents for Richardson's view? Though he doesn't return to the example of the "typical ascetic," we can imagine how his view would handle it. The ascetic's world is presumably "colored" in the same way non-ascetics' worlds are in at least one respect: attractive people stand out to them, and certain kinds of activity with said people seem very desirable. Of course, the drives that constitute his asceticism induce a contrary affective disposition, according to which sex appears as debased and to be avoided. The question, then, is how it is that the latter drives are the person's values? We think Katsafanas begins to speak in terms of "warrant" in order to answer this question. Drives induce action, he tells us, by "making it appear as if" behavior that meet their ends "is *warranted* by the situation at hand" (Katsafanas 2013a: 748). But if Katsafanas means to say that all drives work in this way, then drives will not be something had in common by human beings and other animals. For surely *animals'* drives don't make behaviors appear to *them* as warranted. And yet presumably one reason Nietzsche makes use of the notion of a drive is to emphasize the continuity between human beings and other animals.

What Katsafanas needs, then, is an account as to why only *some* drives make their ends appear warranted. This would in turn explain why the ends of these drives appear to the person not just as desirable but as valuable. One possibility is that the drives that make their ends appear warranted are those that mobilize particular social affects, guilt and shame chief among them. On this view, a drive counts as manifesting one's values if, when the person acts in a way contrary to that drive's orientation, the person experiences certain affects, e.g., guilt.

There would still be a problem for Katsafanas's view, however. For we might still ask what it is that makes the perspective of these drives counts as the person's perspective? Take the ascetic above: he thinks he is trying desperately to maintain his values in the face of temptation. If we accept the picture we've sketched in defense of Katsafanas's view, however, why should we not say that what is really going on is that two (or more) drives are competing for satisfaction (with one side mobilizing the affect of guilt in its favor)? That his decision to abstain is really just a matter of one of his drives having been stronger than its competitors? That what we may think of as a distinction between acting on our values and acting on our (mere) desires is really just a matter of the drives battling for expression (as many have taken *D* 119 to imply)?[4]

The question, then, is this: why should the viewpoint of *these* drives (the ones which lead away from sexual activity) count as the person's viewpoint, and therefore as her values, while the viewpoint of *those* drives (which lead to sexual activity) counts only as the viewpoint of the drives, and therefore as mere desires? It might seem that there is no answer to this question, precisely because Nietzsche was attempting to debunk agency, and especially that involved in acting on values. We've argued elsewhere that Nietzsche's philosophical psychology is meant not to debunk these things, but to illuminate them (Clark and Dudrick 2009). Indeed, it is because we think Nietzsche seeks to explain the

---

[4] Katsafanas writes as though Nietzsche, in his mature work, continues to accept *Daybreak*'s view of the drives, quoting as he does *D* 119. We, however, follow the developmental view according to which much of what Nietzsche says in *Daybreak*—including the agency-debunking aspects of *D* 119—should not be taken as his mature view.

role of values in human motivation that we think he meant for his homuncular descriptions of the drives to be taken seriously. On our picture, the battle for expression isn't merely a battle of strength: one of the factors that leads to which drive gets satisfaction is its political ranking, where it stands in an order of *legitimacy* rather than strength. It is a drive's legitimacy with respect to the other drives that makes it so that its perspective should count as a person's valuation. Having put forward this crude summary of our view, we will now explain it in detail.

Introducing Our View: *BGE* 6

We can begin to articulate our view with a brief discussion of a section Katsafanas uses to support his view, *BGE* 6. That passage opens with a discussion of the importance of values to philosophy. Nietzsche tells us that "to explain how a philosopher's most remote metaphysical assertions have actually been arrived at, it is always well (and wise) to ask oneself first: what morality does this (does *he*—) aim at?" He is not claiming that the philosopher consciously aims to express her values in her philosophy, but rather that, despite what the philosopher herself may think, her values are "the real germ of life out of which the entire plant has grown" (*BGE* 6).

Only at this point in *BGE* 6 does the discussion turn to the drives. In this connection, Nietzsche first concludes from what he has just said about the role of values in philosophy that a "drive to knowledge" is not the father of philosophy. "But," he adds,

> anyone who looks at the basic drives of mankind to see to what extent they may in precisely this connection have come into play as *inspirational spirits* (or demons or kobolds—) will discover that they have all at some time or other done philosophy–and that each of them would be only too glad to present *itself* as the ultimate goal of existence and as the legitimate *master* of all the other drives. For every drive is desirous of ruling: and it is as *such* that it tries to philosophize. (*BGE* 6)

This is the one passage from the published work that Katsafanas quotes in support of his view that Nietzsche has the drives "reason[ing], evaluat[ing], and interpret[ing]." But even if this is true, this is not their most basic activity—to the extent that the drives "reason, evaluate, and interpret," they do it for the sake of something else: to be recognized as "the legitimate master of all the other drives" (*BGE* 6). Though he doesn't mention the will to power here, it's clear that Nietzsche takes it to characterize the drives insofar as they are involved in philosophy. Indeed, *BGE* 6 is a major passage for Richardson's account of will to power as characterizing the drives first and foremost. But we agree with Katsafanas's criticism of Richardson: that if Nietzsche holds that our values are simply the ends at which our drives aim, he has an inadequate idea of values. Nietzsche's idea here appears to be that the person's valuations (at least as they are expressed in her philosophy) are constituted not by the "affective orientation" produced by the drives, as Katsafanas would have it, but rather by the drives' expression of their desire to rule, their will to power. We'll discuss how this is supposed to work below.

Will to Power as Nietzsche's Theory of the Soul

To explain how and why Nietzsche thinks the drives' desire to rule is related to values, we turn to what we take to be the centerpiece of Nietzsche's philosophical psychology and his attempt to reconceptualize the self: *BGE* 12's "hypothesis" that the soul is the political order of the drives and affects. Calling for a rejection of "soul atomism," Nietzsche tells us, "between ourselves," that his aim is not to

> get rid of "the soul" itself and thus forgo one of the oldest and most venerable of hypotheses: as is often the way with clumsy naturalists, who can hardly touch on "the soul" without losing it. But the way stands open to new conceptions and refinements of the soul-hypothesis; and such concepts as "mortal soul," and "soul as subjective multiplicity," and "soul as social [or: political] structure [*Gesellschaftsbau*] of the drives and affects," want henceforth to have citizens' rights in science. (*BGE* 12)

So his rejection of the "atomistic" soul does not lead Nietzsche to side with those naturalists who would dismiss "'the soul' itself," but instead to offer new conceptions of the soul that count as "refinements" of "one of the oldest and most venerable of hypotheses." This raises two important questions. First, what is the difference between keeping the soul and losing it? That is, what does Nietzsche retain of this venerable hypothesis that the clumsy naturalist rejects? And, second: what is that hypothesis? Although Nietzsche never tells us, figuring this out seems necessary if we are to understand his conception of the soul and how it differs from naturalistic theories that lose the soul. We will argue that the hypothesis Nietzsche wants to refine is Plato's, specifically the *Republic*'s theory of the soul.

In advance of our discussion of that theory, we specify some factors that make it seem plausible that *BGE* 12 suggests that Nietzsche's own hypothesis is a refinement of Plato's theory of the soul. First, if Plato's theory is a hypothesis, as we will argue it is, it is certainly one of the "oldest and most venerable." Second, if Nietzsche refers here simply to the bare idea that we have a soul, it is difficult to see why he would even count that as an hypothesis, as opposed to a sheer dogma—what is it posited to explain?—much less as one of the "most venerable of hypotheses." Third, Plato's theory of the soul, divided as it is into three parts, seems like a good model to try to refine if one is interested in rejecting the atomistic soul. And, finally, as we shall argue, there is a relatively clear path from Plato's theory to Nietzsche's.

John Cooper's account of Plato's psychology is helpful for understanding the *Republic*'s theory of the soul as a hypothesis, specifically a hypothesis about human motivation. Emerging in the midst of an attempt to say what justice is (and to show that being just benefits the one who is just), this theory does not explain what justice is in terms of the behavior to which a just person is disposed. Instead, it takes justice to an internal structure—a condition of one's soul—that is responsible for, among other things, one's voluntary behavior. According to Cooper, Plato's psychology denies that an enlightening characterization of such states of the soul can be given in purely dispositional terms, i.e., in terms of how one is disposed to behave. They must be characterized instead, Cooper claims, "in internal, psychological terms, as a condition of a person's action-, choice-, and preference-producing apparatus, specified by reference to interrelations among the different elements of the apparatus itself" (Cooper 1998: 139).[5]

We contend that, like Cooper, Nietzsche sees Plato as postulating an internal or non-observable structure to explain an individual's choices, preferences, and voluntary actions, where the relevant (causal) properties of the system are specified in terms of the interrelationship among the elements of which it is composed. That there is such a structure is precisely the "soul-hypothesis" Nietzsche does not want to renounce. It is Plato's hypothesis concerning what that structure is that he wishes to refine.

Plato's claims, of course, that the soul is composed of three main parts: reason, spirit, and appetite. As Cooper and others have argued, that the soul has parts amounts to the claim that "distinct types of psychological input" have a role in determining human behavior, thus that explanations of voluntary action must take into account three fundamentally different kinds of motivation (Cooper 1998: 121). First is motivation in terms of appetite.[6] According to the standard view, the *Republic*'s account of appetite is in the service of a response to Socrates' argument in the *Protagoras* that "we cannot choose contrary to our belief about the good" (Irwin 1995: 209). Socrates famously argues that so-called examples of incontinence or weakness of will, cases where one's better judgment is overcome by fear or love, for instance, are unintelligible. For why did the person act on his love or fear if he did not believe that it was better

---

[5] John Cooper, "Plato's Theory of Human Motivation," in *Reason and Emotion: Essays in Ancient Moral Psychology and Ethical Theory* (Princeton: Princeton University Press). Page numbers in the text are to this book, which has had great influence on the section of Clark and Dudrick (2012), from which we draw this section of the paper.

[6] *Republic* IX tells us that no single name fits well all the things belonging to the appetitive part of the soul, that it is "named after the biggest and strongest thing in it," namely, "its appetites for food, drink, sex, and all the things associated with them" (580d).

to do so? One could make such cases intelligible if we can distinguish the agent's judgment about what is good from his belief about what is good *for him*. But Socrates evidently denies that we can make such a distinction on the grounds that action is intelligible only if we can explain it in terms of a self-explanatory end, and he assumes that the agent's own happiness (or pleasure) is the only such end (Irwin 1995: 209).

The *Republic*'s answer to Socrates begins by taking the basic biological urges that we share with other animals to be the paradigm cases of one kind or aspect of human motivation. Plato thereby denies that happiness in the sense of pleasure is the only end that makes action intelligible. The appetites have their own ends or objects, towards which human beings can be driven or impelled apart from any judgment concerning their pleasure or goodness or the contribution they make to human happiness. So Plato portrays thirst as something that "drives [one] like a beast to drink" (439b). Although this might seem to imply that appetites cannot be trained or educated, later parts of the *Republic* make clear that this is not the case. Such training happens not by means of coming to believe that certain objects are good, however, but, for instance, by learning that certain things or actions are means to acquiring the objects to which one is driven or that certain of the objects in the relevant class give one more pleasure than others. So, for Plato, it seems, even educated appetites can operate independently of judgments concerning the good.

This is not to say that Plato thinks that such appetites normally operate in independence of judgments about the good, but simply that they *can* do so. In other and perhaps most cases, judgments as to the goodness or badness of the objects of appetite do play a role in the motivation of action, promoting or inhibiting the satisfaction of appetite, but such judgments come from another part of the soul, not from appetite itself. Reason, the part that calculates and loves to learn, is assigned the role of forming beliefs about the good, about what goals are worth pursuing, what appetites worth satisfying. Spirit, the part that desires victory and honor, can be seen as a separate component of the soul because, unlike reason, it does not itself form beliefs about the good. Yet, unlike appetite, except in the cases of animals and infants, it cannot operate in independence of such beliefs. Spirit involves motivation by a desire for victory and honor, and such motivation is not possible without some belief about what constitutes winning or is honorable. So spirit's type of motivation, unlike appetite's, requires an idea of the good which it cannot itself provide. Providing it is, of course, precisely reason's role, and in the ideal case, reason rules the soul in the sense that it has formed the person's belief about what goals are worth pursuing on its own (i.e., rational) grounds, and it has gained the cooperation of the other parts of the soul in such a way that the person acts in accord with reason's idea of the good.

With this sketch of Plato's hypothesis, we can now state our proposal for understanding Nietzsche as refining it. On our view, Nietzsche takes the elements of the soul to be simply the drives and affects. He transforms Plato's appetites into drives and affects, turns Plato's spirit into a property (a second-order drive) of all drives—the will to power—and denies that reason provides an independent source of motivation. Drives are obviously similar to appetites, and "drive" may be even a better word than "appetite" for the kind of motivation Plato attributes to the lowest part of the soul. Motivation by drives[7] seems to be a kind of motivation that humans share with other animals,[8] and drives have their own ends or objects, so that they can motivate behavior in independence of any judgment concerning the goodness of these objects.[9] But why would reducing the soul to Plato's lowest part count as refining rather than simply rejecting of Plato's theory? Our answer is that this is not what Nietzsche does. Although he rejects reason as an independent part of the soul, Nietzsche has the will to power—his equivalent to Plato's spirit—transform the drives in such a way as to make them capable of playing the role played by Plato's reason.

To see how this is supposed to go, consider first what role reason plays for Plato. Reason is the part of the soul that calculates and loves to learn; it is assigned the role of forming beliefs about the good, about what goals are worth pursuing, what appetites worth satisfying. Julia Annas tells us that "'what is most stressed about reason is its capacity *to rule* by virtue of knowing what is best for the soul as a whole and not just itself' (441e, 442c)" (Annas 1981: 133, emphasis added). Because it knows what's best for the soul as a whole, reason is the part of the soul that constitutes the person's viewpoint. When a person acts according to reason, she acts not merely on her desires, but on her values.

Nietzsche does not have a part of the soul designated as rightful ruler: there is no Kantian captain, only a Humean crew, to use Simon Blackburn's image. However, the members of the crew—the drives—have a will to power (*BGE* 6).

---

[7] To say that a piece or kind of behavior is to be explained in terms of a drive is to say that the organism is set up in such a way that, given the presence of certain internal and external clues or stimuli, it is caused to behave in ways that tend to have certain results, precisely the results that are the drives' objects or ends (such as ingesting food in the case of the drive to eat), and that no judgment concerning the goodness of these ends need enter into the process that leads to the behavior.

[8] We leave to the side questions about the teleology of the drives, but we largely agree with John Richardson that Nietzsche's first and most basic move is to appeal to Darwinian natural selection (Richardson 2004). As Richardson has argued convincingly, the behavior directed by the drive does not merely tend to produce the result that is the object of the drive, but it is *designed* to do so, which is to say that the animals engage in the behavior precisely because it tends to have the results that it does.

[9] Here we point out that all of this explains why Nietzsche counts his psychology as a "proper physio-psychology" (*BGE* 23). This is not because he wants to turn psychology into physiology or any other natural science. It is rather because in studying the psyche, he is studying the drives, which are necessarily embodied, whether they are biologically given and modified through human culture or are habits that can exist only within human culture. In either case, they are not "reality" unless they are embodied, and therefore part of our physiology. But this is far from meaning that Nietzsche's psychology reduces psychology to physiology, as we'll see below.

That is, each wants not just to attain its end, but to "command" the other drives so that they "obey" (*BGE* 19). And the fact that this is true of each drive (or perhaps of each specifically human drive) leads the drives to come to be ordered not just causally, but politically—i.e., to form a commonwealth (*BGE* 19), which is what *BGE* 12 calls the "soul." The person's point of view, her values or basic commitments, are constituted by the view not of "reason," but of the politically high-ranking drives. This is so not because they are always the causally strongest drives—weakness of will is a possibility—but because they are recognized as "legitimate *master*" of the other drives (*BGE* 6). Notice that this is not to deny that drives are dispositions—that is what they are insofar as they are part of a causal order, i.e., insofar as they explain behavior. We accept Richardson's account of the kind of disposition that a drive is. But our account aims to respond to the problem for Richardson's claim that the object of a drive is a value raised by Katsafanas (also by Clark and Dudrick 2007, paper 4 in this volume). Our claim is that insofar as these dispositions come to constitute a *person* who is capable of acting on *values*, these dispositions must be taken to be arranged not just causally but politically.[10] This is the beginning of our account of how Nietzsche can find a role for values, for judgments concerning what is good and not merely desired, in human life.

Nietzsche's counts as a refinement of Plato's hypothesis, therefore, because it is like the latter in providing an explanation of how it is that values or judgments about the good can gain a foothold in human motivation. It should also be clear that Nietzsche takes over his homuncular view of the drives from Plato's treatment of the parts of the soul. Julia Annas confirms this reading of Plato, saying that on Plato's view, "each part has desires and pleasures, and tries to gain them, sometimes at the expense of the other two; they conflict, agree, and so on. That is, they are freely described in terms that are normally used only of the person as a whole" (Annas 1981: 142). Now, like Katsafanas, Annas sees that this is potentially problematic. She says that "the parts lead to a regress of explanation if they reproduce, as they seem to, the features of the whole person that needed explanation in the first place" (Annas 1981: 142). Calling this the "Homunculus Problem," Annas uses Dennett's distinction between "two kinds of psychology" in an attempt to show that Plato's use of homunculi is not problematic in this way.

---

[10] "Political" tends to be glossed in purely causal terms, as having to do with such matters as "organization, cooperation, and patterns of domination" (Thiele 1990: 52). What has not been noted and given sufficient attention is that a political order is not just a causal order, but a normative one. That is, the ruler or ruling class in a political order is able to rule not simply because it is stronger. It is stronger, in part, because it is recognized as having the authority to rule, to speak for the whole society. Likewise, we suggest, Nietzsche takes the rank order of the drives to be a political order in this sense, so that one drive has a higher rank than another not in virtue of its causal efficaciousness, its ability to win in case of conflicts, but in virtue of being recognized as having a *right* to win in such cases. It is thus an order of authority or legitimacy rather than one merely of causal strength.

According to Dennett, one might pursue a *"bottom-up"* or *"top-down"* strategy in one's attempt to explain human actions. The "bottom-up" strategy, he tells us, "starts with some basic and well-defined unit or theoretical atom from psychology, and builds these atoms into molecules and larger aggregates that can account for the complex phenomena we all observe" (Dennett 1978: 110). This strategy takes some non-intentional unit (e.g., stimulus-response pairs or neuron signals) and attempts to show how such units can be understood as to constitute intentional, psychological phenomena like human beings acting for reasons. The second strategy is the *"top-down* strategy," which "begins with a more abstract decomposition of the highest levels of psychological organization, and hopes to analyze these into more and more detailed smaller systems or processes" (Dennett 1978: 110). This strategy takes an intentional phenomenon like that of a human being willing an action and attempts to show how it can be understood in terms of simpler—though still intentional—phenomena. Annas rightly claims that Plato can be said to make use of the "top-down" strategy in offering his theory of the soul.

Indeed, it is because it is "top-down" that Nietzsche counts it as a theory of the soul. For it seems reasonable to suppose that what leads the "clumsy naturalists" to "los[e] the soul" is precisely their pursuit of the "bottom-up" strategy. To see this, consider that this strategy is a reductionist one—it seeks to *reduce* intentional phenomena to purely causal phenomena. In trying to do this, the naturalist does not so much explain human agency as explain it away. The "top-down" strategy, however, need not be reductionist in this way. (It would only be so if one held—as Dennett does—that one will eventually descend to non-intentional phenomena.)[11]

---

[11] Dennett holds that the process of "top-down" explanation continues "until finally one arrives at elements familiar to the biologists" (Dennett 1978: 110); it is not clear that Nietzsche would agree. The reason is that the last part of the strategy is ambiguous in an important respect. It might be that to "arrive" at "elements familiar to the biologists" is to account for the *existence* of the intentional phenomenon in question using these "elements." So understood, the "top-down" strategy aims to explain how it is that beings who, e.g., think, desire, and will came into existence via processes that can be understood from a naturalistic perspective. But it might also be that to "arrive" at these elements is to use them to account for the *intentionality* of the phenomenon in question. Understood this way, the strategy attempts to reduce meaning to causal processes. Put another way, where the first version of the strategy attempts to understand how the "space of reasons" arose from the "space of causes," the second version attempts to understand what goes on in the "space of reasons" in terms of the space of causes.

This distinction is important, since on the reading we advance in Clark and Dudrick (2005) and in our 2012 book, Nietzsche cannot accept the second version of this strategy. More specifically, our reading of *GS* 373-4 contends that in those sections Nietzsche puts forward the claim that a complete causal (or "mechanistic") account of the world is not a complete account of the world—such an account will not, that is, provide access to all truths. This is not to deny that all phenomena can be understood in causal terms; it is only to claim that there are true descriptions of the world that cannot be put in purely causal terms. Among these true descriptions are those involving inquiry—thus, one who, like Mr. Mechanic, claims that all phenomena can be understood in causal or mechanistic terms finds himself unable to make sense of his own status as an inquirer. This is what makes his "among the stupidest of all possible interpretations of the world" (*GS* 373).

In her defense of Plato's view, Annas notes that a psychological analysis is not viciously circular simply by virtue of being "top-down." As Dennett puts the point, "Homunculi are *bogeymen* only if they duplicate *entire* the talents they are rung in to explain. If one can get a team or committee of *relatively* ignorant, narrow-minded, blind homunculi to produce the intelligent behavior of the whole, this is progress" (Dennett 1978: 123). The question, then, is whether the activities in which the drives engage are *simpler* than the activities of the person which they are "rung in to explain." Annas thinks that the activities of the parts of Plato's soul are indeed simpler than that which they are to explain. She admits, however, that "there is one snag in the picture": "the more Plato insists that reason is responsible for the welfare of the soul as a whole, the more it expands its capacities until it threatens to become not just a homunculus but a bogeyman" (Annas 1981: 142).

Annas's argument to the contrary notwithstanding, it is not at all clear that Plato's reason has the explanatory value she claims for it. She claims that reason is no bogeyman because "there is no necessary identity between the interests and desires" of reason and of the person as a whole—such identity occurs only in the perfectly just person (Annas 1981: 145). One can still wonder, however, whether Plato is not explaining how it is that a person comes to know and pursue the good by positing a part of the soul whose function it is to know and enable pursuit of the good. And even if this is not a problem, Nietzsche cannot accept reason as an independent part of the soul. For consider that on Plato's view, the person's "desire for the good" is "equivalent to the desire on the part of reason to work out the ends of life *on its own* and to achieve them" (Cooper 1998: 8; emphasis added). This means that for Plato, reason is independent in the sense that it performs its function of knowing and enabling the pursuit of the good without being directed by the appetitive part of the soul. Reason is moved by desire for the good, but this is a desire *of its own*, not "for any particular good," but "for good, as such" (Cooper 1998: 8). But the idea that one might know *anything*—much less "the good, as such"—as the result of reasoning that is in no way directed by interests or affects (except perhaps those of reason itself) clearly runs afoul of Nietzsche's perspectivism, which insists that the use of our cognitive capacities is always directed by interests and affects (Leiter 1994; Clark 1998b, paper 11 in this volume).[12]

---

[12] This is the point of Nietzsche's well-known claim that "there is *only* a perspectival seeing, *only* a perspectival 'knowing,'" that "to disconnect affects one and all, supposing we were capable of this," would be "to *castrate* the intellect" (*GM* III:12). We take the perspectivism expressed in this passage to be about knowledge (not truth, as too many have thought), and to be an empirical claim. Its basis, as Clark claims, is Nietzsche's "naturalistic understanding of the intellect," according to which cognitive capacities originally come into existence because of the evolutionary advantage they confer. No such advantage is conferred by attending to any and all features of reality. Instead, the intellect must be directed to certain features—for instance, those most relevant to human survival and reproduction. And it is precisely affect—interest, emotion, feeling, passion—that turns the mind in a particular direction, focusing its attention on certain features of reality and pushing it to register them as important (Clark 1998b: 74; paper 11 in this volume).

As we interpret it, Nietzsche's perspectivism has as an important corollary that the genesis of our cognitive capacities is naturalistically explicable. But it is difficult to see how a naturalistic explanation could be given for how we came to possess reason, understood as a part of the soul that is independent of interests and affects that are not its own. For Plato, as we have seen, reason explains how human beings are able to know and pursue the good, thus how it is that values can have a role in human motivation. We claim that Nietzsche is able to account for the role of values instead—and without appealing to a faculty that seems to be difficult to account for naturalistically—by attributing a will to power to the drives. It is insofar as the drives develop a second-order drive of gaining power over the other drives that they form a political order that constitutes a human being's values and *"who he is"* (*BGE* 6).

The obvious question here is whether the view we've attributed to Nietzsche succumbs to what Annas calls the "Homunculus Problem." Katsafanas thinks it does: not only is it absurd to think the drives engage each other politically, having them do so would not explain the agency the drives are supposed to explain. On the second point, he says, "First, it is not clear that commanding and obeying are simpler activities than valuing and resisting temptation. Moreover, commanding and obeying require, at the very least, the presence of consciousness. So the type of agency attributed to the drives is still quite robust" (Katsafanas 2013a: 731 n. 7). Our answer to these objections is that commanding and obeying are simpler than valuing and resisting temptation precisely because, unlike the latter, the former can go on *without* the one engaging in them being conscious of that fact. And it is for this reason that it makes sense to think that the drives can engage in commanding and obeying.

To see this, we must be clear about what must be true of an individual's behavior in order for it to be reasonably interpreted as "political." Those who study the social behavior of certain lower animals take them to act politically: chimpanzees, wolves, and other animals are thought to form "dominance hierarchies." As primatologist Franz de Waal points out, this does not imply that the animals in question *take themselves* to form a political order; their "conscious motives and intentions" need not concern their political standing (de Waal 1997: 207). It means only that the behavior of an individual is sometimes best explained not in terms of his brute strength relative to his fellows, but in terms of his rank in the social order. In saying that the drives form a social or political order, then, Nietzsche need not take them to be *conscious* of their political situation. Indeed, it is not clear that he need take them to be conscious, in the Kantian sense that implies the possibility of self-conscious, *at all*. He must only think that their behavior is illuminated by interpreting it in political terms. And this is just what he does think, on our interpretation.[13]

---

[13] We note here that this makes sense of what Nietzsche says about the drives elsewhere in *BGE* One. We've argued (in Clark and Dudrick 2009) that *BGE* 19 gives an account of willing

We pause here to note that this analogy between the political order of the drives and the political order found among certain primates is helpful for understanding an aspect of *BGE* 6 discussed above. Recall that the idea there seemed to be that a person's valuations (there expressed in her philosophy) are constituted by the drives' expression of their desire to rule, their will to power. To see how this might work, consider that, in a primate group, a member of the group will become dominant by "make charging displays, asserting himself" as one to be reckoned with (de Waal 1997: 132). He will, that is, take up the *trappings* of authority in the hopes that, as a result, the others will acquiesce to him and confer upon him *real* (i.e., causally effective) authority. This strategy for gaining and maintaining authority is, of course, not unfamiliar: those who (want to) lead—be they presidents or professors—must project authority in the hopes that they (will come to) have it. The idea, then, is that an interpretation of reality offers some of the drives an opportunity to assert themselves in a comparable way before the other drives.

Understanding this requires that we move between the level of drives and that of the person. Suppose the philosopher described in *BGE* 6 admits to herself that a long-held view of reality is untenable and finds a new interpretation to take its place. How does this happen? What is going on among her drives? The idea is that when she begins to see that there is something wrong with the long-held view, some of her drives are successfully asserting themselves against drives that would preserve the status quo. When she is able to "see" her way to a new interpretation of things, probably as the result of a nagging feeling that the old view is problematic (produced by a recognition of the factors that the insurrectionist drives are highlighting), these drives are vindicated against their rivals—having assumed the airs of authority, they have delivered satisfaction, thus raising their political profile. And because the political status of these drives constitutes the person's values, these values are strengthened.[14]

This is not to say, however, that the process of considering reasons is an illusion or that what appears to be the action of considering reasons is *really just* the drives' expressing a will to power. Nietzsche's account considers a single

---

which makes use of the image of the soul presented here, picturing some drives as commanding other drives to carry out certain actions and to ignore subversive drives who are urging otherwise. The idea, as we understand it, is that when a person acts on the basis of values, the causally effective drive is the one that is also highest in the political ranking—and such an action is therefore reflective of "who she is," i.e., of her values. In fact, *BGE* 19's analysis of willing concerns a case in which a person is inclined to act in a way that contradicts her values, which means that the drive that is causally strongest at the moment is *not* the one that is highest in the political order of the drives. When willing (commanding) is successful, the drives' causal order is brought into line with their normative order through the use of political authority, so that the person's will (the normative order of her drives) is reflected in her action.

[14] That we cannot understand fully what goes on at one of these levels without understanding what goes on at the other is one of the reasons that a "genuine physio-psychology" conceived in terms of the will to power is likely to cause "seasickness" (*BGE* 23).

phenomenon on two different levels, the "macro-level" of the person and the "micro-level" of the drives. When a person acts in accord with her values, her drives operate according to their will to power. But the *person* need not act according to her will to power—it might even be the case that *she* has no such will. It is, however, insofar as the *drives* which constitute her have a will to power that she is a person—a being with values—at all. The drives that constitute the person's point of view are not just those that happen to be the strongest; they are the drives that are accorded legitimacy by the other drives, the drives that have been granted a right to speak for the whole.

GM II on the Origin of the Soul

Even if we are right that Nietzsche offers the political order of the drives as that in virtue of which human beings have values and so are persons, one might still wonder, of course, how Nietzsche thinks a political order of the drives could ever have come about. We should be able to see how this political order comes to be by examining Nietzsche's account as to how human animals first developed a soul. And if the will to power is his theory of the soul, then it should have a crucial role in this account. This is precisely what we find, not in BGE, but in the work Nietzsche calls "a supplement [to] and clarification [of]" *BGE*, *On the Genealogy of Morality*.

Nietzsche's answer to the question as to how the drives form a political order is embedded (though not by name) in *GM*'s Second Treatise: "'Guilt,' 'Bad Conscience,' and Related Matters." To show this, we'll argue first that Nietzsche, like Plato, uses reflection on the state to illuminate the structure of the soul, setting up an analogy between them. Then we'll argue that Nietzsche's account of the development of this soul is to be found in his account of the development of the bad conscience.

That Nietzsche intends his account of the origin of the state to illuminate the origin of the soul becomes evident when we reflect on the following claim:

> The active force that is at work on a grander scale in those violence-artists and organizers and that builds states, is basically the same force that here—inwardly, on a smaller, pettier scale, in a backwards direction, in the 'labyrinth of the breast,' to use Goethe's words—creates for itself the bad conscience and builds negative ideals: namely that *instinct for freedom* (speaking in my language: the will to power). (*GM* II:18)

Nietzsche has just claimed that "the 'state' begins on earth" when packs of blond beasts vented their aggressive drives upon much tamer and probably more numerous nomads by forming them into a political structure. He now claims that the same will to power expressed by these blond beasts also works "inwardly, on a smaller, pettier scale." This smaller scale or level, as we will argue, is that of drives, and the working of the will to power here produces a political order of the drives, which, as Nietzsche has told us in *BGE* 12, is the soul.

To appreciate the analogy Nietzsche is setting up, consider first the creation of the state. The blond beasts are led to create states, as we have seen, by "an instinct for freedom," which, translated into Nietzsche's language, is a will to power. Let's consider the original term first, the "instinct for freedom." Clearly, at the primitive stage of civilization to which Nietzsche refers here, it cannot be anything very sophisticated, and he surely intends it to be something continuous with what can be found among animals. What is found among animals that plausibly fits Nietzsche's phrase is a resistance to restrictions. It is a caged non-domestic animal, and perhaps especially a relatively newly caged one, that we could most easily see as having an "instinct for freedom," which would be equivalent to a resistance to captivity, a drive to escape its cage and return to the wilderness.

Now the blond beasts, unlike the nomads they will form into a state, are not caged, but they are *restricted*. This "pack of blond beasts of prey" is a highly organized "race of conquerors and lords," which has the power to organize the nomadic population on which it descends. These are the same "blond beasts" of which Nietzsche talks earlier in the *Genealogy*, the nobles of *GM* I (if at perhaps an early stage), who (even in non-military life) "are kept so strictly within limits *inter pares,* by mores, worship, custom, gratitude, still more by mutual surveillance, by jealousy," but "are not much better than uncaged beasts of prey toward the outside world. . . . There they enjoy freedom from all social constraint; in the wilderness they recover the losses incurred through the tension that comes from a long enclosure and fencing in within the peace of community" (*GM* I:11). So their "instinct for freedom" is an instinct or drive to return to the "wilderness," where they are able to treat the "others" they encounter as they wish, and therefore to vent upon them the aggressive impulses that they must refrain from directing towards members of their own group. And this is the instinct that moves them, Nietzsche claims, to descend on a nomadic population and form it into a state.

A second point to consider is why Nietzsche calls the "instinct for freedom" a "will to power." One obvious reason is that in forming the state, the blond beasts did not aim to be free from social constraints; they aimed precisely to *impose* such constraints on a population that was largely free from them. Ironically, their "instinct for freedom" led them to drive "an enormous quantity of freedom" out of the world (*GM* II:17), the freedom of the nomads they formed into a state. So Nietzsche's suggestion looks to be that an instinct for freedom, mere resistance to restriction and captivity, becomes directed towards getting power or control over others, and is for this reason appropriately termed a "will to power."

But why would the blond beasts' resistance to captivity lead them to seek power over others? Nietzsche doesn't tell us, and it seems clear that a genealogy of this transformation would need to cite a number of different factors. It seems plausible that one of them, and the main factor Nietzsche wants to bring to our attention here, has to do with military organization. To be part of such an organization one must accept the *authority* of those above one in the military hierarchy, which means acknowledging their right to give orders and obeying these orders. And, according to Zarathustra, those who obey do so in order to be able to command those beneath them (*Z* II:12). This suggests that Nietzsche's story goes something like this. The group organization of the blond beasts was made possible, as we have seen, by developing their natural aggressive instincts in such a way that they were not aimed *inter pares*, but were diverted towards "the other," and especially, the foreigner. To the extent that the point was simply to discharge aggressive impulses, at first there would have been little motive (or ability) for forming these "others" into a society. Why not simply go out in small bands to kill, destroy, and steal? This is what *GM* I:11 suggests actually happened. But *GM* II:16–18 suggests that eventually a more organized military organization took over as the major way of diverting aggressive impulses towards outsiders. As it did, it makes sense that the expression of these impulses would become shaped by the model of military organization and power. If the instinct for freedom was originally a drive to return to the wilderness where one could treat others according to one's own will, it makes sense that under the influence of military organization, the model of what it is to subject others to one's will would become increasingly that of successfully ordering them around from a position of authority.

A final point to note about the creators of the state is that Nietzsche calls them "the most involuntary, unconscious artists there are." This is a very strong statement. The point here cannot be that they are completely unconscious, of course, but only that they are not conscious of what they are creating and that they did not create it intentionally. So the point is presumably that their aim was simply to exert power or control over others, not to bring into existence a stable and (relatively) peaceful society, one that eventually even has the appearance to some of having been established by a social contract (which is, of course, false, as Nietzsche goes out of his way to insist in this section). But that is indeed what they did. Despite their lack of intention, these blond beasts are artists: "their work is an instinctive creating of forms." As a result of that work, "something new stands there, a ruling structure [*Herrschafts-Gebilde*] that *lives*, in which parts and functions are delimited and related to one another, in which nothing at all finds a place that has not first had placed into it a 'meaning' with respect to the whole" (*GM* II:17). The blond beasts and nomads have become "parts and functions" of a "*ruling* structure," clearly meaning "a structure for ruling," one in which authority is recognized and "orders" are given and obeyed, as Nietzsche makes clear. To the extent that there is a "whole," there is a foothold for judgments that can be made about what is to the good or to the advantage of that whole, hence about what is just or fair. As the result of brutish, forcible interaction, the interaction among these primitive humans is no longer simply brute and forced: it has become political.

We will now argue that Nietzsche's account suggests the same three points about the human soul that he makes about the state, first, that it was brought about by the operation of an "instinct for freedom," second, that this instinct is transformed into something that is plausibly thought of as a will to power, and third, that the operation of this instinct unintentionally results in the existence of a "ruling structure." Although Nietzsche does not make all of this fully explicit, it can be seen to follow from what he does make explicit if we compare his account in *GM* II on the origin of the bad conscience with *BGE*'s account of the soul as "the political structure of the drives and affects."

Note, first, that Nietzsche explicitly tells us that his account of the origins of bad conscience is at the same time an account of the origins of "that which man later calls his soul" (*GM* II:16). And the crucial point in that account is that once subjected to the apparatus of the state, the nomads' aggressive drives could no longer be directed towards others without harsh retribution, and yet, "those old instincts had not at all ceased to make their demands!" In a partially similar situation,[15] as we have seen, the aggressive drives of the blond beasts were vented on another population, the nomads. Because there was no external population on which the aggressive drives of the nomads could be vented, however, they "had to seek new and as it were subterranean gratifications. All instincts that do not discharge themselves outwardly *turn themselves* inward ... thus first grows in man what he later calls his 'soul'" (*GM* II:16).[16] The claim, we infer, is that the aggressive instincts that could not be externally discharged—"hostility, cruelty, pleasure in persecution, in assault, in change, in destruction"—were

---

[15] There is one very important dissimilarity here, which is that the blond beasts had a long period of time during which new patterns for discharging aggressive instincts could be developed and made instinctive. In the case of the nomads, the change happened too quickly for new patterns to develop, and the need to deliberate followed from this. See the following footnote for more on this difference.

[16] There is actually another change that is prior to the one here discussed: the onset of the need for deliberation. Whereas previously they had been led by "regulating drives that guided them unconsciously," they were now "reduced to thinking, inferring, calculating, connecting cause and effect" (*GM* II:16).Whereas the "regulating drives" had "guided them with certainty," following these instincts would now expose them to great danger, and because the change was sudden, there was no time to develop a new set of instincts (whether originating in biology or culture) for dealing with the danger. Further, the old "regulating instincts" left no room for uncertainty about what to do, hence no need or room for deliberation. If two drives came into conflict, say the hunger drive and desire for destruction, the organism was set up in such a way—this is presumably the role of the "regulating drives"—that one of them took priority in the circumstances without any need for deliberation. But once severe punishments were in place—as well, of course, as the language, memory, causal reasoning skills, and legal institutions that their effectiveness both presupposes and inculcates—the instincts that made up the physiological order of the drives, and therefore their causal order, were "devalued and 'disconnected.'" The instincts still made demands, as Nietzsche makes clear, but when instincts moved humans in different directions, it was now necessary to deliberate, to decide what to do.

It is actually here that the "inner world," the first person point of view, comes to be—and not with the later "internalizing of man." Instead of acting on instinct (when presented with information about the situation), human beings were now reduced to thinking about it, going over the

also vented upon "another" population, the nomad's other drives, and that this is what explains the origin of the bad conscience.

Nietzsche goes on to make clear that what happened here was the work of the same drive that led to the formation of the state: "this instinct for freedom, driven back, suppressed, imprisoned within, and finally discharging itself only on itself: this, only this, is *bad conscience* in its beginnings." So since it is the instincts that are said to "*turn themselves inward,*" or turn back against their possessors, Nietzsche must be thinking that it is these instincts or drives themselves that have an "instinct for freedom." These resist restrictions to their expression by seeking alternative outlets for their satisfaction. When their *outward* expression is blocked by the restrictions set up within the state and enforced by severe punishment, they are able to find satisfaction by turning *inward*, taking other drives as their objects. But the only way that these aggressive drives could express an "instinct for freedom" in seeking their own satisfaction by turning on *other* drives is by seeking to *deny* satisfaction to these drives.[17]

---

advantages and disadvantages of doing what their various instincts demanded of them. In other words, human beings began to concern themselves with the reasons they had for acting in one way or another. Certainly, Nietzsche would allow that the considerations that are being presented to the person as reasons are being presented as such by the drives. This does not mean, however, that the person is taking as a reason to do *x* that it will satisfy a drive. It is rather that the person is counting as reason to do or not do *x* features of the situation to which a drive prompts her to pay attention: e.g., the pain it risks bringing down on her. It is presumably in this way that one learns the five or six "I will not's" that Nietzsche counts as a major result of the institution of punishments (*GM* II:3).

And yet the "inner world" of deliberation is at this point, Nietzsche tells us, "thin, as if originally inserted between two skins." The point seems to be that having a first-person perspective is not sufficient for having a soul in the sense sufficient for personhood. It is only in terms of change considered above—the "internalizing of man" that the inner world has "spread and unfolded, has taken on depth, breadth, and height" (*GM* II:16).

[17] When the aggressive drives were deprived of satisfaction, their instinct for freedom led them to direct themselves at other drives and to be satisfied by depriving these other drives of satisfaction. Evidence that this is Nietzsche's view is found in the following passage in *GM* II:16:

> The man who, for lack of external enemies and resistance, and wedged into an oppressive narrowness and regularity of custom, impatiently tore apart, persecuted, gnawed at, stirred up, maltreated himself; this animal that one wants to "tame" and that beats itself raw on the bars of its cage; this deprived one, consumed by homesickness for the desert, who had to create out of himself an adventure, a place of torture, an uncertain and dangerous wilderness—this fool, this longing and desperate prisoner became the inventor of "bad conscience." In him, however, the greatest and most uncanny sickness was introduced, one from which man has not recovered to this day, the suffering of man *from man*, from *himself*—as a consequence of a forceful separation from his animal past, of a leap and plunge, as it were, into new situations and conditions of existence, of a declaration of war against the old instincts on which his energy, desire, and terribleness had thus far rested.

Nietzsche here tells us that the nomad deprived of his freedom "tore [himself] apart." He describes this process as "a declaration of war against the old instincts." Of course, the nomad doesn't take "the old instincts" to be the object of his wrath—he takes the object to be himself. His doing so consists in his aggressive instincts, driven by their instinct for freedom, venting themselves on "the old instincts." We discuss the relationship between the "person-level" and the "drive-level" in this situation below.

We shall take up the issue as to *how* the drives can take other drives as their objects below. What is clear at this point is that Nietzsche thinks they do so, and that their doing so is a result of their "instinct for freedom." But does he think that this instinct of the drives becomes a "will to power"? We saw above that he did so in the case of those who formed the state because it led them to impose themselves, in the form of severe restrictions, on the nomadic population by setting up an order of *authority*, a "ruling structure." Does he think something similar happened in the case of the drives? Does he claim that the exercise of their "instinct for freedom" leads *the drives* to impose restrictions on others by setting up a "ruling structure" of commanding and obeying?

To begin to see that it does, let us consider again Nietzsche's description of the "something new" that results from the activity of the blond beasts, with respect to which they are "the most involuntary, unconscious artists there are." Recall Nietzsche's description of it as "a ruling structure that *lives*, in which parts and functions are delimited and related to one another, in which nothing at all finds a place that has not first had placed into it a 'meaning' with respect to the whole" (*GM* II:17). Above we took this to refer to the state; in fact, however, nothing that Nietzsche says makes explicit that he is referring to the state here, much less *only* to the state. We assume this is a description of the state because of the context, but on reflection it becomes clear that context makes it just as possible that it is a description of the soul that grows from the bad conscience (*GM* II:16). Given how Nietzsche writes, it seems unlikely that this ambiguity is an accident; presumably, we are meant to do some thinking here.

A number of features of *GM* II:17 indicate that Nietzsche does intend "ruling structure that *lives*" to apply to the drives that make up the soul. First, consider that if it refers only to the state, it can only be an idealized state, not any state that happens to exist. This suggests that it actually describes the *form* of the state, which should remind us of Plato and therefore of his analogy between the form of the state and the structure of the soul. Second, Nietzsche's use of the plural "forms" in reference to what the blond beasts create ("creating of forms, impressions of forms") gives reason to think he is referring to something in addition to the state here. One who has read BGE well will recognize this as a likely description of the soul as the political order of the drives. Finally, the repeated use of this term here draws our attention to the *other* place in this section where he uses a variant of it, the passage in which he introduces the "blond beasts" as not just "fitting . . . a previously unrestrained and unformed population into a fixed form" (i.e., into a society), but as having worked "until finally such a raw material of people and half-animals was not only thoroughly needed and pliable but also *formed*." They were "*formed*," we suggest, by having a form impressed upon them—i.e., by having their drives molded into a "ruling structure that *lives*."[18]

---

[18] This makes sense: the blond beasts were successful in forming a state *because* they were successful in forming human beings, and their formation of human beings *consisted in* their bringing

Because Nietzsche does indeed think that the drives—like the nomads—come to be organized into a ruling structure of authority, we have reason to think that the instinct of freedom that led the aggressive drives to vent themselves on other drives did indeed become a will to power, a will to control and command. Now, it was relatively easy to see how this worked among the blond beasts: they imposed a military-style organization on the nomads through punishment and threat of the same. But how did the *drives* come to do this to each other?[19]

In order to answer this question, we must examine Nietzsche's account of the development of the "bad conscience."[20] He tells us that it began to develop "in primeval times" when the "relationship of the debtor to his creditor . . . was . . . interpreted into a relationship that is for us modern human beings perhaps

---

about a "ruling structure that lives" among their drives. That said, it goes without saying that these rulers had no idea they were bringing about a political order among the drives of the nomads. To call the blond beasts "the most involuntary, unconscious artists" with regard to this creation is no overstatement! It does seem to be something of an overstatement, though, if we take it to refer only to their creation of the state: surely this "race of conquerors and rulers" (as Nietzsche calls them) saw that what they were doing was conquering and ruling. And while the state they formed is "something new," it is not nearly so new as the bad conscience and beginning of the soul: Nietzsche earlier calls the latter—and not the former—"something so new . . . that the appearance of the earth was thereby essentially changed" (*GM* II:16). We conclude, then, that Nietzsche is referring not just to the state but to the drives as well as when he speaks of a "ruling structure that *lives*."

[19] How the drives act on each other is an issue that interpreters have left completely obscure. Risse (2001: 57) rightly says that those threatened with severe punishment for acting aggressively "are forced to redirect these instincts inward. . . . From now on, [they] treat themselves in ways similar to those in which they used to treat others, and in ways that they themselves are treated by the oppressors [those who instituted the punishments]." So far, so good, but how do they do this? Risse points out that "Nietzsche presents the image of an incarcerated animal that beats itself raw on the bars of its cage." The problem is that this is not a case of one drive suppressing another one, but of an aggressive drive attacking its own body. And this image does not, by itself, help to make plausible how a drive can direct its hostility or aggressiveness towards other drives: it may serve as a *metaphor* for the internalization of the drives, but this metaphor must be unpacked.

[20] In accord with the "two-level" nature of Nietzsche's psychology, he will seek to explain this phenomenon in terms of the behavior of the drives. That said, he will not talk simply about the drives, since *their* behavior can be understood only by keeping the (proto-) person's interpretation of the situation in view. The fact that it may induce a kind of nausea is no objection to our account as a reading of Nietzsche's psychology, however. In fact, it counts in its favor: Nietzsche himself tells us that one of the consequences of accepting his conception of psychology—"as morphology and the *development theory of the will to power*"—is that one "suffers from such a direction of his judgment [*Richtung seines Urteils*] as from sea-sickness" (*BGE* 23). This otherwise puzzling statement fits well with our claim that Nietzsche offers a two-level account of human psychology and that there is a jarring disparity between how the human person appears at each of these levels. When the person is acting on the basis of her commitment to values, the drives that constitute the person are acting on the basis of their desire for power. We can make sense of Nietzsche's claim that the "direction of judgment" required by his psychology will induce "sea-sickness" in this way: like a ship pitching and rolling, the psychologist must constantly shift between the levels of person and drives—"up" and "down," "down" and "up"—in a way that might induce this specific form of nausea.

its most incomprehensible: namely the relationship of *those presently living* to their *ancestors*" (*GM* II:19). Here again an understanding of the situation requires that we move between the level of the drives and that of the person. The notion of "sacrifice" becomes central, and with it a means for the aggressive drives of its practitioners to gain satisfaction: when the (still proto-) person[21] sacrifices his first-born (e.g.), the aggressive drives are venting themselves on another drive (presumably the drive to nurture one's young).

Nietzsche tells us that as the society prospers, the sacrifices deemed necessary become more severe. This continues until the ancestors are taken to be gods and then to be "the Christian god," the embodiment of "the most extreme opposites" the human being "can find to his actual and inescapable animal instincts" (*GM* II:22). At this point, the debt is taken to be impossible to discharge: whereas human beings previously took themselves to have something of value to offer to the gods, they now take themselves to have—more, to *be*—nothing of value. And yet it is with this total self-abasement that actions in accord with genuine values comes to be possible: "He takes all the 'no' that he says to himself, to nature, to naturalness, the facticity of his being and casts it out of himself as a 'yes,' as existing, corporeal, real, as God, as holiness of God" (*GM* II:22). It is here that bad conscience reaches its "most terrible and most sublime pinnacle" (*GM* II:19) and the concepts of guilt and debt are moralized in a way that allows for categorical commitments. It is only now, that is, that human beings become capable of performing actions not because doing so will satisfy some antecedent desire, but because they take doing so to be good.[22]

How does this work? Here we must again alternate between the level of the person and that of the drives. What is going on at the level of the drives when a person abstains from adultery, say, not because he wants his ancestor-spirits to favor him or because he thinks the gods will punish him, but because he thinks it is wrong? The aggressive drives are suppressing a drive (the sex drive, presumably). Their desire for power is satisfied not by giving up some satisfaction here and now for the sake of a promised satisfaction at some time in the future, but simply by saying "no" to the other drive. The drives' doing so is the person's saying "yes"—"yes" to the reality of something the goodness of which is not to be identified with its ability to satisfy his desires.

How does all this lead to the drives forming a political order? Though Nietzsche doesn't make his answer explicit, he gives us the tools for seeing it. We know from what he's said above, e.g., that a drive that is dominated will not cease to make its demands: as a result it will develop its *own* "instinct for freedom," searching for ways to again gain satisfaction. This dogged pursuit of its

---

[21] We argue in our 2012 book that for Nietzsche, a human being becomes a person only when she is capable of acting according to values. As a result, the nomad at this point is not a person. That said, we will, for ease of reference, refer to the nomad as a "person" in what follows.

[22] When the person *fails* to act in accord with such values, the aggressive drives exact payment by venting themselves on other drives, and the person feels guilt.

satisfaction in the face of suppression by other drives leads the dominated drive to become aggressive, directing itself against its oppressors and competitors: that is to say, it develops a will to power. This will to power leads it to seek a place in the newly forming order of dominance, a position from which it might both attain its object and subject other drives. (Securing such a position is a matter of highlighting certain aspects of reality, ones that would help engender in the person a commitment to the pursuit of the drive's object.[23]) If it accomplishes this, the hitherto subjected drive is in a position both to attain its object and to satisfy its will to power by subjecting *other* drives.[24]

This process continues until their will to power leads drives to form a coherent, ordered political structure—one analogous to that which the "blond beasts" made out of the nomads in accord with *their* will to power. Just as he has a naturalistic account of the origin of the state, Nietzsche has such an account as to how the drives come to be in a "ruling structure," and so, to form a soul.[25]

The foregoing provides the basis of an account as to why one who accepts Nietzsche's philosophical psychology must be "beyond good and evil," and this helps us to see why Nietzsche writes the way he does. While we develop this point in our 2012 book, we can only briefly state it here.

Consider *which* drives were denied external satisfaction when social order was imposed: drives to behaviors that threaten social order, especially those associated with aggression and with sex. This means that the will to power would have been strongest among *these* drives and, as a result, *they* would be highly ranked in the political order. It makes sense, then, for Nietzsche to think that values are "essentially identical" with "wicked, apparently antithetical things," as *BGE* 2 puts it, namely aggressive and erotic drives. If values are to be strengthened, then, these "base" drives must be strengthened.

---

[23] The possibility of such a commitment will, of course, require the presence of social practices, including that of holding oneself and others responsible. Nietzsche provides an account of how this and other such practices come to be in *GM* II. See paper 4 in this collection.

[24] This might explain why the drives seek to subject each other via commands, but why do the commanded drives ever *obey*? Zarathustra asks a version of this very question in the "Self-overcoming" section of *Thus Spoke Zarathustra*: "What persuades the living to obey and command, and to practice obedience even when it commands?" He answers: "That the weaker should serve the stronger, to that it is persuaded by its own will, which would be master over what is weaker still: this is the one pleasure that it does not want to renounce." The idea, then, is that the will to power also explains why those characterized by it (i.e., the drives) are willing to obey: obedience is a means to—or a necessary evil that accompanies—being able to command another, to exercise power. Thus the drives come to form a coherent totality, one in which "nothing at all finds a place that has not first had placed into it a 'meaning' with respect to the whole" (*GM* II:16).

[25] Our discussion of *GM*'s account as to how this political order comes to be has shown that Nietzsche takes the ability to act in accord with categorical reasons thus originates with the moralized concepts of "guilt" and "debt" when the bad conscience makes use of the ascetic notions of god and goodness (cf. Clark and Dudrick 2007, paper 5 in this volume). This is not to say, however, that such commitments cannot survive the demise of these concepts and notions.

In *BGE* 23, the final section of *BGE* One, Nietzsche asks us to suppose that someone goes as far as to regard the emotions of hatred, envy, covetousness, and lust for domination as life-conditioning emotions, as something that must fundamentally and essentially be present in the total economy of life, *consequently must be heightened further if life is to be heightened further*—he suffers from such a direction of judgment as from seasickness. (emphasis added)

If Nietzsche is right, then there is no way to increase life in the normative sense without also increasing the potency of these drives. This means that the ideal of purity, of a person who is good and in no way characterized by that which is "evil," is a chimera. If one could rid oneself of these drives, it would be self-defeating: one who succeeded in doing so would thereby sap her commitment to values and also be unable to develop the joyful attitude toward life that Nietzsche encourages in us. Indeed, we argue in our book that Nietzsche writes the way he does both to modify and to strengthen his readers' normative life, their values. As a result, his work must forgo purity and strengthen these "base" drives. To accept this view—both of ourselves and of Nietzsche's work—he tells us that one would have to become unmoored from "moral prejudices and timidities": one would have to be beyond good and evil.

Conclusion

Katsafanas presented two charges against our interpretation of Nietzsche's view of the drives. He claimed that our homuncular reading of the drives (1) deprives them of any explanatory value and (2) leads to a view of the drives that is absurd, if we are to regard them as part of nature. To the first, we've argued that Nietzsche treats the drives as entering political relations in order to explain how human beings have a point of view that may be regarded as that of the person. Put another way, he has the drives commanding and obeying in order to explain how it is possible for human beings to act not just on desires but on values. To the second, we've argued that Nietzsche gives an account as to how the drives came into a political order in *GM* II. Nietzsche's account of the soul in terms of the will to power follows Plato's homuncular account, precisely because it seeks to offer an account that illuminates human motivation in terms that are normatively inflected, rather than reducing it to causal forces.[26]

---

[26] Many thanks to Paul Katsafanas for inviting us to present this paper at the Conference on Late Modern Philosophy at Boston University. We would also like to thank Paul and other conference participants—especially Alexander Nehamas, Fred Neuhouser, Bernard Reginster, and Michael Rosen—for their helpful comments on the paper.

{ SOURCES AND ACKNOWLEDGMENTS }

The original venues for the papers in this collection are as follows:

1. "Nietzsche's Immoralism and the Concept of Morality." In *Nietzsche, Genealogy, Morality*. Edited by Richard Schacht.(c) 1994 by the Regents of the University of California. Published by the University of California Press. Reprinted with permission from the University of California.
2. "On the Rejection of Morality: Bernard Williams' Debt to Nietzsche." In *Nietzsche's Postmoralism: Essays on Nietzsche's Prelude to Philosophy's Future*. Edited by Richard Schacht. Copyright © 2001 Cambridge University Press. Reprinted with permission.
3. "Nietzsche." In *Routledge Companion to Ethics*. Edited by John Skorupski. Copyright © 2010 Routledge. Reprinted with permission from Routledge.
4. "Nietzsche on 'Free Will,' Causality, and Responsibility." Bernd Magnus Lecture, University of California, Riverside. 2009.
5. "Nietzsche and Moral Objectivity." Maudemarie Clark and David Dudrick. In *Nietzsche and Morality*. Edited by Brian Leiter and Neil Sinhababu. Copyright © 2007 Oxford University Press. Reprinted with permission from David Dudrick and from Oxford University Press.
6. "Bloom and Nietzsche." *Nietzscheana* 1(1989): 7–12. Reprinted with permission from Richard Schacht.
7. "Nietzsche's Misogyny." *International Studies in Philosophy* 26, no. 3 (1994): 3–12. Reprinted with permission from *International Studies in Philosophy*.
8. "On Queering Nietzsche." Lecture to the Society for Gay and Lesbian Philosophy. 1997.
9. "Nietzsche's Antidemocratic Rhetoric." *Southern Journal of Philosophy* 37, no. S1 (1999): 119–141. Reprinted with permission from *Southern Journal of Philosophy*.
10. "The Good of Community." Maudemarie Clark and Monique Wonderly. In *Individual and Community in Nietzsche's Philosophy*. Edited by Julian Young. Copyright © 2014 Cambridge University Press. Reprinted with permission of Monique Wonderly and Cambridge University Press.
11. "Deconstructing *The Birth of Tragedy*." *International Studies in Philosophy* 19, no. 2 (1987): 67–75. Reprinted with permission of *International Studies in Philosophy*.

12. "On Knowledge, Truth and Value: Nietzsche's Debt to Schopenhauer and the Development of his Empiricism." In *Willing and Nothingness: Essays on Nietzsche and Schopenhauer*. Edited by Christopher Janaway. Copyright © 1998 Oxford University Press. Reprinted with permission from Oxford University Press.
13. "Nietzsche as Anti-metaphysician." *Routledge Companion to Metaphysics*. Edited by Robin Le Poidevin. Copyright © 2010 Routledge. Reprinted with permission from Routledge.
14. "Nietzsche's Philosophical Psychology: Will to Power as Theory of the Soul." By Maudemarie Clark and David Dudrick. Lecture at the Conference on Late Modern Philosophy at Boston University. 2011. Published here with permission of David Dudrick. This paper includes excepts from Chapters 6, 7, and the Conclusion of *The Soul of Nietzsche's Beyond Good and Evil*, by Maudemarie Clark and David Dudrick, Copyright © 2012 Maudemarie Clark and David Dudrick. They are reprinted with the permission of David Dudrick and Cambridge University Press.

I thank Alexander Nehamas for originally suggesting that I collect these papers and Peter Ohlin for inviting me to submit a collection to Oxford University Press. The papers were written over many years and some changes in both my philosophical views and my understandings of Nietzsche's philosophy. I have been helped along the way by more Nietzsche scholars, philosophers, colleagues, and students than I can possibly remember or hope to acknowledge here. Some few are acknowledged in the footnotes. I have been very fortunate to be part of a very congenial and growing community of philosophers working on Nietzsche, and to be, and remain, a member of two very special philosophy departments during these years: at Colgate for the entire time, and at the University of California, Riverside, for the past six years. I thank my colleagues and students in both departments for their interest, collegiality, and many contributions to my thinking. I owe special thanks to David Dudrick for his collaboration over the past ten years or more and his co-authorship of two of these papers, and to Monique Wonderly, who co-authored one of the papers and did a great deal of work putting the whole manuscript together. Carlos Narziss put together the Index, and I thank him for the tremendous amount of time and thought he put into it. My partner, now wife, Connie Jones, has been with me through the writing of all of these papers and has copy-edited most of them. She claims that Nietzsche has gotten a lot smarter during the years in which I have been working on him. I thank her for that, and for everything else.

{ BIBLIOGRAPHY }

Nietzsche's works

[1850–89] 1986. *Sämtliche Briefe. Kritische Studienausgabe*, ed. G. Colli and M. Montinari. Berlin: Walter de Gruyter.
[1868] 1998. "On Schopenhauer," trans. C. Janaway. In *Willing and Nothingness: Schopenhauer as Nietsche's Educator*, 258–65. Oxford: Clarendon Press.
[1871/2] 1994. "The Greek State," trans. C. Diethe. In *On the Genealogy of Morality*, ed. K. Ansell-Pearson, 176–86. Cambridge: Cambridge University Press.
[1872] 1967. *The Birth of Tragedy*, trans. and ed. W. Kaufmann. New York: Random House.
[1872] 1999. *The Birth of Tragedy*, trans. R. Speirs; ed. R. Geuss and R. Speirs. Cambridge: Cambridge University Press.
[1872] 1979. "On Truth and Lies in a Non-Moral Sense." In *Truth and Philosophy: Selections from Nietzsche's Notebooks of the 1870's*, trans. D. Breazeale. Atlantic Highlands, N.J.: Humanities Press.
[1872–87] 1980. *Sämtliche Werke. Kritische Studienausgabe*, ed.G. Colli and M. Montinari. Berlin: Walter de Gruyter.
[1874] 1983. *Untimely Meditations*, trans. R. J. Hollingdale. Cambridge: Cambridge University Press.
[1874] 1995. "Schopenhauer as Educator." In *Unfashionable Observations*, trans. R. T. Grey, 171–255. Stanford, Calif.: Stanford University Press.
[1874] 1995, 1998. *Unfashionable Observations*, trans. R. T. Gray. Stanford, Calif.: Stanford University Press.
[1874] 1995. "The Utility and Liability of History for Life." In *Unfashionable Observations*, trans. R. T. Grey, 85–167. Stanford, Calif: Stanford University Press.
[1878] 1996. *Human, All Too Human*, trans. R. J. Hollingdale. Cambridge: Cambridge University Press.
[1878] 1997. *Human, All Too Human* I, trans. G. Handewerk. Stanford, Calif.: Stanford University Press.
[1880] 1996. "The Wanderer and his Shadow." In *Human, All Too Human* II, trans. R. J. Hollingdale, 301–95. Cambridge: Cambridge University Press.
[1881] 1997. *Daybreak: Thoughts on the Prejudices of Morality*, trans. R. J. Hollingdale. Cambridge: Cambridge University Press.
[1882/1887] 1974. *The Gay Science*, trans. W. Kaufmann. New York: Vintage Books.
[1882/1887] 2001. *The Gay Science*, trans. J. Nauckoff. Cambridge: Cambridge University Press.
[1883–5] 1982. *Thus Spoke Zarathustra*. In *The Portable Nietzsche*, trans. and ed.W. Kaufmann, 103–439. New York: Viking Penguin.
[1886] 1989. *Beyond Good and Evil*, trans. W. Kaufmann. New York: Vintage.

[1886] 2002. *Beyond Good and Evil*, trans. J. Norman. Cambridge: Cambridge University Press.
[1886] 2003. *Beyond Good and Evil*, trans. R. J. Hollingdale. New York: Penguin Classics.
[1887] 1998. *On the Genealogy of Morality*, trans. M. Clark and A. Swenson. Indianapolis: Hackett.
[1888] 1982. *The Antichrist*. In *The Portable Nietzsche*, trans. and ed.W. Kaufmann, 565–656. New York: Viking Penguin.
[1889] 1968. *Ecce Homo*. In *Basic Writings of Nietzsche*, trans. and ed.W. Kaufmann, 655–791. New York: Modern Library Classics.
[1889] 1982. *Twilight of the Idols*. In *The Portable Nietzsche*, trans. and ed.W. Kaufmann, 463–563. New York: Viking Penguin.
1968. *On the Genealogy of Morals*. In *Basic Writings of Nietzsche*, trans. and ed. W. Kaufmann, 439–599. New York: Modern Library Classics.
1968. *The Will to Power*, trans. W. Kaufmann and R. J. Hollingdale. New York: Vintage.

Other works

Abbey, R. 2000. *Nietzsche's Middle Period*. Oxford: Oxford University Press.
Anderson, L. 1996. "Overcoming Charity: The Case of Maudemarie Clark's *Nietzsche on Truth and Philosophy*." *Nietzsche-Studien* 25: 307–41.
Annas, J. 1981. *An Introduction to Plato's Republic*. Oxford: Oxford University Press.
Anscombe, G. E. M. 1981. *Collected Philosophical Papers*. v. 3. Minneapolis: University of Minnesota Press.
Ansell-Pearson, K. 1994. *An Introduction to Nietzsche as Political Thinker*. Cambridge: Cambridge University Press.
Bergmann, F. 1988. "Nietzsche's Critique of Morality." In *Reading Nietzsche*, ed. Robert Solomon and Kathleen Higgins, 29–45. New York: Oxford University Press.
Bermudez, J., and Gardner, S. 2003. *Art and Morality*. New York and London: Routledge.
Blackburn, S. 1993. *Essays in Quasi-Realism*. Oxford: Oxford University Press.
———. 1998. *Ruling Passions*. Oxford: Oxford University Press.
———. 1999. "Is Objective Moral Justification Possible on a Quasi-realist Foundation?" *Inquiry* 42(2): 213–28.
———. 2005. "Quasi-Realism No Fictionalism." In *Fictionalism in Metaphysics*, ed. M. E. Kalderon, 322–38. Oxford: Oxford University Press.
Bloom, A. 1987. *The Closing of the American Mind*. New York: Simon & Schuster.
Bridgwater, P. 1988. *Arthur Schopenhauer's English Schooling*. London: Routledge.
Brobjer, T. 1998. "The Absence of Political Ideals in Nietzsche's Writings: The Case of the Laws of Manu and the Associated Caste-Society." *Nietzsche-Studien* 27: 300–318.
Brown W. 1990. "Feminist Hesitations, Postmodern Exposures." *Differences: A Journal of Feminist Cultural Studies* 3(1): 63–84.
Carroll, N. 1999. *Philosophy of Art: A Contemporary Introduction*. New York and London: Routledge.
Clark, M. 1976. "Nietzsche's Attack on Morality." Ph.D. Dissertation. Madison: University of Wisconsin.
———. 1990. *Nietzsche on Truth and Philosophy*. Cambridge: Cambridge University Press.

———. 1994a. "Nietzsche's Immoralism and the Concept of Morality." In *Nietzsche, Genealogy, Morality: Essays on Nietzsche's Genealogy of Morals*, ed. R. Schacht, 15–34. Berkeley: University of California Press.

———. 1994b. "Nietzsche's Misogyny." *International Studies in Philosophy* 26(3): 3–12.

———. 1998a. "Nietzsche." In *Routledge Encyclopedia of Philosophy*, ed. Edward Craig, 844–61. London: Routledge.

———. 1998b. "On Knowledge, Truth and Value: Nietzsche's Debt to Schopenhauer and the Development of Empiricism." In *Willing and Nothingness: Schopenhauer as Nietzsche's Educator*, ed. C. Janaway, 37–78. Oxford: Clarendon Press.

———. 1999. "Nietzsche's Antidemocratic Rhetoric." *Southern Journal of Philosophy* 37(S1): 119–41.

———. 2001. "On the Rejection of Morality: Williams' Debt to Nietzsche.'" In *Nietzsche's Postmoralism: Essays on Nietzsche's Prelude to Philosophy's Future*, ed. R. Schacht, 100–122. Cambridge: Cambridge University Press.

———. 2002. Review of *Beyond Good and Evil*, ed. Rolf-Peter Horstmann, tr. Judith Norman, Cambridge University Press. In *Notre Dame Philosophical Reviews*, 12 August 2002.

Clark, M., and D. Dudrick. 2004. "Nietzsche's Post-Positivism." *European Journal of Philosophy* 12(3): 369–85.

———. 2005. "The Naturalisms of Beyond Good and Evil." In *A Companion to Nietzsche*, ed. K. Ansell Pearson, 148–67. Oxford: Blackwell Publishing.

———. 2007. "Nietzsche and Moral Objectivity." In *Nietzsche and Morality*, ed. B. Leiter and N. Sinhababu, 192–226. Oxford: Oxford University Press.

———. 2009. "Nietzsche on the Will: An Analysis of BGE 19." In *Nietzsche on Freedom and Autonomy*, ed. K. Gemes and S. May, 247–68. Oxford: Oxford University Press.

———. 2012. *The Soul of Nietzsche's Beyond Good and Evil*. Cambridge: Cambridge University Press.

Conant, James. 2002. "Nietzsche's Perfectionism: A Reading of *Schopenhauer as Educator*." In *Nietzsche's Postmoralism: Essays on Nietzsche's Prelude to Philosophy's Future*, ed. R. Schacht, 181–257. Cambridge: Cambridge University Press.

Conway, D. 1997. *Nietzsche's Dangerous Game*. Cambridge: Cambridge University Press.

Cooper, J. 1998. "Plato's Theory of Human Motivation." In *Reason and Emotion: Essays in Ancient Moral Psychology and Ethical Theory*, ed. J. Cooper, 118–37. Princeton: Princeton University Press.

Corngold, S. 1983. "Error in Paul de Man." In *The Yale Critics: Deconstruction in America*, ed. J. Arac, W. Godzich, and V. Martin, 90–108. Minneapolis: University of Minnesota Press.

Damasio, A. 1994. *Descartes' Error: Emotion, Reason and the Human Brain*. New York: G. P. Putnam.

Danto, A. 1965. *Nietzsche as Philosopher*. New York: Macmillian.

———. 1998. "Some Remarks on *The Genealogy of Morals*." In *Reading Nietzsche*, ed. R. Solomon and K. Higgings, 13–28. Oxford: Oxford University Press.

Darwall, S. 1987. "Abolishing Morality." *Synthese* 72(1): 71–89.

Davies, S. 2006. *The Philosophy of Art*. Oxford: Blackwell.

Deleuze, G. [1962] 1983. *Nietzsche and Philosophy*, trans. H. Tomlinson. New York: Columbia University Press.

de Man, P. 1979. *Allegories of Reading: Figurative Language in Rousseau, Nietzsche, Rilke, and Proust.* New Haven, Conn.: Yale University Press.

Dennett, D. 1978. *Brainstorms.* Cambridge, Mass.: MIT Press.

Detwiler, B. 1990. *Nietzsche and the Politics of Aristocratic Radicalism.* Chicago: University of Chicago Press.

de Waal, F. 1997. *Good Natured: The Origins of Right and Wrong in Humans and Other Animals.* Cambridge, Mass.: Harvard University Press.

Diethe, C. 1996. *Nietzsche's Women: Beyond the Whip.* Berlin: de Gruyter.

Dorsey, D. 2012. "Can Instrumental Value Be Intrinsic?" *Pacific Philosophical Quarterly* 93(2): 137–57.

Fischer, J. M., Kane, R., Pereboom, D., and Vargas, M. 2007. *Four Views on Free Will.* Walden, Mass.: Blackwell Publishing.

Fodor, J. 1995. "Encounters with Trees." *London Review of Books* 17(8): 10–11.

Foot, P. 1978/1973. "Nietzsche: The Revaluation of Values." In her *Virtues and Vices and Other Essays in Moral Philosophy*, 81–95. Berkeley: University of California Press; originally published in *Nietzsche: A Collection of Critical Essays*, ed. R. Solomon, 156–8. New York: Doubleday.

———. 1994/1991. "Nietzsche's Immoralism." In *Nietzsche, Genealogy, Morality: Essays on Nietzsche's Genealogy of Morals*, ed. R. Schacht, 3–34. Berkeley: University of California Press; originally published in *New York Review of Books* 38: 11, 18–22.

Frankfurt, H. 1999. "On Caring." In *Necessity, Volition, and Love*, 155–80. Cambridge: Cambridge University Press.

Garrett, D. 2005. "Hume, David." In *Routledge Encyclopedia of Philosophy*, ed. E. Craig. London: Routledge. http://www.rep.routledge.com/article/DB040SECT4.

Gemes, K. 2009. "Nietzsche on Free Will, Autonomy, and the Sovereign Individual." In *Nietzsche on Freedom and Autonomy*, ed. Ken Gemes and Simon May, 33–50. Oxford: Oxford University Press.

Gibbard, A. 1990. *Wise Choices, Apt Feelings: A Theory of Normative Judgment.* Cambridge, Mass.: Harvard University Press.

Gilman, S. ed. 1987. *Conversations with Nietzsche: A Life in the Works of His Contemporaries*, trans. D. Parent. Oxford: Oxford University Press.

Gray, J. 1992. *Men are from Mars, Women are from Venus.* New York: HarperCollins.

Guest, S. 2002. "The Value of Art." *Antiquity and Law* 7(4): 305–16.

Hatab, L. J. 1995. *A Nietzschean Defense of Democracy: An Experiment in Postmodern Politics.* Chicago: Open Court.

Hayman, R. 1980. *Nietzsche: A Critical Life.* New York: Oxford University Press.

Hill, K. 1997. "'The Simplest Needs of Life': Nietzsche's Closeted Homosexuality," presented at the Eastern APA in Philadelphia, December 1997.

Hume, D. [1740] 1978. *A Treatise of Human Nature.* Oxford: Clarendon Press.

———. [1740] 1975a. *A Treatise of Human Nature*, ed. L. A. Selby-Bigge, 2nd ed., revised by P. H. Nidditch. Oxford: Clarendon Press.

———. [1748] 1975b. *Enquiry concerning Human Understanding.* In *Enquiries concerning Human Understanding and concerning the Principles of Morals*, ed. L. A. Selby-Bigge, 3rd ed., revised by P. H. Nidditch. Oxford: Clarendon Press.

———. [1751] 1975c. *Enquiry concerning the Principles of Morals*, ed. L. A. Selby-Bigge, 3rd ed., revised by P. H. Nidditch. Oxford: Clarendon Press.

———. [1751] 1957. *An Inquiry Concerning the Principles of Morals*. Indianapolis: Library of Liberal Arts.

Hussain, N. 2004. "The Return of Moral Fictionalism." *Philosophical Perspectives* 18(1): 149–87.

———. 2007. "Honest Illusion: Valuing for Nietzsche's Free Spirits." In *Nietzsche and Morality*, ed. B. Leiter and N. Sinhababu, 157–91. Oxford: Oxford University Press.

Irwin, T. 1995. *Plato's Ethics*. Oxford: Oxford University Press.

Janaway, C. ed. 1998. *Willing and Nothingness: Schopenhauer as Nietzsche's Educator*. Oxford: Clarendon Press.

———. 2009. "Autonomy, Affect, and the Self in Nietzsche's Project of Genealogy." In *Nietzsche on Freedom and Autonomy*, ed. K. Gemes and S. May, 51–68. Oxford: Oxford University Press.

Jones, E. 1955. *Sigmund Freud: Life and Work*, v. 2. New York: Basic Books.

Joyce, R. 2001. *The Myth of Morality*. New York: Cambridge University Press.

Kant, I. [1781, 1787] 1999. *Critique of Pure Reason*, trans. and ed. P. Guyer and A. Wood. Cambridge: Cambridge University Press.

Katsafanas, P. 2013a. "Nietzsche's Philosophical Psychology." In *The Oxford Handbook of Nietzsche*, ed. K. Gemes and J. Richardson, 727–55. Oxford: Oxford University Press.

———. 2013b. *Agency and the Foundations of Ethics: Nietzschean Constitutivism*. Oxford: Oxford University Press.

Kaufmann, W. 1968. *Basic Writings of Nietzsche*, trans. and ed. Walter Kaufmann. New York: Modern Library.

Kekes, J. 1988. "Shame and Moral Progress." *Midwest Studies in Philosophy* 13: 282–96.

Köhler, J. 2002. *Zarathustra's Secret: The Interior Life of Friedrich Nietzsche*, trans. R. Taylor. New Haven, CT: Yale University Press. Originally, *Zarathustras Geheimnis. Friedrich Nietzsche und seine verschlüsselte Botschaft*. Nördlingen: Greno Verlag, 1989.

Korsgaard, C. 1983. "Two Distinctions in Goodness." *Philosophical Review* 92(2): 169–95.

———. 1996. *The Sources of Normativity*. Cambridge: Cambridge University Press.

Lange, F. [1865] 1957. *History of Materialism*, trans. E. C. Thomas. New York: Humanities Press.

Leiter, B. 1994. "Perspectivism in Nietzsche's *Genealogy of Morals*." In *Nietzsche, Genealogy, Morality: Essays on Nietzsche's Genealogy of Morals*, ed. R. Schacht, 334–57. Berkeley: University of California Press.

———. 1995. "Morality in the Pejorative Sense: On the Logic of Nietzsche's Critique of Morality." *British Journal for the History of Philosophy* 3: 113–45.

———. 1998. "The Paradox of Fatalism and Self-Creation in Nietzsche." In *Willing and Nothingness: Schopenhauer as Nietzsche's Educator*, ed. C. Janaway, 117–257. Oxford: Oxford University Press.

———. 2002. *Nietzsche on Morality*. London: Routledge.

———. 2004. "Nietzsche's Moral and Political Philosophy." *Stanford Encyclopedia of Philosophy*. August 26, 2004. http://plato.stanford.edu/entries/nietzsche-moral-political.

———. 2007. "Nietzsche's Theory of the Will." *Philosophers' Imprint* 7(7): 1–15.

———. 2009. "Review of Shaw." *Notre Dame Philosophical Reviews*. January 21, 2009. http://ndpr.nd.edu/news/23891/?id=15105.

Lorraine, T. 1997. "The Eternal Return as Desiring-Machine: Nietzschean Lines of Flight from Oedipal Manhood," presented at the Eastern APA in Philadelphia, December 1997.
MacIntyre, A. 1990. *Three Rival Versions of Moral Enquiry: Encyclopedia, Genealogy, and Tradition.* Notre Dame, Ind.: University of Notre Dame Press.
Mackie, J. L. 1977. *Ethics: Inventing Right and Wrong.* London: Penguin Books.
McGinn, R. E. 1975. "Culture as Prophylactic: Nietzsche's Birth of Tragedy as Cultural Criticism." *Nietzsche-Studien* 4: 75–138.
Miller, A. 2004. *An Introduction to Contemporary Metaethics.* Cambridge: Polity Press.
Nagel, T. 1989. *The View from Nowhere.* Oxford: Oxford University Press.
Nehamas, A. 1985. *Nietzsche: Life as Literature.* Cambridge, Mass.: Harvard University Press.
———. 1998. "Who are the 'Philosophers of the Future'?: A Reading of *Beyond Good and Evil.*" In *Reading Nietzsche*, ed. R. Solomon and K. Higgins, 46–67. Oxford: Oxford University Press.
Owen, D. 2009. "Autonomy, Self-Respect, and Self-Love: Nietzsche on Ethical Agency." In *Nietzsche on Freedom and Autonomy*, ed. K. Gemes and S. May, 197–222. Oxford: Oxford University Press.
Owen, D., and A. Ridley. 2003. "On Fate." *International Studies in Philosophy* 35(3): 63–78.
Pereboom, D. 2007. "Hard Incompatibilism." In *Four Views on Free Will*, ed. J. M. Fischer, R. Kane, D. Pereboom, and M. Vargas, 85–125. Walden, Mass.: Blackwell Publishing.
Pippin, R. 2001. "Morality as Psychology, Psychology as Morality: Nietzsche, Eros, and Clumsy Lovers." In *Nietzsche's Postmoralism: Essays on Nietzsche's Prelude to Philosophy's Future*, ed. R. Schacht, 79–99. Cambridge: Cambridge University Press.
Poellner, P. 2000. *Nietzsche and Metaphysics.* Oxford: Oxford University Press.
Rawls, J. 1971. *A Theory of Justice.* Cambridge, Mass.: Harvard University Press.
Reginster, B. 2006. *The Affirmation of Life: Nietzsche on Overcoming Nihilism.* Cambridge, Mass.: Harvard University Press.
Richardson, J. 1996. *Nietzsche's System.* Oxford: Oxford University Press.
———. 2004. *Nietzsche's New Darwinism.* Oxford: Oxford University Press.
Ridley, A. 2009. "Nietzsche's Intentions: What the Sovereign Individual Promises." In *Nietzsche on Freedom and Autonomy*, ed. K. Gemes and S. May, 181–96. Oxford: Oxford University Press.
Risse, M. 2001. "The Second Treatise in *On the Genealogy of Morality*: Nietzsche on the Origin of the Bad Conscience." *European Journal of Philosophy* 9(1): 55–81.
Robinson, J. 1995. "Startle." *Journal of Philosophy* 92: 53–74.
Rorty, R. 1989. *Contingency, Irony, and Solidarity.* Cambridge: Cambridge University Press.
Rutherford, D. 2011. "Freedom as a Philosophical Ideal: Nietzsche and His Antecedents." *Inquiry* 54(5): 512–40.
Scheffler, S. 1992. *Human Morality.* Oxford: Oxford University Press.
Schopenhauer, A. 1969. *The World as Will and Representation*, 2 vols., trans. E. F. J. Payne. New York: Dover Publications.
———. [1837] 1965. *On the Basis of Morality*, trans. E. F. J. Payne. Indianapolis: Bobbs-Merrill.

———. [1847] 1974. *The Fourfold Root of the Principle of Sufficient Reason*, trans. E. F. J. Payne, 2nd ed. LaSalle, Ill.: Open Court.
———. [1851] 1974. *Parerga and Paralipomena*, trans. E. F. J. Payne. Oxford: Clarendon Press.
Schutte, O. 1984. *Beyond Nihilism: Nietzsche Without Masks*. Chicago: University of Chicago Press.
Searle, J. 1983. "The Word Turned Upside Down: Review of *On Deconstruction: Theory and Criticism After Structuralism* by Jonathan Culler." *New York Review of Books* 30, no. 16 (27 October 1983).
Sedgwick, E. 1990. *The Epistemology of the Closet*. Berkeley and Los Angeles: University of California Press.
Skorupski, J. 1993. "The Definition of Morality." In *Ethics* (Royal Institute of Philosophy Supplement 35), ed. A. Philip Griffiths, 121–44. Cambridge: Cambridge University Press.
Sluga, H. 2014. "The Time is Coming: Nietzsche and the Crisis of Contemporary Politics." In *Nietzsche and Community*, ed. Julian Young. Cambridge: Cambridge University Press.
Solomon, R. ed. 1973. *Nietzsche: A Collection of Critical Essays*. New York: Doubleday.
Spir, A. 1877. *Denken und Wirklichkeit. Versuch einer Ereuerung der kritischen Philosophie*, 2nd ed. Leipzig: J. G. Findel.
Strawson, P. F. 1962. "Freedom and Resentment." *Proceedings of the British Academy* 48: 1–25. Reprinted in G. Watson (2003), *Free Will*. Oxford: Oxford University Press, 72–93.
Strawson, G. 1994. "The Impossibility of Moral Responsibility." *Philosophical Studies* 75: 5–24.
Strawson, G. 2005. "Free Will." In *The Shorter Routledge Encyclopedia of Philosophy*, ed. E. Craig, 286–94. New York and London: Routledge.
Svavarsdóttir, S. 2001. "Objective Values: Does Metaethics Rest on a Mistake?" In *Objectivity in Law and Morals*, ed. B. Leiter, 144–93. Cambridge: Cambridge University Press.
Thiele, L. P. 1990. *Friedrich Nietzsche and the Politics of the Soul: A Study of Heroic Individualism*. Princeton: Princeton University Press.
Vargas, M. 2007. "Revisionism." In *Four Views on Free Will*, ed. J. M. Fischer, R. Kane, D. Pereboom, and M. Vargas, 126–65. Walden, Mass.: Blackwell Publishing.
Waite, G. 1996. *Nietzsche's Corps/e*. Durham, N.C.: Duke University Press.
Warren, M. 1988. *Nietzsche and Political Thought*. Cambridge, Mass.: MIT Press.
Watson, G. 2004. "Responsibility and the Limits of Evil: Variations on a Strawsonian Theme." In his *Agency and Answerability: Selected Essays*, 219–56. Oxford: Oxford University Press.
Wilcox, J. 1974. *Truth and Value in Nietzsche*. Ann Arbor: University of Michigan Press.
Williams, B. 1985. *Ethics and the Limits of Philosophy*. Cambridge, Mass.: Harvard University Press.
———. 1995. *Making Sense of Humanity*. Cambridge: Cambridge University Press.
Young, J. 1992. *Nietzsche's Philosophy of Art*. Cambridge: Cambridge University Press.
———. 2006. *Nietzsche's Philosophy of Religion*. Cambridge: Cambridge University Press.

Young, J. 2010. *Friedrich Nietzsche: A Philosophical Biography*. Cambridge: Cambridge University Press.
———. 2013. "Nietzsche and Women." In The *Oxford Handbook of Nietzsche*, ed. Ken Gemes and John Richardson, 46–62. Oxford: Oxford University Press.
Zimmerman, M. 2002. "Intrinsic vs. Extrinsic Value." *Stanford Encyclopedia of Philosophy* http://plato.stanford.edu/entries/value-intrinsic-extrinsic/.

{ INDEX OF PASSAGES FROM NIETZSCHE'S WORKS }

Note: Locators followed by the letter 'n' refer to notes

Antichrist
  A 13–14, 237
  A 14, 163
  A 58, 197, 197n13, 198

Beyond Good and Evil, 9, 10, 13, 15, 15n7, 18,
  78, 85, 100, 142n1, 146, 162, 164, 165,
  166n2, 167n3, 169, 170, 171, 172, 173, 175,
  176, 178, 182, 183, 234, 258, 260, 261, 277
  BGE I, 87, 246n34, 260, 275n13, 286
  BGE 2, 285
  BGE 6, 257, 261, 262, 267, 271, 272, 275, 276
  BGE 9, 257
  BGE 12, 256, 259, 261, 262, 268, 272, 278,
    280
  BGE 15, 246n34, 258
  BGE 16, 12, 83, 146, 236, 255
  BGE 19, 199, 272, 275n13
  BGE 20, 85
  BGE 21, 5, 8, 48, 67, 75, 76, 77, 78, 79, 80,
    80n2, 81, 82, 83n4, 84, 85, 86, 86n5, 87,
    88, 89, 91
  BGE 23, 271n9, 276n14, 283n20, 286
  BGE 25, 168
  BGE 30, 4, 167, 171n6, 262
  BGE 32, 2, 25, 43, 63, 75
  BGE 34, 249
  BGE 43, 177
  BGE 55, 73
  BGE 75, 155
  BGE 134, 226, 237
  BGE 191, 234n21
  BGE 202, 6, 25n4, 43, 44, 44n7, 63
  BGE 203, 165, 166, 169, 170
  BGE 204, 166
  BGE 206, 2
  BGE 207, 167
  BGE 208, 166, 196
  BGE 211, 117, 121, 125, 160, 167, 169, 187,
    199, 244
  BGE VII, 12–15, 142, 143, 146, 146n3, 147,
    148, 150
  BGE 214, 143

BGE 219, 125
BGE 223, 146n3
BGE 226, 84, 162
BGE 227, 143, 244
BGE 229, 147
BGE 230, 147, 148, 149, 150, 227, 237
BGE 231, 14, 144, 147, 148
BGE 232, 145, 150
BGE 233, 147
BGE 237, 142, 145, 145n2, 149
BGE 238, 142, 146
BGE 239, 147
BGE 252, 227n15
BGE 253, 248n36
BGE 254, 198
BGE 257, 165, 175, 194
BGE 257–8, 169
BGE 258, 166, 192, 193
BGE 260, 33
BGE 268, 157, 158, 180, 199
BGE 284, 248n36

The Birth of Tragedy, 17, 18, 124, 157, 185, 187,
  203, 203n1, 204n2, 207, 208, 209, 210, 211,
  215, 216, 218, 219, 220, 220n7, 221, 225, 250,
  251, 254
  BT P, 17, 210, 220
  BT P:4, 204
  BT P:5, 23, 205n5, 211
  BT 1, 205, 218
  BT 2, 159
  BT 3, 205
  BT 3–4, 2011
  BT 4, 205
  BT 5, 206, 211, 218
  BT 6, 206
  BT 7, 210, 211
  BT 15, 204, 207n6
  BT 16, 218
  BT 16–17, 205–6
  BT 17, 206
  BT 18, 203, 204, 207, 210, 211, 218
  BT 23, 185

Daybreak, 18, 252
  D P, 261
  D P:4, 2
  D P:5, 15, 261
  D 119, 266, 266n4

Ecce Homo
  EH III, UM:2, 2
  EH III, D:1, 2
  EH IV:2, 2
  EH IV:2–4, 23
  EH IV:4, 2
  EH IV:6, 2, 41

The Gay Science, 9, 18, 78, 98, 106, 107, 108, 109, 110, 118, 119, 166n2, 215, 235, 237, 238n24, 240, 241, 242, 254
  GS 1, 113, 114, 115, 116, 117, 119, 120
  GS 2, 114, 119, 126
  GS 7, 108, 240
  GS 17, 194n6
  GS 18, 171, 176
  GS 23, 170
  GS 54, 237, 239, 255
  GS 55, 186, 187
  GS 58, 2, 16, 163
  GS 59, 243n29
  GS 73, 12
  GS 78, 179
  GS 76, 159, 187
  GS 85, 244, 245
  GS 99, 213, 214, 215, 216, 223n11, 225, 227, 235, 243n29, 244
  GS 107, 168, 238n24, 240n27
  GS 108–9, 234
  GS 110, 238, 238n24
  GS 111, 226n14, 238n24
  GS 112, 78
  GS 125, 229
  GS 139, 240n28, 241
  GS 152, 242
  GS 273–4, 273n11
  GS 273–5, 59n22
  GS 229, 107
  GS 293, 243
  GS 294, 243n29
  GS 299, 117, 120, 249
  GS 301, 84, 106, 107, 109, 111, 112, 113, 115, 116, 117, 168n4, 240
  GS 335, 120, 126, 244
  GS 339, 238n24
  GS 345, 5, 67, 68
  GS 354, 157
  GS 356, 170
  GS 357, 234

GS 358, 183
GS 366, 248
GS 373, 248n37, 258
GS 381, 2, 15
GS 382, 244

On the Genealogy of Morality, 3–4, 14, 23, 23n1, 28, 31, 38n13, 53n15, 65, 76, 77, 98, 100, 142n1, 211, 213n1, 259, 277, 285n25
  GM P, 24, 63
  GM P:5, 117, 213
  GM P:6, 24, 116
  GM I, 28, 31, 34, 43, 47, 66, 68, 137, 176, 278
  GM I:1–2, 244
  GM I:2, 66, 77
  GM I:4, 31, 33
  GM I:5, 32, 67
  GM I:10, 14, 33, 67
  GM I:11, 278, 279
  GM I:13, 48, 180, 256, 257
  GM II, 8, 28, 31, 35, 38, 49, 50, 56, 59, 68, 89, 90, 92, 115n7, 161, 277, 280, 285n23, 286
  GM II:2, 35, 37, 49
  GM II:3, 29n6, 35, 281n16
  GM II:3–4, 37
  GM II:4, 35, 35n9, 38, 68, 70, 90, 91
  GM II:5, 29
  GM II:6, 49
  GM II:8, 35
  GM II:9, 35, 36, 56–7, 93
  GM II:10, 36, 37n10, 95, 96
  GM II:11, 26, 95, 125
  GM II:12, 2, 29
  GM II:13, 29, 30, 65
  GM II:16, 70, 115n7, 280, 280–1n16, 282, 285n24
  GM II:16–18, 279
  GM II:17, 36, 198, 278, 279
  GM II:17–18, 38, 282
  GM II:17–20, 71
  GM II:18, 71, 277, 283n18
  GM II:19, 39, 71, 284
  GM II:20, 39
  GM II:21, 6, 37, 38, 39, 57, 69, 71
  GM II:21–2, 92
  GM II:22, 70, 73, 284
  GM II:23–8, 73
  GM II:24, 12
  GM III, 40, 71, 138, 139, 148
  GM III:10, 149
  GM III:11, 72
  GM III:12, 122, 123, 124, 126, 160, 162, 246, 248n36, 274n12

Index of Passages from Nietzsche's Works 299

GM III:16–21, 6
GM III:24–25, 11n4

Human, All Too Human, 8, 9, 10, 18, 24n3, 78, 80, 97, 98, 100, 101, 103, 105, 106, 107, 108, 109, 110, 111, 114, 118, 122, 123, 124, 129, 174, 175, 179, 186, 187, 213n1, 215, 222, 226, 227, 228, 229, 230, 231, 232, 235, 236, 237, 240, 242, 243, 245, 246, 247, 252, 253, 254, 255, 256
HA P, 124
HA P:1, 2
HA P:6, 124
HA I, 104
HA 1, 100, 227, 252, 253
HA 3, 102, 222, 225, 252
HA 4, 102, 225, 225n13, 254
HA 5, 252
HA 9, 101, 222, 223, 224, 232, 237, 252
HA 10, 100, 101, 224, 238, 253, 254
HA 11, 226n14
HA 15, 228n17
HA 16, 224, 225n13, 253
HA 18, 101, 246n34, 253
HA 21, 223n12
HA 29, 100, 101, 103, 105, 107, 224, 228, 246, 253
HA 32, 105, 138, 230
HA 32–3, 122
HA 32–4, 111
HA 33, 105
HA 34, 9, 104, 104n4, 106, 111n6, 123, 129, 186, 229, 230, 239
HA 39, 75, 76
HA 220, 229
HA 222, 225, 229
HA 223, 229
HA 224, 185, 187
HA 259, 155
HA 283, 194n6
HA 371, 105, 230
HA 438, 174, 174n10
HA 509, 179
HA II/P:1, 213
HA II/1:5, 233, 233n20
HA II/2, 174, 186
HA II/2:87, 186
HA II/2:140, 162

HA II/2:284, 186
HA II/2:350, 186

"On Schopenhauer," 219, 219n6
OS, introd, 219
OS 2, 219, 251
OS 3, 219

Thus Spoke Zarathustra, 13
Z II:3, 58
Z II:12, 279, 285n24
Z II:15, 106, 239, 239n26

"Truth and Lies in the Non-Moral Sense," 209, 216, 216n2, 222, 225, 226
TL83, 221
TL 83–4, 221
TL84, 216, 220
TL86, 222

Twilight of the Idols, 187
TI I:37, 188
TI I:40, 188
TI III:2, 255
TI III:3, 226
TI IV, 236, 237, 255
TI VI:1, 52
TI VII:1, 67
TI IX:22–3, 156
TI IX:38, 165
TI IX:24, 196, 196n9
TI IX:50, 195

Untimely Meditations, 189
UM II, 188, 192, 193, 251
UM II:2, 189
UM II:3, 161n3
UM II:6, 122
UM II:9, 189, 251
UM III, 190, 192
UM III:3, 190, 193
UM III:4, 251
UM III:5, 191, 192
UM III:6, 172, 190, 199, 251

Will to Power
WP 818, 198n14

{ INDEX OF NAMES AND SUBJECTS }

Note: Locators followed by the letter 'n' refer to notes

a priori, 78, 85, 100, 138, 160, 205n4, 214, 226–7, 246–7, 252, 257–8
  synthetic a priori, 226
Abbey, R., 10n1
action, 45, 47, 50–1, 59, 77, 90–1, 185, 204, 230, 238, 244, 258, 266, 269–70, 273, 276, 276n13
affect, 9, 11, 12, 14, 123, 129, 160, 162, 163, 230, 234, 242, 243, 244, 246, 249, 265, 266, 268, 274n12
affirmation of life, 18, 33, 72, 73, 137, 193, 203, 204, 207n6, 210–11, 251, 257
agency (*see also* doer), 47, 53, 79, 90, 91, 263, 265, 266, 266n4, 273, 275
aggression, 5–6, 38–9, 57, 71, 186, 285
  animal, 186
  drives, 277, 281, 283, 283n19, 284, 284n22, 285
  impulses, 5–6, 57, 70–1, 72, 278, 279, 280, 281n17
Alexandrian, 210
altruism, 6, 64, 66, 223
amoralism, 2, 44
Anderson, Lanier, 96n9, 249
animal, 12, 70, 72, 73, 90, 114, 115, 158, 172, 186, 190, 191, 227, 233–4, 235, 237, 238, 251, 257, 263, 266, 270, 271, 271n8, 275, 277, 278, 281n17, 282, 283n19
  instincts, 72, 284
  nature, 58, 72
Annas, Julia, 271–5
Anscombe, Elizabeth, 41, 41n2
Ansell-Pearson, Keith, 164, 170, 173n8, 184
anti-realism, 97, 98–100, 102–3, 102n3, 105, 106, 107, 227, 228, 230, 233–4, 237
Apollo, 204, 205
  Apollonian, 203–4, 205, 205n5, 206, 211, 218–19, 220, 220n7, 225, 251
appetite, 259, 269, 269n6, 270–1
aristocracy, 16, 47, 136, 164, 165–6, 167, 169, 170–1, 172, 173–4, 175, 176, 178, 179, 180n12, 181, 182–3, 190, 194
  aristocratic, 16, 47, 136, 164–6, 167, 169, 170–6, 178–9, 180n12, 181, 182–3, 190, 194

art, 6, 13, 54, 102, 111n6, 135, 143, 145, 173, 173n9, 196–8, 203–8, 209, 210, 211, 215, 217, 218–19, 220–1, 222, 223, 225, 228–9, 243, 244, 251, 253, 254, 261, 262n2
Aristotle, 135
ascetic ideal, 4, 5, 7, 8, 9, 11, 11n4, 18, 28, 39–40, 60–1, 71, 72–4, 138–9, 148–50, 192, 211, 257
asceticism, 11n4, 153n1, 211, 265, 266, 285n25
  ascetic interpretation of ethical life, 5, 8, 12, 17, 40, 53n15, 121n11, 150
  ascetic philosophers, 162
  ascetic priest. *See* priest
atheism, 39
atom, 255, 256, 273

bad conscience (*see also* conscience), 28, 35, 37–8, 38n14, 39, 57, 58, 68, 70–1, 259, 277, 280, 281, 281n17, 283, 283n18, 284, 285n25
Basel, University of, 13
Bermudez, Jose, 198
Bergmann, Frithjof, 3, 23, 27–8
bird of prey, 48, 256
Blackburn, Simon, 82, 86n5, 111n5, 129n12, 249n38, 271
blame, 34, 43–4, 46, 47–8, 50, 53, 55, 56, 60, 69, 88–9, 90–2, 244
Bloom, Allan, 10–12, 16, 133–9
blond beast, 277–80, 280n15, 282, 283, 283n18, 285
Brahmins, 168
Breazeale, D., 216n2, 221n8
Bridgwater, P., 231n18
Brown, Wendy, 150
Buddhism, 210–11
Burckhardt, Jacob, 13
Burgard, Peter, 145n2

Carroll, N., 198
caste, 197n13
  ruling caste, 166–7, 169, 170, 175, 176
categorical imperative, 35, 53, 71
causa sui, 67, 78–9, 87, 91, 180, 255–6

causality, 7, 29, 52n15, 77–8, 79, 80–9, 167, 180, 204–6, 204n3, 205n4, 217, 253, 256, 280n16
Clinton, Bill, 179n11
code of conduct, 27, 197n15
cognitivism, 98, 103, 109, 110–11, 120, 126
   non-cognitivism, 9, 18, 98, 106, 107, 109, 110, 111, 118, 119, 120, 122, 127
Colli, G., 23n1, 142n1, 204n2
community, 17, 35–7, 37n10, 37n11, 49, 50, 54, 56–7, 68–71, 92–6, 136, 152n1, 157, 159, 184–8, 188n2, 189, 191–5, 195–200, 195n8, 196n12, 197n13, 200n17
   communitarian, 185, 189, 194, 197n13
compatibilism, 76, 77, 79, 83, 92
Conant, James, 172n7
conscience, 37–8, 38n14, 43–4, 49, 55, 120, 121, 165, 168, 188, 192
   intellectual conscience, 114–15, 120, 126, 130, 214, 245
consciousness, 72, 115n7, 120, 157–8, 217, 264, 275, 279
   ethical or moral, 54, 60
   of guilt, 35, 37, 70, 90
   of power, 96
   of self, 31, 231, 263, 275
conservatism, 1, 2, 9, 10, 11, 16, 17, 184
constant conjunction, 82, 87
contemplative, 72, 111–13, 116, 118, 121, 121n11, 148–9, 168n4, 240–2, 245
Cooper, John, 269, 269n5, 274
Corngold, S., 209n9
correspondence theory of truth, 76, 138, 208, 221–2
Chandala, 197n13
Christianity, 66, 156, 183, 186, 234, 236, 255
   God, 58, 72, 284
   morality, 3, 23, 45, 62, 67, 116, 211
   philosophers, 234
   values, 116, 234
   virtue, 67
coloring, 9, 108, 161, 228, 244, 245n32, 265
compassion, 24, 24n3, 58, 173n9, 213, 214
cruelty, 6, 57, 68, 70–1, 72–3, 143, 147–8, 196n10, 280
culture, 7, 10, 11–12, 16, 27, 30, 64, 70, 133–4, 143, 145n2, 146, 152n1, 153, 155–6, 172–4, 173n9, 185n1, 186–90, 210, 216–17, 221, 235, 250–2, 263n3, 271n9, 280n16
   common, 16, 157, 159, 161–2
   democratic, 162, 166, 177, 181
   Greek, 155, 173n9
   higher and lower, 6, 7, 73, 146, 147, 157, 165, 169, 173–4, 188, 214, 215, 216, 222, 235, 252
   intellectual, 11, 153

Damasio, A., 246n33
Dante, A., 229
Danto, Arthur, 23n2, 28–9, 32
Darwall, Stephen, 41n1, 51–2, 51n13, 51n14, 54, 55, 55n19
Darwin, Charles, 251
   Darwinian, 190–1, 271n8
deconstruction, 17, 203, 207, 207n7, 209, 211, 212n11
debtor-creditor relation, 29, 35–40, 48, 55, 56–9, 68–9, 72, 88, 90, 92–3, 95, 283–4, 285n25
Deleuze, Gilles, 163
democracy, 9–10, 16, 134, 136, 153n1, 160, 162, 164, 165–6, 169, 170–1, 172–7, 178–9, 180n12, 181, 182, 183, 194n6, 248
Dennett, Daniel, 272–4, 273n11
Derrida, J., 207
Descartes, Rene, 232
desert, 29–30, 88, 90
desire, 11, 39, 53, 55, 73, 104, 107, 108, 120, 123, 136, 137, 138, 146, 147, 156, 163, 176–7, 178, 181, 191, 205, 205n5, 206, 228, 230, 233, 242, 245n32, 253, 259, 265, 266, 270, 271, 272, 273n11, 274, 280n16, 281n17, 284, 286
   to believe, 150
   to cause or inflict pain, 70, 93, 147
   for freedom, 78–9, 91
   homosexual, 153n1, 154
   for power, 283n20, 284
   for punishment, 59
   to rule, 268, 276
determinism, 7, 47, 48, 60, 75, 77, 80, 80n2, 81, 82, 84, 87–9, 89–90, 174
Detwiler, Bruce, 164, 165
devaluation, 138, 237
Diethe, Carol, 13n5, 173n8, 173n9
Dionysus, 18, 204–6, 208, 210–11
   Dionysian, 18, 203–11, 218, 220, 251
dissertation, 3, 24n3
doer, 255–6
   evildoer, 91, 94
dogmatist, 125, 155, 222
dominance hierarchies, 275
Dorsey, D., 195n8
drives, 72, 119–20, 148, 153n1, 156, 187, 256, 259, 260n1, 261, 262, 262–8, 270–2, 271n7, 271n8, 271n9, 274, 275–7, 276n13, 277–86, 280n16, 281n17
   aggressive, 277, 281, 283, 283n19, 284, 284n22, 285
   causal order of, 272, 272n10, 276, 276n13, 280n16, 286
   as homunculi, 262, 263–4, 274

political order of, 198, 259, 263, 272, 272n10, 275–6, 276n13, 277, 280, 280n16, 282–3, 286
sexual or erotic, 154, 159, 262, 265
Dudrick, David, 1, 8, 9, 11, 13, 15, 18–19, 78n1, 83n3, 86n5, 111n6, 115n8, 161, 198, 246n34, 259, 260, 266, 269n5, 272, 273n11, 275n13, 285n25
Dühring, E., 124–5
duty, 4, 7, 12, 37, 39, 57, 63, 64, 192

early period, 172
egalitarianism, 16–17, 176, 179, 181–2
ego, 192n3, 255
emotion, 46, 55, 56, 60, 84, 107, 109, 158, 160–1, 198, 233–4, 246, 246n33, 265, 274n12, 286
empiricism, 18, 213–15, 222, 226–8, 230–2, 234–5, 235–7, 239, 245, 247, 249, 258
empirical world, 83n4, 84, 100–2, 103–4, 106, 203–5, 205n5, 216–19, 222–8, 231–2, 237
English psychologists, 77, 244
enhancement (*see also* excellence), 165, 167, 169, 170–1, 173, 175–6, 180n12, 194
Enlightenment, 10, 116, 134, 136
epiphenomenal, 119
equality, 1, 6–7, 9, 16–17, 64, 136, 153n1, 165, 167, 176, 178, 182, 183, 192n3, 262
error theory, 8–9, 97–8, 101–2, 103–5, 106–7, 109, 110–11, 118, 228–30, 234n22, 238–40, 238n25, 249, 254, 255, 257
esoteric, 10–11, 13, 16, 167, 167n3, 171n6, 262
eternal feminine, 145–7, 149
ethics (*see also* morality, comparison with ethics)
noble form of ethical life, 42–4
eugenics, 190–1
Europe, 30, 165–7, 169–70, 174
culture, 250
Europeans, 25, 143, 186
intellectuals, 11
morality, 44
evolution, 101, 160, 187, 190, 224, 246, 251, 274n12
excellence (*see also* enhancement), 7, 17, 64, 96, 176–7, 179–81, 180n12
exceptional individual (*see also* higher human type), 17, 26, 184–5, 186, 187–8, 189, 190, 191, 192, 193, 194, 194n6, 194n7, 195–6, 197, 198, 199, 200, 200n17

faculty, 70–1, 121, 133, 136, 241, 259, 275
Falsification Thesis (FT), 76, 78
fatalism, 7

feeling, 12, 24, 45, 73, 76, 88, 102, 104, 108–9, 110, 113, 115, 117, 120, 122, 127, 144, 145, 145n2, 149, 156, 158–62, 163, 180, 185, 193, 198, 199, 225, 225n13, 228–9, 233, 238n25, 239–42, 244–5, 246, 249, 274n12
aesthetic, 102, 224–5, 254
of equality, 192
guilty, 70
of justice, 90
misogynistic, 145
moral, 76–7, 102, 224
of power, 147
reactive, 125
religious, 102, 224–5, 254
value, 125
feminism, 1, 9, 12–15, 13n5, 16, 141–3, 146–7, 149–50
fictionalism, 110–11
flourishing, 17, 98, 173, 184–8, 192–3, 194n6, 195–6, 196n12, 197n13, 198, 200
Fodor, Jerry, 118
Foot, Philippa, 3, 4, 23–4, 26, 26n5, 27, 28, 38, 45, 45n9, 46, 63
foundationalist, 226
Frankfurt, Harry, 195n8
free spirit, 14, 124, 125, 143, 188n2
free will, 3, 5, 6, 7, 48, 67–8, 75, 76–8, 78–81, 90–2, 101, 217, 223–4, 238, 253–4, 256–7, 279
in the metaphysical superlative sense, 8, 67, 75, 78–80
unfree will, 80–1, 83–4, 86–9, 90, 214
freedom, 4, 27–8, 47–8, 75, 76–7, 80, 80n2, 82, 84, 89, 136, 166, 168, 171, 172, 178, 253, 278
instinct for, 277–83, 281n17
radical, 27–8
French Nietzscheans, 151–2
Freud, Sigmund, 14, 38, 70, 134, 141, 142, 154, 162
Freudian, 55, 153

Gandhi, M., 94
Gardner, Sebastian, 198
Garrett, Don, 82
gay. *See* homosexuality
Gemes, Ken, 75
genealogy, 31, 58, 65, 223, 252, 265, 278
treatment of morality, 28, 49, 73, 100
as method, 28, 31, 50, 92
genetic fallacy, 67
Gibbard, Allan, 45, 46n11, 119, 127
Gilman, S., 153n2
God, 5, 17, 39, 57–8, 61, 71–2, 73, 79, 102, 114, 138, 148, 149, 205n5, 220n7, 242, 254, 255, 285n25

God (*continued*)
  death of, 61, 229, 234
  debt to, 37, 39
  Judeo–Christian, 58, 72, 284
  gods, 11, 39, 58, 135–9, 149, 284
  Greek gods, 58, 72, 135–6
  nonexistence or denial (*see also* atheism), 11, 66
  point of view, 9
  see also Apollo; Dionysus
Goethe, J., 188, 193n5, 229, 277
good, 8, 33, 34, 39, 40, 43, 47, 48, 58, 59, 66–7, 76–7, 99, 104, 109–10, 116–17, 133–4, 158, 171, 176, 180, 181, 181n13, 183, 184
  common, 1, 3–4, 26, 38, 45, 134, 136, 188, 192–3, 195
  life, 185
  person, 7, 24, 26, 58, 64, 67, 182, 188, 269, 286
"good and bad" versus "good and evil", 28, 31–4, 47, 66–7, 68, 76–7
grammar, 255–6
Gray, J., 152
Greeks, 41, 58, 72, 108, 146, 217, 241, 250, 251
  Greek gods, 58, 72, 135–6
  Greek Homosexuality, 155–6
  Presocratic, 217, 250
Grey, R., 172n7
guilt, 4, 5, 28, 35–40, 38n12, 41, 43, 44, 46, 53, 55, 56–60, 59n22, 68–71, 72, 73, 74, 89, 90, 92, 266, 284, 284n22, 285n24
  comparison with shame, 41, 46, 56, 59, 60, 266
  consciousness of, 35, 37, 70, 90

happiness, 6–7, 32, 64, 73, 102, 109, 166, 174, 191, 193, 224, 229, 241, 244, 252, 254, 270
Hatab, Lawrence, 164, 176, 178–82, 180n12
Hayman, Ronald, 154
heaven, 72, 186, 257
  heavenly, 228
Hegel, G., 158, 231
  Hegelians, 189
Heidegger, Martin, 134
Hellenic, 155, 210
Herbart, J., 231
herd, 7, 159, 179, 194n7
  instinct, 65, 68
  morality, 73
heterosexuality (*see also* homosexuality), 155, 162
higher human type (*see also* exceptional individual), 6–7, 64, 65, 73, 112, 113, 157, 165, 173–4, 177, 179, 181, 183, 187, 190, 193, 197n13, 199–200

Hill, Kevin, 16, 151–3, 152n1, 153–4, 156, 157–9, 161–2
history, 2, 4, 6, 30–1, 34, 48, 62, 64, 65, 76, 77, 146n3, 188–9, 236, 237, 239, 251, 255
  of animals, 158
  critical, 188–9
  human, 25, 40, 70, 91, 92, 159
  of philosophy, 134, 138
  prehistory, 120
Hobbes, T., 27, 138
Hoffman, Paul, 96n9
Hölderlin, F., 155
Homeric, 224, 253
homosexuality, 1, 16, 151–2, 153–4, 153n1, 153n2, 154, 155, 156, 157, 162–3
  homosexual desire, 153n1, 154
homunculi, 262, 263–4, 274
Hoover, Edgar, 155
human nature, 114, 161, 245
Hume, David, 27, 45, 48, 76, 82, 85, 87–9, 108, 125, 138, 161, 227, 227n15, 230–1, 231n18, 233, 241, 244–5, 246n34, 249
Humean, 18, 77, 78, 80n2, 81, 84–9, 108, 163, 230–3, 234n23, 236, 240, 271
Hussain, Nadeem, 110–11, 111n5

identity, 49, 53–5, 181n13, 191, 274
imaginary revenge, 33, 138
immoralism, 2–4, 8, 12, 23–4, 25, 27, 41, 42–6, 63, 71
imperative, 35, 53, 71, 257
  categorical, 35, 53, 71
  hypothetical, 35
impulses, 5, 159
  aggressive, 5–6, 57, 70–1, 72, 278, 279, 280, 281n17
  cruel, 70–1, 72
  hostile, 38, 57
  natural, 5
  sexual, 159
incompatibilism, 7–8, 75, 76–8, 79–81, 80n2, 88–9, 89–92, 95–6
intellect, 105, 123, 206, 214, 217, 220n7, 230, 233, 233n20, 234–5, 234n22, 236, 238, 246, 258, 274n12
instincts, 68, 70–1, 72–3, 74, 119–20, 153n1, 211, 233, 234, 279, 280, 280n16, 281n17, 283n19
  aggressive, 279, 280n15, 281n17
  animal, 72, 284
  corruption of, 147, 149
  for freedom, 277–82, 281n17, 284
  herd, 65, 68
  natural, 73, 257
  old, 70, 280n16, 281n17

Index of Names and Subjects

of the rabble, 166
scientific, 166
internalization, 6, 38, 39, 42, 43, 49, 57, 63, 68, 70–1, 72, 73, 280–1n16, 283n19
Irwin, T., 269–70

Jacobson, Daniel, 249n38
Janaway, Christopher, 75, 219n6, 249n38
Jews, 66
Jones, Connie, 249n38
Jones, Ernest, 154
justice, 1, 3–4, 6, 26–7, 28, 36, 37n10, 38, 45, 45n9, 61, 63, 73, 90, 96, 116, 122, 124–6, 146n3, 173n9, 180, 269

Kant, Immanuel, 53, 78, 84–5, 100, 204, 218, 236, 250–1, 255
   Kantian, 6, 18, 45, 56, 64, 83–4, 86, 87n6, 219, 222, 226, 236, 251, 271, 275
   neo–Kantian, 78, 80, 82–3, 83n4, 85–7, 87n6, 89, 222
Katsafanas, Paul, 19, 260, 260n1, 261–2, 262–6, 266n4, 267–8, 272, 275, 286, 286n26
Kaufmann, Walter, 3, 23n1, 23n2, 28, 31, 35n9, 142n1, 145n2, 146, 158, 164, 166n2, 184, 204, 204n2, 213n1, 225n13, 238n25, 239n26, 240, 243n30
Kekes, John, 59n22
King, Martin Luther, 94
knower, 105, 106, 111, 123, 136, 233n20, 239, 242, 243
knowledge, 1, 78, 104, 108, 124, 136, 138, 139, 147, 157, 160, 166–7, 204, 205, 205n4, 207, 213, 215, 217, 218, 218n3, 220n7, 221, 226, 227, 228, 231–2, 233, 235–6, 238, 238n25, 239, 241, 243n29, 244, 245, 246–8, 248n36, 252–4, 257, 274n12
   of art, 206
   drive to, 267
   empirical, 226, 231, 232, 235, 237, 246
   immaculate, 239, 245
   metaphysical, 136, 223–4, 231, 232, 234n23, 235, 254
   perspectival character of, 122, 123
   purifying, 104, 123, 129, 230
   of self, 14–15, 144, 154, 157–8
   of thing in itself, 18, 101, 219, 223–4, 236, 254
Köhler, J., 153n2
Korsgaard, Christine, 53, 53n16, 54n18, 60, 192n4

lamb, 48
Lange, Friedrich, 78, 78n1, 82
last man, 7, 64, 73

later period, 10n1, 235
Leibniz, G., 250
Leiter, Brian, 6–8, 40n15, 43n5, 43n6, 52n15, 64, 75, 76, 78, 79–88, 80n2, 83n4, 96n9, 97, 98–100, 103, 105, 106, 110, 121, 184, 187, 197n13, 199n16, 247n35, 258, 274
lesbian (*see also* homosexuality), 151, 163
liberalism, 9, 10, 10n1, 17, 136, 165–6, 167, 172–3, 178, 182, 183, 184
   left, 10, 12, 16–17
life, 6, 18, 34, 51–2, 60, 65, 104, 112, 114, 119, 123, 124, 158, 168n4, 172, 189, 191, 197n13, 205, 229–30, 239, 240, 242, 249, 257, 258, 267, 274, 286
   communal, 36, 46, 57, 93, 185, 189, 191
   ethical, 4–5, 6, 7, 8, 10, 12, 17, 43–4, 46, 49, 50, 52–3, 53n15, 54–5, 58, 59, 60, 63–4, 65, 73
   good, 185
   higher, 251
   human, 5, 11–12, 50, 55, 56, 60, 113, 137–9, 167–9, 172–4, 272
   philosophical, 11, 137, 213
   Socratic, 135–6
   value of, 105, 138, 185
   see also life–affirmation
libertarianism, 8, 75, 76, 77–8, 79–80, 80n2, 84, 87, 88, 89
life-affirmation, 18, 33, 72, 73, 137, 193, 203, 204, 207n6, 210–11, 251, 257
Locke, John, 85, 134
logic, 48, 52, 78, 204, 204n3, 207, 208, 223, 226, 226n4, 237, 238n25
Lorraine, Tamsin, 151–3, 159, 162–3

Mackie, J. L., 105, 228n16
MacIntyre, Alasdair, 28, 97
macro-level, 277
magnificent tension of the spirit, 18
Magnus, Bernd, 96n9
Maimonides, 136
de Man, Paul, 203, 208–11
Manu, Law of, 197n13
Marx, Karl, 141, 153n1
master morality, 28, 31
McDowell, John, 118–19
McGinn, R. E., 203
metaethics (*see also* cognitivism *and* non-cognitivism), 8–9, 18, 97, 98, 106, 107, 108, 110, 111n6, 118, 161, 233
metaphysical, 1, 5, 6, 17, 18, 56, 62, 98, 98n1, 100–2, 103–4, 110, 114, 148, 149, 163n4, 191, 206, 207, 211, 214, 215, 220–1, 222, 223n12, 224–7, 229, 230, 232, 233, 233n20, 234, 235, 250, 251, 252–4, 254–9, 263n3, 267

metaphysical (*continued*)
  correspondence, 76, 138, 208, 222
  free will in superlative sense, 8, 67, 75, 78–80
  knowledge, 136, 223–4, 231, 232, 234n23, 235, 254
  philosophy, 138
  self, 179, 180
  truth, 218, 220–1
  world, 116, 148, 222–6, 230, 236, 237, 252–4, 254, 257, 259
methodological naturalism, 100, 104, 258
Meysenbug, Malwida von, 15n7
Michelangelo, 229
micro-level, 277
middle period, 10n1, 18, 78, 97, 174, 250, 252
Miller, A., 102n3, 118–19
misogyny, 12, 14, 15, 141, 142–3, 144, 145, 146, 147, 149, 156
modernity, 9, 165
Montinari, M., 23n1, 142n1, 204n2
moral address, 93–4, 95
moral luck, 5, 54, 60
moral, normative, or ethical properties, 8, 9, 97, 98, 100, 102, 103, 104, 105, 107, 109–10, 112, 117, 118
morality, 1, 3–4, 7, 9, 23, 24–8, 24n3, 25n4, 28, 32, 34, 35, 35n8, 38n13, 40, 41, 42–3, 45n10, 46, 47, 48, 49, 50–1, 52, 52n15, 53, 55, 56, 58, 59–61, 63, 64, 65, 68, 71, 73, 90, 92, 102, 103, 121, 214, 225, 256, 267
  authority of, 62
  of compassion, 24
  concept of, 3, 4, 23, 28, 31, 34, 40, 65, 73, 92
  Christian, 3, 23, 45, 62, 67, 116, 211
  critique of, 1, 3, 5, 6, 7, 8, 9, 12, 24–5, 26, 27, 40, 41, 42, 43, 45, 46, 47, 48, 51, 52, 56, 61, 62, 64, 65, 66, 68, 71, 98, 187
  comparison with ethics, 4, 42–44, 45, 46, 53–54
  herd animal, 73
  higher, 43, 44, 63
  history of, 4, 146n3
  Kantian, 45
  master, 28, 31
  naturalistic account of the origins and development of, 5
  naturalizing, 9, 62
  noble, 42, 43
  origin of, 28, 31, 34, 62, 214, 254
  in the pejorative sense (MPS), 6–7, 64, 98, 110
  pre–moral, 10, 43, 68, 73
  slave, 28, 31
  value or evaluation of, 62, 67, 121
  wide and narrow sense of, 4, 8, 25, 43–4, 45, 63, 75, 187

morality of custom, 35, 56, 68
motivation, 37n11, 55, 60, 259, 262, 267, 269–71, 272, 275, 286

Nagel, Thomas, 118–19, 126–7
Napoleon, 188
natural selection, 70, 271n8
naturalism, 5, 8, 9, 18, 35, 60, 62, 78, 81, 82, 83n4, 87n6, 97, 98n1, 99, 100, 101, 102, 102n3, 118, 148, 150, 193, 227, 228, 230, 231, 232, 234, 235, 237, 239, 243, 259, 262, 263, 265, 268, 273, 273n11, 274n12, 275, 285
  methodological, 100, 104, 258
  naturalistic perspective, 9, 101, 263, 273, 273n11
  naturalistic property, 84, 102, 107
Nazis, 133, 139
Nehamas, Alexander, 3, 4, 23, 26–7, 28, 38, 42n3, 184, 261, 286n26
Neuhouser, Fred, 286n26
nihilism, 5, 11, 12, 61, 111, 134, 137–8, 139, 144, 196
  disorientation, 111
  ideal, 60, 61
nirvana, 72, 257
nobles (*see also* morality, noble), 24, 31–4, 40, 43, 66, 95n8, 137, 278
nomads, 5, 70, 277, 278, 279, 280–1, 280n15, 281n17, 282, 283, 283n18, 284n21, 285
non-cognitivism (*see also* cognitivism), 9, 18, 98, 106, 107, 109, 110, 111, 118, 119, 120, 122, 127
norms, 7, 26, 37n10, 38, 45–6, 64, 68, 119, 127–8, 152n1
normative, 1, 17, 19, 45, 46, 98, 103, 116, 117, 118, 121, 127, 129, 228, 259, 286
  authority, 109
  facts, 9, 98, 228, 233
  ideal, 75
  judgments, 127
  life, 286
  objectivism, 103, 106, 109, 111, 121, 127, 129
  order of drives, 276n13
  perspective, 9, 19
  properties (*see also* moral, normative, or ethical properties), 9, 98, 103–4, 107, 109–10, 112, 117, 118
  realm, 45
  subjectivism, 109–10, 111, 117, 118, 127
North American Nietzsche Society, 141

objectivity, 8, 9, 83n4, 95, 97–8, 98n1, 99, 103, 105, 106, 109, 110–11, 118, 121–30, 136, 153n1, 160, 161–2, 219, 230, 234n22, 247, 248n36, 249, 253
  objective world, 99–100, 102, 105, 247, 249

Index of Names and Subjects

obligation, 4, 12, 35, 36, 38, 41, 43, 44, 46, 48–56, 51n14, 56–60, 63, 68, 70, 74
Oedipus complex, 162
  Oedipal, 153, 162–3
Olafson, Frederick, 23n2
ontology, 97, 98, 99, 122, 262
order of rank, 124, 125, 158, 165, 167, 169, 171, 175, 180, 180n12, 194, 198–9, 262, 267, 272, 272n10, 275, 276n13, 285, 285n25
Overbeck, Franz, 65
Owens, David, 80n2

Parmenides, 250
passions, 84, 101–2, 104, 105, 108–9, 119, 160, 177, 224, 228, 230, 233–4, 240–1, 240n28, 243, 246, 252, 254, 274n12
St. Paul, 108, 241
Pereboom, Derk, 75, 90–1, 92
period of Nietzsche's development and works
  early period, 172
  middle period, 10n1, 18, 78, 97, 174, 250, 252
  later period, 10n1, 235
Perry, John, 96n9
person-relative point of view
  first-person, 19, 163n4, 280n16, 281n16
  second-person, 19, 163n4
  third-person, 158, 163n4
persons, 6, 7, 17, 24, 26–7, 29, 29n6, 34, 37, 38, 39, 49, 54, 58, 64, 67, 72, 76, 95, 96, 99, 103, 104, 119, 120, 125, 127, 128, 161, 166–7, 178–82, 187, 230, 239, 256, 258, 259, 263–4, 265–6, 272, 274, 276, 277, 281n16, 283n20, 284, 286
  full-fledged, 263–4
  personhood, 17, 181, 281n16
perspectivism, 9, 28, 122, 123, 124, 127, 128, 160, 245–8, 274–5, 274n12
phenomena, 52, 52n15, 205–6, 207, 218, 232, 273, 273n11
  phenomenal world, 83, 85, 219, 220, 220n7, 231, 240
phenomenalism, 78
philosophers, 11, 12, 16, 67, 97, 113, 117, 121–2, 125, 135–40, 143, 148, 149, 155, 156, 160, 166–71, 168n4, 179, 180, 191, 192, 208, 214, 221, 221n8, 235, 240, 244, 245, 249, 252–3, 255–6, 257, 262, 267, 276
  aristocrats, 167
  ascetic, 162
  new, 121, 121n11, 162, 166–71
  Christian, 234
  critical, 125
  Nietzsche's, 123, 125, 157, 160–2, 187–8, 244, 248n36
  philosopher–king, 26, 199
  of the future, 188
Pippin, Robert, 155

pity, 6, 64, 67, 238n24
  of self, 14
Plato, 26, 103, 156, 162, 199, 250, 255, 269–75, 277, 282, 286
  forms, 100, 102, 114, 206, 218, 218n3, 225, 254
  tripartite theory of soul, 259, 268–70, 269n6, 271, 272, 273–4, 277, 286
  Platonism, 119, 121, 156
Poellner, Peter, 263
positivism, 215, 226, 235, 251, 252
postmodernism, 151, 152, 152n1, 181–2, 216
power, 32, 33, 34n7, 94, 95, 124, 141, 146–9, 152n1, 160, 161, 176, 177, 183, 238–9, 275, 278, 279, 285n24
  consciousness of, 96
  desire for, 283n20, 284
  explanatory, 263–4
  intellectual, 122
  political, 168–9, 176
  quantum of, 256
  will to, 13n5, 69, 142, 147–9, 147n4, 159, 214, 258, 260, 262, 267, 268, 271, 275, 276–7, 276n14, 277–8, 280, 282, 283, 283n20, 285, 285n24, 286
practical attitude, 89
practical necessity, 53–5, 60
practices, 4, 9, 16, 34–5, 65, 68, 72, 92, 95, 117, 119, 121, 121n11, 152n1, 173, 285n23
Presocratic, 217, 250
priests, 5, 34n7, 67, 72, 138, 148, 161, 193, 197n13, 237, 257
promise, 35, 36, 37, 49–51, 51n14, 53, 69, 238n24
psychology, 19, 57n21, 91, 158, 271n9, 272–3, 276n14, 283n20
  drive, 262, 263
  moral, 235
  philosophical, 19, 260, 261, 262, 266, 268, 285
  Plato's (*see also* Plato, tripartite theory of soul), 269
punishment, 29–31, 29n6, 33–9, 37n10, 49, 56–9, 57n21, 67, 68–71, 72, 90–6, 115n7, 191, 280n16, 281, 281n16, 283, 283n19, 284
purpose (*see also* telos), 29–30, 29n6, 113–16, 117, 124, 196–7, 196n10, 198

Raphael, 229
reactive attitudes, 89, 93–6
realism, 97, 106, 119, 233
  anti-realism, 97–100, 102, 102n3, 103, 105, 106, 107, 227, 228, 230, 232, 233–4, 234n22, 237, 239
reason, 11, 60, 108, 133–4, 136–8, 152n1, 163, 233, 234, 234n21, 237, 240, 241, 255, 256, 259, 269, 270–1, 272, 274–5, 280n16

reason (*continued*)
  as activity of drives, 263, 265, 267
  categories of, 255
  errors of, 256, 257
  practical, 54
  pure, 138, 256
  unreason, 159
reasons, 26, 46, 50, 67, 71, 98, 99, 102, 109, 113–16, 115n7, 117–20, 122, 126, 127, 128, 129, 226, 237, 273, 276, 281n16
  categorical, 285n25
  conscious, 72
  space of, 116, 116n9, 117–19, 273n11
  reductionist, 273
Ree, Paul, 14
Reginster, Bernard, 69, 109, 110–11, 122, 123, 124, 286n26
relativism, 11, 134, 138
responsibility, 1, 7–8, 12, 27, 37, 37n11, 47–8, 49, 67, 75–6, 76–8, 79, 80n2, 81, 87–9, 89–92, 92n7, 94, 95, 96, 173–4, 187–8, 197n13, 269, 274, 285n23
resentment, 12, 14, 33–4, 55, 66, 67, 89, 94, 125, 141, 144–5, 150
ressentiment, 14, 15, 17, 66, 95n8, 152n1, 197n13
revaluation of values, 66, 98, 167, 213
revenge, 66, 95, 125, 139, 142, 152, 256, 257
  Chandala, 197n13
  imaginary, 33, 138
revolt, 34, 66–7, 73, 173n9, 183
Richardson, John, 109, 116, 116n10, 200n17, 258, 261, 264–5, 267, 271n8, 272
Ridley, Aaron, 80n2
Risse, Mathias, 65, 283n19
Robinson, J., 246n33
Roman Empire, 197, 197n13, 198
Rorty, Richard, 164, 216
Rosen, Michael, 286n26
Rutherford, Donald, 75

Salomé, Lou, 14, 15, 142
Schacht, Richard, 23
von Scheffler, Ludwig, 153–4, 153n2
Scheffler, Samuel, 55–6, 60
Schleiermacher, F., 231
scholars, 166–7, 171, 194n6, 248
Schopenhauer, Arthur, 18, 24n3, 33, 78, 78n1, 103, 106, 122, 156, 161, 172, 172n7, 189, 190, 204, 205–7, 205n4, 205n5, 211, 213–15, 216–21, 218n3, 218n4, 218n5, 219n6, 220n7, 222n10, 223, 225, 227, 228, 230, 231, 231n18, 232–5, 233n19, 233n20, 234n22, 234n23, 235–6, 240, 244, 245–6, 250–1, 258
Schutte, O., 146

science, 10, 100, 101, 102, 104, 114, 128, 142, 160, 164, 166, 167, 183, 204, 206, 208, 214, 215, 216–19, 218, 218n5, 221–2, 221n9, 223n11, 224, 226, 227–8, 229, 230, 231, 232, 233, 235–6, 237–8, 238n25, 239, 240, 242–4, 243n29, 245, 246–7, 248–9, 248n37, 250, 251, 252, 253, 255, 258–9, 268, 272n9
  genealogy as, 265
  political, 135
  scientist, 81, 83n4, 136, 166–7, 171, 194n6, 221, 221n8, 245, 256
  viewpoint of, 106, 107, 258–9
Searle, John, 207, 207n7
Sedgwick, Eve, 151–2, 154
self, 27, 39, 48, 58, 71, 148, 179–81, 263–4, 268
  abasement, 284
  affirmation, 31–2, 33, 66, 139
  aggression against the, 58, 71, 72, 74
  assertion, 133
  blame, 46
  concern for, 64
  confidence, 66, 95
  consciousness, 14, 31, 231, 263, 275
  contempt, 88
  creation, 48, 153
  crucifixion, 73
  cruelty, torture, or maltreatment, 5, 58, 59n22, 71, 72, 73
  deception, 101–2, 224, 232, 252, 254, 257
  denial, 72, 73, 138, 257
  determination, 174
  governance, 6, 257, 259
  identification, 154
  ignorance, 154
  indulgence, 11
  interest or selfishness, 2, 7, 257
  knowledge, 14, 15, 144, 154, 157–8
  metaphysical, 179, 180
  misunderstanding, 112
  overcoming, 153, 175, 279, 285n24
  pity, 14
  punishment, 39
  purify the, 5
  reference, 247
  reliant, 167
  selfhood, 179, 181, 263–4
  understanding, 113
self-contradiction, refuting, or defeating, 14, 23, 48, 78–9, 203, 208, 210, 286
Sellars, Wilfrid, 116n9
sex, 16, 153–4, 163, 177, 264, 265–6, 269n6, 285
  desire, 154, 155
  drive, 262, 284
  impulses, 159

orientation or sexuality (*see also* heterosexuality *and* homosexuality), 151–2, 154, 155, 156, 157, 181, 181n13, 182
roles, 147
sexism (*see also* feminism and misogyny), 12, 15
shame, 41, 46, 56, 59, 59n22, 60, 266
Shylock, 69
Sils Maria, 15
skepticism, 2, 43, 82–3, 84, 87, 88, 152n1, 157, 160, 162, 216, 223, 223n12, 252
skeptic, 125
Skorupski, John, 45–6, 45n10
slaves, 66, 165, 167, 169, 171, 192, 194n6
slave morality, 28, 31
slave revolt (*see also* revolt), 34, 66–7, 73
slavery, 41, 171, 173, 174, 175, 194, 194n6, 233
Sluga, Hans, 199n16
Socrates, 134–5, 187, 203, 204, 204n3, 250, 269, 270
Solomon, Robert, 3, 23, 26n5, 45n8
soul, 32, 58, 66–7, 158, 161, 175, 177, 180, 180n12, 198–200, 205n5, 232–3, 255, 258–9, 260, 261, 262, 263–4, 270, 272, 273, 274, 276n13, 277–8, 280, 281n16, 282, 283n18, 285, 286
atomism, 268–9
higher states of, 17, 73, 175–6, 177, 178, 180, 182, 194, 199
immortal, 101
mortal, 268
parts of the, 198–9, 200, 259, 269–71, 272, 274, 275, 282
philosopher's, 156
Plato's tripartite theory of the, 259, 268–70, 269n6, 271, 272, 273–4, 277, 286
superiority or nobility of, 32, 66–7, 176
space of causes, 116, 116n9, 119, 273n11
space of reasons, 116, 116n9, 117–19, 273n11
Spinoza, Baruch, 232
Spir, Afrikan, 78, 116n9, 246n34
spirit, 125, 143, 146, 147, 148, 149, 154, 155, 156, 173n9, 267, 269, 270–1
free, 14, 124, 125, 143, 188n2
higher, 157, 178
magnificent tension of the, 18
pure, 39, 72
spirits, 159, 189, 284
spiritual type, 6, 73, 183, 187, 193
spiritualization, 33, 113, 125, 138, 147, 149, 174, 177, 183
Stoics, 64, 257
Strauss, Leo, 10–11, 10n2
Strawson, Galen, 76, 79, 92

Strawson, Peter, 8, 76, 89–90, 92–4, 95
Stein, Heinrich von, 15
strong will, 87
subjectivism, normative, 109–10, 111, 117, 118, 127
sublimation, 33, 74, 101, 150, 153n1, 224, 227, 232, 253
substance, 78, 224, 238, 253–4, 255
substratum, 256
suffering, 7, 29, 29n6, 39, 57, 57n21, 64, 69–71, 72, 94, 95, 110, 116, 191, 192n3, 205, 251, 281n17
superego, 55, 70
Svavarsdóttir, Sigrún, 126–7

teachers of the value or purpose of existence, 113–16, 115n7, 117, 118, 119
teleology, 114, 115, 124
of drives, 271n8
telos, 169, 171, 173, 182–3, 194, 197
Thales, 136, 139
Thiele, Leslie Paul, 263, 272n10
thing in itself, 12, 18, 82–5, 100, 101, 103, 107, 138, 204–5, 210, 216–22, 220n7, 221, 222–5, 231–2, 234n23, 236–7, 251, 252–4, 255
traits of character, 26, 32–3, 67
true world, 100, 103, 223, 225, 228, 229, 235, 236, 237, 247, 252, 253, 255–6, 273n11
truth, 1, 3, 14, 18, 23, 32, 33, 67, 76, 101, 104–5, 107, 108, 111n6, 119, 133, 135–6, 137, 138–9, 142, 143–4, 145–6, 147–50, 155, 159, 160, 181–2, 181n13, 203–11, 207n6, 213–14, 215, 216–17, 218–19, 220–2, 221n8, 221n9, 222–3, 226, 228, 237, 238–9, 241, 242, 244, 245–6, 247–8, 248n36, 250–1, 252, 253, 256, 257, 273n11, 274n12
empirical, 216, 221–2, 223, 226
god of, 211
metaphysical, 218, 220–1, 226
ultimate, 204, 205
untruth, 77, 104–5, 111n6, 238n25, 239
will to, 5, 11n4, 13n5, 18, 61, 73, 111n6, 143, 148, 149
type of human, 165, 183, 189
contemplative, 72, 148, 149
creative, 7
enhancement of, 165, 167, 169, 170–1, 173, 175–6, 177, 180n12, 194, 194n6
exceptional, 188, 192, 194n6, 199
higher, 6, 7, 64–5, 73, 165, 172, 173, 174, 179, 183, 187, 190, 193, 197n13, 199
lower, 179, 199
non–reflective, 72
spiritual, 6, 73
splendid, 26, 45n9, 63

unconscious, 43, 141, 154, 279, 280n16, 282, 283n17
unfree will, 80–1, 83–4, 86–9, 90, 214
United States, 10, 10n2, 11, 179, 179n11
untouchables. *See* Chandala
utilitarianism, 6, 48, 56, 64

values, 5, 8, 9, 11, 17, 18, 25–6, 25n4, 27, 28, 31, 32, 39, 44, 58, 60–1, 63, 71, 72, 84, 98, 107, 108, 109, 110–13, 111n6, 116–20, 121–2, 124–7, 128, 129, 133–4, 136–8, 148, 158–9, 160, 161, 162, 163, 166, 167–9, 168n4, 170–8, 180, 180n12, 182, 184, 191–2, 192n4, 195–9, 195n8, 196n11, 196n12, 198n15, 200, 200n17, 204, 207–8, 211, 212, 213–15, 222, 228, 229–30, 232–4, 233n20, 234n22, 238, 239–40, 241, 242, 243, 244–5, 248n37, 249, 256, 257, 258–9, 263, 266, 267–8, 272, 275, 276, 276n13, 277, 283n20, 284, 285–6
  acting on, 271–2, 284n21, 284n22
  aesthetic, 4, 26, 63, 204, 207
  American, 134, 136
  anti-realism, 98–9, 103, 106, 227–8, 230–1, 232, 234, 234n22, 237–8, 239, 241
  aristocratic, 174, 178, 180n12, 182
  artist, 196, 198
  Christian, 116, 234
  creation of, 16, 109, 110, 111–13, 116–18, 120, 121–2, 123, 125, 129–30, 133, 188, 248n36
  democratic, 169
  of drives, 263, 265
  Enlightenment, 116
  eternal, 166
  ethical, 5, 46, 99, 107, 112–13
  of existence, 113–16, 115n7, 117, 118, 119
  higher and lower, 101, 182–3, 223–4, 229, 252–4
  highest, 17, 101, 138, 162, 170, 171, 172, 181, 184, 186, 190, 195, 200, 223
  in-itself, 72, 106, 109, 112, 117, 168n4, 239
  instrumental, 191, 192n4, 195–6, 195n8, 196n11, 197, 200
  intrinsic, 17, 138, 172, 191, 192, 192n4, 195–8, 195n8, 196n11, 196n12, 200, 200n17
  judgments, 100, 110, 118, 124, 127, 129, 165, 230, 239, 245, 272
  legislation of, 154, 157, 160–1, 167–8, 169–70, 187, 199, 244
  moral, 4, 5, 8, 25–6, 32, 43, 45, 60, 62, 97, 98–9, 100, 103, 228n16
  of morality, 24, 62, 63, 67–8
  noble, 66
  objectivity of, 8, 9, 98, 106, 111, 121, 124, 126–7

realism, 97, 106
  realm of, 26, 133
  revaluation of, 66, 98, 167, 213
  universal, 3, 4, 28
  will to value, 18
Vargas, Manuel, 92
verificationalist, 226
violence, 29n6, 70, 87, 93–4, 104, 159, 165, 167, 169
virtue, 4, 32, 43, 44, 58, 66, 67, 74, 108, 110, 124, 128, 137, 138, 143, 148, 149, 150, 161, 162, 177, 180, 188, 241, 244, 253, 257, 262n2
  ascetic, 40, 150
  Christian, 67
  higher, 177, 178, 180, 188, 262n2
  intellectual, 135
  moral, 32, 34, 40, 46, 47, 135, 137
  nonmoral or noble, 40, 66
  pagan, 34
  slave, 66, 73
  weak, 142
Voltaire, 10

de Waal, Franz, 275–6
Wagner, Richard, 188, 214–15, 220, 223n11
Waite, Geoff, 164n1, 167n3
Warren, Mark, 164
Watson, Gary, 89, 93, 94, 95
weak will, 87
weakness of will, 259, 269, 272
Weber, Max, 97, 134
Wilcox, John, 23n2, 203, 211n10
will, 72, 80–1, 80n2, 83–4, 105, 109, 133, 134, 147, 148, 157, 160, 163, 210, 214, 220n7, 230, 232, 233n20, 236, 246, 251, 255, 256, 258, 259, 273n11, 276n13, 277, 279, 285n24
  blind, 205, 217
  drives having a, 263, 275–6
  free, 3, 5, 6, 7, 48, 67–8, 75, 76–8, 78–81, 90–2, 101, 217, 223–4, 238, 253–4, 256–7, 279
  negation of the, 210, 211
  nihilistic, 138, 139
  philosopher's, 157
  to power, 13n5, 69, 142, 147–9, 147n4, 159, 214, 258, 260, 262, 267, 268, 271, 275, 276–7, 276n14, 277–8, 280, 282, 283, 283n20, 285, 285n24, 286
  Schopenhauer on the, 18, 156, 205, 205n4, 205n5, 206–7, 211, 214, 217–18, 218n3, 218n4, 219, 220, 220n7, 221, 232–4, 233n19, 233n20, 234n22, 235, 236, 251, 258
  to self–maltreatment, 71
  striving, 205
  strong, 87

to truth, 5, 11n4, 13n5, 18, 61, 73, 111n6, 143, 148, 149
unfree, 80–1, 83–4, 86–9, 90, 214
to value, 18
weak, 87
weakness of, 259, 269, 272
world as, 211
will to power (*see also* power), 13n5, 69, 142, 147–9, 147n4, 159, 214, 258, 260, 262, 267, 268, 271, 275, 276–7, 276n14, 277–8, 280, 282, 283, 283n20, 285, 285n24, 286
 drives having a, 275–6
 instinct for freedom, 277–82, 281n17, 284
will to truth, 5, 11n4, 13n5, 18, 61, 73, 111n6, 143, 148, 149
will to value, 18
Williams, Bernard, 4–5, 8, 41–2, 42n3, 42n4, 42–6, 47–8, 48–56, 53n17, 56, 58, 59–61, 63, 68, 128, 235
Williams, Christopher, 249n38
Wisconsin, University of, 3, 24n3
Wittgenstein, Ludwig, 158, 255
women, 12–14, 13n5, 14n6, 15–16, 114, 141–7, 145n2, 149–50, 153–4, 155–6, 158, 162–3, 180n12, 243n29
Wonderly, Monique, 17
world, 8–9, 18, 79, 82, 84–5, 86, 87, 100–2, 103–5, 106–7, 109, 112, 114, 115–16, 117, 118, 120, 121n11, 126, 127, 129, 148, 149, 161, 162, 163, 168n4, 169, 183, 190, 198n14, 204, 205, 206, 214, 217–20, 222, 224, 225, 226, 228–30, 233–4, 233n19, 235, 237–8, 238n24, 239–40, 241, 242, 243–4, 246, 247, 249, 251, 253, 255, 256, 257, 258, 265, 273n10
 empirical, 83n4, 84, 100–2, 103–4, 106, 203–5, 205n5, 216–19, 222–8, 231–2, 237
 inner, 205, 280–1n16
 metaphysical, 116, 148, 222–6, 230, 236, 237, 252–4, 254, 255, 257, 259
 natural, 9, 56, 85, 114, 115–16, 120, 138, 148, 227, 254, 257, 263
 noumenal, 83n4
 objective, 99–100, 102, 105, 247, 249
 other, 138, 249
 phenomenal, 83, 85, 219, 220, 220n7, 225, 228, 231, 240, 251, 255
 second, 100, 103–4, 106, 223, 240, 249, 250, 252–3
 true, 100, 103, 223, 225, 228, 229, 235, 236, 237, 247, 252, 253, 255–6, 273n11
 two-worlds, 250, 254, 257, 259
 as will, 211

Young, Julian, 13–16, 13n5, 14n6, 17, 184, 185–8, 185n1, 188–91, 188n2, 192–4, 194n7, 195–6, 196n9, 196n12, 197n13, 198, 199–200, 260

Zarathustra, 58–9, 106, 239, 245n31, 279, 285n24
Zimmerman, M., 192n4